MASS MEDIA

FORCES IN OUR SOCIETY

THIRD EDITION

edited by
FRANCIS H. VOELKER
LUDMILA A. VOELKER
St. Cloud State College

HARCOURT BRACE JOVANOVICH, INC.
New York San Diego Chicago San Francisco Atlanta

ISBN: 0-15-555122-1
Library of Congress Catalog Card Number: 77-79659
Printed in the United States of America

ACKNOWLEDGMENTS

In addition to the individuals and companies cited in the text, the editors would like to thank those listed below for permission to use material in this book:
Part opening art: François Colos

Page 26: Ken Karp
Page 36: Logo design by Don Menell
Page 37: **Viva** Magazine The International Magazine for Women
Page 38: Smithsonian Institution—**Smithsonian** Magazine
Page 41: **National Lampoon**
Page 43: Ms. Magazine Corporation
Pages 52–59: Photos by W. Eugene Smith, Magnum
Page 61: The Boston **Globe**
Page 64: © 1974 The Louisville **Courier-Journal.** Reprinted with permission.
Page 65: The Miami **Herald**
Page 66: (top) The Milwaukee **Journal**
Page 66: (bottom) **Newsday**
Page 69: **The Wall Street Journal**
Page 77: Wide World Photos
Page 99: National Broadcasting Company
Page 159: Wide World Photos
Page 189: CBS News
Page 203: (upper left) National Broadcasting Company
Page 203: (upper right) National Broadcasting Company
Page 203: (lower left) CBS News

Page 464 constitutes a continuation of the copyright page.

PREFACE

As the end of the 1970s approaches, we find ourselves reflecting on what has happened to the world—and the world of mass media—since we first thought about a book called **Mass Media: Forces in Our Society.** A decade ago we began looking for material on the mass media as negative and positive shapers of our society. Often the articles were hard to find since the media, as subjects for study, were largely ignored.

Now, however, the public has awakened. Evidence of media power abounds: A former president of the United States lives in the seclusion of a West Coast villa because two newspaper reporters wouldn't stop searching for the truth. Women and minorities are finding new opportunities in government, education, the arts—and the media—because the public consciousness has been raised through attention given them in all media. And, perhaps the best example of all, leaders in many fields have finally become concerned enough about the excessive display of violence in our media to form groups to combat the trend.

The list could go on. The point is that not enough people used to care, but in this age of consumer awareness people are beginning to realize the power of the media and are making intelligent use of them.

Like its predecessors, **Mass Media: Forces in Our Society,** Third Edition, is intended to foster intelligent selection and appraisal of the media. Most of the articles and illustrations reprinted in this edition were published in the 1970s. They present a variety of viewpoints on contemporary media by such writers as Michael J. Arlen, Jack

Anderson, Daniel J. Boorstin, Nicholas Johnson, Pauline Kael, Michael Novak, Newton Minow, George Gerbner, and Alvin Toffler. Among the new topics considered in this edition are women in film, electronic newsgathering, the current development of American music, black journalism, confidentiality of news sources, "Doublespeak," and television commercials. It is our hope that the selections in this edition will help students better understand the complex nature of the mass-media languages.

The focus and scope of the Third Edition remain the same as in the Second Edition. Part 1 consists of an essay by Theodore Peterson that gives a historical perspective on the development of the mass media in the United States. Part 2 deals with the print and electronic media, covering a wide spectrum: magazines, photo essays, newspapers, books, television, radio, popular music, and film. Part 3 looks at the media performing their three major roles as informers, entertainers, and persuaders. Finally, Part 4 treats the broader implications of the media—their overall impact on our society and the possibilities for the future.

Besides serving as a text for courses on the mass media, this book is designed as a reader for composition courses. At the end of each section are questions to stimulate discussion or to serve as topics for composition; these questions are followed by bibliographies that direct students to related materials. In addition, each section in Parts 2 and 3 concludes with a "mini-case study"—a collection of writing and visual materials dealing with a subject treated in the section. One of the mini-case studies is new to this edition; one has been revised. These studies can be used to stimulate student writing and media projects or as takeoff points for further research. In addition, there is an Instructor's Manual that offers techniques for the effective use of the textbook in courses on both mass communications and composition.

We would like to express our appreciation to our many students of both mass communications and composition for their interest in **Mass Media: Forces in Our Society.** They continue to inspire us. Also, we would like to thank our colleagues across the country whose comments on the First and Second Editions have been helpful in the selection of materials for this revision. Finally, we want to express our gratitude to the editorial staff at Harcourt Brace Jovanovich for their patience, cooperation, and helpful criticism. Their genuine interest has made it easier for us to share our concerns about the mass media through this book.

Francis H. Voelker
Ludmila A. Voelker

CONTENTS

The Entertainers 271

The Persuaders 330

Part One
Introduction

Mammoth Uncovered in Siberia
Is Remarkably Well Prese

MOSCOW, July 23 (AP)—A bull
operator in Siberia has found a pr
toric baby mammoth so well prese
in permafrost that it looks as thou
died only yesterday, Izvestia reports

The Government newspaper said
the mammoth, an early form of elep
had been put in a special cold cha
and was being studied by a comm
headed by the academician Nikolai
at an institute in the Siberian port
of Magadan.

"The impression is that the mam
died not 9,000 or 10,000 years ago,
only yesterday," Izvestia said in des
ing the find.

Moscow reacted harshly. In a re
of the book the political weekly
Times accused Mr. Carrillo of anti-S
ism and warned that his ideas, if
into practice, would split the interna
al Communist movement. The denu
tion drew protests from the Spa
French, Italian and Yugoslav Comm
Parties. New Times, in a later a
explained that it had not meant to
for excommunication of the Sp
party or any other "fraternal party."

Analysts of Communist affairs s
that Moscow's criticisms were w
heartedly endorsed only in Czechos
kia and East Germany. The respon
Mr. Carrillo's interpretation seemed
biguous in Poland and surprisingly l
in Bulgaria, where the Moscow li
normally followed without question

By PAUL HOFMANN
Special to The New York Times

Although their political views
somewhat similar, Mr. Jayewardene
nounced Jai-eh-WAR-deh-na) and
Desai contrast sharply in manner
new Sri Lanka leader is urbane and
ernized, while Mr. Desai is an a
who adheres firmly to his rigid int
tation of the teachings of the late M
das K. Gandhi.

Continued on Page 31, Column 1

Mr. Carrillo, secretary general o
Spanish Communist Party, has w
a controversial book, "Eurocommu
and the State," that is being read, t
lated, excerpted and discussed throu
Eastern Europe. In Prague, and pe
elsewhere, it is being clandestinely
tributed in what are known as padl
editions, the Czechoslovak equivale
Samizdat, unauthorized publicatio
the Soviet Union.

The 70-year-old Mr. Jayewardene
was sworn in as Prime Minister
today, is widely known here as a "d
ishta," or "righteous one," althous
opponents sometimes call him "Y
Dick" because of his anti-Commu
The contrast between him and
Bandaranaike is as marked as the
tween Prime Minister Morarji R.
of India and his vanquished predec
Indira Gandhi.

Continued on Pag

on Page 32, Column 1

In "Eurocommunism and the St
which appeared in Spain earlier this
Mr. Carrillo criticized the Soviet sy
declaring that it was not "a ge
workers' democracy" and had proc
'deformations and degenerations.'
also deplored the Soviet military i
vention in 1968 that ended Alex
Dubcek's experiment in liberalizing
munism in Czechoslovakia.

ge 6, Column 1

olumn 1

A publishing venture by a grou
dissident writers and editors, the
locked editions are turning out type
ten copies of texts that are banne
the rigorously pro-Moscow Czechos
Communists.

Continued on Page 32, Column 3

The fact that both leaders won be
of an image of cleanliness is cons
part of a political trend in South
Neither Mrs. Bandaranaike nor

Continued on Page 34, Column 1

Continued on Page 30, Column

We are surrounded by the mass media. Statistics provide ample evidence. Each year over 40,000 new books are published in the United States. Ayer's **Directory** lists more than 9,800 periodicals published in our country and more than 11,000 papers, including 1,813 dailies with a combined circulation of nearly 62 million. More than 39 million comic books are circulated by only six of the comic book publishers. Movie box office receipts total over $2 billion annually with an average of 23 million admissions per week. More than 413 million radios are tuned to 8,034 AM and FM stations, and more than 71 million phonographs play more than 10,000 new singles and LPs each year. Americans in 97 percent of the nation's homes spend over six hours daily viewing their 120 million TV sets, selecting shows from the programming offered by 962 UHF and VHF stations.

As a result of the explosive growth of the mass media in the recent past, they have become a natural part of life in the 1970s. However, the mass media should not merely be accepted as natural; each person should become aware of how they influence the shaping of his or her own being and the environment in which he or she lives.

The mass media are important forces in our society. They provide information and entertainment and, at the same time, have persuasive powers that are capable of effecting radical changes. The media do more than present ideas; each medium also uniquely shapes what it presents. As John Culkin has said:

> Each medium has its own language, audience, methods of production, economics, and distribution. Each must be judged within these limits. The print media pose problems far different from the broadcast and image media. Movies differ from TV both in style and in distribution. Television and radio operate on channels belonging to the public and, therefore, have a different responsibility to that public than the strictly private enterprise products of print and film.*

Modern technology has radically altered the media. No longer must the media assume the past tense, historical approach. Because of the new media, an event and its media coverage are often simultaneous, giving us an opportunity to experience events that people in previous times could know of only historically. The fact that people the world over **saw** Neil Armstrong's first step on the moon may have been the real "giant leap for mankind." Today's emphasis on technology allows society's attention to be focused on the present in light of the future, as contrasted with what Marshall McLuhan has called the "rear view mirror" concept of the present held by previous generations. Changes in the media have caused us to alter our time perspectives.

Many other social changes evident today are at least partially attributable to the mass media. They—in particular the electronic media—provide a global view that has allowed us to become involved in concerns far beyond the scope

* John M. Culkin, "Mass Media Study in the Schools," **Teaching English in Today's High Schools**, ed. Dwight L. Burton and John S. Simmons (New York: Holt, Rinehart & Winston, 1970), p. 439.

of earlier generations. In recent years natural tragedies like the earthquakes of Turkey, Guatemala, and Romania became world concerns within minutes of their happening. As a result of media coverage, people from all over the world responded to the obvious needs of the victims. The current energy shortage, reported as a world concern, is perhaps the strongest illustration of this global view. Political opinions too have been changed largely by the fact that the electronic media can provide seemingly uninterpreted news. Media coverage of President Jimmy Carter's statements on human rights not only informed Americans of his concern for the status of people in other countries as well as at home but also alerted world leaders to America's position. Earlier, the Viet Nam war became unpopular, in part because it was so vividly portrayed by the media. An informed electorate pressured politicians who began to speak out against the war in increasing numbers. Because of media coverage, Watergate became a household word, and a president was forced from office. The resulting stress on openness and honesty in government ushered in a new era in American politics. It is difficult to believe that phenomena of these proportions could have occurred without the mass media, especially without the electronic media.

The media have influenced entertainment and the arts as well. The camera, for example, has driven the poet and painter to do more with their pen and brush than simply picture reality. Disc jockeys and promotional campaigns have swayed the musical tastes of millions of listeners, while fan magazines have created cults. The viewer, listener, or reader is frequently unable to distinguish among information, entertainment, and persuasion; an advertisement may both inform and entertain at the same time it persuades. And finally, the quality of media presentations varies widely. While critics often disparage the mass media, it must be remembered that the media have enormous appetites for new materials, making almost impossible demands on the creativity of writers and performers. The media user's responsibility, then, becomes one of selectivity.

In the introductory article to this text, Theodore Peterson, University of Illinois journalism professor and author of **Magazines in the Twentieth Century** and other media books, outlines the very complex nature of the mass communications media, how they profoundly influence society, politics, economics, and culture, and how these factors, in turn, influence the media. It is these influences that have given rise to much of the criticism leveled at the mass media, which Peterson attempts to counter.

WHY THE MASS MEDIA ARE THAT WAY

by THEODORE PETERSON

In the past few years a good many persons have been lining up, like sailors at a shooting gallery, to draw a bead on the various mass media of communication. A. J. Liebling, for one, has published his essays about our "monovocal, monopolistic, monocular press." Newton Minow has spoken about television fare with such vehemence and frequency that he has given the term "wasteland" a currency that T. S. Eliot never did. And Robert Lekachman, in the greatest heresy of all, has charged that our good magazines, our *Harper's* and *Atlantic* and *Nation,* are not good enough, are not the equal of their British counterparts.

Editors, publishers, and broadcasters have learned to live with this criticism, but they have seldom learned to like it. Their reactions have varied from surprised hurt and mild petulance on the one hand to red-faced indignation and savage counterattack on the other.

I cannot agree with those publishers and broadcasters who seem to think that finding fault with the mass media is somehow un-American, like setting out poisoned Ken-L-Ration for Lassie. My aim is not to argue that the American mass media are the best in the world, although I think they are. It is evading the issue to say that our media are the best or even good. The word "good," after all, has many meanings, as G. K. Chesterton reminds us with his remark that a man who shoots his grandmother at five hundred yards may be a good shot but not necessarily a good man.

The truth is that I sometimes agree with what the critics have to say about press performance. But when I do, I often have the uneasy feeling that they are right for the wrong reasons and that one may as well look to Dr. Seuss for richness of character and complexity of plot as to look to them for sensible prescriptions. So what I propose to do is to touch on a major stream of press criticism that I think is bound to be futile, to examine its assumptions and shortcomings, and then to suggest, a little hesitantly, a direction that I think holds greater promise.

The strain of criticism that strikes me as essentially futile blames publishers and broadcasters for all of the shortcomings of the mass media. In its many variations, this line of criticism sees the men who own and operate the media as merely foolish, as irresponsible, or as downright evil. The common denominator of the variations is that the media are bad because the men who own and operate them are in some way bad.

That idea is almost as old as printing itself. In the sixteenth century, even before the newspaper came to England, critics were grumbling about the half-penny chroniclers who scampered off to scribble verses for its precursor, the broadside. When newspapers did appear, the men who ran them came in for some abuse. Samuel Johnson, who had opinions on all subjects worth having opinions about and on a good many that were not, delivered his views on newsmen in 1758: "The compilation of Newspapers is often committed to narrow minds, not qualified for the task of delighting or instructing; who are content to fill their pages with whatever matter, without industry to gather, or discernment to select." His observations were mild compared with the American variety, especially those in the period of bitter partisan journalism in the late eighteenth and early nineteenth centuries, when the press deserved all of the criticism it got. James Ward Fenno, an old newspaperman himself, said in 1799:

> The American newspapers are the most base, false, servile, and venal publications, that ever polluted the fountains of society—their editors the most ignorant, mercenary and vulgar automations that ever were moved by the continually rusting wires of sordid mercantile avarice.

In our own century, by far the great bulk of press criticism, I think, has blamed the owners and operators for the shortcomings of the media. A good deal of it arises from what we might call the conspiratorial theory of press malfunction—the notion that publishers and broadcasters have conspired with big business to promote and to protect their mutual interests, that in exchange for suppressing and distorting media content they share in such handsome rewards as advertising contracts, social position, and political prominence.

Will Irwin set the themes for much of such criticism in a series of articles about newspapers that he wrote for *Collier's* back in 1911. Advertisers had come to realize their power over the press, he said, and in some instances they had been taught it by the newspapers themselves. To attract customers for advertising space, some papers had made concessions to advertisers. In time advertisers came to take these concessions as special privileges—insertion of publicity; biased news accounts; suppression of news harmful to the advertiser, his family, his associates, and his business interests; and, in rare instances, a complete change in editorial policy. Irwin was perceptive enough to recognize that many shortcomings of the newspaper arise not from the harmful influence of advertising but from the commercial nature of the press, and he observed that simply because publishers are businessmen, the newspapers they control might be expected to reflect the viewpoint of business.

Irwin was followed by a succession of critics who reiterated his charges, although not always with his perception. In 1912, after he had already clubbed the packing industry with his wooden prose, Upton Sinclair brought out *The Brass Check,* which likened the press to a vast brothel in which truth was the virtue for sale. *The Brass Check* has been almost as durable as its author, who has written a book for each of his eighty-four years, for it went through several editions and was revised in 1936. Sinclair's pitch was that the "Empire of Business" controls journalism by four devices—by direct ownership of the press, by ownership of the owners, by advertising subsidy, and by direct bribery.

The "empire of business" idea was a favorite one in the Depression of the 1930s, when businessmen were low in popular esteem, and critic after critic described how knights of that empire worked hand in hand with the press to thwart the common good. Harold L. Ickes contended that publishers made up America's House of Lords, a body enriching and enhancing the power of the economic royalists whose ideology had a well-filled purse as its core. George Seldes saw the lords of the press as polluting the fountain of truth by suppressing news or distorting it and plotting evil behind closed doors at meetings of the American Newspaper Publishers Association. Ferdinand Lundberg wrote scathingly of Imperial Hearst, and other writers did portraits of other publishers in acid.

Today critics seldom speak of "lords of the press," a term that sounds a little dated, but they sometimes do number media owners among "the power elite." And quite a few critics evidently do assume that Sinclair and Seldes and Ickes were right in blaming the owners and operators for a good share of what is wrong with the media.

Their line of thought, let me confess, is rather appealing. For one thing, there is enough truth in it to make it seem valid. The media *are* big business, and their outlook *does* tend to be that of big business generally. For another thing, the way to improvement is then comparatively easy: Somehow, through punishment or persuasion, we must make the media owners pure of heart; then the press will be as great as publishers say it is during National Newspaper Week, and television will become man's greatest achievement since the pyramids. Charles Dickens had a similar explanation for the ills of nineteenth-century England, and his solution was equally simple: Let evil-doers be shown their errors, and they will join their nobler fellows in a merry dance of brotherhood around the Christmas tree.

Criticism that does little more than blame the men who own and operate the mass media is bound to be futile, I think, for it rests on debatable if not downright erroneous assumptions.

One is that most owners and operators lack a sense of social responsibility. Now, some publishers do show a deeper concern over what paper costs than over what they print on it, and some broadcasters do regard the public airwaves as their personal, exploitable property. Even so, I am prepared to argue that most publishers and broadcasters have a greater sense of public responsibility than a good many critics give them credit for having—one as high as that of most leaders in business and government, and perhaps higher. At times their standards of performance may not be the ones that most intellectuals would set if they were running the media, but the eggs that make one man's soufflé make the next man's omelet.

A second assumption is that the nature of the communications system is determined primarily by the men who now own and operate the media. They of course do have a good deal to say about what the mass media pump out. But in one sense what they choose to include and omit, as I will try to show, is not entirely of their own doing.

Let me make it abundantly clear that I am not suggesting that publishers and broadcasters are sacrosanct, like Harvard, J. Edgar Hoover, and the Marines. I am not defending the shortcomings of the media for which they can be held accountable. What I am saying is this: Criticism that concentrates on them and their motives at best can explain only a small part of reality and at worst can obscure a genuine understanding of why the mass media are what they are.

Jay Jensen, in an article in the *Journalism Quarterly,* argued that genuine criticism of the press must begin with an understanding of the mass media as an institutional order.[1] His approach enables us to see the mass media from an entirely different perspective. It changes our focus from the transitory, short-term effects of the media to the relationships of the communication system to society in their most fundamental form. It enables us to see that the communication system performs certain objective functions quite irrespective of the intents and interests of the men who operate it.

For criticism to be valid and fruitful, Jensen said, it must meet three re-

[1] Jay W. Jensen, "A Method and a Perspective for Criticism of the Mass Media," *Journalism Quarterly 37* (Spring 1960), 261–66.

quirements. First, it must be objective. It must be conducted without bias or censure arising from ideological presuppositions. Second, it must take into account the influence of social, political, and cultural forces in the historical development of the media. And finally, it must put the media into the context of their environment; it must take note of the demands, values, aspirations, and life interests of the society in which the media operate.

Criticism meeting those three tests can come about, he said, if we will look at the mass media from an institutional perspective. Man has devised various institutions to help solve different aspects of the problem of human existence. Each institution is a complex pattern of values and behavior designed to meet some persistent and pressing social need. The family exists to sustain life, the church to give it meaning and direction. An institutional order is simply a larger and more complex pattern of values and behavior, for it is made up of several institutions by which man attacks the overall problem of existence. In that functional sense, then, the mass media are an institutional order. They are a way of dealing with one phase of existence—the necessity for social communication. So wrote Jensen.

In a sense, human societies arose from and are maintained by communication. What makes man unique among all creatures is his capacity for creating symbols. Throughout history, in all societies, mankind has had certain fundamental means of communicating—gesture, imitation, what Sapir calls social suggestion, language. Using them, both primitive man and civilized man have surrounded themselves with a web of symbols.

Man, in fact, seems to have some inner compulsion to create symbols. They give him his image of himself and locate him in the vast stream of time. As Kenneth Boulding reminds us, a dog has no idea that there were dogs before him and that there will be dogs after him. But man, through his symbolic creations, has a sense of the past that stretches centuries behind him and a concept of the future. Symbols are man's chief means of communicating with his fellow man, the carrier of the social process. Through them, he can express his fears, his hopes, his plans, his ideas of the world he lives in, and through them he achieves the consensus that is necessary if he is to get along with his fellow men. They are the means whereby man copes with his environment and gives meaning to his existence.

Man's propensity for creating symbols has given human beings a whole new environment. For man, alone of all creatures, reacts not just to his physical surroundings but to a pseudo-environment, a symbolic environment, and it may be more important than the actual one in governing what he thinks and does. Only with comparative rarity does man deal with physical reality at first hand; for the far greater part, he deals with ideas about reality. In short, he interposes a symbolic system between himself and his purely physical universe. This is not to say, of course, that he moves in a world of utter fantasy. The symbols he has developed are his attempts to organize his sensations and experiences into some meaningful form, to bring some order and meaning to his existence, and thus to deal with his environment. And indeed through the use of symbols man can alter and shape his environment.

What one sees from the institutional perspective is that the mass media are but one aspect of human communication in general. Like the semaphore and tribal drum, they are technical extensions of this primary social process that I have been talking about. As purveyors of symbols, the mass media help society to function. They are carriers of the values, the beliefs, the distinctive tone of the society in which they operate. As Walter Lippmann observed some forty years ago, they interpose a sort of pseudo-environment between man and physical reality. But if they are a force for stability, they are also a force for change. And because they are technical extensions, they can transmit their message across vast sweeps of space and time.

What one further sees from his institutional perspective is that the mass media are not really autonomous but are adjuncts of other orders. Looking back through history, one sees how various dominant institutions, unwittingly or by conscious design, have used the media to maintain and strengthen their power. So it was when the church used the printing press to reinforce and extend its influence. So it was when the Crown held the press of England in thrall. So it is today in Soviet Russia, where the mass media are an adjunct of the political order, or in the United States, where they are an adjunct of the industrial.

What one sees still further, however, is that the media are a force for disrupting the status quo as well as for perpetuating it. Under the bejeweled but firm hand of Queen Elizabeth I, the press was a means of consolidating the power of the Crown and of achieving the nationalism that echoes so gloriously through the chronicle plays of Shakespeare. Yet in the hands of dissidents the press became a powerful weapon for wresting the scepter from the monarch and reducing his presence on the throne to the largely ceremonial. Or consider another instance. When printing came along, its immediate effect seems to have been to disseminate and perpetuate the very superstitions that scientists were trying to combat. In the November 1962 issue of *The American Behavioral Scientist,* Livio C. Stecchini summarized the effects in this way:

> In the sixteenth century books of geography consolidated the outmoded conceptions, just when navigators and discoverers were revealing completely new worlds. The press was greatly responsible for the general wave of opposition to the Copernican doctrine. Copernicus' book *De revolutionibus orbium coelestium,* published in 1543 A.D., was not reprinted for twenty-three years, while in the interval there appeared a cataract of popular works on astrology. Not until the beginning of the seventeenth century did the

non-academic public, reading in vernacular, become sufficiently enlightened to make it possible for Galileo to impose his views by appealing especially to them. The surprising epidemic of witch trials which began in the sixteenth century can be blamed partly on enterprising publishers who discovered that there was an excellent market for books on magic and witchcraft.

Yet true as all of that may be, few persons would dispute the subsequent influence of the press on the dissemination and advancement of learning.

If we look at the press from an institutional perspective, we should be especially concerned, I think, with the forces that have helped to make our mass communications system what it is. From here on, I would like to talk about two environments in which our communications system grew up. Both of those environments, as I will try to show, have played a tremendous part in determining the nature of our communications system. On the one hand, the mass media have been conditioned by an environment that exists largely in the minds of men. They have been profoundly influenced, that is, by the way we have answered such fundamental questions as the nature of man, the ideal relationship of man to the state, and the nature of truth and knowledge. On the other hand, the media have been shaped by such powerful social and economic forces as the rise of democracy, urbanization, and the industrial and technological revolution.

The classical libertarian theory of the press derived from the ideas of the Enlightenment, and among its several assumptions are these: That man is a creature of reason who wants to know the truth and will be guided by it, that he can find truth by applying his reason, that he is born with certain inalienable natural rights, and that he forms governments of his own volition to protect those rights, and that hence the best government is that which governs least.

In brief, the libertarian theory of the press came to be something like this: The press must have only the most minimum of restraints imposed upon it because man can find truth only if there is free trade in information and ideas. No one need worry about the wide arena of freedom, though, for the natural workings of things provides certain built-in correctives and safeguards. If some parts of the press lie and distort, if some parts abuse their freedom, other parts will find it expedient or profitable to expose them. And, after all, man puts all information and ideas to the powerful test of reason. He may find some truth amidst falsehood, some falsehood amidst truth, but over the long pull truth will prevail.

The government should keep its hands off the press for several reasons. For one thing, free expression is a natural right, one the state must preserve and protect. For another, the state has traditionally been a foe of liberty and is always likely to use the press for its own selfish purposes. For yet another thing, the state by intervening would surely upset the delicate dialectic by which truth emerges. The press, then, is best left in private hands, to make its own way in the market-place, free from the pressures of any one group or interest. In short, freedom under libertarian theory consists simply of the absence of restraint; to put it another way, a negative freedom is an effective freedom.

As that theory evolved, certain social functions came to be ascribed to the press. The press, for instance, is charged with enlightening the public and providing it with some entertainment. It is charged with servicing the political system by carrying the information and discussions that the electorate needs for its decisions. It is charged with protecting individual rights by sounding the alarm whenever they are threatened or infringed. It is charged with servicing the economic system, largely through advertising, and with earning its own financial support.

In the twentieth century especially, many of the assumptions of traditional theory have been seriously challenged if not indeed actually undermined, and some of us have found signs that a new theory of the press, a social responsibility theory of the press, has begun to emerge. But social responsibility theory is still largely theory, and our traditional ideas still guide a good deal of thinking about the press and still influence its workings in many ways. Let me give just one rather detailed example.

One tenet of Anglo-American theory is that the government should stay out of the communications business. My purpose is not to debate whether or not that idea is a good one. My point is that the idea has profoundly affected the nature of our communications system, although someone from another society may find it as quaint as we find the Yurok salmon fisherman's belief that he must not eat in his boat. From his parochial viewpoint, the Yurok has good reason for that bit of dietary abstinence: eating on the water violates his tribe's belief that various channels of nature must be kept apart. From our parochial viewpoints, so ingrained are the laissez faire doctrines of Adam Smith and the experiences of men who fought for press freedom in the past, we think we have good reason for keeping the government's hands off communications; for control necessarily follows support, we reason, and the government can weigh the scales on which truth is measured. In each case, a sacrosanct belief has affected life's crucial affairs—getting enough to eat in one, communicating with our fellows in the other.

Let me give just one illustration of how our faith in laissez faire has affected our communications system. Broadcasting depends upon the use of a limited number of channels, and other countries have handled the ownership of radio and TV facilities in various ways. The assumption is that the airwaves belong to the people. There is nothing in the nature of the medium demanding that it be left to private entrepreneurs, or, if it is, that its programs be surrounded by and punctuated with pleas to buy this product or that.

But broadcasting costs money, and someone has to pick up the tab. In our society the financing, described crudely, goes something like this:

Broadcasters pay for programing and all of the equipment for transmitting it, but they are more than reimbursed by advertisers. Presumably the advertisers are not out of pocket, though, for they are reimbursed by listeners and viewers, who also must invest in receiving equipment. So ultimately the consumer bears the cost of broadcasting, but his money is channeled through private rather than governmental hands. True, the government regulates broadcasting, but the Federal Communications Commission has severe legal and practical limitations on its powers.

So strong is the conviction that communications must be kept in private hands that the federal government was reluctant to assign frequencies for educational and other non-commercial broadcasting. When it did, it acted in accord with the negative tradition of our press theory. It simply granted schools and communities permission to operate stations, but it made no provision for getting them on the air or keeping them there. Many stations got their money from state funds, a form of government support that was only partially taboo, since the cause was "education."

Once a year the Yurok suspends his tribal taboos, and in 1962 Congress waived one by authorizing the expenditure of $32,000,000 to encourage the growth of educational TV. Even though that sum was only about 60 percent of what Procter & Gamble spent on network TV in 1961, Congress hesitated for months before actually appropriating just a small part of it.

Although critics have found fault with our system of broadcasting, attack is not my aim here. My object is simply to show how an idea, central to public thinking about the press, has contributed to the nature of the system.

It is not just ideas, however, that have given us the sort of communications system we have. Social, economic, and political forces shaped the media too, and a combination of ideas and these other things made the media what they are.

In a way, it is not surprising that the mass media should be described as an adjunct of the industrial order. The rise of journalism paralleled the rise of capitalism, and printing itself was one of the earliest forms of mass production. Many early printers in England and America were primarily businessmen. Indeed, the fight for press freedom in England arose not just from political causes and the philosophical principles of free inquiry; it also came about from the trade demands of London printers and stationers who wanted to pursue wealth without state interference.

Today our communication system is characterized by bigness, fewness, and costliness. Small units have grown into huge ones. The *Reader's Digest,* for instance, began publication in a Greenwich Village basement in 1921 with a capital of $5,000 and a list of 1,500 charter subscribers. Today it publishes more than forty editions around the world, and its domestic edition alone reaches slightly more than one in four of U.S. adults. As the media have grown, there has been need for fewer of them. Three networks serve the great majority of TV stations, and two major wire services supply the great bulk of international, national, and regional news to the nation's dailies. As the media have grown, they also have become costly. A century ago one could start a metropolitan daily like the New York *Times* for $50,000 to $75,000. Today one can spend more than a million getting a daily going in a medium-sized town such as Jackson, Mississippi, and then have it fail.

In all of those things, the media are not much different from other businesses and industries. Bigness, fewness, and costliness are characteristics of much of our economic order. The electronics industry is dominated by a few huge complexes, and the automotive industry has its short list of giants. Most cities have a few large department stores, and it would be about as quixotic to establish a new one as to run a Republican in an Alabama election.

What happened is that the media were moulded by forces that conditioned American industry generally and that tremendously affected other social, economic, and political institutions. These forces wrought a powerful revolution that affected virtually every aspect of American life, especially after the Civil War, although their foundations were laid long before that.

Those forces, closely interrelated, were the rise of democracy, the spread of popular education, the industrial and technological revolution, urbanization, and, in this century, the redistribution of income.

In the nineteenth century, the electorate broadened as restrictions on voting gradually broke down, although it was not until 1920 that women got the right to vote. Meanwhile, qualifications on the right to hold office were giving way; no longer did a candidate need to own property or meet religious tests before he could hold office. One result of all of this was that the common man, for the first time in history, achieved effective political power. Another was that he was called upon, at least in theory, to make innumerable decisions that once had been made for him, decisions that required information, decisions that countless special pleaders were anxious to help him make.

A concomitant of universal suffrage was the spread of free popular education. By 1850, in principle if not in practice, the issue of a common-school education for all children at public expense was settled in the North and in parts of the South. In the half-century after 1860, the number of high schools increased a hundredfold, from 100 to 10,000, and a growing proportion of children entered their classrooms. After the Civil War, assisted by the land-grant movement, colleges began a period of expansion that has made the bachelor's degree a commonplace. All of this gave the media a vast audience equipped at least with the rudimentary tools of literacy and at best with far-ranging intellectual interests.

Between the end of the Civil War and the start of the new century, industrialization and mechanization hit America with all the force of revolution. So pervasive were the changes they brought about that a man of George Washington's time would probably have been more at home in the Holy Land of Jesus Christ than in the America of Teddy Roosevelt. A web of shiny rails held the nation together, and factories sprouted up where once corn had grown. Inventor after inventor came up with machines and gadgets to do the tasks that man once had performed by hand. Steam power replaced water power, electricity and the internal-combustion engine replaced steam. In the sixty years after 1850, the average manufacturing plant increased its capital more than thirty-nine times, its number of wage earners nearly seven times, the value of its output more than nineteen times.

Beneath much of that change, of course, lay a system of mass production and mass distribution. The system depended upon standardization and mass consumption; so long as consumers would accept goods tailored to averages instead of to individual preferences, they were treated to a profusion of products at relatively low cost. Mass production changed the conception of markets from areas to people. The typical manufacturer no longer produced only for his own locality; he sought out buyers wherever they lived. Now, all of the characteristics of mass production—greater use of product, standardization, and so on—had implications for the mass media, as I plan to show.

But one is so important that I wish to mention it now—the development of advertising. For one thing, mass production and mass distribution needed some kind of inexpensive mass salesmanship. For another thing, the media and appeals that worked when markets were regional or local did not suffice when markets became widely-scattered consumers. For still another thing, manufacturers had no great need of advertising when their production was barely above subsistence level. But as assembly lines turned out a seemingly endless flow of products of seemingly endless variety, as consumption became essential to keeping the stream of goods flowing, manufacturers had to make consumers conscious of dimly-sensed needs and desires, had to channel human drives to exploit the psychic values of their wares, had to make the consumer want to consume. For yet another thing, as unlabeled merchandise gave way to the brand-name product, the manufacturer saw the financial advantage inherent in his name and trademark. If he could convince the consumer that his product was more desirable than all others, he could charge a premium for it. Advertising grew, and as it did the media clutched at it for financial support.

Along with the industrial and technological revolution came the crowding of Americans together in cities. Farm workers put down the plow to tend the machines of the factory. Boat after boat brought immigrants seeking new opportunities—some 11½ million of them in the thirty years before 1900—and although many of them huddled together on the coast, many others ventured inland, some no doubt encouraged by the special rail fares that let them journey from New York to Chicago for as little as a dollar. All in all, the nation's population just about doubled between 1870 and 1900, and the city became home for an increasing proportion of it. Gathered in one place, people were natural markets for the media. And the immigrant, in many ways, had an influence on the media. The foreign-language newspaper, for instance, provided a link with the homeland and with others from it, helped adjustment to a strange land but also encouraged reading of regular American dailies. The early movies, low in price and heavy on pantomime, were an ideal medium for the foreign-born struggling with a new tongue and wanting escape from the drudgery of the factory.

In our own century, we have seen a redistribution of income so apparent that it probably is unnecessary to document it. It is true, of course, that despite all of our talk about the affluent society, poverty stubbornly exists and many Americans still live in actual want. It is also true that disparities of income still exist, although not on the grand scale of 1900 when Andrew Carnegie's personal tax-free income of $20,000,000 was at least 20,000 times that of the average workingman. The middle-class American is considerably better off financially than he was in 1900, and that point is important to the mass media, not only because he has money for TV sets, transistor radios, and newspaper and magazine subscriptions but also because he has money for the advertisers' washing machines, hi-fi sets, and automobiles.

My little excursion into history has turned up little that is unfamiliar, I am sure. I have dwelt on the past at such length because critics have looked back to it surprisingly little when they have tried to explain why the media are what they are. My pitch is that the communications industries, like other industries, were affected by the social and economic forces I have just outlined; they changed, in short, from personal craft industries to impersonal mass-production industries, and today they share many of the characteristics of other mass-production enterprises.

First, the mass media usually carve out little markets of their own, much as manufacturers and retailers do. The publisher of a confessions magazine no more expects every literate American to curl up with his tales of sin and redemption than an overalls manufacturer expects every American to wear his blue jeans. Each has a pretty clear idea of who is a good prospect for what he turns out, and he fashions his product accordingly.

Usually the market of a medium coincides with that of its advertisers. A newspaper typically concentrates its circulation in the trade area served by local retailers, for instance, and a magazine like *Farm Journal* aims at people who buy the tractors and chemical fertilizers extolled on its advertising pages. Even TV programers do not necessarily expect the people who guffaw at the Beverly Hillbillies to sit entranced by Meet the Press.

Media that do not carry advertising quite often pick out specialized markets, too. The book clubs neatly illustrate the point. Sired by that middle-aged grandfather, the Book-of-the-Month Club, their tribe has multiplied to include clubs for antique collectors, gardeners, cooks, farmers, educators, salesmen, executives, Civil War buffs and other amateur historians, Irishmen, outdoorsmen, drama and art lovers, science fans, yachtsmen, writers, Catholics, Jews, Lutherans and other Protestants, young children, teenagers, and grapplers of prose in its original French and Spanish.

A second consequence is what we might rather grandiosely call a democratization of content. In simple words, the mass media as a whole turned from a class audience to a mass audience and adjusted their content accordingly. Newspapers began their transition from sober organs for the mercantile class to lively sources of news for quite literally the man on the street in the early nineteenth century. Magazines began their change about a half-century later. Movies, radio, and television, born into a world of cities and technology, went after a mass market from the start.

As I have already said, the media seek out their own little publics. But in speaking to those publics, the media tend to address themselves to some center point, to some common denominator of taste, interest, and capability. In the nature of things a publisher or broadcaster must conduct his business pretty much as any other manufacturer must. A magazine publisher and a refrigerator maker, say, both want maximum saturation of their chosen markets. The media need audiences to exist, and to get and hold them they must please the majority of their chosen market. They can no more tailor their product to the specifications of a single individual or tiny group than can the dressmakers in New York's garment district. Overall, then, they tend to reflect the concerns, values, beliefs, and tastes of the great majority, and therein lies their essential conservatism.

Third, the mass media have become standardized in content and in technique. Newspapers across the land are pretty much alike in size, format, and overall appearance; in the ways in which they get their news; in the ways in which they write it, headline it, and present it; even in the relative play they give to national and international events. Magazines depend upon a pattern of content that carries over from issue to issue, and the big ones play a relatively small scale of major themes. Television programs are remarkable more for their basic sameness than their variety; the past season offered more than a dozen series in which Western badmen found death on the dusty streets of frontier towns, for instance, and depending on how one counted them, between twenty-three and thirty situation comedy series. And TV programs themselves, as any viewer knows, are developed in familiar, standardized ways. This standardization seems an almost inevitable result as the media increased their reach, their speed, and their efficiency by adopting such techniques of mass production as division of labor and mechanization, but consumer convenience and expectation also have probably played some part.

Fourth, as content became democratized, as technological advances enabled speedy output, there has been an increased use of the media. Today the typical American spends more time looking at and listening to the mass media than at anything else except his work or sleeping, and the typical youngster leaving high school has spent more time in front of a TV set than in the classroom. Newspapers, magazines, radio, and television all penetrate deep into the population.

Fifth, the media have become more efficient, just as many other mass-production enterprises have. The telegraph, wireless, train, and plane have enabled the media not only to take the entire world for their beat but to cover it with astonishing swiftness. Until the middle of the last century, England was still two or three weeks away, and at home news was slow in traveling from one part of the country to another.

When Andrew Jackson successfully defended New Orleans in the War of 1812–14, New Yorkers did not read about the outcome until a month afterwards. And as they learned from their papers five days later, the battle itself had been fought two weeks after the peace treaty was signed

"Every now and then Roger likes to cut himself off from all media."

in London. But when the Korean War broke out in June, 1950, Jack James's United Press dispatch reached Washington almost at once —several minutes before the State Department's own cable, in fact.

New means of communication and improvements in the old ones have made possible vast audiences for the media. High-speed presses and mechanical typesetting allowed newspapers and magazines to seek their large circulations, and the electronic media have put a speaker into instantaneous touch with millions of persons. We often forget how very recent some of these changes are. In my own childhood, in 1919, when President Woodrow Wilson wanted to sell the Treaty of Versailles to the nation, he spent twenty-seven days traveling more than 8,000 miles in seventeen states to deliver forty formal speeches and many more informal talks, only one of them with benefit of public address system. In December, 1962, when three TV networks carried "Conversation with the President," John F. Kennedy was in instantaneous touch with an estimated 21,960,000 American homes, according to A. C. Nielsen figures.

Finally, the mass media, like other industries, have used the assembly-line technique of division of labor. Once even the publisher of a metropolitan daily could operate as James Gordon Bennett did in 1835, when he gathered his own news, wrote it up, handled business affairs, and waited on customers at a desk made of two barrels with a plank across them. By the 1870s those days were largely gone, and by the 1890s the large-city dailies had staffs about as specialized as they are today. All of the other media, too, have come to depend upon a variety of specialists to put together the finished product. As they have, the individual employee has lost most of whatever chance for self-expression he ever had. He became one of a team turning out mass-produced images, and too large an investment rides on his efforts for him to produce with anything but the market in mind.

Those, then, are the forces that have joined to give us the sort of communication system we have, and in large measure they are responsible for the many strengths we too often take for granted. They have contributed to the development of a communication system that reaches virtually the entire population and that in the aggregate makes available an astonishing amount of entertainment and an astonishing array of information, viewpoint, and interpretation on a wide array of subjects with incredible swiftness and superb technical skill. They have contributed to the important part that the media have played in bringing about our high material standard of living.

But in large measure those forces also are responsible for the faults that have sent many a critic reaching for his thesaurus of epithets. They have contributed to the superficiality, the sameness, the blandness, and the blindness that characterize a good deal of media content. They have contributed to the bigness, fewness, and costliness that some critics see as jeopardizing the free trade in information and ideas, putting control of a powerful social instrument into the hands of the few and converting the personal right of press freedom into a property right.

All of what I have said, I immodestly think, has some implications for those who are serious in their criticism of the mass media.

First, those who examine the press should try to achieve objectivity in two meanings of the term. On the one hand, as they set out to discover what the mass media are and why they are what they are, they should leave their ideological baggage behind, much as a good cultural anthropologist does. They should look deep into the past for clues to present understanding. They should examine the interrelationships of the media with other parts of society. On the other hand, they should explore the objective social functions that the media perform, quite apart from those ascribed by normative press theory. As Jensen suggested, the media have a reality of their own. Although they are man-made creations, they have developed certain objective functions distinct from the tasks assigned them by their operators and by society. Desirable or not, those functions exist, and it is the duty of the serious critic to understand them.

Second, critics should put up for serious examination our traditional theory of the press, which in many ways seems out of joint with the times. That theory may have been adequate in the eighteenth and nineteenth centuries, when both the world and the communication system were far less complex than today, but one might ask if it is in accord with contemporary thought and reality. Some such examination has already begun; and as publishers and broadcasters themselves have discarded parts of traditional theory as outmoded, there are indications that a new theory of social responsibility is emerging. As a part of this intellectual overhaul, which should begin with the questioning of basic assumptions, I hope we could also re-examine some of the notions that have long surrounded traditional theory. For instance, are we right in the notion that although the media have a responsibility to enlighten the public, the public has no special responsibility to be enlightened? Are the media right in their notion that in enlightening the public, the demands of the market are the best test of how well the job is being done? Are we right in the notion that bigness is necessarily badness? Does a multiplicity of communications units necessarily mean a multiplicity of viewpoints? Are small media operators necessarily more socially responsible than large ones? Does control necessarily follow financial support?

In conclusion, let me say that I am not proposing that we grant the media absolution for all their sins, venal or otherwise. Some, I know, will read my message that way. In looking at the press from an institutional perspective, some will conclude that publishers and broadcasters are swept inexorably along by powerful, impersonal social and cultural forces and that there is nothing that they or we can do about it. That conclusion implies a degree of predestinarianism I am quite unwilling to accept. Man with brain and hand has given the media the milieus in which they operate, and man if he will can change them.

Part Two
The Media

While Part 1 gave a general overview of the workings of the media, Part 2 separates them according to type. This is important, since each medium uniquely shapes what it presents. In other words, the means of communication is an intrinsic part of the message conveyed. (Marshall McLuhan went so far as to say that the medium **is** the message.) Thus the nature of a society is profoundly affected by the types of media that are prevalent in it. From the time of Gutenberg until the twentieth century, print was predominant. This meant that messages appeared in a spatial context (on the printed page) and that the visual sense was emphasized. Today these orientations are changing; we are experiencing a virtual revolution in communications. Walter Ong wrote that "a new age is upon us, and its shift from sight-emphasis to increased sound-emphasis spans this entire area from the diffusion of the word to the exploration of one's surroundings."*

This shift from sight to sound has occurred largely because of the development of electronic media. Ong described some of the implications of these new media:

> In their whole trend, modern developments in communications, while they have not slighted the visual, have given more play to the oral-aural, which a purely typographical culture had reduced to a record minimum in human life. The sequence of the development running from silent print through audiovisual telegraph to the completely aural radio is an obvious instance of increasing aural dominance. Even television belongs partially in this visual-to-aural series, being only equivocally a regression to visualism. For the visual element in television is severely limited. The amount of detail feasible on a television screen is far less than that visible on a movie screen and not remotely comparable to that tolerable and easily discernible in photographs. Details on television have to be filled in aurally, by explicit vocal explanation or by suggestion through music and sound effects. Silent television is hardly an engaging prospect.†

This emphasis on the aural sense is not the only way in which the electronic media shape our messages. In his article "The New Languages" (pp. 409–423), Edmund Carpenter refers to print as an "embalming process" and describes the printed message as inflexible and permanent. In contrast, the electronic media, with their messages conveyed partially or entirely by sound, cannot communicate with such precision. Logical thought is giving way to multisensory perception. The TV generation tends to respond to a communication with "I feel" rather than "I know."

But the print and electronic media do not operate in isolation; they are shaped by each other. The newer media not only have become alternatives to print but also have caused the print media to change. For instance, the immediacy and urgency of interviews conducted on radio and television probably inspired the intimate question-and-answer interviews that are becoming increasingly popular in the print media. The electronic media have also increased the variety of ways in which literature can be experienced.

* Walter J. Ong, **The Barbarian Within** (New York: Macmillan, 1962), p. 225.
† **Ibid.**

No longer is a book considered an object to be preserved in libraries. A poem is no longer merely set on a printed page; it may now be read aloud—often by the poet himself—and conceived as a media "production" in quadraphonic sound.

The print media, in turn, influence the electronic. For example, the magazine format has been adopted by some television news programs. A more significant change—which can be at least partially attributed to the influence of the print media—is in the audiences the electronic media attempt to attract. The electronic media tend to be associated with mass audiences and the print media with small, select audiences, but this distinction seems to be blurring. The broadcast networks and commercial film industries have recently been adopting a marketing approach that has traditionally been associated with the print media: aiming their programs and films at small, homogeneous audiences rather than at the masses. For example, radio stations direct their programming toward one segment of a community, some even distinguishing between early teen-agers and late teen-agers. Experimental and "art" films now compete with films designed to fit a formula attractive to wide audiences. The steady diet of escapism offered on commercial television is now spiced with shows that have socially significant themes. Although films like **Jaws** and television shows like **Kojak** or **Happy Days** are still in the majority, a viewer now has access to quality productions that draw a relatively small audience. Lina Wertmuller's **Seven Beauties** did not enjoy the broad appeal of **Network** or **Rocky,** but it did serve an important segment of the film-going audience. The same was true for television's **American Short Story** series.

Part 2 considers the different technical and physical capabilities and limitations of the print and electronic media. Each medium has its own biases that enable it to perform uniquely. While the verbal messages of the print media tend to stimulate sequential, logical thought, the aural and visual images of the electronic media lead to immediate, emotional responses. In reading the selections, the media student should keep in mind not only the differences between the print and electronic media but the implications of those differences. It is impossible to make an accurate evaluation of a communication without considering the unique characteristics of the medium through which it was presented.

The Print Media

The American Periodical Press and Its Impact

by ROLAND E. WOLSELEY

Journalism Professor Roland Wolseley discusses magazines in the United States, reaffirming that they are an important medium today. He considers both the impact of particular magazines and the impact of the magazine industry as a whole.

While this article was being written the world of the periodical press in the U.S.A. was the maker of front-page news. One of the country's oldest and most famous magazines, *The Saturday Evening Post,* died of malnutrition, i.e., of lack of advertising revenue. At its death, almost its 150th birthday anniversary, it had more than three million subscribers and newsstand buyers; a few months before it had in excess of six million, but half the subscription list was dropped in an economy move that was unsuccessful.

Too much circulation is a disease from which a number of American magazines have suffered in the past two decades. On the surface it appears to be a paradoxical situation. Generally speaking, in all print journalism it has for years been the rule that the higher the circulation the higher the advertising rate and consequently the greater the income. This formula still is followed, by and large. But an enormously expensive magazine to manufacture and distribute by the millions of copies each week (in recent years every other week), as was the *Post* and as were such other giants of circulation that succumbed at mid-century (*Collier's, Coronet, American,* and *Woman's Home Companion* were among them) must enlarge the formula to include 'if costs of production and distribution are kept in ratio.'

Once, too, magazines and newspapers could take for granted that if they offered an advertiser the readers he wanted they could count on him to buy the space to reach those readers. But today there is a new type of competitor: broadcasting, and particularly television. It can tell an ad-

The American Periodical Press and Its Impact: From *Gazette,* International Journal of the Science of the Press, vol. 15 (1969). Reprinted by permission.

vertiser that he can reach the mass of the people through television sets, of which in the U.S. there now are more in use than there are motor cars or telephones. Since television's arrival as an advertising competitor, two decades ago, magazines of mass circulation have had problems.

All this about the failure of widely-known American magazines may leave the impression that the periodical press is in an unhealthy state. But this conclusion has no basis in fact. On the contrary, the health of this industry as a whole is sound. The animal kingdom was not destroyed, centuries ago, when the dinosaurs, and almost all other huge animals, died out. Similarly, some of the giant magazines have not been able to adjust to new competition, new tastes, new climates of opinion, and a changing economic order. But there are at least 20,000 periodicals in the U.S.A., and the handful of huge-circulation publications is only a small, if widely-publicized, minority.

To understand the American periodical press and its impact it is necessary to see it whole. Only a few generalizations can be made about the entire industry, for it is in many segments. In fact, neither the industry itself nor the public at which it is aimed agrees on what that industry includes. To most Americans the word *magazine* (the term *periodical* is not much used) connotes a publication, weekly or monthly, intended either for all persons, as is *The Reader's Digest,* or for a large portion of the population, as is *McCall's* or *Ladies' Home Journal,* both multi-million circulation periodicals for women. And many persons employed in this consumer or general area of magazinedom take the same narrow view. In fact, the most widely used reports and studies of the industry usually cover only the consumer books (in the jargon of the publishing business a magazine often is called a *book,* to the utter confusion of outsiders), as if the thousands of small periodicals did not count. This situation came about, of course, because the bulk of the dollar investment in advertising space is in the consumer area: these magazines have been the big money makers. Actually the majority of the consumer magazines do not have large circulations despite their broad content.

Just what kind of publication the others are considered by the owners of the consumer magazines is not clear. Those others exist, just the same, and are far greater numerically and in the long run have a different and perhaps greater impact.

Depending upon how you count them, the consumer magazines may number as few as three and as many as 900. Perhaps *The Reader's Digest,* with 27,000,000 circulation, is the only true American consumer magazine left. The figure 900 is reached by including those that attempt to reach a wide public. The majority have small circulation and little advertising. They print trivia. They include sensational, sexy adventure magazines for boys and men; various fan publications for the worshippers of cinema idols, sports stars, and other entertainers; various collections of thin articles about hobbies; and numerous attempts to catch the teen-agers' coins with magazines telling the girls how to apply cosmetics and the boys how to become a professional football player.

The remaining 19,100 are for the most part the actual core of the magazine press. That figure, in round numbers, includes about 10,000 known as industrial periodicals but more commonly called house organs or company magazines, and are ignored by the entrepreneurs in the business because they do not accept advertising and are given to readers, who are employees of a company, its customers, its dealers, or its prospects. Also in the 19,100 are 2,500 business magazines, that is, commercially-published periodicals catering to the business world and ranging from the austere *Fortune,* published by Time Inc., to the highly specialized *Roads and Streets,* issued by the Reuben H. Donnelley Corp., which has 17 others equally specialized. And it also includes about 400 published by associations, embracing the *National Geographic* and the *Journal of the American Medical Association,* two of the most profitable enterprises in the business.

To these can be added about 1,500 that deal with religion, 300 magazines of education at different levels, 200 about labor, and the remaining thousands that are devoted to such subjects as science, specialized sports, all of the arts, and various juvenilia.

In America, it appears, if three or more people get together their first act is to form a committee and their second is to launch a publication; generally it is a magazine.

The periodical press in the U.S. therefore is overwhelmingly composed of specialized journals. Yet those who trace the press's current fortunes insist upon judging it by the fate of a minority of large periodicals hardly typical of the entire industry.

The situation is made even more complicated by the realization by some of the larger publishing companies that issue consumer magazines that the specialized field is a less risky one and that a mixture of operations is desirable. Cowles Communications, Inc., for example, is a widely diversified firm that issues several mass magazines (including *Look* and *Family Circle,* with 7,750,000 and 6,000,000 circulation, respectively) but also has a clutch of business periodicals which it calls 'Magazines for Industry'; these include *Candy Marketer, Food & Drug Packaging, Bottling Industry,* and nine others. Another large firm, Condé Nast, is best known for its popular *Vogue, Mademoiselle,* and *Glamour.* But only insiders realize that it also issues *Analog,* a science fiction periodical, and *House and Garden,* whose function is obvious from its title. Similarly, the Hearst firm, one of the ancients of American magazine journalism, has *Good Housekeeping* as well as *Motor* and *American Druggist,* among others, in its group of more than a dozen.

The picture of the industry must include certain trends. One relates to advertising. In each of the past four years the gross income from advertising has exceeded one billion dollars. Year by year the intake was higher. Actually it is more, for those who do the adding include mainly the consumer magazines. But at the same time the number of pages of advertising sold has decreased, the decline in 1968 from 1967 amounting to 2 per cent, for example. There has been some question about the soundness of an industry where such a situation exists. But it is a debatable situation and of concern, perhaps, largely to businessmen who insist on quantity, who measure success by numbers: number of subscribers, number of readers, number of advertisers, numbers of pages of it sold, and numbers of dollars brought in. They are so fascinated by numbers that they neglect quality and fail to see the danger of the numbers game, as did *The Saturday Evening Post* and several other magazines, before it is too late. Within the bitterly competitive consumer magazine business however, the worry about losses in amounts of advertising sold is justified, if for no other reason than that buyers of general advertising space tend to place their orders with periodicals already swollen with copy. They give little thought to any obligation to support a publication that may be in temporary distress so as to keep competition alive, if not a voice heard. In other words, the successful publication becomes still more successful and its rivals are killed off by advertisers who flock to the leader.

The worshippers of numbers stand in strong contrast to one of the great American editors, Frederick Lewis Allen, who was at the helm of *Harper's,* for many years a leading serious magazine. Writing in his magazine in 1950, Allen said: 'Our circulation . . . is a practically microscopic figure when set alongside the circulations of the monster slicks and digests. But it includes so many people who write, speak, teach, edit, manage, and govern that we may perhaps be permitted to remind you that the ignition system is a very small part of an automobile.'

The American periodical press is an industry which is fundamentally sound so long as printed communication is vital and has not been replaced by electronic means of communication. It also is a highly segmented and diversified industry. Few generalizations therefore can be made about its impact as a whole. Easier to point out are the effects of the various types of periodicals. The main obstacle to a clear, broad answer is that tools or techniques for the measurement of effect or influence still are rudimentary. Some progress has been made in noting the effect of single elements that can be isolated: certain advertisements of specific articles, for example, but little reliably beyond that. Some studies have been made which indicate effects within the segments, however, and these can be put on the record for what they may be worth.

The impact of the American periodical press also has been technological and social. The large, mass-circulation magazines have influenced the smaller magazines, which in many instances seek to imitate their appearance and to emulate the high quality of their printing, layout, and make-up. They also have influenced magazines around the world. Europe, for example, is given to publishing magazines resembling *Life* and *Look,* and almost no heavily industrialized country is without its imitator of *Time* (*The Link* in India, *Elseviers* in the Netherlands, *Tiempo* in Mexico, *Der Spiegel* in Germany, and *L'Express* in France, for example).

The social effect has to do with the discharge or failure to discharge its social responsibilities. These responsibilities the magazine press shares with all communications media, printed or electronic. They include the obligation, in a political democracy such as is the U.S.A., to provide the people with a fair presentation of facts, with honestly held opinions, and with truthful advertising. All but the subsidized periodicals hold—or seek to hold—to these goals within a certain framework: that of the business order, the private initiative, profit-making system.

As business institutions, commercial magazines, consumer and specialized alike, have influenced the progress of the business world by stimulating the desires for products and services on the part of readers through advertising and editorial content. This result has in turn affected the living standards of readers, influencing their decisions about how they dress, what they eat, and how they use their spare time. The enormous consumption of cosmetics by American girls and women is in part due to the years of commodity advertising in magazines for those readers. The sale of motor cars is heavily influenced by the advertising and special editorial content about new models.

What might be considered the official concept of the influence of the general magazines has come from the Magazine Advertising Bureau of the U.S.A. Placed first among general effects is the shaping of public opinion. 'The national magazine does not have the spot news function of either the newspaper or the radio,' MAB said. 'But being edited with deliberation, it is read with equal deliberation, and therefore has the unique ability to form a *mature* public opinion, nationally.' It also is a reflector of American life or what the owners think is American life. Said the MAB: 'Life is not the daily headlines of the newspaper, nor is it the artificial dramatics thrown out daily, hourly by radio. The solid values of the lives of millions of American families are reported by the national magazine, unsensationally but vividly and accurately, in articles and fiction, in pictures and illustrations.' The contrast with television, even sharper, might have been added.

James Playsted Wood, a magazine official and writer of several books on periodicals, reminds us that the magazine is read more persistently than any other medium, is less perishable, and is read attentively. It provokes results, receives reactions. Much magazine material later goes into books and motion pictures; reprints are made.

'The character of a given magazine limits its audience,' he says, 'thus, to some extent, the spread of its influence, its educational force, its persuasion to belief, and possibility to individual or social action.'

Wood properly qualifies his generalization by using the word *given*. The effects of the comic magazines are unlike those of the literary, and within the specialized magazine world the effects of one technical journal only in a superficial way resemble those of another.

Led by *The Reader's Digest,* condensed material and pocket-size magazines have stimulated popularized reading by the middle-class public, have spread certain social positions and attitudes, and have increased demand for short, quickly-read publications. The digest made the portable magazine among the most popular of those published, one of them being of world influence.

With magazines of seven and eight million circulation setting the pace, the women's group, with which may be associated the service and shelter books (*Woman's Day* representing service, with its many recipes, and *Better Homes,* the shelter group) has been principally responsible for influence wielded by advertising departments on homes and families of the middle class. They have to some extent standardized housekeeping tools, widened the variety of cookery, introduced or popularized certain habits, such as more frequent bathing and shaving, use of deodorants, and hair coloring, and called attention to books, motion pictures, and art works, considerably broadening their effect. Not a minor result has been the introduction of fictional stereotypes; most heroes and heroines of fiction in women's magazines seldom are realistic, although there is a trend away from that in a few. Consumer magazines try to exert influence through their advertising and editorial policies. *Esquire* in 1968, after the assassinations of Dr. Martin Luther King, Jr. and Senator Robert F. Kennedy, adopted a policy of accepting no gun advertising of any kind. This decision came after a campaign against gun advertising launched by *Advertising Age,* a business weekly. *McCall's,* with a circulation of more than eight million, on the day of Senator Kennedy's assassination, stopped its presses and inserted a two-page editorial calling on its women readers to support stronger gun control legislation, help stop excessive violence on broadcasting programs and in films, boycott certain toys, and follow other policies.

The confession magazine, more and more an imitator of the slick ones in content, has had a changing influence. In its early days it played a psychological role: it offered spiritual release for uneducated or immature readers (whether adults or adolescents) enabling them to experience adventures of the more daring and unorthodox without personal risks. Now, except for a surviving group offering stories of sex adventures and crime detection, it is achieving on its own economic level a standardization in reader habits and practices similar to the women's slicks.

The circulation and advertising leaders among men's magazines have turned away to some extent from tales of wartime bravery to tales of bedroom exploits, holding as admirable man's sexual domination of women and gratification of his dreams of wealth, power, and comfort. They encourage their readers to a hedonistic philosophy of life and to be primarily patrons of entertainment.

The religious magazines, less given than they once were to regularizing moral concepts, now are influencing their readers to apply their religious principles to social concerns as well as to personal conduct. Some have helped bring social movements into existence, such as the civil rights groups, and mustered support for social legislation in various areas of human activity: conscientious objection to war, better housing, and employment opportunities for minorities, for example.

American literary magazines have started movements, erected critical standards, and founded schools of criticism, introduced new writers, maintained the following of older ones, and provided an outlet for work not marketable to the public through general or consumer periodicals.

Magazines for juveniles have had definite effects, since their readers are in formative years. A youngster's heroes once were provided almost solely by books and magazines; today radio, television, cinema, and recordings also have strong influence, perhaps stronger. The religious juvenile publications have built concepts of right and wrong in human conduct and of individual responsibility at home and in the church or temple. They have aroused loyalties. The secular juveniles in more recent times have been simplified versions of magazines for grown-ups. Their effect has been at once to create little adults and to encourage youthful independence and also standardization of mores among adolescents. The comics have appealed to childish imaginations so effectively, and with so much question-

"Sorry, sonny, but I already get 'Cosmopolitan.'"

able content, that they have been treated as social phenomena to be studied as seriously as are educational practices.

The effects of specialized magazines are vertical rather than horizontal. A clothing publication or a food magazine affects the profession, industry, business, or other group it serves by conveying news created by the group, evaluating trends within, providing an outlet for ideas, and stimulating business through advertising. Business periodicals have taken dramatic stands to correct what they consider evils. The company magazine (house organ, as often dubbed) has established itself as a bulwark or dam against ideas that its publishers deem undesirable or has helped to stimulate business.

These influences and effects have not escaped criticism. The adverse critics say that the magazines, particularly the consumer type, are too much inclined to give the public what it wants, they deprive the public of the fullest knowledge of facts and ideas; through advertising content they stimulate desires for possessions that cannot be gratified by the average reader's income. Nor is that all the criticism. The critics go on to say that the periodicals present only conventional or ultra-conservative viewpoints, that they evade their duty to provide leadership in solving social problems, that they are time-wasting, distracting the reader from more valuable uses of his leisure, and that they knuckle in to advertisers.

The favorable critics, on the other hand, counter that magazines have helped produce the high standard of living in the U.S.A. through their advertising content, have helped to stimulate mass consumption of goods and, thereby, mass production; have therefore contributed toward the lowering of the cost of living; that they have merchandised, as one proponent has put it, new ideas; and that they have played a part of importance in every national crisis, whether it be flood, war, depression, or recovery from such disasters.

As with so many arguments, this collection is not a clear case for either pro or con. To begin with, most critics of either side are talking exclusively about the consumer magazine, and, as usual, overlooking all the rest, which as we know are in the U.S.A. fifty times as numerous, and in some instances just as influential. Accepting the consumer scope, some parts of each set of criticisms may be accepted as true.

A business society such as that of the U.S.A. prevents the majority of the magazines, consumer or specialized, from fulfilling the role of the institution wholly devoted to the welfare of society as are, for example, the church, school, and the professions of medicine and nursing. It is left for the periodical press to play a part short of full devotion to the commonweal.

John Peter picks the

John Peter, writing from the standpoint of magazine management, believes that the following consumer magazines are today's most innovative and influential. His list of trendsetters reflects the growing tendency to specialization in an attempt to serve our society's diverse interests and needs. This trend is also apparent in radio (See Kirkeby, pp. 150–152) and in the specialization of newspapers (See Malloy, pp. 212–218).

There are many criteria for selecting a list of the top ten magazines, and none of them is completely just.

One is circulation. That list would read *TV Guide, Reader's Digest, National Geographic, Family Circle, Woman's Day, Better Homes & Gardens, McCall's, Ladies' Home Journal, Playboy* and *Good Housekeeping*. The top ten in advertising revenue would be *Time, TV Guide, Newsweek, Sports Illustrated, Reader's Digest, Better Homes & Gardens, Business Week, Woman's Day, Family Circle* and *Playboy*. The top ten in profitability would be something else.

My list is of the ten most innovative and, from a magazine-making standpoint, influential magazines in the United States—not including business or professional publications. These ten are trendsetters which tell us something about the future of magazines from a publishing, editing and design standpoint. They were all launched in relatively recent years and all have enviable performance records. (Innovative magazines that attract neither readers nor advertisers do not set many trends.) The order of listing means nothing. They are all good.

It's evident from this list that there is no single success formula. There are some general interest publications though special interest successes predominate. There are publications ranging from weekly to quarterly in frequency. There are those with traditional and new journalism, with solid service and dream stuff. They all have clearly defined appeals.

It is abundantly clear, with publishing expenses rocketing, readers will be paying an increasing share of the costs. This means an all-out emphasis on the editorial product. The premium will be on the content and quality of the writing, the value of the service—less tricky layouts and more meaningful photographs and graphics. From these ten, there seems every indication that people will pay for a good product. But it had better be good.

Quarterly circulation, 100,000; advertising revenue over $100,000; subscription $10 per year; 60 percent renewals on first notice.

William Kemsley liked backpacking, writing and independence. He combined all these to launch *Backpacker* magazine in March 1973. In two years, it is at the financial break-even point.

By any yardstick, *Backpacker* has to be considered a special interest publication—a very special interest publication. Kemsley took an unorthodox approach to this. He developed the publication and then worked out the frequency. "Six issues were more than I could afford and two issues a year were too few." He went quarterly. He estimated that backpackers would pay $8 to $10 for the right magazine. The subscription price is set to carry the cost of the publication. Kemsley originally planned the magazine to be independent of advertising. He draws a hard advertising line, turning down categories that would clash with the health and environmental views of his readers.

Like *Smithsonian* (another of my picks), only more so, *Backpacker* has many of the qualities of a book. The laminated cover simply carries the name and the number rather than the date. With a small staff it relies largely on outside authors. "I figured," Kemsley says, "I could get any expert in the world to write, if I could create an exciting, prestigious product. I wrote out a list of the very best people. I don't think I've had a 'no' yet, and I haven't paid a lot of money." The same applies to the stunning photography. "They are all enthusiasts."

Editorially, the most expensive thing in the magazine is the consumer rating of equipment made by the staff, and it's worth it. "If subscribers bought the best sleeping bag according to our recent test, they would save $55—more than five times the price of the magazine."

This consumer research and authoritative know-how is mixed with hiking adventure and history—"the gods and heroes of the outdoors." *Backpacker* is beautifully produced with straightforward typography, functional graphics, color photography and rough stock special inserts. "Backpackers," Kemsley says, "have it on their coffee tables and sell it to their friends."

VIVA

Monthly circulation 800,000; advertising revenue $1,000,000; single copy price $1.25 (94 percent); subscription $16 per year (6 percent).

In any selection of the top ten it would be difficult to ignore the box office success of sex magazines. Bob Guccione, publisher of *Penthouse,* launched *Viva* in 1973—a magazine for the other sex with the same proven formula. A substantial cover price, backed with by-product sales such as *Viva*'s book club, is designed to carry the costs with advertising for profits.

Editor and assistant publisher Kathy Keeton, at a reputed salary of $335,000 per year, produces "a magazine for women liberated in mind and body. While regular women's magazines," Keeton explains, "have done a terrific job in the traditional feminine interests—decorating, fashion and beauty—women have gone out in the world today and become intellectually liberated and sexually liberated."

The *Viva* advertising rate card puts it this way—"*Viva* recaptures the quality of dreams, fulfills the fantasies and reflects the lifestyle of the women of the 70s. . . . Viva la Difference!"

Viva mixes brand-name authors with photos of male nudes. Keeton explains, "When we didn't go all out in the first two issues women wrote in calling it a cop-out. Yes," she says, "men read *Viva.* Some buy it for their wives but there are better homosexual books around if that is the interest."

Viva is an unusually handsomely printed and produced publication. In a campy style it sets a high level of design and layout. "Why not a beautiful magazine for women?" Keeton observes.

Biweekly circulation, 150,000; advertising revenue $1,300,000; single copy sales price, 50 cents (5 percent); subscription, $9.50 (95 percent).

Noting that a surprising number of fashionable women subscribed to their trade paper, *Women's Wear Daily,* Fairchild launched *W* as "The National Newspaper of Fashionable Living" in 1972. It's a special interest magazine in newsprint format with stunning upscale demographics—medium income $30,000 with 28 percent exceeding $50,000. In the midst of all the enthusiasm about the youth market, *W* touts a 47-year-old median age level.

Editorially, *W* does not break with any traditions. It is a lively mixture of jet set gossip and plush interiors which go back to early *Town and Country* days. Its extra strength is in delivering the latest fashions fast—scooping the women's fashion magazines with the speed of a newspaper. The *Women's Wear Daily* staff provides double coverage on these assignments.

The photos, sketches and typography, in traditional style, look fresh on the impressive color offset, billboard-size newspaper format.

Psychology Today

Monthly circulation, 1,000,000; advertising revenue $5,900,000; single copy price, $1; subscription, $6.

This special interest magazine was launched in 1967 as Nicholas Charney and John Veronis "took psychology public." In many ways it was the prototype of the new special interest publication trend. It charged the reader a good price for the product. It did not invent but it maximized selling by-product items to readers. It was a surprise success.

The success has to be credited to the Charney-Veronis publishing team. But the continued success must be credited in no small part to the quality of the editorial content. With nine PhD's on the masthead, editor T. George Harris says, "The audience is aware of the authenticity of the writing but not the PhD nature of it. What readers want is a sense of authority—that this is the legit from someone who has a right to know."

Psychology Today sets the pace for reader participation tests. "It invites the readers as experts in a subject they are the experts on, their life, to be part of a research project. Basically the magazine organizes a community of interest around our special interest."

The design of *Psychology Today* reflects the psychological nature of the subject with strong graphic illustrations and some of the most creative concept photography in magazines today.

Smithsonian

Monthly circulation, 635,000; advertising revenue, $2,500,000; no single copy sales; subscription $10 per year with 70 percent renewal rate.

Smithsonian was a publication so easy to underestimate that the savvy *Washington Post* declared it dead before its first issue was out. To others the idea of a respected national institution issuing a publication for its members may have seemed sound but few expected it to be one of today's thriving publishing successes.

Smithsonian was launched in the spring of 1970 with $50,000 from an anonymous donor plus the credit backing of the Institute. In four and one-half years its circulation has tripled and advertising revenues have doubled each year.

From a publishing standpoint, it started with the advantages of the name of a nationally known institution and a prestigious mailing list. It reconfirmed the reader appeal of membership in a club rather than simply subscribing to a magazine. With *National Geographic* today reaching a circulation of 8,800,000 perhaps this should not have needed confirmation.

In one sense *Smithsonian* is a book club. The publication is a keepsake, status item planned to break even on reader revenue. With single copy sales the thing, *Smithsonian* is strictly subscription only.

With special interest magazines the style, *Smithsonian* talks about its general interest appeal. Its promotion describes it as "The Renaissance of the Curious Reader." More than anything it reflects the wide-ranging interest of its very professional editor, Edward K. Thompson, hired by Smithsonian secretary S. Dillon Ripley to launch the magazine. Thompson, former managing editor of that general-interest magazine *Life,* was instructed that "we should be interested in the kind of things the Smithsonian is interested in." Since the Smithsonian is a miscellany of 11 museums and galleries popularly known as "the nation's attic," this was a broad mandate. Thompson broadened it to include "all the kinds of things the Smithsonian *should* be interested in."

Solid editing and good writing is the common ingredient of the unpredictable mix of natural and physical science, fine and folk art and also history "when it's relevant today." This editorial craftsmanship is matched in *Smithsonian*'s book-like design. Traditional typefaces are sensitively employed in straightforward layouts. Lush paper and printing makes the most of the striking four-color photography and art. *Smithsonian* is fresh evidence of the audience for a publication which combines the variety and readability of a magazine with the quality and longevity of a book.

Rolling Stone

Biweekly circulation, 400,000; 1974 estimated advertising revenue, $8,000,000; single copy price, 75 cents (70 percent); subscription $12 per year (30 percent).

Jann Wenner launched *Rolling Stone* in 1967 with $7,500 as a San Francisco rock music publication. Now age 28, Wenner has transformed his tabloid newsprint magazine into a general interest magazine covering contemporary American culture, politics and arts with special interest in music.

Rolling Stone proves that the tabloid newspaper format doesn't have to look cheap or be sold cheaply. It moved to four-color offset printing a while ago with circulation and advertising benefits. On new presses, it can now go to a bulky 64 pages. *Rolling Stone* has spawned three foreign editions in England, Germany and Japan. Its Straight Arrow book division is breaking into the black with 15 to 20 titles a year.

Editorially, *Rolling Stone* is a lifestyle magazine with 50 percent still devoted to music news and criticism. Wenner attributes part of its growth to the fact that it billed itself as an alternate—not an underground—publication covering news not printed by the so-called straight press. With writers like Hunter Thompson, *Rolling Stone* developed a reputation and won awards for solid reportage in new journalism style. At a time when shorter articles are the trend, these in-depth pieces frequently run 10,000 to 20,000 words long. This attracts good writers who like to write at length.

The shift from straight music to lifestyle reportage is underscored by the opening of a Washington, D.C., editorial office. "Politics," explains advertising director Joseph Armstrong, "was once in the music. Now politics are separated from the music that is going introspective—'Who am I?' 'What am I doing?'—but the young are still very interested in politics."

The design of *Rolling Stone* is surprisingly formal and restrained. Traditional serif typefaces top huge areas of solid text. Graphics are in the pop art style, but the superb staff photography follows the incisive photojournalistic style.

New York

Weekly circulation, 355,000; estimated advertising revenue in 1974, $7,000,000; single-copy price, 50 cents; subscription, $14.

New York began as the Sunday supplement of the *New York Herald Tribune*. When the paper folded, the supplement editor, Clay Felker, used his severance pay of $6,575 to buy the rights. With the help of a Wall Street friend, Armand Erpf's $1.1 million and a talented staff of *Trib* expatriates, Felker hit the stands in April 1967 with the first issues of *New York* magazine.

From a publishing standpoint, *New York* is a special interest magazine. It is by no means the first but is the prototype example of the flourishing breed of city magazines. The size of the city gives *New York* a built-in circulation and advertising advantage. Nevertheless, its circulation universe is limited to those who have a special interest in the particular city. This focus, along with its weekly frequency, has provided a steady and tidy income from a source frequently neglected by magazines—classified advertising.

Editorially the magazine is Clay Felker's world or Clay Felker's New York which he sees as the center of the world. "As long as there's an audience for the way I see it," Felker says, "I think that's enough." He maintains, however, the magazine is "a collaborative effort in which the editor is not the main person." Yet in a magazine abundant with talent, nobody doubts who *is* the main person. Felker has a keen editor's knack of attracting and developing able writers. From the Sunday supplement he brought writers like Tom Wolfe, Jimmy Breslin, Peter Maas, Gail Sheehy and Gloria Steinem. They pushed a personalized brand of writing known as new journalism [see "New? Journalism?" FOLIO March/April 1974]. It was these well-written investigation pieces that made readers buy and try *New York*. But what turned them into subscribers was the service stuff. *New York* became a manual on "how to survive in New York." It carries regular reviews of books, art, theatres, movies, television and food. Also, its selection of "bests" from door locks to pastrami sandwiches have set a trend. *New York* didn't invent the idea but no one else pushes "lists" with such frequency and elan.

No *New York* influence is more pervasive than that of design. Milton Glaser is not only the design director but an original partner, significantly listed second to Felker on the masthead. Glaser's use of out-of-fashion typefaces and abundant rules, hairline and otherwise, as well as what can only be described as his Push Pin Studio graphics has set the style for a whole generation of magazines.

Monthly circulation 800,000; advertising revenue $5,000,000; single copy price $1; 90 percent newsstand, 10 percent subscriptions at $6.95 per year.

Humor magazines like *Judge, Life, College Humor* and *Ballyhoo* once flourished in the United States. Aside from that comic book phenomenon, *Mad, National Lampoon* was the first in years. It was launched four years ago in 1970, when two former editors of the *Harvard Lampoon,* Doug Kenny and Henry Beard, teamed up with Twenty First Century Communications, Inc.

National Lampoon reflects the changing style of young American humor. Editorially it relies heavily on satire lapsing into sick humor. Parodies of other magazines, a regular newsstand success with the annual issues of the

Harvard Lampoon, are staples with *National Lampoon.* Burlesque advertisements, a standard ingredient of parody publications, run to mail order types in contrast with the real thing for records and hifi equipment. Vice-president of sales Gerald Taylor says, "There is nothing funny about the way the ads sell."

The magazine is staff-written. Humor writers, perhaps with talent absorbed today by TV, are hard to come by. *The New Yorker,* once famous for humorous writers like Thurber, Parker and others, now has the reputation for solid reporting.

Since a high percentage of the humor is visual, presentation plays an important part. The makeup is a scramble of underground newspaper style typography, burlesque standard formats and comic-book techniques. This editorial package attracts 18- to 25-year-old males and "has a fantastic passalong." Taylor explains: "What do you do when you hear a good joke? You pass it along."

Ms.

Monthly circulation, 400,000; advertising revenue, $1,000,000; single copy price $1 (40 percent); subscriptions $10 per year (60 percent) with renewals at 75 percent.

Gloria Steinem started *Ms.* when staff writers on *New York* and a group of women's liberation advocates who first thought of a newsletter, turned to the idea of a magazine as being a more populist vehicle. *Ms.* was tested when Clay Felker offered to distribute 300,000 copies bound into his *New York* year-end issue. It sold out in ten days and *Ms.* received 50,000 subscriptions in the mail. With this response, another test and minority backing by Warner Communications, the first regular issue appeared in July 1972.

From the startup *Ms.* was designed to be self-financing, principally out of copy sales. This income is bolstered by advertising revenue and successful book and record sales. Profits go to The Ms. Foundation for Women, Inc.

Ms. is a woman's magazine with a dedicated following. Editorial offices receive more than 200 letters a day. Direct response advertising has proven very strong.

In keeping with its readership commitment, *Ms.* runs a high editorial ratio—65 percent editorial vs 35 percent advertising. *Ms.* set out to encourage new women writers and has published more than 450 so far.

In design, *Ms.* wanted to look like no other woman's magazine. With a mixture of typographic styles, photos and graphics, it has managed to look like no other magazine at all. It has its own style.

"We made some hard promises to keep," publisher Patricia Carbine reports, "but so far we are coming through on all levels."

People

Weekly circulation, 1,000,000; advertising revenue, $2,250,000; single copy sales price 40 cents; subscription $15.

With the "People" section of *Time* magazine consistently racking up high readership, the idea of a magazine about people has been around Time Inc. quite a while. In August 1973 a task force produced an issue to test in 11 cities. On the basis of solid sales, *People* was put into orbit in March

1974. It is a compliment to the management of a large, established organization that *People* is such an innovative publication. The lessons of *Life* have been learned. *People* has a healthy cover price and avoids rising postage rates with newsstand and supermarket single copy sales. A spontaneous trickle of subscriptions comes in from the small type in the publishing indicia, but subs is not the way they plan to go (though they did have a year-end holiday gift subscription promotion).

Guessed by outsiders to be after the blue-collar market discovered by the tabloid newspaper *National Enquirer, People* proved out with surprising upscale demographics—income 49 percent over $15,000, 18-30 age bracket with 49 percent college background. Managing editor Dick Stolley describes *People*'s audience as characterized by "real awareness."

People, like TV, is highly pictorial using news pegs but telling each story, naturally, through people. The text is brief. Stories run one and two pages. Only the biography is longer, with 2,000 words. The characterization, "a five-minute magazine," is unfair but admittedly a person can read it in an hour.

Following a close-up, full-color portrait cover, the 50-page editorial minimum is all black-and-white. The flush left, ragged right, sans serif typography provides an informal breezy look. Pictures are informal and action-oriented portraits executed by photo services and freelance photographers. Large department labels, designed to signal the brevity of the articles, are executed with a sense of typographic fun.

HOW MAGAZINES

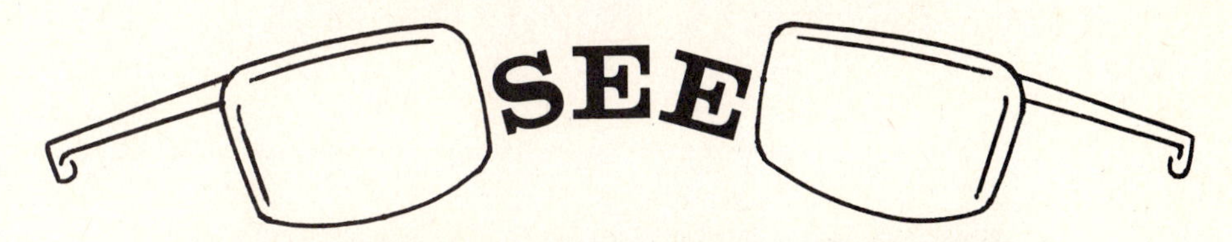

THEMSELVES

One way to determine a magazine's self-image is to look at the way it presents itself to potential new readers. These two advertisements are declarations of the basic appeal of two very different magazines.

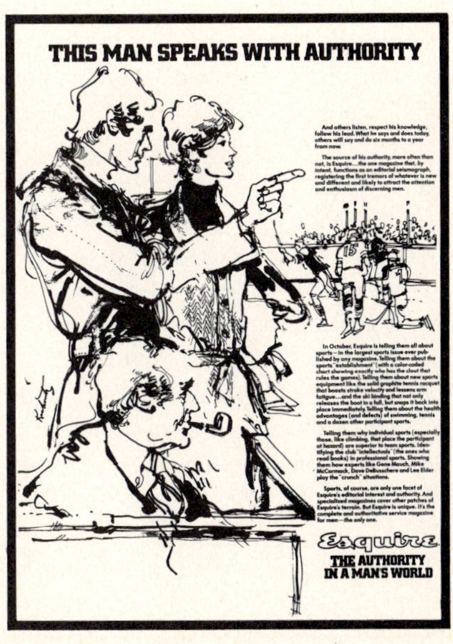

THE BLACK MAGAZINES

by ROLAND E. WOLSELEY

In this article, Wolseley surveys the magazines that aim primarily at the black reader and points out the need for more publications written by and for blacks. He questions the purpose of current black magazines and their effect on their intended audiences.

Since *Freedom's Journal* was founded in 1827 as the first black publication in the United States, the journalism of the Negro people has been dominated by their newspapers. But the rise of the civil rights movement, the somewhat better coverage of the black community by white papers, the education now more readily obtainable by black citizens, and other causes have been bringing about the acceptance of the magazine as an important medium as well.

The new, re-segregating black society (the readers should substitute *Negro, Black, Afro-American,* or *non-Caucasian,* as desired, so there need be no arguments over nomenclature) will require many more specialized journals as well as the general periodicals it now possesses. White society for years has been giving the giants of magazinedom a hard time but supporting in increasingly large numbers various specialized publications. Among black readers the same trend to specialized magazines already can be noticed. Now available, for example, are the recently begun *Negro Heritage, Black Theatre, Urban West,* and *Soul Illustrated.*

As more black businesses are established—banks, investment houses, manufacturing firms—publications to serve their many interests are inevitable.

The world of religion has for a century or more issued dozens of magazines for black readers. Fraternal and other organizations have been pub-

The Black Magazines: From *The Quill* (May, 1969). Reprinted by permission.

lishing for years; one of the most important and influential periodicals in all Negro journalism is *The Crisis,* a monthly issued since 1910 by the National Association for the Advancement of Colored People. First edited by W.E.B. DuBois, its circulation has hovered around 80,000 in recent years; it fails to get the attention it deserves because it is passed over as merely the house organ of the NAACP, which is only one of its functions. Another has been to print the writings of some of black literature's most important writers: Langston Hughes, Paul Lawrence Dunbar, and James Baldwin, for instance.

The Negro magazine has been traced as far back as 1837, Frank W. Miles, one of the few historians of black magazines, reporting that the "first magazine to be both owned and edited by a Negro" was the *Mirror of Liberty,* a quarterly begun that year by David Ruggles. Owning, editing, and intention are important to black historians, some of whom rule out a periodical owned by whites but intended for black readers or edited by whites for blacks. Thus an even earlier magazine, *The National Reformer,* while edited by William Whipper, a Negro, was owned by the American Moral Reform Society, and so is not acceptable. The generally accepted first is *The African Methodist Episcopal Church Magazine,* founded in 1842. It, note, is specialized. The first general one is a Boston publication, *The Colored American,* begun in 1900.

All other general ones after that failed until *Ebony* and *Sepia* came into the field and today head the list. Behind them were several noble efforts, including *Our World, Bronze World,* and *Opportunity.* Since there is no limit to the possibilities for exploration of black history, culture, personalities, art, and the present condition of the Negro people, it is likely that the half dozen general magazines of today will flourish.

There are the four well-publicized Johnson Publishing Co. periodicals, led by *Ebony.* That picture monthly now is in the group of about 60 U.S. magazines that have more than one million circulation (it has 1,200,000). The other three are *Jet,* a peppy, vest-pocket-size weekly newsmagazine, shy on advertising but long on news nuggets; *Tan,* a sensational, somewhat squishy women's and confession book like *True Story* and *True Confessions* before they became service magazines for the workingman's wife, now a person of medium affluence; and *Negro Digest,* a money-losing maverick of the Johnson family because it is militant in behalf of the Negro whereas the others urge him to join what E. Franklin Frazier, the sociologist, once called the black bourgeoisie.

Although *Ebony* is John H. Johnson's best known publication, it was not his first. *Negro Digest,* which he began in 1942 after mortgaging his mother's furniture for $500, was followed by *Ebony* three years later, and then came the others, including two that did not pan out: *Hue,* for the small pocket or purse, was devoted largely to entertainment subjects, did well for a time, and then faded, having difficulty obtaining ads, as *Jet* still does; *Ebony International,* intended for English-reading Africans, lasted only a few issues, running into political and ideological complications.

Johnson now is a V.I.P. in the white Magazine Publishers Association (the black magazine firms have no organization of their own, as the Negro newspaper publishers have had for many years) but it took him almost two decades to gain recognition just as it took a long time for him to amass the advertising which now makes his publishing firm one of the most lucrative. It unquestionably is the dominant company in black magazinedom and perhaps all Negro journalism.

Less widely known than the Johnson magazines but economically successful in a more modest way is another quartet, issued by the Good Publishing Co. in Fort Worth, Texas. Under the rule that the publisher must be black as well as the staff and readers these four may not qualify as Negro magazines, since George Levitan, the publisher, is white. Putting this technicality aside, they are four that must be noted. More given to exploitation of Negro emotionalism than exploration of Negro history and culture, these include *Sepia,* a monthly which attempts to rival *Ebony* but has one-twentieth of its circulation and far less advertising. Its companions are *Jive, Hep,* and *Bronze Thrills,* all lively and physically smaller than *Sepia,* which like *Ebony* is *Life*- or *Look*-size. They are monthlies and delight in printing realistic confession pieces with such titles as "A Den of Homosexuals" and "I Was a Nurse Abortionist" but also serious articles on the Negro in the Peace Corps and about the Riot Committee Report and the unrest in the colleges.

In recent years we have seen the rise of the magazine with the largest circulation among all black publications of this country: the ably-produced *Tuesday,* a four-year-old magazine supplement to white newspapers circulating in black neighborhoods, with a distribution of about 2,000,000. Physically resembling *This Week,* it is found in the Cleveland *Plain Dealer,* the Milwaukee *Journal,* the Chicago *Sun-Times,* and other large papers in Boston, Los Angeles, Detroit, and Philadelphia, among others, and puzzles whites who read these dailies and do not see *Tuesday* in their Sunday copy. That happens because it is sometimes inserted only in the copies that go to readers in the black part of the community. W. Leonard Evans, its editor and publisher, explained its philosophy in its third anniversary issue. He pointed out that the Negro income in the U.S. collectively represents $32,000,000,000. "We are poor individually, wealthy collectively," he wrote, and then presented the solution to the inequity:

> The solution is simple enough, if men of good will and honest concern are willing to invest their time, their money, their talents and knowledge. And they must, for time is running out in our black communities (this was September, 1968) . . . *Tuesday,* for one, refuses to believe that despair is necessary. There must be hope for our people, our communities, our nation, our world. We believe

these few ideas and proposals can help provide a solution. Once the black communities become economically profitable like others in our nation through the utilization of their creative and intellectual capacities then, and only then, will the true meaning of freedom be realized.

Tuesday is giving its readers a goal, attempting to create a particular image or at least something to which to aspire. It is difficult, however, to say what the black magazines as a group are saying or what image of himself or of other blacks the Negro reader is getting because the black periodical is much less standardized than is the black newspaper. In *Ebony* he is reflected as an aspirant to recognition by whites as being as capable as they in business, industry, sports, and the arts. He is portrayed as wanting *things*—swank cars, natural hair (or wigs), handsome suits and glamorous dresses, leisure for vacations, and other white middle class pleasures. The critics of the Johnson mass-appeal magazines (therefore excluding *Negro Digest*) accuse them of being too unrealistic, of building false hopes, of constructing a wonderland into which the black citizen really cannot hope to enter for many, many years. To be sure, Johnson's editors are changing this slightly; they are becoming more aware of the revolution now going on and they glorify personal success less than they did a decade ago, but it still is dominant. In edging into this new position they are running into new trouble. A reader in Isle of Palm, S.C., wrote this complaint:

". . . I'd like to protest the insults I receive every time I read it. Not an issue goes by but that you refer to the Caucasian race in the most insulting terms . . . Whitey, Charley and Honkie . . . ." He goes on to say that he feels "we are all Americans; not black, white, yellow or red" and accuses *Ebony* of preaching bigotry and violence.

A Canadian reader calls the magazine discriminatory because whites are excluded from it. "For you to be proud that you are a black man is just as wrong as for me to be proud I am a white man. We are men," he writes, adding: "You are the ones now giving importance to the coloring of the skin, the very crime you condemn the whites for."

In any of the four issued by the Good firm the image is of a superstitious young man or woman, intent on a good time, not too well educated and somewhat puzzled by life's every day problems. The Johnson reader has left the ghetto and the Good reader is perhaps on the fringe of the ghetto rebellion. He has many emotional and mental conflicts, it appears, and turns to *Bronze Thrills* or *Hep* for help or escape.

Beyond these popular-mass-aimed magazines are the specialized ones for hairdressers, businessmen, scholars, and others of particular purpose where there is no image-building but mainly service and information. As with so many other special sections of the magazine world, the black magazine industry has its own scholarly journals which rarely are seen by anyone except the few specialists themselves but influential nonetheless. These include the quarterlies called *Journal of Negro History, The Journal of Negro Education,* and *Phylon.* Similar in some ways but less objective is *Freedomways,* with a political and literary emphasis. All conform, more or less, to the physical pattern of the American scholarly journal.

Phylon, issued at Atlanta University, is somewhat more given to including literary as well as scholarly work. Like *The Crisis,* it was edited by W.E.B. DuBois, whose long activity in journalism is overlooked because of his noted career as a sociologist.

The *Journal of Negro Education* is 38 years old. Issued from Howard University, which sponsors others dealing with religion and the university's own life, it is produced by the Bureau of Educational Research. Less expensive than most such journals, it has the traditional purposes of these quiet, thick quarterlies and lists a large staff almost all of which, as is customary with these periodicals, is to lend prestige. Topping it is Charles H. Thompson, former dean of the Graduate School at Howard and founder and editor emeritus of the *Journal.*

The content is substantial, as is illustrated by the number dated Summer, 1968. The theme is race and equality in American education, with articles by Dr. Thompson; Robert L. Carter, the general counsel for the NAACP; Charles V. Willie, chairman of the sociology department at Syracuse; Lee S. Shulman, professor of educational psychology at Michigan State; John H. Fischer, president of Teachers College; and others from Harvard, Howard, Columbia, and Yeshiva.

A handful of new, small local weeklies or publish-when-we-cans, something like the white underground magazines, is entering the black journalistic scene. They can be placed in the magazine category as readily as the newspaper, even though printed on newsprint (so could the pioneering *Freedom's Journal,* for that matter). They are almost newsless tabloids, with long think pieces, and bear such names as *The Black Voice, Afros Expressions, The Plain Truth, The Liberated Voice,* and *The Ghetto Speaks.* Their number is unknown, for they come and go as subsidy permits. Often the more unrestrained call for violent revolution; all are given to sprawling generalizations about Negro affairs and rest their views on few facts.

These black underground publications are the lost souls and opportunities of Negro journalism. Unable or unwilling to become actual newspapers or magazines, which their communities usually need, they follow the easier formula of printing long magazine-type articles, lengthy editorials, and many free columns and much publicity from favorite causes. Little editing is done, the publications often are a typographical mishmash and reflect scarcely more than the prejudices of the non-journalists who usually are behind them. Unprofessional as they are, however, they are significant voices of dissent merely because they are vehicles. Since their crusades at times are justified, it is a pity that ineptness weakens them. So they disappear, remembered as well-meant but amateurish periodicals.

What is a pity—or maybe, depending upon what one thinks of their viewpoints, it is not—is that the readers in the ghetto are not being reached in any large numbers by these muckraking publications. What does the ghetto resident read in the way of magazines? Not much has been learned about that. From the few research studies made, it appears that the middle class Negro reads more or less the same white magazines as whites and to them adds perhaps two or three black periodicals: a general, consumer book; one provided by an organization to which he may give support, such as the NAACP; and possibly one of ideas about black culture. The ghetto resident reads few magazines of any color but if he comes from the revolutionary or militant group within it he may read one of the local weekly magazines of the underground type or perhaps a national monthly aimed at dissident blacks. If the ghetto resident reads a magazine at all it is likely, from his own group, to be *Ebony*.

As the swing toward separatism continues, the black publication, be it newspaper or magazine, is likely to flourish. If that swing should be reversed the turn to the black publication may be halted. But it seems unlikely that the probing of their past and the reporting of their present situation will leave the black people of America devoid of ongoing interest in their history and their culture. Because of their physical characteristics magazines may be able to satisfy that interest more effectively than any other medium.

Waste water from the Chisso chemical company.

W. Eugene Smith: MINAMATA

by ARTHUR GOLDSMITH

The large magazines like **Life** and **Look,** which frequently ran articles composed primarily of photographs, are no longer published, but the importance of the photo journalist has not diminished. This photo essay from **Popular Photography** tells the story of W. Eugene Smith and his crusade to expose the effects of mercury poisoning on the citizens of a fishing village on Japan's Minamata Bay. Smith's photographs express better than words ever could the anguish and the suffering of the victims at Minamata.

Gene Smith is a Rome plow of photojournalism: a super bulldozer cutting swaths through the jungle of human complacency and indifference. He needs big themes. He is not living at his fullest, as a photographer or a human being, unless passionately committed to a cause, a crusade, a major work with the potential for being, in his own words, "a catalyst to emotions and thinking." He found his most recent theme in 1971 at Minamata, a fishing village in the south of Japan.

What he discovered, and what apparently energized his powers to a degree not seen since his Pittsburgh essay, was the gruesome effect on human

W. Eugene Smith: Minamata: From *Popular Photography* (February, 1974). Reprinted by permission.

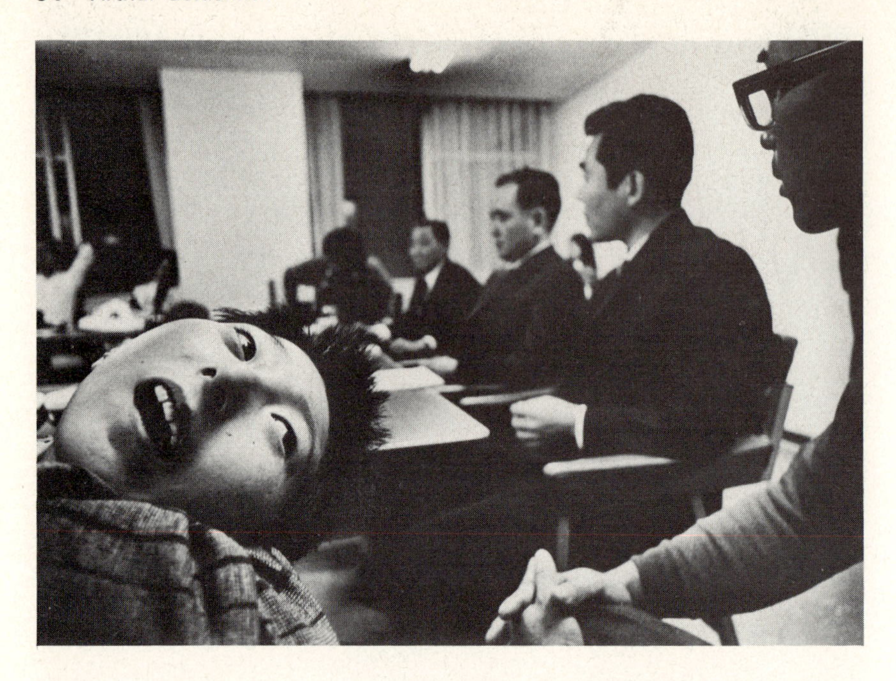

Minamata patients at the Environmental Disputes Coordination Commission.

beings of mercury poisoning, caused by the dumping of waste products into Minamata Bay by the local Chisso chemical company. The fish were poisoned, which in turn afflicted a number of the inhabitants of Minamata, who depend on the adjacent waters for much of their nourishment and livelihood. That is a tragic human story of suffering in itself, but behind it, and also deeply involving Smith, are the political and social aspects as the victims and their families confronted the power establishment of industry and government with a plea for justice. Smith and his half-Japanese wife, Aileen, have been documenting these events ("scandal" is the word commonly applied to the Minamata situation) ever since: a self-assignment which ranks with the most significant projects of his career, and also, in the event, one of the most personally dangerous. He was severely beaten by Chisso-hired goons while photographing a meeting between Minamata citizens and representatives of the chemical company. . . . As a consequence of the beating, his eyesight appears to be permanently impaired.

Although it is a work still in progress, many of Smith's Minamata photographs have been published, in a major story for **Life** magazine, in Japanese publications, and elsewhere. A 200-print exhibition of photographs (50 of them by his wife) has been touring Japan. Most recently, a portfolio of 12 reproduction prints from Smith's total coverage has been published by Sojyu-Sha Publishers and distributed by Orion Books. (*W. Eugene Smith:*

Minamata, 12 x 16 in., $7. Orion Books, Export Dept., P. O. Box 5091, Tokyo International, Japan.)

The portfolio prints, a selection from which are reproduced here, illustrate three aspects of the tragedy: the physical act of pollution, the ghastly effect of mercury poisoning on its victims and their families, and the demonstrations and confrontations as retribution is sought. The double-dot offset reproduction is adequate, but nothing short of high-quality sheet-fed gravure could do justice to the original prints, which are vintage Smith, with the rich and luminous blacks so characteristic of his style and so appropriate for the emotional tone of what he is communicating here. However, at the portfolio's relatively modest price, it is within reach of students and teachers concerned with ecology, and they, perhaps more than photographic collectors, should find these images of value for classroom study and dialog. A comprehensive, although typo-plagued, biography of Smith is included, as is background information on the Minamata situation.

"These really aren't pictures you'd want to hang on your wall to enjoy," was a comment I heard from a number of people who saw the portfolio. Indeed they are not, in the sense of being visions of beauty or happiness. It is an exceedingly bad trip that Smith has documented. But that is not the point: this is visually powerful documentary photography of a currently hot situation. From the standpoint of purpose, the catalytic immediacy of the pictures transcends, for the moment, the possibly more enduring esthetic values. (We tend to forget when looking at a "classic" documentary photograph such as Dorothea Lange's *Migrant Mother,* quietly hung on antiseptic off-white museum walls, that it shows the suffering of a live individual human being, that it was a politically loaded "controversial" image when it first appeared, that Lange's purpose in making it was to right a social injustice.)

In comparison with some of Smith's other major projects, his World War II coverage, for example, or the Pittsburgh essay, his Minamata work is an exploration in depth rather than breadth. By the very nature of the subject, he is limited to a narrower spectrum of events and environments, a claustrophobic nightmare, in effect. The images tend to become repetitious even within the context of a small portfolio like this because they are variations on a relatively confined theme. But their cumulative weight, and the impact of some individual images, is overpowering. In that village of invisible poison, Smith found our self-polluting, self-destroying civilization expressed in microcosm. The process of destruction was singularly gruesome and highly visible. In documenting that, and the incredibly blind and callous attitude of the authorities in the face of what was happening, Smith transformed the Minamata scandal into a metaphor for the human race struggling against its own suicidal obtuseness.

The horror is crystalized in the images of the victims. It is chilling enough to read a description of the poison's effect (the "strange" disease, the "ugly" disease, it was called): the creeping numbness of lips and fingers, the slurring

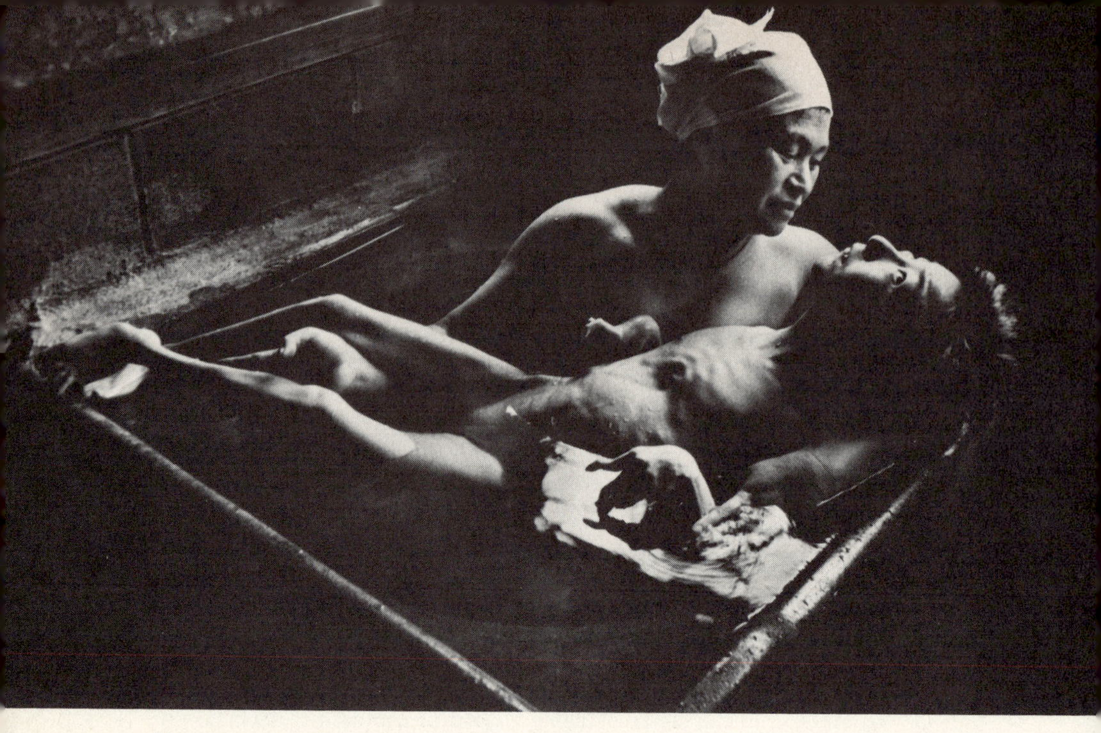

Mercury-poisoning victim and his mother.

of speech, the loss of motor control, the lapse into unconsciousness, uncontrolled shouting, and ultimately death as the nervous system is eaten away, the brain cells reduced to pulp. But it is something else to witness the speechless horror in the eyes of the victims, to see, close up, a person's hand deformed into a twisted claw, to feel the despair of parents, wives, and husbands. Then to realize this is not something caused by war or natural calamity, but something preventable and unnecessarily done to humans by humans.

But do images like this, searing as they may be, and rendered with the superb visual and technical skill of a photographer like Smith, actually have an effect on human behavior?

In a statement in the portfolio, Smith expresses a cautious optimism. "Photography is a small voice at best . . . Photographs right no wrongs, they cure no illness. Then why photograph? Because sometimes—just sometimes—a photograph or photographs can strike our senses into greater awareness. It must depend on the viewer, but to some—photographs can demand of emotions enough to be a catalyst to thinking. As a catalyst to emotions and thinking, someone among us, or perhaps many among us, may be influenced to give heed to reason and to understanding until a way will be found to right that which is wrong, to inspire a dedication for the search to cure an illness. For the rest of us it may perhaps give a greater sense of understanding and compassion for those who are alien to our own life."

But perhaps photography is not such a small voice. We really do not know, there being a lack of research in this area and great difficulties in attempting to measure the effect of any communications input on public opinion and behavior. The direct, short-range effects of Smith's Minamata photographs appear to be considerable. At the very least they sound a loud alarm bell waking us to the dangers of a particularly hideous form of pollution. Largely as a result of Smith's work, "Minamata" is a household word in Japan. The very degree of violence inflicted upon Smith is a measure of the power of his photographic documentation. "He grabbed me and kicked me in the crotch and cameras, then hit me in the stomach . . . Then they picked me up and dragged me out and slammed my head against concrete." You don't do that to still a small voice. A case of overkill for a small voice. Someone in authority must have felt otherwise. As a result of the beating and attendant publicity, Smith has become something of a national folk-hero in Japan, and people stop him on the streets for his autograph, which is small consolation for impaired vision and the threat of total blindness. So a story was told, through photographs, a pollution scandal exposed, through photographs, and public opinion aroused, through photographs, in the finest tradition of documentary photography. (It should be noted that the process involving mercury was discontinued by Chisso in 1968, when a new production method was adopted. However, it is believed that there still is around 600 tons of mercury in Minamata Bay.)

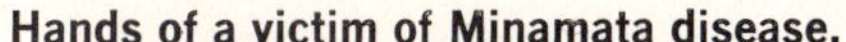
Hands of a victim of Minamata disease.

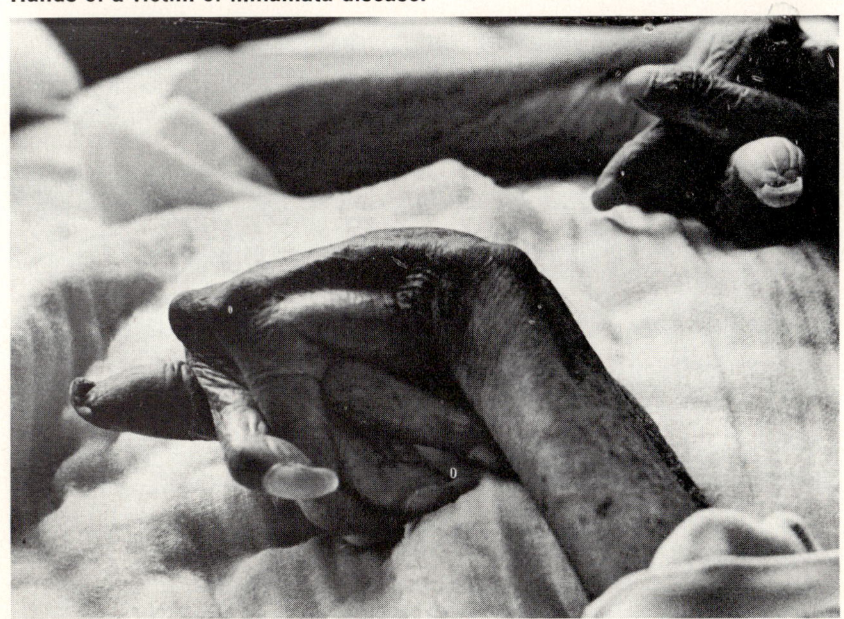

Demonstrators, end of Minamata disease trial, 1972.

But for the long run, who knows? Perhaps Smith's own expressed caution about the impact of photographs is the realistic guide. Goya's *Horrors of War* were created years ago, and despite their power, the bloodiest wars of all time have been fought since. The air raid which motivated Picasso, in compassion and outrage, to paint his *Guernica,* was on a scale hardly to rate a newspaper mention by contemporary standards of slaughter. It is naive to expect that the work of even the greatest artist/documentarian will have a directly measurable effect in resolving such complex and deep-rooted problems as war, social injustice, or pollution. But then, why photograph? Because the camera is a powerful tool. Because there may indeed be a long-range effect, in the altering of the threshold of human perception, in heightened awareness, in helping create a climate within which it is more possible for human behavior to change in creative, productive ways.

In the meantime, Smith's pictures should warn us. Mercury poisoning is not limited to Minamata. Cases have been reported elsewhere in Japan, and there is a likelihood it may already exist in the U.S. and elsewhere in the world to a greater degree than has yet been detected or exposed. These nightmare visions captured on strips of 35-mm film in Minamata are likely to haunt us for a long time to come. One hopes, along with Smith, that they will help catalyze the effective answer which can prevent more of them.

Fishing in Minamata Bay.

The Ten Best American Dailies

from **TIME**
THE WEEKLY NEWSMAGAZINE

What follows is **Time** magazine's appraisal of the ten large metropolitan newspapers that have been most successful in their efforts to "cover national and international news as well as to monitor their own communities." While many may disagree with **Time**'s choices, analysis of the bases for them will contribute to a definition of the role of the press.

Nowhere else can one find so miscellaneous,
so various an amount of knowledge
as is contained in a good newspaper.
Henry Ward Beecher, 1887

Fair enough, but what is a good newspaper? It does not help to reverse Beecher's apothegm and define a good newspaper as one that prints a miscellaneous, various amount of knowledge. All papers do that. But if the knowledge is undigested, or simply wrong, more is not better. Journalistic quality is thornier matter. A newspaper in its variety may be superb and terrible at the same time, even on the same page.

Playwright Arthur Miller has a briefer definition: "A good newspaper is a nation talking to itself." But most American papers cannot speak that loudly. The sheer size of the U.S. has precluded the development of a truly national press like Britain's. The New York *Times* and the *Wall Street Journal* try to speak to the country at large, but almost all of the 1,760 dailies in the U.S. tailor themselves to the contours of their localities.

Ten years ago, TIME listed its choice of the ten best newspapers in the U.S. In alphabetical order, they were: the Baltimore *Sun,* Cleveland *Press,*

Los Angeles *Times,* Louisville *Courier-Journal,* Milwaukee *Journal,* Minneapolis morning *Tribune,* New York *Daily News,* New York *Times,* St. Louis *Post-Dispatch,* and the Washington *Post.* Reviewing the nation's major dailies today, TIME correspondents and editors found marked change; five of the 1964 selections have been replaced by other papers that have improved sharply.

These ten papers stand out, in TIME's view, for several reasons. They make a conscientious effort to cover national and international news as well as to monitor their own communities. They can be brash and entertaining as well as informative. They are willing to risk money, time and manpower on extended investigations. Through "Op-Ed" pages and dissenting columns they offer a range of disparate opinion. TIME made its selections on the basis of editorial excellence rather than commercial success, but economically these papers range from the sound to the very prosperous.

The Boston Globe

Morning (circ. 293,000), evening (185,000) and Sunday (625,000).

Historically, Boston has been a bad newspaper town. The old saw used to run that the city's best newspaper was the New York *Times.* Some Bostonians might give that title to the widely respected *Christian Science Monitor,* though it is now largely a journal of commentary rather than of breaking news. For nearly a century, the *Globe* offered no competition, but it improved abruptly after Tom Winship, 53, became editor in 1965. The following year the *Globe* won a Pulitzer Prize for its campaign to block a federal judgeship for Francis X. Morrissey, a crony of Joseph P. Kennedy's. Its four-man "Spotlight" investigative team picked up another Pulitzer for a 1971 exposé of municipal scandals in neighboring Somerville. The *Globe,* which had not backed a presidential candidate since 1900, changed policy by declaring for Humphrey in '68 and McGovern in '72. It was the third U.S. daily (after the New York *Times* and the Washington *Post*) to publish excerpts from the Pentagon papers.

The *Globe* is known as "a writer's paper"—permissively edited, and allowing a variety of tone and approach. In George Frazier, whose columns are a continuing tirade against lapses in taste, morals and common sense, it has one of the few genuine eccentrics left in daily journalism. Music Critic Michael Steinberg's running quarrel with Erich Leinsdorf's direction of the Boston Symphony was a major factor in the maestro's departure in 1969. Sport Columnist Bud Collins is easily the best tennis reporter in the country.

With a five-man bureau in Washington, the *Globe*'s national coverage is excellent. It is somewhat weaker in covering Boston's own sprawling suburbs. Overall, the *Globe* is one of the country's most improved papers during the past decade.

Chicago Tribune

THE WORLD'S GREATEST NEWSPAPER

Morning (circ. 681,766) and Sunday (1,157,032).

Gone from the front page are the old-fogyish editorial cartoons, as well as the proclamation that this is the "American Paper for Americans." The comic strip *Moon Mullins* no longer adorns the first page of the sports section, and most of the Shavian experiments in phonetic spelling (*frate* for *freight*) are a thing of the past. Thanks to its flamboyant long-time publisher, Colonel Robert McCormick, the *Tribune*'s history is as colorful as that of any paper in the nation. But its raucous eccentricities have given way to a calmer tone and a less polemical approach to events.

The *Trib* has always excelled at local investigative reporting—for which Chicago provides ample raw material—and it keeps bearing down hard. Under the direction of George Bliss, 55, muckraking teams have scored an impressive number of exclusives, including the Pulitzer-prize-winning exposé of 1972 Cook County vote frauds and an eight-part series on police brutality that resulted in several indictments.

Major credit for the paper's new orientation goes to Clayton Kirkpatrick, 59, a 34-year veteran of the paper who became editor in 1969. Kirkpatrick toned down the *Trib*'s Republican war cries, which were sometimes as audible in news columns as in editorials, and balanced them with other viewpoints. The paper supported Nixon in 1972 but gave regular front-page coverage to McGovern. The *Trib* has occasionally endorsed Democrats for local and state offices. "We are no longer backing a particular point of view all the time," says Kirkpatrick. "We are using balance."

Los Angeles Times

Morning (circ. 1,036,911) and Sunday (1,226,132).

With the strike-crippled *Herald-Examiner* as its only metropolitan competition, the chief threat facing the Los Angeles *Times* could be lethargy. It is fat (average daily size: 106 pages) but not exactly sassy. It carries more advertising linage than any other U.S. daily (1973 total: 117,450,860 lines), yet it gives the impression of just falling short of its great potential. Its metropolitan staff of 96 has problems making sense of its turf—4,800 sq. mi. of overlapping municipal governments that constitute a city editor's nightmare.

Since assuming control from his father in 1960, Publisher Otis Chandler, 46, has expanded the paper's scope and built up its national reputation. Its network of foreign correspondents is sizable (19), and their files home carry more life than most. In his regular features from Moscow, Murray Seeger offers cross-cultural information in the style of Alistair Cooke. The paper's Washington bureau has had several Watergate scoops, including the first interview with Alfred C. Baldwin, who was manning a listening post when the burglars were caught. That exclusive earned Bureau Chief John Lawrence a 2½-hour jail term after he refused Judge John Sirica's order to turn the interview tapes over to the Watergate prosecutors. With Baldwin's permission, the material was later submitted.

The Courier-Journal

Morning (circ. 230,956) and Sunday (363,917).

The advertisement shows a fist slamming down on a table. The caption: "What this town needs is another newspaper!" Oddly enough, the ad appears in the *Courier-Journal;* it and its sister evening *Times* are the only newspapers in Louisville. This ad was placed and paid for by the *Courier-Journal,* which is uneasy about its news monopoly. A press monopoly is

never desirable, but the *Courier-Journal* handles its responsibility well. Its history of enlightened service goes back to "Marse Henry" Watterson, the *Courier-Journal*'s first editor in 1868, and later to Publishers Robert and George Barry Bingham, a father and son who played a major role in coaxing Kentuckians into accepting peaceful integration.

Grandson Barry Bingham, Jr., 40, the current editor and publisher, has maintained the paper's public-spirited tradition. George Wallace, for instance, has called it the "Curious-Journal" because of its liberal approach to racial issues. On the eve of the second Nixon Inaugural, Bingham editorially urged citizens to march on Washington and demand an end to secret Indochina bombings. The *Courier-Journal* was the first U.S. daily to hire a full-time editorial ombudsman to monitor the paper's fairness and accuracy. It also retains an advertising ombudsman to weed out false or misleading claims.

The paper's state coverage often gets measurable results. *Courier-Journal* stories showing how some back-country lawyers reaped huge profits from miners in black-lung-disease cases are expected to bring legislative action this year. The paper even takes on thoroughbred racing, a sacrosanct Kentucky institution. A 1972 series exposed apparent conflicts of interest on the part of some racing officials, ownership of a horse by convicted felons and the operations of bookies. The racing hierarchy was outraged, but reforms were prompt.

The Miami Herald

Morning (circ. 404,846) and Sunday (507,777).

A cargo plane loaded with Christmas trees crashed into a Cuban neighborhood in Miami one Saturday night last month, killing nine people. At the time, *Herald* Editor Larry Jinks was at a party and the paper had only three men on duty in its newsroom. Upon hearing the news, Jinks took a carload of reporters from the party to the crash site, had 30 men on the story by 3 a.m. Their work, plus five pictures, appeared in nearly one-third of the Sunday morning press run.

Such hell-for-leather legwork has become almost routine at the *Herald,*

the strongest link in the Knight newspaper chain.[1] Pulitzer-prize-winning Reporter Gene Miller has the *Herald*'s carte blanche to travel to big stories: the Attica prison insurrection, the Howard Johnson rooftop shootout in New Orleans, the court-martial of Lieut. William Calley. After nearly three years of digging into Miami operations of the Federal Housing Authority, *Herald* reporters tracked down the existence of an alleged political slush fund for Florida Senator Edward J. Gurney. Although the paper backed Nixon in 1972, it has kept reporters busy looking into Bebe Robozo's Florida finances.

The *Herald* excels in covering Miami's rich ethnic mix: Southern WASPS, Cubans, blacks and Jews. It is particularly alert to its Cuban communities; Reporter Roberto Fabricio spent a week in Spain last year, came back with an exclusive series on some 30,000 Cuban refugees there who were having trouble getting U.S. visas. Many had relatives in Miami. It daily flies 8,000 copies into Latin America, prints eight separate inside editions for the eight areas of southern Florida where it stations news bureaus.

[1] The other Knight dailies: the Akron *Beacon-Journal,* Boca Raton (Fla.) *News,* Bradenton (Fla.) *Herald,* Charlotte (N.C.) *News and Observer,* Columbus (Ga.) *Enquirer* and *Ledger,* Detroit *Free Press,* Lexington (Ky.) *Herald* and *Leader,* Macon (Ga.) *News* and *Telegraph,* Philadelphia *Inquirer* and *Daily News,* and the Tallahassee *Democrat.*

THE MILWAUKEE JOURNAL

Evening (circ. 305,005) and Sunday (543,992).

For years the *Journal* was locked in an acrimonious conflict with popular Milwaukee Mayor Henry Maier. The paper's extensive coverage of Father James Groppi's open-housing marches in 1967 and 1968 blurred the mayor's liberal image. When the *Journal* later criticized the concentration of all Milwaukee's model-cities strategy inside the mayor's circle, Maier proposed antitrust legislation against the Journal Co.'s news empire (it also owns the city's other daily, the morning *Sentinel,* plus radio, TV and

rural cable stations). Yet the paper endorsed him for re-election to a fourth term in 1972, support which the startled mayor quickly repudiated.

Like 80% of *Journal*-backed candidates, Maier won. But the paper's heavy influence on Milwaukee voting patterns cannot be explained away by its monopolistic hold on the city. It has a long tradition of fair-minded coverage (a recent *Journal*-commissioned poll found that 60% of its readers feel that the paper is balanced. The remainder were evenly split between those who find it pro-Democrat and those who find it pro-Republican). Editor Dick Leonard insists that his reporters keep daily tab on all issues affecting Milwaukee. So close is its monitoring of local government that the pace of city office work slows perceptibly shortly after 1:30 each afternoon when the *Journal* appears—officials are checking to see what their colleagues are up to.

The paper's civic pride can occasionally be cloying. It goes into annual paroxysms of praise over such events as the state fair and the Fourth of July circus wagon parade (sample lead: "The parade wasn't long and the route was short, but the enthusiasm . . ."). Although it does send reporters and editorial writers on international fact-finding tours, the paper's thrust is unabashedly local.

Newsday

THE LONG ISLAND NEWSPAPER

Evening (circ. 450,000) and Sunday (360,000).

Newsday is easily the nation's best suburban newspaper. Only 33 years old, it has grown up and prospered with Long Island. Its tabloid format is an innovative blend of newspaper and newsmagazine. The contents conform: heavy on interpretive reporting and features, light on spot or breaking news stories that commuting readers have already seen in

the Manhattan press or heard on their car radios. *Newsday* combines solid local coverage with ambitious national and international undertakings. It invested a year of reporting, for instance, to produce a sophisticated 13-part feature called "The Real Suburbia." (Among its findings: suburban housewives "overwhelmingly" say they are happy rather than bored or lonely, most new residents are not driven away by city problems but are attracted to suburban living.)

Owned by the Times-Mirror Co., which also publishes the Los Angeles *Times, Newsday* takes an independent political line. But in recent years it has been no friend to the Republicans. A 1971 series by the paper's investigative team (whose trophy room contains 17 top awards, including three Pulitzers) concluded that some of Bebe Rebozo's financial "deals" had "tarnished the presidency." Perhaps as a result, White House Correspondent Martin Schram was excluded from the President's China trip, and Publisher William Attwood, Editor David Laventhol and Robert Greene, who led the investigation, were all treated to IRS audits of their tax returns. On its way to becoming a paper of national influence, *Newsday* has also built an enviable economic base; it now carries more advertising linage than any of New York City's three dailies.

The New York Times

Morning (circ. 940,027) and Sunday (1,508,116).

There is no other U.S. daily quite like the *Times*. Its total news staff is by far the largest (about 650), its scope and coverage the most exhaustive, its influence on national and world leaders daunting—as its publication of the Pentagon papers demonstrated.

But under A. M. ("Abe") Rosenthal, 50, managing editor since 1969, the *Times* has loosened up and varied both its appearance and its coverage. Boxed and horizontal layouts now interrupt the long gray columns of old. Perhaps the single most important innovation is the Op-Ed page, an editorial feature that the *Times* did not invent; characteristically, though, its Op-Ed page, introduced in 1970, quickly became a model national forum of contrasting ideas and attitudes. The section is now edited by Charlotte Curtis, 45, who had previously transformed the *Times*'s routine women's page into a sophisticated minidaily on modern living styles.

Lately, too, there has been a greater range in the newspaper's tone. John Corry's thrice-weekly column on moods and minutiae of the city is occasionally sentimental, but it is fresh, impressionistic reportage. With a welcome minimum of liberation cant, Judy Klemesrud and Deirdre Carmody have unearthed an impressive number of offbeat stories about how women's lives are changing. Lesley Oelsner has done expert law reporting on such complex issues as court challenges and sentencing and the juvenile justice system.

Since New York is still the cultural capital of the world, the *Times*'s critics understandably exert formidable power. Theater Critic Clive Barnes can easily kill a Broadway play with a negative notice, which may be the reason why many readers find his prolix reviews generally far too kind. Ada Louise Huxtable, now part of the nine-member editorial board, is probably the most influential commentator on architecture in the country. The *Times* has also broadened its cultural reviews to include regular coverage of rock and other outgrowths of the counterculture that would not have made its pages a few years back.

The last decade has not all been triumph at the *Times*. It was badly outdistanced by the Washington *Post* on Watergate. Not until the *Times* in 1972 hired Seymour Hersh, who first exposed the My Lai massacre, did its Washington bureau do much in the way of investigative reporting. Shrinking profits have twice prompted Publisher Arthur Ochs ("Punch") Sulzberger to send somber Yuletide messages to employees warning of economies ahead. Its editorial staff has been trimmed slightly.

These problems have not substantially affected the finished product. The *Times* is still the nation's single most informative paper, and it is commendably blessed with a passion for accuracy in things both great and small. If gasoline is abbreviated as "gas" in headlines, the word is decorously draped with quotation marks.

THE WALL STREET JOURNAL

Morning (circ. 1,300,000).

In 1939 the *Journal* submitted to the Pultizer Prize board a series attacking antiquated building codes. The material was returned, along with the comment that "trade papers are not eligible for consideration." The *Journal* has outgrown its "trade" classification (it finally won a Pulitzer in 1947), though it is obviously a specialty paper for the business and economic community. It has also emerged as one of the most distinctive voices in U.S. daily journalism. The *Journal*'s editorial page is the country's most widely quoted source of conservative opinion. Its front page has a capacity for surprise unmatched by any other paper. News and financial items are ticked off with smart, bulletin-like precision. These columns are

bracketed by serious financial comment, offbeat personality profiles and flights of pop sociology. In a given week, the *Journal*'s left-hand column will take up subjects as diverse as the trend toward naming rival products in advertising, and the not-quite-emerging nation of Afghanistan (headline: DO THE RUSSIANS COVET AFGHANISTAN? IF SO, IT'S HARD TO FIGURE WHY).

At a time when any self-respecting paper must do aggressive investigative reporting, the *Journal* ranks high. Jerry Landauer scooped the country last August with the story that Spiro Agnew was under criminal investigation. Stanley Penn has produced major exclusives on the tangled finances of Robert Vesco and Howard Hughes.

The *Journal* publishes four regional editions in nine printing plants across the U.S., runs a mammoth and complicated delivery system to ensure same-day service to most subscribers. The paper still sticks to line drawings in preference to photographs—a tradition that happens to be thrifty and that bypasses pressure to print glossies of executives. In 1972 Managing Editor Frederick Taylor outlawed the word "reform" on the conservative principle that not all change is for the better. The *Journal* has enormous impact on its main beat. On the day it ran a grim front-page report listing the expected impact of the Arab oil boycott, industry by industry, the stock market dropped 24 points.

The Washington Post

Morning (circ. 532,000) and Sunday (701,671).

Appearing to speak at schools, *Post* staffers customarily receive standing ovations before they utter a word. Such celebrity for print journalists is unprecedented, but so is the story to which the *Post* led an indifferent nation. Thanks largely to the tireless digging of Watergate Reporters Bob Woodward and Carl Bernstein, the *Post*'s work on the nation's worst political scandal has won awards beyond the staff's counting. But obscured by Watergate is the *Post*'s broader challenge to the New York *Times* for national pre-eminence. Under Executive Editor Ben Bradlee, 52, the *Post* has tripled its 1965 news budget of $4,000,000, recruited some major talent. Bradlee's news-department staff of 379 is still smaller by almost 300 than the *Times*'s, but it has a we-try-harder zeal. In one important re-

spect the *Post* is clearly superior to the New York *Times:* its nine editorial writers, led by Editor Philip L. Geyelin and Deputy Meg Greenfield, produce wise, reasoned, dispassionate commentary. The paper's political staff, under Pulitzer-prize-winning Columnist David Broder, is perhaps the most knowledgeable in the country.

Less successful is the style section, of which Bradlee is quite proud. Actually, it is a somewhat erratic blend of the good, bad and incongruous. Columnists Nicholas von Hoffman and Art Buchwald are mixed with meandering reviews of the arts—plus Ann Landers. The *Post* has some trouble serving its fragmented local area; it is not only the sole morning daily in the District of Columbia, its suburban circulation makes it the largest morning paper in Maryland and the largest paper—period—in Virginia. Publisher Katharine Graham has not let the rigors of Watergate coverage stiffen her sense of humor: "Wherever I go, someone inevitably declares that this has been a banner year for journalism and the *Post*. That's true, though in much the same sense that tropical storm Agnes was a great time for disaster agencies."

THE BOOK AND THE GREAT COMMUNITY

by WALLACE E. STEGNER

The following excerpt from Wallace Stegner's book **The Sound of Mountain Water** focuses on the role that books play in providing a sense of history. Stegner feels that this sense is lacking in today's cultural climate, partly because of the electronic media's emphasis on the present.

. . .

This is not the great age of books. They have been for a good while now drifting from the north before the breath of the media, and writers as well as librarians have been growing coats of protective hair. A rather small percentage of Americans read books, and many of those who do read, read nonbooks, or treat real books as if they were nonbooks. The paperback revolution that has made everything available has also tended to make everything expendable, like a used magazine. The American device of built-in obsolescence is operative even in literature. And there is always Marshall McLuhan, confidently predicting the Gutenberg Götterdämmerung, the end of print, with all that it has historically meant in terms of sequence, rationality, and tradition. If you are bent upon losing your head rather than keeping it, you do not need the alphabet.

Yet a librarian could be forgiven for thinking that the trouble is not too few books and too few readers, but too many of both. The presses of America alone turn out 25,000 titles a year, and what respectable library can confine itself to the books of its own nation? These days, if we read, we must read the world, and that will multiply the titles by a factor of six or eight, or ten. Assuming that not all of these are frivolous, or irrelevant to the concerns of educated Americans, and assuming that we have money to buy them and shelves to put them on, there is still the massive problem of selection. You can't preserve them all. Anyone who has had a stack card in the Library of Congress, and has pursued one single book through those labyrinthine miles of stacks, under streets and into annexes and through annexes of annexes, knows the nightmare of total inclusiveness. Then there is the problem of what to throw away, and when. One explosive science, biology, proliferates into print at so frenzied a pace that the mere abstracts of a mere month's articles fill a volume the size of a telephone book. Much of that, indispensable this year, is worthless next. Here the problem is not to store knowledge permanently, but to store it briefly and then throw most of it away.

If we solve the difficulties of selection and space and money and disposal, there is still the problem of retrieval, and that multiplies as readers do. Only 15 percent of Americans read books, but that 15 percent equals 30

"On second thought, Master Gutenberg,
I think I'll wait for the paperback."

"Yes, it has redeeming social value, Mr. Barnes. Unfortunately, it has no redeeming commercial value."

million people. Watch the bedlam activity in a great metropolitan library such as the New York Public, and you conclude that your notion of the librarian as ruminative, tranquil, rubbersoled, quietly dusty, gently helpful, needs revision. These people are required every day to build a great haystack in which, ever afterward, they will be able to find every single needle.

But if those were the only difficulties attending the preservation and distribution of books, no one would be dismayed. They may be eased by decentralization, miniaturization, standardized cataloging procedures, computerized retrieval, and other means; and if they cannot be completely solved, that should not bother us. Neither can any other real problem. What is harder for a book-centered generation or a book-centered intellectual class to cope with is the contemporary cultural climate that increasingly disregards the book and depreciates the traditions it reflects.

This climate, described and in fact celebrated by McLuhan, may be, as he thinks, a function of the mass media. In its neglect of print in favor of the image, and in its growing neglect of the eye in favor of the ear, it very probably is. The image is immediate, it needs no complicated symbolic system such as words to communicate its message; and the ear is at least as immediate as the image, and increasingly appealed to. You will find plenty of American homes without bookshelves, but few without a television set, a radio, and probably a stereo. But in its general rejection of the conventional, its emphasis on the present and distrust of the past, its faith in the spontaneous, innovative, and impromptu, as well as in its lively inventiveness, the generation raised on the media is only extending to the limit, and perhaps to absurdity, tendencies that have always been distinctly American, and that in fact have traditionally distinguished western nations from the nations of the East.

. . .

The Commission for the Year 2000, looking into present and future for the American Academy of Arts and Sciences, remarks that "a sense of historical time is absent from American thought." We have not only looked with suspicion on the dead hand of the past, we have been unwilling to admit that we cannot make the most profound social changes by a simple act of will or law. Instant Reform is as American a product as instant coffee. We have been as willing to legislate morality, or try to, as we have been to tear down obsolete buildings or retool plants. Thus contemporary dissenters show a family resemblance to the dissenters who left England for Holland in the 17th Century, and left Holland for America, and left the Atlantic colonies (or Nauvoo, to bring the parallel closer home) for the wilderness. In repudiating their heritage they assert it, for it is a heritage of questioning and rebellion. The Haight-Ashbury district, the capital of the Flower People, has its relationship not only to all bohemians, but to the Massachusetts Bay Colony, mad as that comparison seems.

No young person respects history as much as do people who have lived a little of it. "Why do you care where you came from or what your ancestors did?" a girl asked me when I was trying to explain to a group of students my reasons for writing a somewhat personal history book, *Wolf Willow*. "Isn't it what you *are* that matters? *Now?"*

Now. It is a big word with the young, almost as big a word as wow. Between them, those two words seem sometimes to comprehend the responses of a whole generation. Television's greatest hour, the show that above all others satisfied the demand for instantness as well as violent sensation, was Jack Ruby's shooting of Lee Harvey Oswald. The characteristic modern art form is the happening, which can't be programmed or repeated, but only joined in, participated in. Musicians celebrate silence over sound, or noise over music. Painters assert accident over design, a fiercely pure nonart over any sort of technique or manipulation. Pop artists transfer real objects into the art frame with so little organization or change that as Wright Morris suggests, the result differs hardly at all from window dressing. And the Berlin artist who exhibited himself as "a perfect living total work of art" was not thinking of himself as the complex end-product of biological, historical, and cultural forces, and still less as a creator or maker. He was thinking of himself as a happening. He would be right at home in San Francisco.

There is an obvious reason why the young have been able to seize power from the old in this generation as they have not been able to in the past, and the reason is not the media. The young now simply outnumber us, they find they can outvote us as the immigrant Irish found, about 1870, that they could outvote the Boston Yankees. They can not only outvote us, they can outbuy us, outmarch us, outshout us, and in general handle us. They are wooed by advertisers and politicians, they put the fear of God into university administrations, they challenge parents and police.

. . . In 1970, more than half [of all Americans were under 25]. Possessed of the power of numbers, they have naturally learned to exercise it. And it is easy for a generation coming of age in a time of bitter social crisis, and having a somewhat inadequate knowledge of history, to think that it invented idealism and commitment. It is easy to discard elderly counsels along with elderly error and timidity and failure. To trust no one over 30 becomes not only a declaration of personal independence but a moral imperative. Iconoclasm can become as compulsive as any other form of conventional behavior, and the voice of the young hormone is sometimes mistaken for the voice of God. The elders, outvoted, disregarded, held in contempt, watch this youth revolution from the sidelines, dismayed and aghast. Or else they try to join it, adopting cosmetically young ideas and some version of Carnaby Street costume or Haight-Ashbury hairdo, in order to get rich from it or win its votes.

I have said that the majority of Americans read no books at all. The youth who trusts no one over 30 may, since he is often an intellectual of sorts, but he does not read the books his elders admire. He reads in some counter-tradition, Zen or otherwise, and quotes from the Tibetan Book of the Dead, or he reads his own kind, books written in the spirit of intransigent modernity—purified of moral taboos, conventional "taste," traditional techniques, and sometimes coherence. Time, a traditional means of order, is melted down into the simultaneity of solipsism or the drugged consciousness. Form means nothing—what is admired is anything that turns the reader on, and this may be better done by irrational than by formal means. Greek rationalism sets as Afro-Asian mysticism rises, and words that were coined to convey meanings are made to serve as substitutes for strobe lights and over-amplified guitars. The virtue of anything—art, costume, life-style, sexual habits, entertainment, conversation—inheres in its novelty, its capacity to shock or titillate, and its promotion of states of ecstasy.

All of which only reminds an elder with some historical sense of Robert Frost's remark that there are no new ways to be new.

Nevertheless the elder must reserve judgment. This generation is probably as good as other generations, and will make its own contributions. But it cannot long continue the pretense that it is breaking entirely with the Establishment and the past. It will have to rediscover history, it will have to reestablish contact with the tradition it aspires to alter drastically or to destroy. Above all, it will have to acknowledge the absurdity of its cult of total individual freedom. The irresponsible individual "doing his thing" without reference to other individuals or to society is neither new or viable. Neither is the activist bent upon instant and total reform by means which amount to threat and coercion. Anarchy, pursued very long, is a form of suicide both individual and social.

For no risk, as Josiah Royce once said, is ever private or individual, and no accomplishment is merely personal. What saves us at any level of human life is union, mutual responsibility, what St. Paul called charity. The detached individual, Royce wrote,

> is an essentially lost being. That ethical truth lies at the basis of the Pauline doctrine of original sin. It lies also at the basis of the pessimism with which the ancient southern Buddhism of the original founder of that faith . . . viewed the life of man. The essence of the life of the detached individual is, as Gotama Buddha said, an unquenchable desire for bliss, a desire which hastens to enjoyment, and in enjoyment pines to feel desire. Train such a detached individual by some form of high civilized cultivation, and you merely show him what Paul called "the law." The law thus shown he hereupon finds to be in opposition to his selfwill. Sin, as the Pauline phrase has it, "revives."

The Buddha, unlike some of his contemporary western followers, found the salvation of the detached individual to lie in the resignation of all desires. Our own tradition pushes us toward the more dynamic solution of an organized and indoctrinated social interdependence, St. Paul's "charity." More of that human bond than he knows remains in the dropout who has "had" this civilization and wants no more of it. More of it than he would admit survives in the activist bent upon tearing down the imperfect political and social structure and erecting a perfect society where it stood. More of it than he imagines motivates the hippie who believes he has emancipated himself into total freedom and the life of pure sensation. Except for a few minor matters such as Christian faith and chastity, he is a dim copy of St. Francis of Assisi.

So there is virtue in the creation of a great library, even in a time which questions or repudiates so much of the tradition, which has made a specialty of the nonbook, which has cultivated instant communication and has taken speed-reading courses that will let it read *Hamlet* in 12 minutes—if it hasn't already read *Hamlet* in comic book form. Bright as the media are, they have little memory and little thought: their most thoughtful programs are likely to take the form of the open-end discussion, a form as inconclusive and random as the happening. Thought is neither instant nor noisy, and it is not very often tribal or communal in the fashion admired by McLuhan. It thrives best in solitude, in quiet and in the company of the past, the great community of recorded human experience. That recorded experience is essential whether one hopes to reassert some aspect of it, or attack it. "Like giants," Robert Frost said, "we are always hurling experience ahead of us to pave the future with against the day when we may want to strike a line of purpose across it for somewhere."

MINI-CASE STUDY

Daniel Schorr: Defender of the Fourth Estate?

On February 11, 1976, **The Village Voice** appeared on newsstands throughout the nation. Its lead story, "The CIA Report the President Doesn't Want You to Read," popularly called the Pike Report, began a news media-government furor that was not to be resolved until the House Ethics Committee decided not to press contempt charges against Daniel Schorr, who provided **The Village Voice** with the report.

Schorr, then a CBS news correspondent, was the principal character in the drama, which began as a story about secrecy in government and turned into a celebrated case of freedom of the press.

This mini-case study provides a brief glimpse of the Schorr case as it was reported in the print media. A variety of sources are represented: a front page news story with a side bar, a newspaper editorial and a letter-to-the-editor in response, newspaper columns, opinion magazine editorials, a magazine news story, and, finally, a news magazine guest essay in which Schorr tells his own story.

The order of the selections follows the normal progression of a developing story. The news columns provide the facts as quickly as they are ascertained, followed by the editorial/opinion pages, which provide newspaper columnists space to express their opinions. News magazines summarize the events of a week, and sometimes offer comment, while opinion magazines have comment as their chief purpose.

These are but a few of the hundreds of articles that were carried in newspapers and magazines during the seven months between Schorr's action and its denouement. It will be evident that the print media have a difficult task when following an extended story, especially one like that of Daniel Schorr, where the issue of the public's right to know became clouded with the issue of whether a journalist should be paid for supplying a secret report. Additional articles are listed in the bibliography at the end of this section.

SECURITY QUESTION

by STEPHEN ISAACS

Large segments of the secret report of the House intelligence committee were printed yesterday in a 24-page supplement to The Village Voice, a weekly tabloid newspaper published in New York.

Publication of the 338-page report was blocked Jan. 29 by a vote of the House after Ford administration officials claimed that its disclosure would damage the national security.

Many members of the House, as well as critics of America's intelligence-gathering apparatus, have expressed doubt about some contents of the report and the quality of the investigation that produced it.

The report snipes again and again at Secretary of State Henry A. Kissinger, contending he placed one obstacle after another in the way of the committee's getting material and, when he appeared before it, lied.

The report at one point says that "Dr. Kissinger's comments . . . are at variance with the facts."

It describes Kissinger as having a "passion for secrecy" and as trying "to control dissemination and analysis of data."

In sum, the excerpts of the House panel's report describe the American intelligence community as often inept, not out of control (as has often been charged), and as frequently considering itself beyond the laws of the land.

For instance, then-President Johnson in 1967 blocked the CIA from offering further covert assistance to educational or other private voluntary institutions, after disclosures that the CIA had been sneaking money to the National Students Association.

The Village Voice excerpts quote CIA deputy director Carl Duckett as testifying that the CIA still maintains covert contracts with "a small number of universities."

The report talks of most of the CIA's covert activities as haphazard and in effect lacking any master plan, saying that "the overall picture . . . does not support the contention that covert action has been used in furtherance of any particular principle, form of government, or identifiable national interest."

"Instead," the report continues, "the record indicates a general lack of a long-term direction in U.S. foreign policy. Covert actions, as the means for implementing a policy, reflected this Band-aid approach, substituting short-term remedies for problems which required long-term cures."

Yet at another point the report claims that "all evidence in hand suggests that the CIA, far from being out of control, has been highly responsive to the instructions of the President and the assistant to the President for national security affairs."

What is absent, the report suggests, is any kind of controls on the CIA and its fellow intelligence-gathering agencies.

The report makes much of the fact that the intelligence community has never been frank about how much it spends, which the committee claims is "at least three to four times the amount reported to Congress."

That means it all costs about $10 billion a year, says the report, with almost no controls, no checks, no balances.

As a result, says the committee, the CIA has been able to do some unusual things with the taxpayers' money, including developing "a huge arsenal of weapons and access to ammunition . . . giving it a capability that exceeds most armies of the world," having put at least $75 million into Italian politics, and serving in effect as a discount shopper for some foreign officials.

The CIA's budget, it says, "appears as only a single line item" in the budget, giving the agency "an unusual advantage" in its ability to transfer money from area to area unimpeded.

The committee points out that the General Accounting Office, because of the CIA's penchant for secrecy, cannot even balance the CIA's books, "let alone analyze its efficiency," and that last year the CIA, National Security Agency and Defense Intelligence Agency all refused information the GAO was seeking.

* * *

'Voice' Melodrama

by WILLIAM CLAIBORNE AND LAURENCE STERN

After a week of clandestine melodrama complete with secret code names (Operation Swordfish) and covert working headquarters, Village Voice publisher Clay Felker went to press with a 24-page supplement under the titillating headline:

"THE CIA REPORT THE PRESIDENT DOESN'T WANT YOU TO READ."

By the time the circumstances of the Voice exclusive seeped to the surface there appeared to be some question whether it was more important as a substantive scoop or a journalistic morality play.

Felker, reflecting the secretive mood in the offices of New York magazine, which was the operations center for the Voice leak, said

'Voice' Melodrama: From *The Washington Post* (February 12, 1976).

laughing "as far as I know, it landed on the back doorstep in a basket." Both publications are directed by Felker.

But other sources familiar with the hush-hush developments of the story say that CBS correspondent Daniel Schorr, who covered the intelligence committee for his network, was instrumental in transmitting the report to Felker.

It was also learned that a Washington-based organization of journalists, The Reporters Committee for Freedom of The Press, had agreed to accept "passively" any cash proceeds from publication of the report by arrangement with Schorr.

Schorr, who recently displayed the title page of the still-secret House committee report on television as he described some of its contents, said yesterday that he was obliged "to deny on the record that I have a copy of the report."

The CBS correspondent also denied that he had discussed the report with Felker. "I have no knowledge of how The Village Voice acquired its copy. I had no connection with it and I do not mean by that to state that I have a copy."

He added that whatever conclusions viewers might gather from having seen the report's title page on the screen "is something that they are inferring."

Schorr told a fellow CBS reporter on a CBS radio broadcast that he had a copy.

Schorr also acknowledged that in a conversation he had recently with a Washington Post editor he said he possessed the House report. He added, however, that he regarded it as a "business conversation" and off the record. Both Schorr and Post Assistant Managing Editor Harry M. Rosenfeld agreed that nothing was said about the conversations being off the record.

Schorr denied, on the record, having made any approach to the reporters committee under which he would assign it the proceeds from the report's distribution. The reporters committee agreed, after a telephone poll of its trustees, not to say anything publicly because of the "confidentiality" of its conversations with Schorr.

"God, I'm never going to get involved again with a bunch of reporters," said one trustee of the organization which is dedicated to promoting freedom of the press. "Off the record, it's a - - - - mess."

Schorr, it was learned, first talked with a CBS colleague and member of the reporters group, Fred Graham, about the financial arrangement within the past two weeks. The commentator began considering offering his exclusive copy of the report for paperback publication after it came into his possession two weekends ago.

"Dan proposed that the reporters committee receive whatever profits were generated by the sale," acknowledged one trustee. ". . . Some of the group didn't want to be associated in print or any way with release of that document (but) we had no objection to a passive role" in accepting funds.

Efforts by the trustees of the reporters committee yesterday to agree on a statement ended in a collective decision to have "no comment."

"We had no objection, however, to passive role," the trustee added. "We've accepted proceeds from a variety of sources."

During the discussions with the reporters committee, Schorr consulted a lawyer in New York on his legal position in making the report public. He was advised that there was no immediate criminal liability against him although he might be subject to contempt of Congress proceedings should he refuse to tell a congressional committee the source of his copy.

Schorr conceded that he may have made a mistake in showing the title page of the report to his viewers. "I guess I was boasting," he said.

Schorr obtained access to the report, according to one authoritative account, after the House intelligence committee voted to refer the document to the House for a publication decision. The New York Times obtained its access earlier. Schorr spent his limited time with the document, Xeroxing rather than reading, according to the account.

He thought he and the Times both had copies until Times columnist William Safire called for help on details in the report concerning CIA involvement with the Kurds. At that point, Schorr confided to an acquaintance, the realization began to dawn upon him that he alone was the possessor of a copy of the House document.

At one point in an on-and-off-the-record conversation, Schorr volunteered, when asked what he intended to do with the proceeds of publication of his copy of the report:

"On the record, I would not have been willing to benefit personally from the sale of the report but would have been willing to sign the proceeds over to a First Amendment-oriented group."

For Felker the first installment of Operation Swordfish, as the report was code-named, began last Thursday when he learned it was available to him and he dispatched a staff worker to Washington to get a copy. Asked yesterday if he was specifically denying or refusing to comment that Schorr made it available to him, Felker chuckled.

"I stand on what I said," he repeated. "It was left on the doorstep."

There was never any debate, Felker said, against running the report. "There was a big split in Congress on what to do . . . We feel, in an election year, this is the time to contribute to that debate."

By coincidence, the 24-page section of excerpts was included in the Voice's first experimental national edition. It was also the third 160-page issue in the weekly newspaper's history.

When he learned of the publication of the excerpts in the Voice, House intelligence committee chairman Otis Pike (D-N.Y.) said he suspected the material was leaked by the executive department to incriminate Congress.

from The New York Times

Selling Secrets

The winding trail of the secret intelligence committee report from its origins in the House of Representatives to the pages of The Village Voice raises at least as many ethical issues for journalists as it poses sleuthing problems for those in the executive branch or in Congress who may be inclined to trace this leak back to its spout.

CBS correspondent Daniel Schorr now admits that he transmitted the report to The Voice through a still unnamed intermediary. The *quid pro quo* was an arrangement under which money passed from The Voice to the Reporters' Committee for Freedom of the Press, a group dedicated to defense of the First Amendment.

In his journalistic capacity Mr. Schorr had every right to seek access to the Pike committee report and to communicate the information in his possession to viewers of CBS News. Where he did responsible journalism a disservice was in making the report available for cash sale. The Reporters' Committee, in turn, did itself and its mission little honor in becoming a willing recipient of the proceeds of such a transaction.

To put it bluntly, while reporters and news organizations have rightly declined to accept the Government's judgment on what documents it is appropriate to publish, it is flatly wrong for reporters to be involved in any commercial traffic in such documents.

The attempt to launder the transaction by devoting the proceeds to high constitutional purposes just does not work. The damage to journalism lies in the willingness to be involved in such commerce in any manner, and the fact that the crusading Voice and the Reporters' Committee—both of which, in other circumstances, would probably be among the first to denounce "checkbook journalism"—receive the benefit deepens rather than eradicates the stain.

Of Secret Documents

by DANIEL SCHORR

To the Editor:

Let's look more closely at the issue of commerce in secret documents, raised in the form of an attack on me in your Feb. 15 editorial, "Selling Secrets." What you are really accusing me of is not selling secrets in the customary, or Times way.

Distribution of information, like other economic activities in a capitalistic society, generates profit. That is true of information whose value is enhanced because it is not generally available.

The Times, having had access to the same unreleased report of the House Intelligence Committee which is now a subject of controversy, reported extensively on its contents, reaping profit in prestige, and possibly circulation.

Do you consider that The Times was "selling secrets"?

Or, do you wish to narrow the question (though why?) to the text of the report, published elsewhere than in one's place of usual employment?

Then we are talking about something like the paperback book published on the Pentagon Papers after they had been so brilliantly covered by The Times. Did that book represent "selling secrets"?

My problem, which seems to have landed me in so much trouble, at least on The Times editorial page, was how to avoid making a profit.

I found myself unexpectedly, because of a surprise action by the House, in possession of possibly the only available copy of a report, bearing no classification on its face, its principal sensations already divulged, tied up in a confused parliamentary situation.

My problem was that doing nothing would mean that I would be suppressing a report that might be interesting as a matter of public record. It had nothing more of national security significance, certainly nothing that would endanger any individual.

But, because of the current climate about "secrets," I was advised that finding a book publisher would be difficult. I was told that the one clear opportunity for publication was offered by Clay Felker, publisher of The Village Voice.

I had then to consider, since taking money was unthinkable to me, whether Felker should be the sole beneficiary. If our system inevitably creates profits, should Felker enjoy them exclusively?

So, I suggested it would be appropriate for him to make some gesture to the free press idea which had animated me by a "voluntary" contribution to the Reporters' Committee, which provides legal defense in First Amendment cases.

Is it not really unbecoming, if not downright hypocritical, for a paper that has so successfully profited from secrets to apply a term like "laundering" to one who is trying to avoid a profit and divert it to a cause he believes in?

DANIEL SCHORR
Washington, Feb. 16, 1976

The Secret Report Caper

by CHARLES B. SEIB

If the CIA's dirty tricks department had been assigned to cast a shadow over the press, it couldn't have done a better job than did a covey of journalists earnestly committed to the integrity and high purposes of their calling.

I'm talking about the Secret Report Caper, featuring Daniel Schorr, a star reporter for CBS News, and the Reporters Committee for Freedom of the Press.

Here's the plot:

Schorr, who has a way with government secrets, obtained a copy of the House intelligence committee's unreleased report on the CIA and other intelligence operations. It was a pretty good coup, and Schorr did a series of radio and television reports on it. Then it became even more of a coup when the House decided on grounds of national security that the report should not be issued. Schorr had not just beaten his colleagues to a soon-to-be-released document; he had a permanent exclusive.

What to do? First, he decided that the report should be published —not just the guts of it, which he and others had reported, but all of it, or at least large sections, word for word and in print. Schorr says he made that decision as a matter of "journalistic conscience" because, as the only person outside of official circles with a copy of the report, "I could not be the one responsible for suppressing (it)."

Second, he decided that the report, now officially bottled up by the House, was worth money. Since he had no wish to profit from it himself, how about helping some worthy cause? And what more appropriate cause than the Reporters Committee for Freedom of the Press?

He approached the committee's leaders and proposed that it accept the proceeds of the sale. They agreed and gave him the name of a lawyer who could help him in his negotiations with publishers.

And so it came to pass that on February 11, the Village Voice, a New York liberal weekly, printed 24 pages of excerpts. The content was less than sensational. The hardest news was a charge that Secretary of State Kissinger made statements "at variance with the facts."

Nevertheless, the publication set off a storm. President Ford angrily offered to help the House find the leak. Kissinger declared that "a new version of McCarthyism" was rampant. House committee sources hinted that maybe the CIA had leaked the report to make Congress look bad.

Then, with fine irony, there was a leak within the leak. The Washington Post reported, in effect, that Schorr was the source of the Voice's text even though he was denying it on the record. It also reported the deal with the Reporters Committee.

Schorr is angry at The Post and the Reporters Committee. He says The Post story, which he called "unconscionable," used off-the-record material. He also says that his discussions with the Reporters Committee were confidential and should not have been disclosed.

The Post denies that it broke any agreements with Schorr, and the Reporters Committee says it never felt that its arrangement with Schorr could or should be kept secret.

The day after the Post story appeared, Schorr confirmed that he did indeed provide the Village Voice text and that he had made the arrangement with the Reporters Committee.

To bring the story up to date as of this writing, CBS has said that Schorr has been taken off the intelligence story, but that "as always we will back our guy."

Rep. Samuel Stratton (D-N.Y.) wants the House to find Schorr in contempt for releasing a secret House report. So before it's over, CBS may get the opportunity to back its guy.

It's a pretty funny story, if you like black comedy: news people arguing bitterly over what was on the record and what wasn't, and a group with the loftiest journalistic mission—defense of the First

Amendment—agreeing to accept proceeds from the sale of a secret government document.

But before the laughter dies and the press' notoriously short attention span wanes, journalists concerned about the good name of their trade would do well to try to clean up the mess.

There is, for example, that money. At this writing it apparently is hovering between the Village Voice and the Reporters Committee. Schorr has said it is a "substantial" amount, but he won't say how much.

Think how the press—Schorr included—would move in on a situation like this if someone else had been doing the dealing.

Retroactive judgments are easy and often unfair. Nevertheless, I'll offer a couple:

Schorr should have recognized that the dollar sign is a danger sign in journalism. The buying or selling of news inevitably taints the product. His own network has had experience with that truism. (It should be noted that CBS was not involved in Schorr's marketing of the text; he says he acted entirely on his own after the report's use to the network was over.)

As for the Reporters Committee, no matter how much it needed funds, it should have recognized the untenable position it was getting itself into. Its argument that the deal was acceptable because the committee was to be just a "passive" recipient of the money is naive—and doesn't quite jibe with the suggestion of a negotiator to Schorr.

The story is not over. Schorr may have further problems with the House and with his bosses.

But whatever happens, the cause of free journalism has been damaged. News people should be laughing with tears in their eyes.

As for those dirty trick boys at CIA, their laughter should be tempered by envy. Even the most devious of them couldn't have dreamed up a "poisoned well" scheme like the Secret Report Caper.

News Leaks and Hypocrisy

by JACK ANDERSON

We have been treated lately to two particularly gross spectacles of governmental hypocrisy.

One is the raising from the dead of the House Ethics Committee, not to pursue its hoary mandate to keep congressional corruption down to tolerable levels, but to hound newsman Daniel Schorr for pirating out to the public a committee report on intelligence fiascos.

The other has been the wailing of Secretary of State Henry Kissinger that press leaks were making foreign diplomats reluctant to deal with the United States. The leaks that he felt impaired the national security happened to be derogatory toward Kissinger.

At the same time, it was revealed that his most trusted aide had leaked extensive quotes from classified memoranda of conversations between Kissinger and Middle Eastern leaders, who thought they were negotiating in confidence. These leaked quotes made the Secretary appear a genius among pedestrian diplomats.

There are two simple rules of government, apparently, concerning the public's right to know: 1) classify and suppress sensitive information if it's unfavorable to officialdom; 2) declassify and leak sensitive information if it's favorable to officialdom.

Consider the Schorr case. CBS newsman Schorr glommed onto the text of a report that the House Intelligence Committee intended to release. As a movement to suppress it began building up in the House, Schorr rushed out the following highlights:

The CIA had flopped badly in not anticipating either the 1973 Yom Kippur war or the 1968 Tet offensive; intelligence information had sometimes been manipulated for the political purposes of the White House; Henry Kissinger had done his best to stonewall the House probe. The inescapable conclusion was that congressional supervision over intelligence agencies, entrusted to the most prestigious figures in Congress, had been an abject, negligent and inexcusable failure.

The report thus did not deal in real, live spy secrets but with old, rusted conspiracies. Oh, foreign feathers might be ruffled by the disclosure, and our adversaries in the world might receive some peripheral benefit. But this was nowhere near the benefit our country would reap from exposing, and thus creating the climate for correcting, the incredible lapses of our covert organizations in both effectiveness and adherence to the law.

When the House voted to suppress the report, Schorr arranged to have it published in the Village Voice. We won't attempt to unravel here the secondary flap caused by Schorr's effort to get the publication to pay for the report with a charitable donation to the Reporters Committee for Freedom of the Press. But we agree with Schorr on the public's right to know about the CIA fiascos.

The publication of the report brought down upon Schorr's head the most disingenuous outburst of sanctimony seen since the palmiest days of the Watergate coverup. Secretary Kissinger cried "McCarthyism" and mourned for the nation's future; President Ford offered to put the FBI at the disposal of the House until the perpetrators of truth were brought to justice; a vast braying went up that press leaks must stop before our foreign policy became paralyzed.

The act was going great until the untimely disclosure that Kissinger's office had been ladling out massive doses of classified material that lionized the Secretary, page after page of confidential diplomatic conversations.

This wholesaling of secrets for no loftier cause than to puff up Kissinger caught the secrecy buffs with their indignation down. There was no dispatch of FBI agents by Ford, no pronunciamentos by Kissinger that diplomacy had been rendered impossible, no talk of hearings or prosecution or contempt action as in the Schorr case.

Instead, there was a congenial huddle of veteran Foggy Bottom leakers; and then Kissinger aide Alfred Atherton, long noted for his meticulous observance of Kissinger's orders, obligingly took the fall. There had been a "substantial misunderstanding" of Kissinger's instructions, said the State Department, but the leakers were motivated by "good intentions." Atherton was patted on the wrist with an official reprimand and then invited to lunch with Secretary Kissinger and the Israeli Foreign Minister.

Meanwhile, the House Ethics Committee, after a decade of stalwartly looking the other way to avoid investigating dozens of House members publicly accused of bribe-taking, kickbacks, campaign fraud, conflicts of interest and abuses of government perks, suddenly roused itself from the torpor and asked for $350,000 to probe a crime it could enthusiastically pursue: the smuggling to the American people of forbidden truths about bureaucratic misbehavior and congressional laxity.

Perhaps some good can be wrung from the committee's new-found zeal for investigation. While it is in the mood to investigate something and possessed of funds, staff and subpoena power to do it, we are prepared to offer the committee several cases of real violations of congressional ethics, each one guaranteed to merit a bona fide probe in contrast to the current shabby harassment of a newsman.

The revival of the House Ethics Committee shows that it's not crimes against the public but embarrassment of the government that provokes official ire, just as the Atherton charade again reveals the double standards on the uses of classified information. Both incidents illustrate the dangerous mind-set of government, which laughs off official abuses of power while massing its armament against the proper challenges that freedom must make to pretensions of sovereignty. It is a mind-set the people in the press must resist in this, our bicentennial year, if we are to preserve our freedoms for another 200 years.

The Schorr Sham

The House of Representatives voted last week, amid blustery talk of prosecution, to investigate CBS correspondent Daniel Schorr for his admitted role in giving *The Village Voice* part of a secret House committee report on US intelligence excesses. And now CBS has put him out to pasture for an "indefinite period," which many in Washington suspect will have no end. The networks have always been more comfortable being supine than being brave, and we may soon see the big media reverting to their pre-Watergate coziness with power.

There are at least three embarrassing questions mocking the House action. To begin with, Schorr most probably got the report from someone in the House itself. If the members are so worried in this case about their integrity, they might properly begin with themselves, and not with a newsman whose professional obligation is to cast light on the dark corners of government. But that only begs a second question: what were these secrets, and what did their publication damage? The national security? The reputations of the CIA and Henry Kissinger? The sanctity of a private deal between the Pike committee and the Ford administration? The political safety of some congressmen who're now worried about a backlash on the intelligence issue? After all the scandalous abuses of the past three years and after all the revelations of outrage committed in the name of national security, secrecy and its central tool, the classification system, still reign supreme in the US government. Bureaucrats and cabinet officers can cover their mistakes, sometimes their crimes, with the soft smudge of a rubber stamp, and Congress, in awe of authority, submits, leaving itself as powerless as ever in foreign affairs. The vast majority of the House committee report "secrets," like most foreign policy secrets, were well known abroad, to the Soviets, the French, the British, the Israelis, the Iranians, and assorted other intelligence services. The secrets were to be guarded from the American public, which could not to be trusted to let the Forty Committee and CIA stations operate in their customary autonomy, free of the messy intrusions of democracy. Until the House reforms the classification system, until secrecy is brought into proportion with real national security interests, gestures like the Schorr vote are a sham.

There is a final and probably more difficult question in all this. If errant journalist Schorr is to be censured by an indignant House, what about all those officials who have lied to the members and their committees? Did any of our representatives think it ironic that at the same time they adopted their Schorr resolution, the Justice Department let the statute of limitations run out on former CIA Director Richard Helms for his alleged responsibility in an "official" burglary? . . . Members of Congress have been an audience for perjury and deception by foreign policy officialdom many times. And not one lie or liar has been so much as officially chided by the Congress.

Editorial cartoon by Bill Sanders. Reproduced through the courtesy of Field Newspaper Syndicate

from NATIONAL REVIEW

The Week

■ The worm turns. CBS reporter Daniel Schorr, who regularly sermonizes on the public's right to know, has come upon an exception to this right. He thinks it "unconscionable" of the *Washington Post* to have revealed

The Week: From *National Review* (March 19, 1976). Reprinted by permission of National Review, 150 East 35 Street, New York, N.Y. 10016.

him as the *Village Voice*'s source for the Report of the House Committee on Intelligence. That information, harumphs muckraker Schorr, was off the record and should not have been disclosed. Why did CBS suspend Schorr? That's easy. One CBS official told the *Post* that by giving the report to the *Voice,* Schorr "could reinforce the conviction some of our conservative affiliates have that while CBS news management is not politically oriented, underneath them are some reporters who wear their hearts on their left sleeves."

from Time

Schorr Signs Off

Almost from the day last February that CBS suspended him for passing a copy of the secret Pike committee report on CIA operations to New York's *Village Voice,* Daniel Schorr suspected that he would never again appear as a CBS correspondent. Then came his eloquent defense of a reporter's First Amendment rights last month before the House ethics committee, which had demanded that he identify his source. "To betray a source would be to betray myself, my career and my life," he declared. "I cannot do it."

He did not have to. The committee decided not to punish him, and CBS seemed ready to take him back. Said Schorr: "It appeared to me, from the ashes of all the trouble we'd had, that a whole new era might arrive."

Deep Tube. It never arrived. After consulting his wife Lee and his lawyer Joseph Califano—the only people to whom Schorr identified his Deep Tube, he handed his resignation to CBS News President Richard S. Salant. Schorr was afraid that CBS would keep him on until the memory of his ethics committee performance had faded and then quietly fire him. He also thought that he would not be able to fit in easily again at the CBS Washington bureau. "I would doubt my ability to function effectively if reinstated," explained Schorr, who first joined the CBS News staff 23 years ago. "My reinstatement would be a source of tension within an organization whose future success I still care about."

Not everyone at CBS was eager to see Schorr return. Some executives were still fuming over Schorr's remarks to Duke University students, in January 1975, implying that CBS had pressured Walter Cronkite, Eric Sevareid and Dan Rather to go easy on Richard Nixon the night he announced his resignation from the presidency—a charge all three deny. Worse, for several hours last Feb. 11, Schorr let his bosses believe that fellow correspondent Lesley Stahl leaked the Pike report. Some of the people Schorr worked with in the CBS Washington bureau have never forgiven him. Said a correspondent: "It's one thing to deceive management. It's another thing to shit on your colleagues."

Schorr, 60, will be paid his full salary (close to $70,000 a year) through 1978, when he will begin receiving a pension. He plans to give speeches (at $3,000 each), lecture next spring at the University of California (Berkeley), and finish a book. Schorr is free to leave the CBS payroll and join another network, but he insists that he is finished with television. Says he: "I have a terrible hunger for direct contact with people, and I want to see those little words in print that I can go back to next day and say, 'That's what I wrote.' "

from Newsweek, October 11, 1976

MY TURN

Covering My Own Story

Daniel Schorr

For seven months I was transformed from practitioner of the press to defender—and target—of the press. Now I know what it looks like from the other side of the barricade.

I can see the irony of my position last February, when CBS suspension and Congressional investigation turned me from news reporter into news story. Life changed abruptly with photographers at the door, the first unlisted telephone number in my life and an invitation to the annual Gridiron Dinner, not as roaster but as roastee. It was to hear Clark Mollenhoff sing, "I want a leak just like the leak they gave to dear old Dan."

Traveling around the country, trying to explain what I had done with the Pike committee report and why, I found it hard, at first, to keep a straight face when interviewers poked microphones at me or confronted me from the wrong side of press-conference tables. At one airport, I actually came up behind a cluster of cameras waiting for me and inquired about who was arriving.

The reporters' questions never seemed to vary, as though a printed list was preceding me from town to town, and they seemed to be all the wrong questions. They were directed not toward my issues of security vs. disclosure, the free press vs. the bad government, but whether I was too abrasive, who in CBS didn't like me, how much I had been paid for the Pike report, and why I had chosen the Village Voice. (I cherish the question that was asked only once—whether I had picked the Voice because my daughter works there. My daughter, you see, is 6.)

ISSUES OR ERRORS

With a *déjà entendu* memory from the other side of the fence, I began muttering about reporters not caring for the big issues, just about gossip and trivia, preferably damaging. Ah, McGovern, how I could weep with you now! Ah, Nixon, I see what you meant about being kicked around! To one campus audience I said, full bitterly, "I'm fighting for freedom of the press, and maybe I should also be fighting for freedom *from* the press."

But my role reversal and bad press involved more than wry irony. They clearly influenced the course of events. The proposal for a House investigation originated with Rep. Samuel Stratton on the day he read an editorial in The New York Times denouncing me for "selling secrets." My suspension by CBS caused one member of the House ethics committee to say that the committee could hardly be less stringent with me than my own employer. Critical comments in the press made me seem fair game to a House anxious to demonstrate against leaks and for national security.

Not contesting some errors of judgment on my part, I wondered why these errors of detail dominated press discussion rather than the developing issue for the press—a confrontation with Congress that might parallel the "prior restraint" confrontation with the Executive over the Pentagon papers. There was also, from the start, the possibility of the first clash with Congress in this century over confidential sources.

THE PRESS AND THE PEOPLE

My probem, friends in the press advised, was that I had made the press establishment feel threatened by breaching several of its cardinal rules. I had made my own decision about publishing the Pike report, causing many editors to worry about the precedent for staff discipline. Though meeting all my employer's needs, I had disposed of a document that raised questions of property rights. (I had assumed it was the public's property.) I had involved television in an argument with Congress, when Congress was looking balefully at the broadcast industry anyway. And I had flaunted the idea of press disclosure when disclosure was retreating before a secrecy backlash, and the press was fretting about public hostility to the news media.

But, while getting a bad press, I was getting a good public. I was sympathetically received when I explained that I believed in national security, but not in the debasement of national security for cover-up. I was understood when I said the press may have saved our free institutions when the government had been corrupted and silenced by a Nixon conspiracy that necessarily included a conspiracy to discredit the press. I was cheered when I said that at issue was not my right to report, but the public's right to know.

"It's an election year," Majority Leader Thomas (Tip) O'Neill had told me on Jan. 29, when the House voted to suppress the Pike report, "and they're voting their American Legion posts." It reflected the conventional wisdom that the public was sick of four years of Watergate and CIA disclosure. And I had apparently gotten the press into trouble by raising my head when it was time to duck.

I was getting a different signal from the grass roots, though—a more complicated signal. Indeed, Americans were worried about whether too much investigation and disclosure were hampering the FBI and CIA from seeing to their personal and national safety. But, the trauma of Watergate and distrust of an uncontrolled government lingered, and Americans were not ready to close the door on everything asserted to be "secret" and hand the key trustingly to anybody—the President included.

And I found that while Americans were deeply, though vaguely, concerned about the power of the press, fearful of being manipulated by "the media," they valued the press when the chips were down. They trusted the government less than they trusted the press, and they wanted the press to watch the government vigilantly—including Congress.

CONFRONTATION

None of this was the conventional wisdom in Washington, and few in Congress, or the press, believed it. So, acting on the conventional wisdom, the House ethics committee, by subpoenas, moved toward confrontation. That action, with the implied menace of jail for contempt, provided the necessary dramatic focus to forge a belated solidarity in the press in defense of its interests. More important, it brought a spontaneous outpouring of public outrage.

What had initially seemed attractive to politicians in an election year—upholding secrecy and giving comeuppance to the press—suddenly began to look counterproductive when constituents were finally roused to express themselves. More than many of its own practitioners had realized, the First Amendment was alive and well in the heart of America.

Schorr resigned from CBS News last week in the wake of the controversy over his role in divulging the secret Pike committee report on the CIA. A House panel investigating the leak had decided earlier not to charge him with contempt.

THE PRINT MEDIA

STUDY QUESTIONS

1. In "The American Periodical Press and Its Impact," Wolseley says that the national magazine is either "a reflector of American life or what the owners think is American life." What problems might arise if there were discrepancies between the two? Can you think of a magazine in which such discrepancies are apparent?

2. What composite picture do you get of Americans from looking at Peter's list of top ten magazines?

3. Few general magazines exist today. What factors in our society have brought about the shift from general interest to specialized magazines? New media? Advertising? Changing interests? Affluence? Does the specialized magazine have a greater influence on society than one with mass appeal?

4. Can you find evidence that supports Wolseley's conclusion that most magazines do not fully serve the public?

5. In "The Black Magazines," Wolseley points out that more than any other medium, the magazine may be able to help black people in their search for a place in society. Can the same be said of other groups—women, political radicals, racial and ethnic minorities, workers, artists, intellectuals, youth?

6. Stegner is pessimistic about America's cultural climate if the tendency to overlook the traditional media—especially books—in favor of newer media continues. Do we need books? What can books do that the other print media cannot? That the electronic media cannot?

7. In what ways do the different print media complement each other in making it possible for the public to get the whole story?

8. Although the mini-case study on Daniel Schorr is an example of the variety of ways the print media treat a subject, the ramifications of Schorr's actions have not been fully explored. Should a reporter enjoy personal benefit from a story? Did the media tell the whole story?

BIBLIOGRAPHY FOR FURTHER STUDY

Bagdikian, Ben H. "The Myth of Newspaper Poverty." *Columbia Journalism Review* 11 (March/April, 1973), 19–25.

———. "Newspapers: Learning (Too Slowly) to Adapt to TV." *Columbia Journalism Review* 12 (November/December, 1973), 44–51.

———. "Publishing's Quiet Revolution." *Columbia Journalism Review* 12 (May/June, 1973), 7–15.

Consumer Magazine and Farm Publication Rates and Data. Skokie, Ill.: Standard Rate and Data Service, Inc., published monthly.

Directory: Newspapers and Periodicals. Philadelphia: N. W. Ayer & Son, published annually.

Editor & Publisher International Year Book. New York: Editor & Publisher, published annually.

Glessing, Robert J. *The Underground Press in America.* Bloomington: Indiana University Press, 1970.

Hornby, William H. "Beware the 'Market' Thinkers . . . " *The Quill* (January, 1976), 14–17.

Janssen, Peter A. "*Rolling Stone's* Quest for Respectability." *Columbia Journalism Review* 12 (January/February, 1974), 59–65.

Joyce, Donald Franklin. "Magazines of Afro-American Thought on the Mass Market: Can They Survive? *American Libraries,* VII (December, 1976), 678–83.

Leamer, Laurence. *The Paper Revolutionaries: The Rise of the Underground Press.* New York: Simon and Schuster, 1972.

Lewis, Roger. *The Outlaws of America: The Underground Press and Its Context.* Baltimore: Penguin Books, 1972.

Literary Market Place: The Business Directory of American Book Publishing. New York: Bowker, published annually.

Madison, Charles G. *Book Publishing in America.* New York: McGraw-Hill, 1967.

Morris, Monica B. "Newpapers and the New Feminists: Black Out as Social Control." *Journalism Quarterly* 50 (Spring, 1973), 37–42.

Newspaper Rates and Data. Skokie, Ill.: Standard Rate and Data Service, Inc., published monthly.

Peter, John. "The Rise of the City Magazine." *Folio* (November/December, 1973), 61–64.

Petersen, Clarence. *The Bantam Story.* 2nd ed. New York: Bantam Books, 1975.

Peterson, Theodore. *Magazines in the Twentieth Century.* 2nd. ed. Urbana: University of Illinois Press, 1964.

"The Pike Papers." *Time* (February 23, 1976), 55.

Schorr, Daniel. " 'The Daniel Schorr Affair': A Reply." *Columbia Journalism Review* 15 (July/August, 1976), 48–49.

"Schorr Under Siege." *Time* (March 1, 1976), 42.

Schuneman, R. Smith. *Photographic Communication: Principles, Problems and Challenges of Photojournalism.* New York: Hastings House, 1972.

Steinfels, Peter. "The Schorr Witchhunt." *Commonweal* (March 26, 1976), 198ff.

Stern, Laurence. "The Daniel Schorr Affair." *Columbia Journalism Review* 15 (May/June, 1976), 20–25.

Stone, I. F. "The Schorr Case: The Real Dangers." *The New York Review of Books* (April 1, 1976), 6, 10.

"Tale of Two Leaks." *The Nation* (March 27, 1976), 354–55.

Talese, Gay. *The Kingdom and the Power.* New York: The World Publishing Co., 1969.

Tebbel, John. *The American Magazine: A Compact History.* New York: Hawthorn, 1969.

"Text of Opening Statement by Daniel Schorr Before House Committee." *The New York Times* (September 16, 1976), 69.
Welles, Chris. "The Numbers Magazines Live By." *Columbia Journalism Review* 14 (September/October, 1975), 22–27.
Wolseley, Roland. *Understanding Magazines.* Ames: Iowa State University Press, 1969.

THE ELECTRONIC MEDIA

Television: More Deeply Than We Suspect, It Has Changed All of Us

by DANIEL J. BOORSTIN

Daniel J. Boorstin, author and historian, warns that television will destroy many admirable aspects of our society unless we can overcome the segregation, the isolation, that it causes.

Just as the printing press democratized learning, so the television set has democratized experience. But while our experience now is more equal than ever before, it is also more separate. And no Supreme Court ruling can correct this segregation, no federal commission can police it. It is built into our TV sets.

Segregation from One Another

When a colonial housewife went to the village well to draw water for her family, she saw friends, gathered gossip, shared the laughs and laments of her neighbors. When her great-great-granddaughter was blessed with running water, and no longer had to go to the well, this made life easier, but also less interesting. Running electricity, mail delivery and the telephone removed more reasons for leaving the house. And now the climax of it all is Television.

For television gives the American housewife in her kitchen her own private theater, her window on the world. Every room with a set becomes a private room with a view—a TV booth. Television brings in a supply of information, knowledge, news, romance, and advertisements—without her having to set foot outside her door. The range and variety and vividness of these experiences of course excel anything she gets outside, even while she spends hours driving around in her automobile. At home she now has her own private faucet of hot and cold running images.

But always before, to see a performance was to share an experience with a visible audience. At a concert, or a ball game, or a political rally, the audience was half the fun. What and whom you saw in the audience was at least as interesting, and often humanly more important, than what you saw on the stage. While watching TV, the lonely American is thrust back on herself. She can, of course, exclaim or applaud or hiss, but nobody hears except the family in the living room. The other people at the performance take the invisible forms of "canned" laughter and applause.

And while myriad island audiences gather nightly around their sets, much as cave-dwelling ancestors gathered around the fire, for warmth and safety and a feeling of togetherness, now, with more and more two-TV families, a member of the family can actually withdraw and watch in complete privacy.

Segregation from the Source

In the 1920s, in the early days of radio, "broadcast" entered the language with a new meaning. Before then it meant "to sow seeds over the whole

surface, instead of in drills or rows," but now it meant to diffuse messages or images to unidentified people at unknown destinations. The mystery of the anonymous audience was what made sensible businessmen doubt whether radio would ever pay. They had seen the telegraph and the telephone prosper by delivering a message, composed by the sender, to a particular recipient. They thought the commercial future of radio might depend on devising ways to keep the radio message private so that it could be sent to only one specific person.

The essential novelty of wireless communication—that those who received "broadcast" messages were no longer addressees, but a vast mysterious audience—was destined, in the long run, to create unforeseen new opportunities and new problems for Americans in the age of television, to create a new sense of isolation and confinement and frustration for those who saw the images. For television was a one-way window. Just as Americans were segregated from the millions of other Americans who were watching the same program, so each of them was segregated in a fantastic new way from those who put on the program and who, presumably, aimed to please. The viewer could see whatever they offered, but nobody (except the family in the living room) could know for sure how he reacted to what he saw.

While the American felt isolated from those who filled the TV screen, he also felt a new isolation from his government, from those who collected his taxes, who provided his public services, and who made the crucial decisions of peace or war. Of course, periodically he still had the traditional opportunity to express his preference on the ballot. But now there was a disturbing and frustrating new disproportion between how often and how vividly his government and his political leaders could get their message to him and how often and how vividly he could get his to them. Even if elected representatives were no more inaccessible to him than they had ever been before, in a strange new way he surely felt more isolated from them. They could talk his ear off on TV and if he wanted to respond, all he could do was write them a letter. Except indirectly through the pollsters, Americans were offered no new modern avenue comparable to television by which to get their message back. They were left to rely on a venerable, almost obsolete 19th-century institution, the post office.

Segregation from the Past

Of all the forces which have tempted us to lose our sense of history, none has been more potent than television. While, of course, television levels distance—puts us closer and more vividly present in Washington than we are in our state capital and takes us all instantly to the moon—it has had a less noticeable but equally potent effect on our sense of time. Because television enables us to be there, anywhere, instantly, precisely because it fills the instant present moment with experience so engrossing and overwhelming, it dulls our sense of the past. If it had not been possible for us all to accompany Scott and Irwin on their voyage of exploration on the moon, we would have had to wait to be engrossed in retrospect by the vivid chronicle of some Francis Parkman or Samuel Eliot Morison, and there would then have been no possible doubt that the moon journey was part of the stream of our history. But with television we saw that historic event—as we now see more and more of whatever goes on in our country—as only another vivid item in the present.

Almost everything about television tempts the medium to a time-myopia—to focus our interest on the here-and-now, the exciting, disturbing, inspiring, or catastrophic instantaneous now. Meanwhile, the high cost of network time and the need to offer something for everybody produce a discontinuity of programming, a constant shifting from one thing to another, an emphasis on the staccato and motley character of experience—at the cost of our sense of unity with the past.

But history is a flowing stream. We are held together by its continuities, by people willing to sit there and do their jobs, by the unspoken faiths of people who still believe much of what their fathers believed. That makes a dull program. So the American begins to think of the outside world as if there too the program changed every half hour.

Segregation from Reality

Of all the miracles of television none is more remarkable than its power to give to so many hours of our experience a new vagueness. Americans have become increasingly accustomed to see something-or-other, happening somewhere-or-other, at sometime-or-other. The common-sense hallmarks of authentic first-hand experience (the ordinary facts which a jury expects a witness to supply to prove he actually experienced what he says) now begin to be absent, or to be only ambiguously present, in our television-experience. For our TV-experience we don't need to go out to see anything in particular. We just turn the knob. Then we wonder while we watch. Is this program "live" or is it "taped"? Is it merely an animation or a "simulation"? Is this a rerun? Where does it originate? When (if ever) did it really occur? Is this happening to actors or to real people? Is this a commercial? A spoof of a commercial? A documentary? Or pure fiction?

Almost never do we see a TV event from what used to be the individual human point of view. For TV is many-eyed, and alert to avoid the monotony of one person's limited vision. And each camera gives us a close-up that somehow dominates the screen. Dick Cavett or Zsa Zsa Gabor fills the screen just like Dave Scott or President Nixon. Everything becomes theater, any actor—or even a spectator—holds center stage. Our TV perspective makes us understandably reluctant to go back to the seats on the side and in the rear which are ours in real life.

The experience flowing through our television channels is a miscellaneous mix of entertainment, instruction, news, uplift, exhortation, and guess what. Old compartments of experience which separated going to church, or to a lecture, from going to a play or a movie or to a ball game, from going to a political rally or stopping to hear a patent-medicine salesman's pitch—on television, such compartments are dissolved. Here at last is a supermarket of surrogate experience. Successful programming offers entertainment (under the guise of instruction), instruction (under the guise of entertainment), political persuasion (with the appeal of advertising) and advertising (with the appeal of drama).

A new miasma—which no machine before could emit—enshrouds the world of TV. We begin to be so accustomed to this foggy world, so at home and solaced and comforted within and by its blurry edges, that reality itself becomes slightly irritating.

Here is a great, rich, literate, equalitarian nation suddenly fragmented into mysterious anonymous island-audiences, newly separated from one another, newly isolated from their entertainers and their educators and their political representatives, suddenly enshrouded in a fog of new ambiguities. Unlike other comparable changes in human experience, the new segregation came with rocket speed. Television conquered America in less than a generation. No wonder its powers are bewildering and hard to define. It took 500 years for the printing press to democratize learning. Then the people, who at last could know as much as their "betters," demanded the power to govern themselves. As late as 1671, the governor of colonial Virginia, Sir William Berkeley, thanked God that the printing press (breeder of heresy and disobedience) had not yet arrived in his colony, and prayed that printing would never come to Virginia. By the early 19th century, aristocrats and men of letters would record (with Thomas Carlyle) that movable type had disbanded hired armies and cashiered kings, and somehow created "a whole new democratic world."

With dizzying speed television has democratized experience. Like the printing press, it threatens—and promises—a transformation. Is it any wonder that, like the printing press before it, television has met a cool reception from intellectuals and academics and the other custodians of traditional avenues of experience?

Can TV-democratized experience carry us to a new society, beyond the traditional democracy of learning and politics? The great test is whether somehow we can find ways in and through television itself to break down the walls of the new segregation—the walls which separate us from one another, from the sources of knowledge and power, from the past, from the real world outside. We see clues to our frustrations in the rise of endless dreary talk-shows, as much as in the sudden increase in mass demonstrations. We must find ways outside TV to restore the sense of personal presence, the sense of neighborhood, of visible fellowship, of publicly shared enthusiasm and dismay. We must find ways within TV to allow the anonymous audience to express its views, not merely through sampling and statistical averages, but person-to-person. We must find ways to decentralize and define and separate TV audiences into smaller, more specific interest-groups, who have the competence to judge what they see, and then to give the audiences an opportunity to react and communicate their reactions. We must try every institutional and technological device—from more specialized stations to pay TV, to cable TV, and other devices still unimagined.

Over a century ago, Thoreau warned that men were becoming "the tools of their tools." While this new-world nation has thrived on change and on novelty, our prosperity and our survival have depended on our ability to adapt strange new tools to wise old purposes. We cannot allow ourselves to drift in the channels of television. Many admirable features of American life today—the new poignance of our conscience, the wondrous universalizing of our experiences, the sharing of the exotic, the remote, the unexpected—come from television. But they will come to little unless we find ways to overcome the new provincialism, the new isolation, the new frustrations and the new confusion which come from our new segregation.

The Careening of America

Caution: Television Watching May Be Hazardous to Your Mental Health

by NICHOLAS JOHNSON

Nicholas Johnson, former FCC Commissioner and well-known media critic, sees danger in television programming and commercials because they promote a life-style in which a person's worth centers on "conspicuous consumption of mass-produced goods, rather than the growth of individuality." Possible solutions, according to Johnson, lie in such alternatives to commercial broadcasting as cable TV, pay TV, public broadcasting, and economical videotape equipment.

The general semanticist Alfred Korzybski described three categories of mental health: sane, insane, and unsane. His point was that most of us, while not *in*sane, are *un*sane. That is, we are not living up to our potential as human beings; we are not fully functioning. The so-called "human potential movement," including the late Abraham Maslow, argues that even the *healthy* human beings among us function at perhaps 5 per cent of their potential.

Reflect: How many people do *you* know whom you think of as "fully functioning personalities"? How many are there in whose daily lives there is a measure of beauty, contact with nature, artistic creativity, some philosophical contemplation or religion, love, self-fulfilling productivity of some kind, participation in life-support activities, physical well-being, a spirit of joy, and individual growth? That's what the world's great theolo-

The Careening of America: This article first appeared in *The Humanist* July/August 1972 issue and is reprinted by permission.

gians, psychiatrists, poets, and philosophers have been telling us human life is all about. But few of us have come close to realizing that potential.

As an FCC commissioner, I think I have a responsibility to examine the possibility that this potentiality gap may be related in some way to the operation of radio and television.

It is, of course, preposterous to suggest—or even suspect—that television is responsible for everything wrong with America, or that it is the sole cause of any individual problem. We had social problems before we had television, and since its coming we have made some progress of which we can be proud. But it would be equally shortsighted to ignore the finds of the many task-force reports and academic studies that link television, in greater or lesser degree, to virtually every national crisis.

Television programming is not, of course, the only influence on a child; but the fact remains that it is a large one. The average child will have received more hours of "instruction" from television by the time he enters first grade than he will later spend in college classrooms earning a B.A. degree. By the time he is a teenager he will have spent 15–20 thousand hours with the television set and will have been exposed to 250–500 thousand commercials. It would seem simple common sense to assume that this exposure has its influence; in any event, since "hard-headed businessmen" are willing to bet three billion dollars a year in advertising budgets on the proposition that it is having an effect, they at least are effectively estopped from arguing the contrary.

We are all vaguely aware that Big Television is allied with Big Business. But you may not be aware of the full reach of that alliance. The most influential broadcast property—talent, programs, studios, network contracts, and stations—are actually owned by big business, lock, stock, and barrel. Each of the three networks is a major industrial-conglomerate corporation. The time on the stations is purchased by big business—virtually all the available programming and advertising time on 7,500 radio and television stations. The entire enterprise, programs as well as commercials, revolves around the consumer mechandisers who find the medium the most effective way to sell their wares. The top talent (let alone the executives) are paid salaries that place them well up in the ranks of America's wealthiest businessmen.

Very little is programmed anytime during the broadcast day that is in dissidence with this overall domination by big business. Procter and Gamble's editorial policy provides that "There will be no material that may give offense, either directly or by inference, to any . . . commercial organization of any sort." The only exceptions are tokenism: an occasional news item (carefully kept out of prime time; network news is programmed as early as 5 P.M. in many sections of the country), or an even rarer documentary. Even these programs are larded with commercial messages sold for as much as the networks can extract. History—the moon walk, election returns—is also "brought to you by" some commercial sponsor. Whatever the benefits of news, documentaries, and live coverage, for those millions of American families whose television watching is limited to prime-time series shows, or soap operas during the day, Procter and Gamble's policy reigns supreme.

You may think, "Of course big business dominates television—so what? It may be separating a few fools from their money in exchange for products of questionable worth—a hazard of any foray into the marketplace. There are occasional fraudulent or misleading ads, but that's the Federal Trade Commission's problem. What other cause for concern is there?"

In the process of trying to answer that question, I have become more and more aware of the extent to which television not only distributes programs and sells products, but also preaches a general philosophy of life. Television tells us, hour after gruesome hour, that the primary measure of an individual's worth is his consumption of products, his measuring up to ideals that are found in packages mass produced and distributed by corporate America. Many products (and even programs), but especially the drug commercials, sell the gospel that there are instant solutions to life's most pressing personal problems. You don't need to think about your own emotional maturity and development of individuality, your discipline, training, and education, your perception of the world, your willingness to cooperate and compromise and work with other people; you don't need to think about developing deep and meaningful human relationships and trying to keep them in repair. "Better living through chemistry" is not just DuPont's slogan—it's one of the commandments of consumerism. Not only do the programs and commercials explicitly preach materialism, conspicuous consumption, status consciousness, sexploitation, and fantasy worlds of quick shallow solutions, but even the settings and subliminal messages are commercials for the consumption style of life.

The headache-remedy commercials are among the most revealing. A headache is often the body's way of telling us something's wrong. What is wrong may have to do with the bad vibes one picks up working in big corporations' office buildings, or shopping in their stores. The best answer may be to stay out of such places. Obviously, such a solution would be as bad for the corporate state generally as for the headache-remedy business in particular. So the message is clear: Corporate jobs and shopping trips are as American as chemical additives in apple pie. You just keep driving yourself through both; and when those mysterious headache devils appear for no reason at all, you swallow the magic chemicals.

But what's true of the magic-chemical ads is true of commercials and programs generally. Look at the settings. Auto ads push clothes fashion and vacations. Furniture-wax ads push wall-to-wall carpeting and draperies. Breakfast-cereal ads push new stoves and refrigerators. Not surprisingly, the programs do the same—after all, they're paid for by the same guys who pay for the commercials.

In fact, there's a rather intricate "corporate interlock" of jobs, products, and life-style. Once you come into the circle at any point you take on nearly all of it, and once you're in it's very difficult to get a little bit out. The choices you are left are relatively meaningless—like which color and extras you want with your Chevrolet, scotch or bourbon, how "mod" your ties will be, and which toothpaste you'll use. It all fits: corporate white-collar jobs, suburban home, commuting by automobile, eating in restaurants, and the clothes. There is the canned "entertainment" of radio and television for boredom, bottled alcohol and aspirin for pain, and aerosol cans of deodorant and "room freshener" to maintain the antiseptic cleanliness of it all. You wear your office, your home, and your car as much as your clothes and deodorant. And from the corporate layers of externals comes your very identity—and the smothering of your soul.

I would be the first to acknowledge that we are, of course, talking about matters of personal taste. People should be free to choose the life they want. Certainly it ought not to be the business of government to choose life-styles for its citizens. But two facts remain. First, the wholly disproportionate—if not exclusive—emphasis of television is pushing only one point of view. The choice you'll never know is the choice you'll never make. Many Americans are not sufficiently informed of the alternatives to make an intelligent choice of the life they most want. Second, independent students of our society—wholly apart from their own personal preferences—

"Say, let's generate a little excitement around here! What's on television?"

believe there is a correlation between the philosophy preached by television and many of our social problems.

The gospel of television simultaneously seems to create tremendous anxiety and alienation in the poor, and emptiness and neuroses in the affluent. As we are sold the products we are given the belief that our worth as individuals turns on our capacity to consume. We are given a shot of anxiety for free, told to buy more to make it go away, and find the feeling only gets worse.

But apart from the content, the mere act of television-watching is a passive activity. When we turn it on we turn ourselves off. If it is true that passivity and a sense of powerlessness are among the most dangerous epidemics in our society today, the television set is suspect at the outset regardless of what's programmed on it. The only exceptions would be programs like Jack LaLanne's exercises, or Public Broadcasting's offerings of Laura Weber's guitar lessons and Julia Child's cooking programs. Television could urge us to get up, turn off the set, and go live a little. It could help us to lead more interesting, more informed, more fulfilling lives. With rare exceptions, it doesn't.

Humanness as an Alternative

I think television could—and should—help us understand the alternatives to the conspicuous consumption, chemical, corporate life-style. Not because I'm "right," but because there *are* alternatives; people are entitled to know about them, and experience them if they choose. And today's televised theology seems to be contributing very little to life, or liberty, or the pursuit of happiness—which somebody once thought *was* the business of government.

Suppose you don't want to drop out or camp out. Maybe you want to step in, try to make things a little better, or just earn a living. What then? How can we make life *in* a corporate state more livable and more human? It became obvious to me that if I were going to criticize television for not offering alternative life-styles, I would have to be able to find the answer to that question. So I set about it.

Camping in the West Virginia mountains for two weeks reaffirmed my latent but basic commitment to the psychic values of simplicity. You not only "get along with" substantially fewer "things" when camping in the woods, you actually enjoy life more because it is not so cluttered with objects. The experience gave me a way of thinking about simplicity, objects, and natural living that I had not had before. And it impressed upon me, for perhaps the first time, a sense of the interrelated totality of "life-support activities."

By life-support activities I mean the provision of those things that are necessary to sustain physical life for ourselves: food, clothing, shelter, transportation, and so forth. These are the kinds of activities that I became most fully aware of in the woods, because I had to, and because they can be most easily comprehended when reduced to their basics. And yet I used to give almost no attention to these kinds of activities. Food simply appeared on my dinner table ready to eat. The house I lived in was purchased; it was warmed or cooled by some equipment in the basement that I knew very little about, and was attended to by repairmen when necessary. Clothing was something I found in closets and dresser drawers; it was cleaned and mended by my wife, the maid, or a cleaning establishment. Transportation was provided by the municipal bus system for commuting, and by FCC drivers during the day. At my office I was not only surrounded by machinery—copying machines, electric typewriters, dictating machines, and so forth—but also by people paid to operate them for me, answer my telephone, and bring me coffee.

I had, in short, taken very nearly all my life-support activities—"my life"—and cut them up into bits and pieces which I parceled out to individuals, corporations, and machines around me. The upshot was that there was very little of it left for me to live. This was extraordinarily "efficient" in one sense. That is, I was working at perhaps 98 per cent of the ultimate level of professional production of which I am capable. But what I concluded was that it was bad for life. For I was *living* only a small percentage of my ultimate capacity to live.

In an industrialized urban environment it is easy to forget that human life still is, as it was originally, sustained by certain basic functions. I think *some* participation in the support of your life is essential to a sense of fulfillment. I do not, however, think that you need to do everything for yourself. For one thing, you cannot trace everything back to first elements. You can build your own furniture. But are you going to saw your own boards from your own trees? Are you going to insist upon having planted the trees? Are you going to insist on making your own nails from your own iron ore? Even the most deeply committed do-it-yourselfers reach some accommodation with civilization.

In the second place, you simply don't have time to do it all. To raise and can all your own fruits and vegetables, for example, would take substantially more time per year than most people are prepared to give to it—especially if you are also personally constructing your own home, weaving your own material and making your own clothes, and walking everywhere.

In the third place, many conveniences of urbanized life are there anyway and you might as well use them. They can save you time you might spend in other, more satisfying ways. There's no point to cooking in your fireplace every night—or on your corporate-cookout charcoal grill—if you have a gas or electric range sitting in your kitchen.

So my conclusion is that you ought to try to do a *little bit* of all your life-support activities, and a substantial amount of whichever one or two of them appeal to you the most and make the most practical sense for you.

I have taken to buying and preparing my own simple foods, doing some modest mending of clothes, preparing some logs I intend to make into furniture, and providing my own transportation by bicycle. Undoubtedly other activities will fit better with your own life pattern.

If you start looking around for simplification, ways to make you less possession-bound and give you more chance to participate in your life, the opportunities are endless. Start by searching your house or apartment for things you can throw away. Ask yourself, "If I were living in the woods, would I spend a day going to town to buy this aerosol can?" Look for simple substitutes. Bicarbonate of soda, for example, can substitute for the following products: toothpaste, gargle and mouthwash, burn ointment, stomach settlers, room freshener, icebox cleaner, children's clay, baking powder, and so forth. And it only costs 12 cents a box! Get the idea?

Look for unnecessary electrical and other machinery and appliances. Bread can be toasted in the broiler of the stove. Carving knives and toothbrushes really need not be electrically powered. Put fruit and vegetable waste in a compost heap instead of down an electric disposal. I took up shaving with a blade, brush, and shaving soap instead of an electric razor. It's kind of bloody, but it's more fun. On the same principle, you can easily ignore most of the products in your supermarket and do a little more food preparation from basic ingredients.

Personally, I'm not interested in giving cooking or any other of these activities a lot of time. I'll walk up to a mile in dense urban areas because I can move faster that way than in a car—as well as get exercise, not pollute, help fight the automotive life-style, save money, and do a "life thing" (transportation) myself. But I'm not going to walk 20 miles into the suburbs—at least not often. I can make cornbread with baking soda in 20 minutes, about the time it takes to go to the store, or put supper on the table. But I won't often take the time to make yeast bread, unless there's somebody there to visit with, or something else to do at the same time. I make my own muesli (rolled oats, wheat germ, raisins, and so on) in less time than it takes to open a box of Captain Crunch, but I don't often take the time to crack and pick walnuts to add to it.

It is often possible to find activities that serve more than one function at the same time. Bicycle riding is perhaps my best example.

As you may have observed, my own reasons for adopting (and sharing and urging) the kind of approach to life I have been describing could be described as almost hedonistic. I ride a bicycle because I enjoy it more than driving a car. It makes me *feel* better. It gets my lungs to breathing and my heart to pumping. Dr. Paul Dudley White and others have long advised it as a means of warding off heart attacks. If you can use a bicycle to get to and from work, you can have the added satisfaction of knowing that you are providing one of your own life-support activities: transportation. In my case, I bicycle along the C & O Canal tow path, so that it also provides my daily time in a natural setting with canal, river, trees, birds, changing seasons, and sky. I find this time especially good for doing some of my best thinking (something I found very difficult to do during an earlier phase when I was jogging). So it also serves as a time when I compose little poems and songs, get ideas for opinions and speeches, and think about matters philosophical.

Bicycling has many peripheral benefits. It is cheap; you can buy an entire bicycle, brand new, for the cost of operating an automobile for a couple of weeks. The costs of operation are negligible, perhaps a penny or two a day. During rush hours, it is a significantly faster means of transportation than automobiles or buses, as "races" in numerous cities have demonstrated.

It happens that bicycle riding has some significant social advantages over the automobile, too. Compared to the car, the bicycle is a model citizen. It does not kill or maim; it does not pollute; it does not deplete natural resources; it makes no noise; and it takes up a great deal less space.

Why do I bicycle? Who knows? In one sense it makes no difference why people think they are doing what they are doing. If others' activities are consistent with what you think is constructive and delightful you can take some satisfaction from their joining with you. Most people don't think very precisely about their motivations, or the philosophies underlying their actions. It is probably just as well. It makes life more spontaneous and lighthearted. Besides which, if the truth were known, we often do things for other than the reasons we think we do; or for a complicated interrelationship of reasons that are sometimes consistent, sometimes inconsistent, and often constantly changing. Nevertheless, whatever the peripheral benefits may be, it seems to *me* that bicycling is just one example of a more satisfying, fulfilling, and joyful way to live *in* the corporate state.

Whether the truths I am dealing with are biological or metaphysical, my own experience supports the lessons of the world's great teachers. If man is to develop the rich individuality and full potential of which he is capable, he needs more than the hollow values and products of consumerism. He needs not only productive "work," but also love, beauty, creativity, contemplation, contact with nature, and participation in the support of his own life. When we live our lives in ways that take us too far from those basic truths, we begin to find ourselves in all kinds of troubles that ultimately show up in social statistics. And the evidence seems to suggest that as we return to a richer and more natural life, our problems subside. Whether or not that is enough for you, it is enough for me.

Central to all that I suggest is the necessity that you work it out for yourself. You need to discover who you are; what feels right and best for you. You not only need to walk to the sound of a different drummer, you need to be that different drummer. You need to write your own music. You need to look inside yourself and see what is there. I think some time in the woods is useful for this purpose; but camping may not be right for you, for a variety of quite sensible reasons. The purpose of self-discovery is not to stop copying Howard Johnson and start copying Nick Johnson, or anybody else. The point is to find your own soul and kick it and poke it with a stick, see if it's still alive, and then watch which way it moves.

I see evidence all around us that people are in fact rejecting materialism and looking for more meaningful lives for themselves. Without the internal or external direction of an ideology or an operating manual, ordinary people by the thousands are, in a violent spasm of reaction, simply casting off the chains of corporate control of their lives. The point is not that I find this encouraging—although I do. The point is not even that I think the system may be capable of righting itself—although it may. The point is that the actions of all these people are simply additional evidence that the corporate life is, like war, unhealthy for children and other living things.

Nevertheless, I do not foresee a meaningful revolution without—at least—a good old-fashioned political battle. My principal disagreement with the Greening of the Third Reich concerns the prediction that new attitudes are going to bring the downfall of the corporate state, and that they constitute a new and powerful political movement. I think not. I think we are talking about 10 to 30 per cent of the population at best, and that while it will have a substantial impact, meaningful reforms are still going to require more conventional political action and legislation. There will continue to be a majority of people who, for a variety of reasons, can't or won't break out of the corporate trap. They would rather continue to tell themselves that they really want to drive that car, and smoke those cigarettes, and use that hair spray. Under it all may be the fear that if they went out in search of themselves they might come back empty-handed. Almost any alternative is preferable to that nightmare.

Creative Lives and Commercialized Television

Earlier I mentioned the opportunity for creativity as one aspect of a full human life. Because it is a quality that is especially related to television, it deserves a little fuller discussion.

Creativity is an essential quality of humanness in two respects. If a person is to have his own individuality, his own unique self, it will be expressed in creative and artistic ways most honestly and fully. If you do not give him the opportunity to be creative, you are in a very meaningful sense depriving him of the opportunity to be human. Second, and equally important, is the concept of Ezra Pound and Rollo May that the artist is the "antenna of the race." Throughout history some of the most perceptive analysis and forecasting has been done not by public officials or social scientists, but by the artists.

If you accept this thesis that creativity is central to humanness and society's well-being, I believe that you should be extremely concerned about the impact of commercial television. When a nation takes its most powerful soap box–theater–lecture hall and turns it over exclusively to the sale of snake oil, it is not only depriving its citizens of the opportunity to grow and develop as people, it is also cutting off their vision of their future.

The tendencies toward lack of diversity, reality, and controversy are only reinforced by the oligopolistic uniformity inherent in the current patterns of ownership. In the nation's 11 largest cities there is not a single network-affiliated VHF television station that is independently and locally owned. All are owned by the networks, multiple station owners, or major local newspapers—and many of these owners are large conglomerate corporations as well. Compounding this problem, most national news comes from the two wire services, AP and UPI, each serving approximately 1,200 newspapers and three thousand radio and television stations. Newspaper cross-ownership figures are also depressing. Of the 1,500 communities with daily newspapers, for example, 96 per cent are served by single-owner monopolies, and approximately 28 per cent of all television stations are owned by newspapers. In 1945 there were 177 cities with separately owned dailies; by 1966 there were only 43—one-third as many.

Equally important is the already-dominant network monopolization over the production and purchase of television programming. For all practical purposes, any writer, director, or producer of television programming has only three buyers for his product: ABC, CBS, and NBC. The networks customarily purchase both the first-run and the syndication rights—the entire package of ownership and control. The networks are involved in every aspect of programming production: the choice of a theme, the designation of the writer, the rewriting of the script, the choice of actors, director, and producer, and the day-to-day shooting and censorship of the series. It is no accident that the three networks and their 15 wholly owned and operated television stations earn more than 50 per cent of all television revenues (in an industry of 642 television stations), and more than one-third of all profits.

The inhibitions on creative television programming inherent in the industry's present structure are only part of the problem. Equally important are the inhibitions on individual expression that are built into our present system. Individuals need to express themselves—to communicate to others, to share thoughts and ideas, to build a sense of community, to overcome the alienation caused by a highly urbanized, industrialized, mechanized life. Yet speech depends on access to a medium of communication. A soap box in the town square is no longer sufficient. Ideas must be communicated to society as a whole, and they cannot be unless the structure of television permits and encourages the participation by individuals with something to say.

Communications in the Creative Society

Given the extraordinary political and economic power of Big Broadcasting, radical restructuring of the commercial television networks and stations will come slowly, if ever. For the foreseeable future, commercial television will continue to exert perhaps the most influential impact on our nation of any single industry. Unless we continue to try to reform commercial broadcasting, we cannot have much of an impact. But the fact that the impact will be minimal does not detract from the necessity of making the effort. Broadcasting reform groups in Washington and throughout the United States are mushrooming, and chalking up an impressive record of accomplishments.

Let me itemize a few of our present rules and decisions. There are at least *some* limits on television station ownership—no one can own more than seven stations, of which no more than five can be VHF (channels 2 through 13). The FCC has announced that it intends to forbid future acquisitions of television-radio combinations in the same community. Commonly owned AM and FM radio stations in communities of over 100 thousand people cannot duplicate programming simultaneously for more than 50 per cent of the time. Cable-television system owners must permit the origination of programming. The Commission has provided that networks can no longer control more than three hours of prime-time programming each evening, a policy that opens up the market a crack for independent suppliers. And, of course, the advent of new technology has significantly increased the number of broadcast voices in the country—AM radio was first augmented by FM radio; then came VHF television, then UHF television (channels 14 through 83), and now cable television, with a potential for an unlimited number of channels.

The Public Broadcasting Corporation constitutes a somewhat more significant institutional restructuring. Although it necessarily has the rigidities of any large institution, and the local public television stations tend to have as directors and corporate contributors the same kind of men who control commercial broadcasting, it is nevertheless directly dependent neither on commercial sponsorship nor on attracting the largest possible mass audience.

Pay, or subscription, television could offer another significant change. The only meaningful use of the marketplace mechanism in audience control of programming today is in the listener-supported community radio stations run by organizations like Pacifica. Those stations are dependent upon the financial contributions of the listeners—who obviously are free to listen to the station without contributing, should they choose. They are also free to stop their contributions on the merest whim. How many commerical stations in this country would continue in operation if they had to rely upon voluntary contributions from the audience for all their operating costs? Pay television would offer an even more precise marketplace mechanism. If one million people are willing to pay one dollar apiece to watch a show that can be produced and distributed at a profit with gross revenues of one million dollars, they would have at least some chance of watching the program. Under the present system, they do not. A combination of pay television with cable television, with its potential for a larger number of fragmented audiences, makes such an approach even more viable.

One reform holds out perhaps the greatest potential for meaningful impact: The Justice Department, or the Federal Communications Commission, could order the abolition of network ownership of stations and the present restrictive affiliate contracts. There is a very striking analogy in the motion-picture business. During the 1930's and 1940's the motion-picture industry had the kind of control of theaters that the networks now have of their owned and affiliated stations. The large studios owned the talent, the books, the studio lots, the films, the distribution facilities, and the theaters. They produced movies according to formulae, and then pointed to the number of people who came to see the films as evidence that the companies knew what the public wanted.

In the Paramount divestiture case [*United States* v. *Paramount Pictures,* 334 U.S. 131 (1948)] the Department of Justice successfully argued in court the proposition that major motion-picture studios should not own theaters. Of course, the coming of television at about the same time also had a great impact upon the motion-picture business; but nevertheless, once the theaters were sold and the distribution channels opened up, there was a burgeoning of independent filmmakers. Not only did the motion-picture industry discover that the cost of producing films could be significantly reduced (*Easy Rider,* which will gross about 30 million dollars, was produced for about 300 thousand dollars), it also discovered a new flowering of creativity, diversity, and effervescence the like of which the industry had not seen for decades.

The parallel to the present network television is striking enough that the Justice Department finally, in 1972, filed against the networks an action comparable to the Paramount divestiture case.

Nevertheless, no such reforms are adequate to create the kind of flowering of creativity we seek, nor do they affect the fact that television programming is created to sell products and maximize profits. Big Business controls Big Television, which in turn influences the Congress and the Federal Communications Commission. And even if they did not, no matter how effective the FCC might be, the regulation of large corporations by a large governmental agency can do very little to humanize the product of radio and television programming.

What we seek are two goals. First, we want the opportunity for every American citizen who cares to do so to be able to express himself creatively in the television medium. Second, we want every American citizen at least to have the *opportunity* to see on television the product of the very best creative individuals (as distinguished from corporate committees). Fortunately, there is a potential answer. Even more fortunately, it is one that may be economically, politically, and socially viable.

Creative expression requires some new and cheaper television equipment—which is already on the market—and a vast increase in the number of training programs for its use. In 1967, Sony introduced on the American market a do-it-yourself television kit—including television camera, video tape-recording equipment, and television set—for scarcely more than the first color television receiving sets had cost (about one thousand dollars). Since that time an alternate-television movement has sprung up across the country—principally centered in New York and San Francisco.

With a whole generation of filmmakers coming along that would like to work in the television medium, there is reason to believe that this movement may be in for a boom. Audio tape recorders are widspread today; videotapes and discs are about to come on the market. (Even for the home-movie buff, videotaping has a number of advantages over film.) And the prices on the equipment will probably continue to decline as demand increases. Hopefully, institutions such as city recreation departments, community colleges, universities, and high schools will begin acquiring this equipment and providing training programs for those who would like to use it.

But how do we take the best of their output—and that of the more professional creative people in television—and make it available to all the American people? That is where cable television comes in—or at least cable television with a twist. Up to now, cable television has been largely conceived and utilized as an alternative means of distributing over-the-air commercial television signals. As such it is merely a part of the problem. What cable television also offers—in terms of greater profits to the cable operators as well as greater service to the customers—is an alternative approach to program distribution.

Cable-television operators could be treated like the telephone company, and required to make channels available on their systems to anyone who wants to use them for the distribution of television programs. The telephone company cannot tell you that they are temporarily out of telephones when you ask to have one installed, nor can they refuse to install one because they don't like what you talk about. The same principles, tariff agreements, and traditions could apply to the cable-television industry. The cable-television operator could post prices (of course, charging more for 8 P.M. than for 4 A.M.), and anyone who could pay the rates could get a channel. As a result, he would make money not only from the monthly fees paid by subscribers, but from the leasing charges paid by those who used his channels. Because the cost of adding additional channels to a system is minimal (a 40-channel system costs only about 10 per cent more than a 20-channel system), there is no reason why channels could not be made available free to those unable to pay for them. Some channels could be allocated free to community purposes on a permanent basis—to the local school system, the city council, police and fire training, and so forth. In fact, something like these proposals have now been adopted by the FCC.

There then would be a large number of alternative ways of funding programming. (1) There still would be programming from the networks and commercial stations. (2) There would be the programming of the

Public Broadcasting System and the local public television stations. (3) Advertiser-funded programming could be provided by independent producers. (4) There could be subscription television (for which the viewer would pay an additional fee); this would be funded directly by the audience. (5) Foundations might wish to lease channels on a permanent or spot basis for projects of their own, including the showing of programs produced with their grants. (6) There would be the channels set aside for community purposes. (7) Finally, some channels would be available at no charge to citizens who were engaged in nonremunerative efforts or otherwise unable to pay for them.

This blend of new technologies—cheap videotaping equipment and unlimited-channel cable distribution systems—holds the promise for a practical flowering of the creative society. Whether it comes about will depend upon individual citizens and community-action groups seeking unlimited-channel provisions in the franchises granted by city councils to local cable-television systems, and upon regulations ultimately promulgated by the FCC and acts of Congress.

Summary and Conclusion

Television is involved, in one way or another, in virtually everything that is right and wrong with America. It has decidedly more influence on our information, politics, education, moral values, aesthetic taste, and mental health than any other institution in the history of our country. Because of its influence, and the Federal Communications Commission's responsibility to regulate broadcasting "in the public interest," it is necessary for me, an FCC Commissioner, to keep a constant watch on the possible implications of television in new developments in our society.

There is presently a considerable body of evidence—as well as personal experience—that a great many Americans are experiencing stresses and strains formerly unknown. As we examine the programming and commercials of television, we see that they are encouraging a particular life-style—one in which conspicuous consumption of mass-produced goods, rather than the growth of individuality, is held out as central to one's worth as a human being. Alternatives to that life-style get little time and attention on television—principally because they run counter to the profit motive of those who control the system. There is considerable evidence that a great many Americans are beginning to cast those standards aside, and trying to bring more humanness and creativity into their lives. Commercial television, as now structured, is the keystone of the corporate system, which makes such efforts very nearly impossible. The combination of the new, cheaper videotaping equipment and the possibility of cable-television systems that would make available as many channels as demand warranted, offers a potential solution to this problem.

There are many researchers and writers in this country who know far more psychiatry and political science than I do, and they report that we are in serious danger as a people. They predicted the social disintegration we are now experiencing some 10 or 20 years before it happened: the nervous breakdowns and mental illness, the alcoholism and drug addiction, the unwanted illegitimacy and divorce rates, the crime and the violence. They told us that these symptoms would occur because human beings have to be able to grow and develop as individuals; that they need whole lives in which love, productivity, dignity, and creativity can play a daily role. They say if people do not lead full and whole lives they will not only suffer as individuals, but will make a society that is bad for everyone else. In other words, the "quality of life" does not just mean getting the smoke out of the air. That's necessary for us as animals; pollution is as bad for cows and citrus trees as it is for people. But the "quality of life" for human beings has to do with the smog inside our minds. The same people who are putting the garbage in the air are putting the garbage in our heads.

I have hope we may have begun to evolve the tactics for talking back to our corporate state. I welcome your interest and support, for we are talking about nothing less precious than your life and mine.

WHAT TV DOES TO KIDS

by HARRY F. WATERS

Since television's early days, there has been only a slight effort made to study its effects on children. Not until the later 1970s did television's influence on the young become a serious concern to various groups in our society—among them, leaders in medicine and the social sciences, educators, television executives, and perhaps most importantly, parents. **Newsweek** correspondent Harry F. Waters provides a comprehensive report of the situation in early 1977.

His first polysyllabic utterance was "Bradybunch." He learned to spell Sugar Smacks before his own name. He has seen Monte Carlo, witnessed a cocaine bust in Harlem and already has full-color fantasies involving Farrah Fawcett-Majors. Recently, he tried to karate-chop his younger sister after she broke his Six Million Dollar Man bionic transport station. (She retaliated by bashing him with her Cher doll.) His nursery-school teacher reports that he is passive, noncreative, unresponsive to instruction, bored during play periods and possessed of an almost nonexistent attention span—in short, very much like his classmates. Next fall, he will officially reach the age of reason and begin his formal education: His parents are beginning to discuss their apprehensions—when they are not too busy watching television.

The wonder of it all is that the worry about television has so belatedly moved anyone to action. After all, the suspicion that TV is turning children's minds to mush and their psyches toward mayhem is almost as old as the medium itself. But it is only in recent years—with the first TV generation already well into its 20s—that social scientists, child psychologists, pediatricians and educators have begun serious study of the impact of television on the young. "The American public has been preoccupied with governing our children's schooling," says Stanford University psychologist Alberta Siegel. "We have been astonishingly unconcerned about the medium that reaches into our homes. Yet we may expect television to alter our social arrangements just as profoundly as printing has done over the past five centuries."

The statistics are at least alarming. Educators like Dr. Benjamin Bloom, of the University of Chicago, maintain that by the time a child reaches the age of 5, he has undergone as much intellectual growth as will occur over the next thirteen years. According to A. C. Nielsen, children under 5 watch an average of 23.5 hours of TV a week. That may be less than the weekly video diet of adults (about 44 hours), but its effects are potentially enormous. Multiplied out over seventeen years, that rate of viewing means that by his high-school graduation today's typical teen-ager will have logged at least 15,000 hours before the small screen—more time than he will have spent on any other activity except sleep. And at present levels of advertising and mayhem, he will have been exposed to 350,000 commercials and vicariously participated in 18,000 murders.

The conclusion is inescapable: after parents, television has become perhaps the most potent influence on the beliefs, attitudes, values and behavior of those who are being raised in its all-pervasive glow. George Gerbner, dean of the University of Pennsylvania's Annenberg School of Communications, is almost understating it when he says: "Television has profoundly affected the way in which members of the human race learn to become human beings."

A Question of Air Pollution

Unquestionably, the plug-in picture window has transmitted some beneficial images. Last month's showing of "Roots," for example, may have done more to increase the understanding of American race relations than any event since the civil-rights activities of the '60s. And the fact that 130 million Americans could share that experience through the small screen points up the powerful—and potentially positive—influence the industry can have on its audience. In general, the children of TV enjoy a more sophisticated knowledge of a far larger world at a much younger age. They are likely to possess richer vocabularies, albeit with only a superficial comprehension of what the words mean. Research on the impact of "Sesame Street" has established measurable gains in the cognitive skills of pre-schoolers. And many benefits cannot be statistically calibrated. A New York pre-schooler tries to match deductive wits with Columbo; a Los Angeles black girl, who has never seen a ballet, decides she wants to be a ballerina after watching Margot Fonteyn perform on TV.

Nonetheless, the overwhelming body of evidence—drawn from more than 2,300 studies and reports—is decidedly negative. Most of the studies have dealt with the antisocial legacy of video violence. Michael Rothenberg, a child psychiatrist at the University of Washington, has reviewed 25 years of hard data on the subject—the 50 most comprehensive studies involving 10,000 children from every possible background. Most showed that viewing violence tends to produce aggressive behavior among the young. "The time is long past due for a major, organized cry of protest from the medical profession in relation to what, in political terms, is a national scandal," concludes Rothenberg.

An unexpected salvo was sounded last week when the normally cautious American Medical Association announced that it had asked ten major corporations to review their policies about sponsoring excessively gory shows. "TV violence is both a mental-health problem and an environmental issue," explained Dr. Richard E. Palmer, president of the AMA. "TV has been quick to raise questions of social responsibility with industries which pollute the air. In my opinion, television . . . may be creating a more serious problem of air pollution." Reaction was immediate: General Motors, Sears Roebuck and the Joseph Schlitz Brewing Co. quickly announced they would look more closely into the content of the shows they sponsor.

The AMA action comes in the wake of a grass-roots campaign mobilized by the national Parent-Teacher Association. The 6.6 million-member PTA recently began a series of regional forums to arouse public indignation over TV carnage. If that crusade fails, the PTA is considering organizing station-license challenges and national boycotts of products advertised on offending programs.

'The Flickering Blue Parent'

In their defense, broadcasting officials maintain that the jury is still out on whether video violence is guilty of producing aggressive behavior. And they marshal their own studies to support that position. At the same time, the network schedulers say they are actively reducing the violence dosage. "People have said they want another direction and that's what we're going to give them," promises NBC-TV president Robert T. Howard. Finally, the broadcast industry insists that the responsibility for the impact of TV on children lies with parents rather than programmers. "Parents should pick and choose the shows their kids watch," says CBS vice president Gene Mater. "Should TV be programmed for the young through midnight? It's a real problem. TV is a mass medium and it must serve more than just children."

But the blight of televised mayhem is only part of TV's impact. Beyond lies a vast subliminal terrain that is only now being charted. The investigators are discovering that TV has affected its youthful addicts in a host of subtle ways, varying according to age and class. For deprived children, TV may, in some cases, provide more sustenance than their home—or street—

life; for the more privileged, who enjoy other alternatives, it may not play such a dominating role.

Nonetheless, for the average kid TV has at the very least preempted the traditional development of childhood itself. The time kids spend sitting catatonic before the set has been exacted from such salutary pursuits as reading, outdoor play, even simple, contemplative solitude. TV prematurely jades, rendering passé the normal experiences of growing up. And few parents can cope with its tyrannical allure. Recently, Dr. Benjamin Spock brought his stepdaughter and granddaughter to New York for a tour of the Bronx Zoo and the Museum of Modern Art. But the man who has the prescription for everything from diaper rash to bed-wetting could not dislodge the kids from their hotel room. "I couldn't get them away from the goddamned TV set," recalls Spock. "It made me sick."

Small wonder that television has been called "the flickering blue parent." The after-school and early-evening hours used to be a time for "what-did-you-do-today" dialogue. Now, the electronic box does most of the talking. Dr. David Pearl of the National Institute of Mental Health suspects that the tube "has displaced many of the normal interactional processes between parents and children . . . Those kinds of interactions are essential for maximum development." One veteran elementary-school teacher in suburban Washington, D.C., has noticed that her students have grown inordinately talkative when they arrive for class. "At home, they can't talk when the TV is on," she says. "It's as if they are starved for conversation."

The Passive Generation

Even more worrisome is what television has done to, rather than denied, the tube-weaned population. A series of studies has shown that addiction to TV stifles creative imagination. For example, a University of Southern California research team exposed 250 elementary students—who had been judged mentally gifted—to three weeks of intensive viewing. Tests conducted before and after the experiment found a marked drop in all forms of creative abilities except verbal skill. Some teachers are encountering children who cannot understand a simple story without visual illustrations. "TV has taken away the child's ability to form pictures in his mind," says child-development expert Dorothy Cohen at New York City's Bank Street College of Education.

Parenthetically, nursery-school teachers who have observed the pre-TV generation contend that juvenile play is far less imaginative and spontaneous than in the past. The vidkids' toys come with built-in fantasies while their playground games have been programed by last night's shows. "You don't see kids making their own toys out of crummy things like we used to," says University of Virginia psychology professor Stephen Worchel, who is the father of a 6-year-old. "You don't see them playing hopscotch, or making up their own games. Everything is suggested to them by television."

Too much TV too early also instills an attitude of spectatorship, a withdrawal from direct involvement in real-life experiences. "What television basically teaches children is passivity," says Stanford University researcher Paul Kaufman. "It creates the illusion of having been somewhere and done something and seen something, when in fact you've been sitting at home." New York Times writer Joyce Maynard, 23, a perceptive member of the first TV generation, concludes: "We grew up to be observers, not participants, to respond to action, not initiate it."

Conditioned to see all problems resolved in 30 or 60 minutes, the offspring of TV exhibit a low tolerance for the frustration of learning. Elementary-school educators complain that their charges are quickly turned off by any activity that promises less than instant gratification. "You introduce a new skill, and right away, if it looks hard, they dissolve into tears," laments Maryland first-grade teacher Eleanor Berman. "They want everything to be easy—like watching the tube." Even such acclaimed educational series as "Sesame Street," "The Electric Company" and "Zoom" have had some dubious effects. Because such shows sugar-coat their lessons with flashy showbiz techniques, they are forcing real-life instructors into the role of entertainers in order to hold their pupils' attention. "I can't turn my body into shapes or flashlights," sighs a Connecticut teacher. "Kids today are accustomed to learning through gimmicks."

For the majority of American children, television has become the principal socializing agent. It shapes their view of what the world is like and what roles they should play in it. As the University of Pennsylvania's Gerbner puts it: "The socialization of children has largely been transferred from the home and school to TV programmers who are unelected, unnamed and unknown, and who are not subject to collective—not to mention democratic—review."

What does TV's most impressionable constituency learn from primetime entertainment? No one can really be sure, but psychologists like Robert Liebert of the State University of New York, one of the most respected observers of child behavior, don't hesitate to express sweeping indictments. "It teaches them that might makes right," Liebert says flatly. "The lesson of most TV series is that the rich, the powerful and the conniving are the most successful."

The View from the Victims

Whatever the truth of that, the tube clearly tends to reinforce sex-role stereotypes. In a Princeton, N.J., survey of sixteen programs and 216 commercials, it was found that men outnumbered women by three to one and that females were twice as likely to display incompetence. By and large, men were portrayed as dominant, authoritative and the sole source of their family's economic support. "These roles are biased and distorted, and don't reflect the way a woman thinks or feels," complains Liebert. "And it's just as bad for blacks."

It may, in fact, be even worse for blacks. Not only do black children watch more TV than whites, but they confront a far greater disparity between the illusions of videoland and the reality of their own lives. Two yet-to-be-published studies conducted by University of South Carolina psychology professor Robert Heckel found that young black viewers regard whites as more competent than blacks, and model their conduct accordingly. In one study, black children were shown a TV film of an interracial group of peers choosing toys to play with—and then given the same toys to pick from themselves. All the blacks selected the toys chosen by whites in the film, even though many of those toys were smaller or inferior in quality. "On TV, the competent roles tend to go to whites, particularly young white males," explains Heckel. "Thus black children regard whites as someone to copy."

A classic example of such racial imprinting is Rowena Smith, a 14-year-old Los Angeles black who remains glued to the tube from school recess to 11 each night. Rowena's favorite TV characters are CBS's Phyllis and her teen-age daughter. "They get along so good," she sighs. "I wish me and Mom could talk that way." When Rowena was scolded for getting her clothes dirty, she indignantly told her mother that "the kid in the Tonka truck ad gets dirty all the time." Rowena's first awareness of the facts of non-TV life came after she ran away for two days—and her mother gave her a licking. "When TV shows runaways," she complains, "they don't show the part about being beaten." Nowadays, Rowena is more skeptical about television, but she has become increasingly concerned about her 8-year-old brother. He wistfully talks about getting seriously injured and then being reassembled like the Six Million Dollar Man. "This kid really *believes* TV," sighs his sister. "I gotta keep an eye on him 24 hours a day."

Indeed, call on the children themselves to testify and the message comes through clear—and sometimes poignantly. A vidkid sampler:

Fourteen-year-old, Los Angeles "Television is perfect to tune out the rest of the world. But I don't relate with my family much because we're all too busy watching TV."

Eleven-year-old, Denver "You see so much violence that it's meaningless. If I saw someone really get killed, it wouldn't be a big deal. I guess I'm turning into a hard rock."

Nine-year-old, San Francisco "I'd rather watch TV than play outside because it's boring outside. They always have the same rides, like swings and things."

Fifteen-year-old, Lake Forest, Ill. "Sometimes when I watch an exciting show, I don't blink my eyes once. When I close them after the show, they hurt hard."

Thirteen-year old, Glastonbury, Conn. "When I see a beautiful girl using a shampoo or a cosmetic on TV, I buy them because I'll look like her. I have a ton of cosmetics. I play around with them and save them for when I'm older."

Ten-year-old, New York "It bugs me when someone is watching with me. If your friend is bored, you have to go out or make conversation. That's hard."

It would be preposterous, of course, to suggest that television alone is responsible for everything that is wrong with America's young. Permissiveness at home and in school, the dispersion of the extended family, confusion over moral standards and the erosion of traditional institutions—all help explain why Dick and Jane behave as they do. Moreover, any aspect of child psychology is enormously complex, especially when it comes to measuring cause and effect. There is always the temptation among social scientists to set up their experiments in a way guaranteed to reinforce their preconceptions. Nevertheless, there is one thrust of reliable study—into video violence—that has produced an unmistakable pattern of clear and present danger.

Paranoia and Propaganda

The debate over the link between TV violence and aggressive behavior in society has had a longer run than "Gunsmoke." Today, however, even the most chauvinist network apologists concede that some children, under certain conditions, will imitate antisocial acts that they witness on the tube. Indeed, a study of 100 juvenile offenders commissioned by ABC found that no fewer than 22 confessed to having copied criminal techniques from TV. Last year, a Los Angeles judge sentenced two teen-age boys to long jail terms after they held up a bank and kept 25 persons hostage for seven hours. In pronouncing the sentence, the judge noted disgustedly that the entire scheme had been patterned on an "Adam 12" episode the boys had seen two weeks earlier.

Convinced that they have proved their basic case, the behavioral sleuths on the violence beat have switched their focus to less obvious signs of psychic dysfunction. They are now uncovering evidence that the tide of TV carnage increases children's tolerance of violent behavior in others. In one experiment, several hundred fifth-graders were asked to act as baby-sitters for a group of younger kids—shown on a TV screen—who were supposedly playing in the next room. The baby-sitters were instructed to go to a nearby adult for assistance if their charges began fighting. Those who had been shown a violent TV film just before taking up their duties were far slower to call for help than those who had watched a pro-baseball telecast. "Television desensitizes children to violence in real life," observes University of Mississippi psychology professor Ronald Drabman, who

". . . Eric says he's been appointed media analyst for the third grade, specializing in non-public programming!"

helped conduct the study. "They tolerate violence in others because they have been conditioned to think of it as an everyday thing."

Beyond that, some researchers are finding that TV may be instilling paranoia in the young. Three years of tests directed by Gerbner, who is perhaps the nation's foremost authority on the subject, established that heavy TV watchers tend to exaggerate the danger of violence in their own lives—creating what Gerbner calls a "mean-world syndrome." As for children, he reports that "the pattern is exactly the same, only more so. The prevailing message of TV is to generate fear."

And now a word about the sponsors. The late Jack Benny once quipped that television is called a medium because nothing it serves up is ever well-done. But as the child watchers see it, the not-so-funny problem with TV commercials is precisely that they are so well put together. "Everybody has had the experience of seeing a 2-year-old playing on the floor, and when the commercial comes on, he stops and watches it," notes F. Earle Barcus, professor of communications at Boston University. "TV ads probably have more effect on children than any other form of programing."

Junk Food for Thought

The hottest battle involves the impact of child-directed commercials on their audience's eating habits. More than 70 per cent of the ads on Saturday and Sunday-morning "kidvid" peddle sugar-coated cereals, candy and chewing gum. Laced with action-packed attention grabbers and pitched by an ingratiating adult authority figure, such messages hook children on poor eating habits long before they develop the mental defenses to resist. "This is the most massive educational program to eat junk food in history," charges Sid Wolinsky, an attorney for a San Francisco public-interest group. "We are creating a nation of sugar junkies."

Research has also established that as the kids grow older their attitudes toward commercials move from innocent acceptance to outrage about those ads that mislead and finally to a cynical recognition of what they perceive as adult hypocrisy. According to a study by Columbia University psychology professor Thomas Bever, TV ads may be "permanently distorting children's views of morality, society and business." From in-depth interviews with 48 youngsters between the ages of 5 and 12, Bever concluded that by the time they reach 12, many find it easier to decide that all commercials lie than to try to determine which are telling the truth. Concludes Bever: "They become ready to believe that, like advertising, business and other institutions are riddled with hypocrisy."

Who is to blame and what, if anything, can be done? The networks argue that the number of violent incidents portrayed on TV has declined by 24 per cent since 1975. That figure has been challenged, but there is little question that the networks have instituted some reforms. The number of "action-adventure" series has decreased of late, and the weekend-morning kidvid scene is gradually being pacified. Such superhero cartoon characters as CBS's "Superman" and NBC's "Granite Man" have been replaced with gentler fare; ABC even canceled "Bugs Bunny" and "Road Runner" because of their zap-and-whap antics.

There is also considerable merit to the broadcasters' argument that parents are to blame if they don't regulate their children's viewing habits. By the time the Family Hour experiment was struck down by the courts last year, it had already proved unworkable because so many parents refused to cooperate. Nielsen found that 10.5 million youngsters under the age of 12 were still hooked to the tube after 9 p.m., when the Family Hour ended. And a recent Roper study reported that only two-fifths of the parents polled enforced rules about what programs their children could watch. "Parents who take active charge of most of the elements of their children's upbringing allow a kind of anarchy to prevail where television viewing is concerned," says Elton Rule, president of ABC, Inc.

The Public Strikes Back

In rebuttal, public-interest groups point out that TV stations have been granted Federal licenses to ride the public airwaves—a highly lucrative privilege that carries a unique responsibility. In addition to the nationwide pressure being exerted by the AMA and the PTA, local organizations like the Lansing (Mich.) Committee for Children's Television have persuaded local stations to drop gory shows from their late-afternoon schedules. But no one has achieved more reform than the activist mothers of Action for Children's Television, based in Newtonville, Mass. ACT is largely credited with persuading the networks to reduce time for commercials on children's weekend shows from sixteen to nine and a half minutes an hour, to halt the huckstering of vitamins on kidvid and to end the practice of having the hosts deliver the pitches. ACT's ultimate—perhaps chimeric—goal is to rid kidvid of all advertising. "We feel it is wise to separate children from the marketplace until they are ready to deal with it," explains Peggy Charren, ACT's indefatigable president.

The shrewdest reform movement is aimed at persuading network programmers and advertisers that violence really doesn't sell. J. Walter Thompson, the nation's largest advertising agency, has begun advising its clients to stop purchasing spots on violent series—pointing out that a sampling of adult viewers revealed that 8 per cent of the consumers surveyed had already boycotted products advertised on such shows, while 10 per cent more were considering doing so. To help viewers identify the worst offenders among the shows, the National Citizens Committee for Broadcasting now disseminates rankings of the most violent series. At last body count, the bloodiest were ABC's "Starsky & Hutch" and "Baretta," NBC's "Baa Baa Black Sheep" and CBS's "Hawaii Five-O."

On the brighter side, some educators have begun harnessing commercial TV's power in positive ways. The movement first took hold a few years ago in Philadelphia's school system, which started tying reading assignments to TV offerings. For example, scripts for such docu-dramas as "The Missiles of October" and "Eleanor and Franklin" were distributed to more than 100,000 Philadelphia students in advance of the TV dates.

From Violence to Social Values

The children watched the shows while following along in the scripts, and discussed them in class the next day. The program has worked so well—some pupils' reading skills advanced by three years—that 3,500 other U.S. school systems are imitating it. This week WBNS-TV, the CBS affiliate in Columbus, Ohio, is transmitting four hours of classroom programming each day aimed at 96,000 local students whose schools are closed due to the natural-gas shortage. . . .

Prime Time School TV, a nonprofit Chicago organization, has come up with the most innovative approach: PTST uses some of TV's most violent fare to implant positive social values. In one seven-week course, pupils were given questionnaires and told to fill them out while watching "Kojak,"

"Baretta" and the like. The questions, which were subsequently kicked around in class, dealt with everything from illegal search and seizure to forced confessions. "One boy told us that we had ruined television for him," reports PTST official Linda Kahn. "He couldn't watch a police show any more without counting the number of killings." Says PTST president William Singer: "We are saying that there are alternatives to merely railing against television, and this is just one of them."

Life Without the Tube

Unfortunately, the options available to the individual parent are considerably more limited. A few daring souls have simply pulled the plug. Charles Frye, a San Francisco nursery-school teacher and the father of five boys, decided he would not replace his set after it conked out in 1972. Frye's brood rebelled at first, but today none of them voices regret that theirs is a TV-less household. Fourteen-year-old Mark fills his afternoon hours with tap-dancing lessons, Sea Scout meetings and work in a gas station. Kirk, his 13-year-old brother, plays a lot of basketball and football and recently finished "Watership Down" and all four of the Tolkien hobbit books. "I know of no other children that age who have that range of interests," says their father.

Short of such a draconian measure, some parents are exercising a greater degree of home rule. Two years ago, the administrators of New York's Horace Mann nursery school became distressed over an upsurge of violence in their students' play. Deciding that television was to blame, they dispatched a letter to all parents urging them to curb their children's viewing. "After we sent the letter, we could see a change," recalls Horace Mann principal Eleanor Brussel. "The kids showed better concentration, better comprehension, an ability to think things through." Sheila Altschuler, one of the mothers who heeded the school's request, noticed that her 4-year-old son began making up his own playtime characters instead of imitating those on the tube. "If I didn't feel it was kind of freaky, I wouldn't own a set," allows Altschuler. "But these days it's a matter of conformity. Kids would be outcasts without TV."

Clearly, there is no single antidote for the vidkid virus. For the children of the global village, and their progeny to come, TV watching will continue to be their most shared—and shaping—experience. Virtually all the experts, however, agree on one palliative for parents of all socioeconomic levels. Instead of using TV as an electronic baby-sitter, parents must try to involve themselves directly in their youngsters' viewing. By watching along with the kids at least occasionally, they can help them evaluate what they see—pointing out the inflated claims of a commercial, perhaps, or criticizing a gratuitously violent scene. "Parents don't have to regard TV as a person who can't be interrupted," says behavioral scientist Charles

Corder-Bolz. "If they view one show a night with their kids, and make just one or two comments about it, they can have more impact than the whole program."

Reduced to the essentials, the question for parents no longer is: "Do you know where your children are tonight?" The question has become: What are they watching—and with whom?

FROM

POGO PRIMER FOR PARENTS

by WALT KELLY

There are a few things to practice not doing. Do not be afraid of your t.v. set. These things are probably here to stay. Do not be afraid of your child. He is not here to stay. He is a precious visitor. Do not wind your child up and set him to watch the t.v. unguided. Do not wind the t.v. set up and set it to watch your child. A machine is a bad sole companion. It needs help. You can help it. Love your child.

Reprinted from Walt Kelly, *Pogo Primer for Parents* (U.S. Department of Health, Education, and Welfare, 1961), p. 23.

MEDIA MEANS

by JAMES W. THOMPSON

STRANGE,
how MEDIA MEANS,
Sitting mid-morning—
so clock announced
in a scream a six
stopped by a slap
on the back by a hand
designed to web
air space of stage—
in slum, a warm
significant personage
dignifies & "smoke"
makes supreme;
(as flames from several
7 day lights set such
objet d' art as Africa
affords the *connoisseur,*
this one a lover
not copious w/coin
of the realm
but replete w/taste,
to pulsate beneath
the naked sun of a
red 100 watt, beating
the trail of incense
which clouds its glare
in gentle gloom/
a Frankincense & Myrrh
perfume to match
the furred feeling
of the CASTRO,
contoured through use
and such abuse
as bodies meaning
to be heard extend) speaking
to Young Blacks
whom MEDIA has made
B E L I E V E
that a Black Blues Chord
played by BLACKS
is an
A C I D R O C K T U N E
that White imitation
of a very black feeling/
I was forced to scream:
INTEGRATION IS DREADFUL
when you don't control
the media which makes
ZOMBIE/ISM a constant
condition.) IT SELLS IMAGES—
imitations of REAL
and REALITY imitates
IT:
Black folks imitating
white folks
who
imitate
THEM!

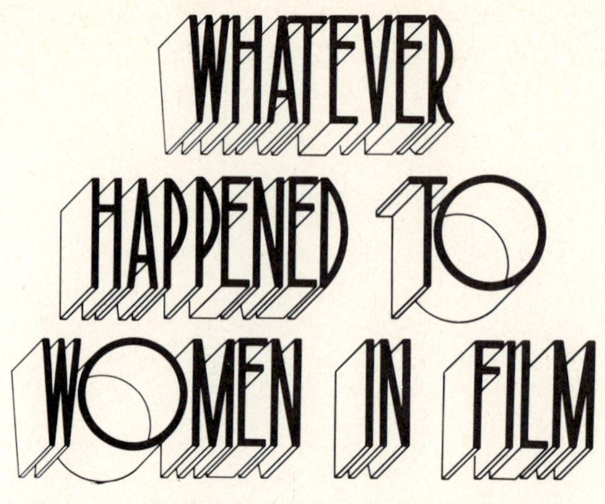

by JEANNE BETANCOURT

Acknowledging that the "image of women in film reflects popular beliefs," Jeanne Betancourt, author of **Women in Focus,** analyzes the kinds of roles women have played in films since the 1920s. She urges that the film industry more accurately depict women as well as reflect all aspects of human experience. In addition, she calls for a new consciousness in film criticism along with a greater involvement in all aspects of film production.

It's easy to point a finger at the film industry for its stereotyped and restrictive treatment of women. The reason it's easy is that it's true. But it's equally true that Hollywood films are made to sell, and you can't sell what the people won't buy. So films are a mirror of societal norms and preferences; if women are treated narrowly by "the industry," it is because they are being similarly treated by the society. What we have is the chicken-and-egg dilemma: Did the flappers flap more because of the movies, or did the movies flap more because of the flappers?

The question is difficult—perhaps impossible—to answer. But this much is certain: As with other aspects of our culture, the image of women in film reflects popular beliefs, and by so doing reinforces these beliefs. Having said that, however, it is still valid to analyze the role of women in film—not for the sake of argument or gospel, but because the current interest in feminism and sex-stereotyping requires that we understand the impact of this influential medium on how women are viewed and how these views are validated. Whether it is the female characters portrayed, the actresses who portray them, or the behind-the-camera influences, the

Women in Film: From *Media & Methods* (October 1975). Reprinted by permission of *Media & Methods* magazine.

marriage of women and movies has been one of convenience rather than concern. Somewhere between "the girl next door" and the "bawdy broad" lies a complex reality that the celluloid world has hardly noticed.

Early Film Images

The films of the '20s presented the flapper as free socially, but not intellectually. With limited career opportunities, she usually got married before the last fade out. And though she kept late hours, drank and danced, there were definite boundaries beyond which she could not go. In films like *Flaming Youth* (1923) and *Wine of Youth* (1924), she exemplified Victorian virtues draped in beads and fringe.

There was a brief time, between the beginning of the talkies and the establishment of the 1933 Production Code, when some aggressive and accomplished women artists (among them, Garbo, Dietrich, Hepburn, West) enhanced their roles through charisma, fine acting, and great lines. They openly displayed an unabashed sexuality that was more adult than their flapper precursors, and certainly more inspiring than the freckle-faced, pony-tailed cuties of the '50s.

After the Production Code's restrictions, film actresses still played characters who were professionally aggressive. But they were no longer sexually aggressive. The Code directed that screen characters (read "women") suffer for their sexual transgressions, their "sins of the flesh." Thus, the end of Mae West and the beginning of Shirley Temple.

A Change of Focus

Along with World War II came a rash of "working women" films, typified by the Maisie character of Ann Sothern. With the best male actors and the male population off to war, Hollywood set out to appeal to the independent, female audience. Films reflected the camaraderie and strong character essential to women of that period. Independence, hard work, hope, energy, and mutual support were suddenly "feminine" virtues. This was also the time when the Hollywood soap opera films emerged—the "women's films." These tearjerkers, while superficial, often carried an engrossing plot; they had strong women and were the vehicle for many film careers. They showed women helping one another deal with the hardships of that lean and lonely period. Frequently they presented the story of the war widow: *Something for the Boys* (1944), *Watch on the Rhine* (1943), and *Since You Went Away* (1945) had heroic and loving women.

The '40s also gave us the Evil Woman—the woman who would do anything (frequently for the wrong man), regardless of who got hurt. These were the "dames"—Davis, Hayworth, Darnell, Peters, Arden, Turner, Malone, Stanwyck—and they all had their turn as they appeared in films like *Double Indemnity* (1944), *Dark Mirror* (1946), and *Lady from Shanghai* (1947).

The Films of the Fifties

Women growing up in the '50s rarely realized that their mothers had run the country from 1941 to 1945. "Home and hearth" were the focal points once again, and the movies reflected this. Movie heroines were vacuous, vivacious, and virtuous. Naiveté was in. Debbie Reynolds, Doris Day, and Natalie Wood reflected the powerless '50s woman. They went directly from mortarboard to wedding veil. The *other* actresses were the "bad girls"—Monroe, Gardner, Jones, Russell, and often Taylor. ("Good girls" were not to model themselves after these villains. After all, they were not the kind of girls that boys married.) These actresses even contrasted physically with the light and lively crowd. They were darker (or more bleached), bustier, and believe it or not, even more stupid. The possibility of translating either of these images—saint or whore—into real life was frustrating, masochistic, and dismal. Many women active in the feminist movement today seem to be retaliating against these ridiculous images as well as the conditions they mirrored.

Yet, some actresses transcended and even transformed their roles. As Marjorie Rosen points out in her book *Popcorn Venus,* Audrey Hepburn always brought to her roles a certain flair and independence that shone through such Cinderella dramas as *Roman Holiday* (1953), *Sabrina* (1954), *Funny Face* (1956), and *Love in the Afternoon* (1956). She conveyed, by look and movement, more intelligence and maturity than her contemporaries. Doris Day, too, had a spark of aggressiveness and sometimes even played a career woman. And the staunch independence of Katharine Hepburn remained a powerful reminder that "kids and cooking" were not the only options.

But even these actresses did not reflect the rebellion, introspection, and disillusionment of the '50s that appeared in the roles played by Montgomery Clift, Marlon Brando, and James Dean. Women's roles in the '50s to early '60s rarely got beyond "Whither thou goest, I will go."

Women in Films Today

But at least there were women in those films. Today's directors, instead of dealing with the emancipated woman or expressing the struggle of women as people, seem more inclined to eliminate women from the screen completely. Even some of the old stereotypes don't work quite so well any more; in place of "boy meets girl" we have "boy meets boy" in such films as *Easy Rider, Midnight Cowboy, Rancho Deluxe, The Sting, California Split, Mean Streets, M*A*S*H, French Connection, Dirty Harry,* and *Papillon.*

Where are the women in these films? They are practically reduced to extras, unimportant characters with as much persona as the set. Lacking even the mystique of the star system to add dimension to their meager roles, today's actresses merely titillate and disappear. Certainly there are still women in films—there are always a few around, if only to be raped in the sex-and-violence flicks. Yet, the outrage and stunned reaction to the male rape in *Deliverance* contrasted starkly with the calm acceptance of female rapes presented and accepted so voyeuristically in films like *Clockwork Orange* and *Straw Dogs.*

Why is sex in film today often synonymous with sadistic violence against women? Since women are demanding economic and political equality, is this a way to strengthen the chauvinistic libido? Is it a strategem for assuaging the disillusionment of men who must acknowledge that women are not just all freckles or all chest, but are complex and individual human beings? Ignoring the reality of women as persons can hardly resolve the movie-generated conflict in the male mind between the loveable Debbie Reynolds in perky print dresses and the lusty Marilyn Monroe in clinging low-cut gowns.

The Aging Actress

Another way that current movies deny the personhood of women is by not allowing the great actresses of the '30s and '40s to age on the screen. Actresses of extraordinary talent and experience—whose male counterparts still get fine roles—find themselves portraying horrified and horrifying screamers in *Straight Jacket* (Crawford), *Whatever Happened to Baby Jane?* (Davis, Crawford), *Hush . . . Hush, Sweet Charlotte* (Davis, deHavilland), *The Nanny* (Davis), *Die! Die! My Darling* (Bankhead). Molly Haskell observes in her book *From Reverence to Rape:*

> It was considered perfectly normal for Fred Astaire or Cary Grant to go on playing romantic leads from one generation to another, while their early partners were forced to play mothers or character parts, or go wilting into retirement. Fred Astaire was paired romantically with Ginger Rogers in the '30s, Rita Hayworth in the '40s, and Cyd Charisse and Audrey Hepburn in the '50s, while Cary Grant went with Katharine Hepburn in the '30s, Ingrid Bergman in the '40s, Grace Kelly in the '50s, and Sophia Loren in the '60s.

With a few exceptions—Gena Rowlands in *A Woman Under the Influence,* and Ellen Burstyn in *Alice Doesn't Live Here Anymore*—the image of women in the American feature length film has yet to be developed. Perhaps as the social context changes, Hollywood will see a financial advantage in showing women as strong, independent-minded people, ready to grow and change or shrink and disappear in the face of conflict—as male characters do. On the horizon is only the promise of a film adaptation of Erica Jong's best seller, *Fear of Flying; Amelia,* a film about Amelia Earhart masterminded by Shirley MacLaine; and *Rooster Cogburn,* a sequal to *True Grit.* The redeeming quality of the latter is that it features John Wayne riding side by side with Katharine Hepburn. Is it a sign of the times that they are putting Wayne with his contemporary, rather than perhaps Candice Bergen?

Feminist Film Criticism

Despite the painfully slow change in Hollywood, the feminist perspective is already being expressed in film criticism. Marjorie Rosen's book, *Popcorn Venus: Women, Movies and the American Dream,* and Molly Haskell's *From Reverence to Rape: The Treatment of Women in the Movies,* are receiving wide distribution. Haskell's reviews regularly appear in *The Village Voice* and *Viva;* Rosen writes for *The New York Times* and *Ms.* Here in *Media & Methods,* Susan Rice's articles have often underscored the sexism that permeates many of the Hollywood productions. . . . Each of these writers has used her feminine consciousness to develop a realistic and sensitive perspective on new films and on the industry in general. Perhaps, as the times change and sexism becomes less popular and acceptable, other critics will reflect this trend. Even the most blatant chauvinist may be forced to consider the image of women in film —if such is the popular attitude.

The Women Who Make the Movies

Where are the women who make movies? Actually, there haven't been and still aren't many of them. In 1974, of the nearly 3,000 persons in the Producer's Guild, only eight were women, only 23 of the more than 2,000 Director's Guild members were women, and only 148 women were listed among the almost 3,000 members of the Writer's Guild.

Despite these dreary statistics, and the situation they reveal, there are women who made milestone contributions to the film industry. Lotte Reiniger invented silhouette animation in 1926. Leontine Sagan's *Maedchen in Uniform* (1931) was the first collectively made film. During the years she worked for Hitler, Leni Riefenstahl made one of the best known and most frighteningly effective propaganda films, *Triumph of the Will* (1934) as well as a full-length film on sports, *Olympia* (1936). Nicole Verdres created the first compilation film, *Paris 1900* (1946). Germaine Dulac was one of the leaders of the French avant garde, and Agnes Varda is the mother of the New Wave in France. Maya Deren is widely recognized as the catalyst and one of the most important figures in the postwar experimental film movement in America.

Even with this impressive history, however, women have made few inroads into current filmmaking circles. Areas where they are accepted by the film industry are those of editing and scripting—all that writing (typing?) and cutting and gluing (patience!) is considered appropriate "women's work" apparently. But camera work, sound work, directing, producing? Not much is available for women in these functions. In 1975, it still looks as if women who want careers in these fields will be pioneers and must come in through the back door. Some local unions are supportive and encourage women applicants, but they are precious few. The National Organization for Women (NOW) is making extensive and intensive efforts not only to improve the image of women in the media but also to fight discrimination toward women in the media job market.

A direct result of the women's movement in the late '60s and early '70s is a developing group of women filmmakers whose works often reflect feminist concerns. The support their short films receive through festival, community, club, library, and school use has given a number of female artists an opening, albeit a narrow one, into filmmaking careers. (Of the 75 Blue and Red Ribbon winners at the 1975 American Film Festival last June, 16 were directed or co-directed by women.) The most successful of these efforts have combined a deep conviction and sincerity with a growing mastery of film forms. In many of these works the exploration and development of a filmic vocabulary is motivated by a stirring of the will to communicate a deep and personal sensibility. They are, as Maya Deren put it, "driven by that which motivates any artist or writer, the conviction that her medium has infinite potentialities for conveying her particular perceptions of life."

One of the popular myths about women filmmakers is that each is a feminist and will make "good" films about women—or that all male directors are insensitive sexists. Obviously, women can make "bad" (and "good") films just as men can. The point is that they ought at least be allowed the opportunity. Right now, that opportunity exists mostly in the 16mm short fiction and documentary format, where the filmmaker can work alone or with a small group of like-minded professionals. Those who want careers as feature-length film directors face a formidable obstacle in that such productions require extensive support systems. Unless these systems are staffed by persons who welcome a balanced image of women and men as persons, efforts to develop strong female characters will prove frustrating if not impossible. Few artists work well in an environment where everyone calls them "Honey."

Conclusion

The real point at issue in discussing the image of women in film is not recrimination or retribution. Nor is it to replace violent and sadistic male characters with violent and sadistic female roles. On the contrary, some of the traditional male roles also need to be reexamined—and less role-bound images developed for everyone.

We need to see more movies on maturing love and the variances in relationships as lovers grow older together, more films about parents and children dealing with the real consequences of divorce. There are not enough films about the joys and loneliness of living and growing old alone, about a single man or woman coping with the conflicting demands of career, personal needs, and relating to others.

In other words, if the film industry is to continue as the reflection and reinforcement of the social milieu, it needs to explore every facet of the human experience. And excluding or restricting women from that exploration is unfair—not just to the women, but to film as an art form as well.

by RONALD P. KRISS

In 1971 **Business Week** described cable TV as "a grubby infant." Several years later, the cable still finds that it has not been allowed full development. **Time** magazine senior editor Ronald P. Kriss focuses on the political struggle over the future of television. He cites some of the major problems in determining cable's role in the communications industry.

Until the last decade or so, over-the-air broadcasters regarded cable television, with tolerant condescension, as a convenient auxiliary that brought clear pictures—including pictures of detergents, deodorants, and dandruff cures—into thousands of otherwise unreachable homes and thus provided a rationale for raising advertising rates. Cable still serves that function, but broadcasters no longer regard the industry merely as "a grubby infant," as *Business Week* described it in 1971. For now, after twenty-seven years, cable is assuming the menacing aspect of a rival medium.

The vast potential of cable has long been recognized. Where over-the-air broadcasting—even with U.H.F. channels—is limited to a comparative handful of frequencies, cable can potentially deliver up to eighty interference-free channels over long distances. The implications are enormous. The promised abundance and versatility of cable has stimulated planners to talk of a "wired nation"—a universal medium that would not only carry greatly expanded educational, cultural, and civic programming but would permit two-way communication with its audience and bring into being dial-a-libraries, facsimile newspapers, remote-controlled shopping, data transmission, banking by wire, electronic mail delivery, and instant national referenda.

Although most observers assume that eventually such uses of cable will

Cable TV: The Bottled-Up Medium: From *Columbia Journalism Review* (July/August 1976). Reprinted by permission of the *Columbia Journalism Review* and the author.

come to be, they have remained vague about cost and timing. As Les Brown put it in *The New York Times:* "Whether cable will become a medium unto itself, instead of an aid to TV reception, has never been a question; the question has always been when. Optimists still predict it will happen in the 1980s; pessimists give it longer, some not until the 21st century."

Back here in the 1970s, the question of cable's emergence is more narrowly drawn: will cable be permitted to develop as technological and economic circumstances permit, or will government regulation, supported by over-the-air broadcasters, impede or halt its progress? During the first half of 1976 this issue has produced an unbecoming dogfight between broadcast and cable, and it looks as if a reluctant Congress will have to attempt a settlement.

Until recently, broadcasters have had little cause for alarm, because government has supervised cable to the point of strangulation. The chief regulatory body, the Federal Communications Commission, is not wholly to blame; Congress left a legislative vacuum and the F.C.C. moved in. Moreover, it moved in with the concept that cable was, and always would be, subservient to broadcasting. Partly as a result of this attitude, cable's growth has been slow; barely a quarter-century after its inception it has attained a "penetration," as broadcasters call it, of only 15.3 percent of American homes, compared with 97.5 percent for over-the-air television.

Now there is a growing consensus in the government that cable has been shackled too long, but it is a difficult time to do anything about it. Although Congress has responded to the extent of trying to draft new—and long overdue—legislation, the odds are that no law will emerge before the national-convention recess, and probably not before 1977, if then. A presidential election year is hardly prime time for any legislation affecting broadcasters, let alone something as touchy as this. As agencies of a White House fine-tuned to the campaign, the F.C.C. and the Office of Telecommunications Policy are unlikely to push for policy changes, and the dependence of members of Congress on broadcasters is even more obvious.

Moreover, the opposing sides offer little ground for consensus. Broadcasters depict cable as a parasite, a shameless freeloader living off conventional television's sweat and ingenuity. The cable industry sees the broadcasters as a coddled, over-protected special interest that rakes in outrageous profits, thanks mostly to its fortuitous possession of a limited resource, the airwaves.

The two sides were put on a collision course last February, when the Communications Subcommittee of the House Committee on Interstate and Foreign Commerce issued a staff report on cable TV. It was the first comprehensive congressional study of the industry since the early 1960s, and the authors pulled few punches: "The FCC has continually refused to confront the basic issues presented by cable television and is not likely to unless Congress provides the impetus," they wrote. They accused the F.C.C.'s

Erratum

Study Questions appearing on page 262
should be disregarded.

The appropriate Study Questions for
The Informers begin on page 268.

Cable Bureau and Broadcast Bureau of being "shills" for the industries they were supposed to oversee, and they charged the commission itself with "following a protectionist policy."

"It has chosen to interpret its mandate from the Congress," they wrote, "as requiring primary concern for individual broadcasters rather than for the needs of the audience being served." The F.C.C., the authors went on, kept a tight rein on cable TV "largely because of its threatened impact on conventional broadcasting."

To rectify this situation, the report urged in a statement particularly chilling to broadcasters that the government abandon its reliance "on any particular technology as the chosen instrument of national communications policy." Specifically, the report recommended:

☐ Amending the Communications Act of 1934 to cover the cable industry and to acknowledge its importance in the national communications system.

☐ Easing the rigid rules curtailing cable's ability to pluck signals from distant transmitters and the restrictions on programming for pay television.

☐ Requiring that cable operators pay reasonable fees to copyright owners, which they do not now do. ("Cable's growth," the report rightly noted, "cannot be based on such an unfair foundation.")

☐ Enacting a "rural telecommunications act," patterned on the Rural Electrification Act that brought light to the nation's countryside, to finance low-interest loans for building cable systems in remote areas.

None of the parties was entirely pleased. Some of the cable operators grumbled about the copyright proposal. Independent critics complained that the rural loan provision would leave the government deeply involved in cable's activities. But the sharpest outcries came, naturally, from the broadcasters. The National Association of Broadcasters branded the report as an effort "to replace the great system of over-the-air broadcasting in the United States with a wired nation which would cost over $200 billion in construction costs alone." (When broadcast lobbyists *really* get worked up, they put the cost of wiring the nation at $1 trillion. Estimates cited in Ralph Lee Smith's *The Wired Nation,* published in 1972, ranged from $15 billion to $123 billion, depending on the extent of the system and its range of services.) ABC warned that the existing television structure "should not be undercut by a subsidized wire service at tremendous additional cost which would serve only the small minority who can afford it and will have access to it." In a similar vein, NBC complained that the report betrayed "an elitist approach" that departed from the basic American concept of "a free broadcast system."

Progress since has been slow. The Communications Subcommittee had intended to hold hearings in March, when Washington was still buzzing about the staff report. But political infighting helped delay the fifteen-day hearings until mid-May, when the report had had time to cool.

There were other problems. Pressed by Ronald Reagan, that archenemy of Washington, President Ford had made a point of relaxing the federal government's regulatory hand. The White House sent Congress proposals for "deregulating" the airline, rail, and trucking industries, and cable TV was next on the list. For months, the White House had been studying proposals aimed at increasing competition between cable and over-the-air television. But ideology had to give way to prudence. As Paul W. MacAvoy, a member of the president's Council of Economic Advisers and a leading advocate of deregulation, told *The New York Times:* "The industry screamed bloody murder." The White House backed off.

MacAvoy hastened to add, however, that the industry's rage was not the chief reason for hastily dropping cable deregulation. "Those who propose change," he said, "have the burden of coming up with the evidence about its probable impact." The pro-cable forces had not produced convincing evidence; one subcommittee source referred to a "research gap." The broadcasters, meanwhile, had come up with hair-raising figures. In a White House memo that was leaked in April, MacAvoy quoted the N.A.B. as saying that if cable TV were permitted to import an unlimited number of distant signals into an area, "over half the stations in the country would be driven out of business."

Since 1949, when it was developed independently by engineers in Pennsylvania and Oregon, cable has grown steadily. By January 1, 1961, there were 640 cable systems, serving 650,000 homes. A decade later, the number of systems had increased to 2,500; the number of subscribers had grown to 4.9 million. Today some 3,450 systems are wired, by means of 190,000 miles of cable, to 10.8 million homes in all fifty states plus the Virgin Islands, Puerto Rico, and Guam.

What may be more significant is that while cable is available to only 30 percent of U.S. homes, fully half of these have been wired. According to some estimates, by 1981 cable will be available to 50 or 60 percent of U.S. homes. If half of those homes were wired, that would mean close to 25 million subscribers to cable TV.

While cable was growing, Congress kept hands off. In the absence of specific legislation, the F.C.C. began to take charge of the industry, usually to protect local stations.

In 1972 the F.C.C. issued a ruling that managed both to alarm broadcasters and nearly kill cable. Since 1966 the commission had maintained a freeze that barred cable systems from entering the "top 100" TV markets (led by the New York metropolitan area, with close to six million TV households) without express F.C.C. approval. The 1972 order lifted the freeze, but at the same time required cable systems plunging into the top 100 to provide at least twenty channels, half of them reserved for educational, cultural, and public-access programs.

The cable operators thought it was the breakthrough they had been seeking. True, they weren't all that happy about having to maintain public-access channels and to provide those who sought access with video equipment to boot. "The industry," one civic-minded cable spokesman said loftily, "cannot afford to sacrifice itself on the altar of public good." Still, they foresaw a bonanza in the big cities—and nearly went bust. In rural areas, cable could be strung for as little as $3,500 a mile; in cities, it has been known to cost as much as $80,000 a mile. In rural areas, one of cable's prime attractions was improved reception; but many big cities already had excellent reception—except for New York, with its skyscrapers, and Los Angeles and San Francisco, with their canyons and valleys.

Cable operators were also authorized to introduce pay television, which had been tried experimentally, and usually unsuccessfully, in the 1960s. Under it, subscribers may pay either a flat monthly surcharge or a per-program fee for first-run films, sports events, and other attractions. At the beginning of 1973, pay systems had only 16,000 subscribers throughout the U.S. By the beginnning of 1976, there were 500,000.

From the first, broadcasters demanded stern "anti-siphoning" rules to keep pay TV from outbidding the networks for top attractions. As the House Communications Subcommittee puts it, "Siphoning is a word used by broadcasters, no doubt because it evokes the image of a cable operator robbing the broadcaster of his programming." One critic of the broadcasters notes that with pay TV accounting for perhaps 1 percent of all TV homes, "Anti-siphoning regulations are akin to protecting an elephant's feeding rights against interference from a mouse." To the broadcasters, however, this is a mouse that someday, soon, may roar: according to ABC officials, figures compiled by the Stanford Research Institute show that by 1985 the pay TV industry may be able to spend nearly $900 million to acquire programs; the three networks spent $1.1 billion in 1974 for that purpose.

Despite cable's financial struggle in the big cities, it had one very important thing going for it. From the early 1970s, in the universities, the courts, and government offices, a feeling seemed to be growing that cable should be at least partly freed from restrictive regulations and given a make-it or break-it chance in the marketplace.

Late in 1971, an eighteen-month, $500,000 study commissioned by the Alfred P. Sloan Foundation gave powerful impetus to this feeling. *On the Cable: The Television of Abundance* saw little risk that either many local stations or networks would wither as cable audiences grew. But the report went on: "If over-the-air television is to fall victim to technological change, it is in no different position from any other enterprise in which investments have been made, and possesses no greater right than other industries to protection from technological change." No greater right than, say, the radio or film industries possessed when television happened along and mugged them both.

Four years later, yet another blow for cable was struck by the Committee for Economic Development, a private, non-partisan organization of 200 business and educational leaders which produces thoughtful, well-researched policy payers on a variety of current issues. Noting that business "has a stake in the diversity of voices competing in a free market," the C.E.D. urged: "In the transition from scarcity to greater abundance and diversity, broadcast policy should rely more on competitive market forces and less on government regulation. Fair competition among the technologies should be encouraged." The C.E.D. did have a major caveat. "There are cogent arguments," it said, "for protecting the established broadcast service if a competitive system deprives the public of present benefits without offering the prospect of future improvements. What is needed, therefore, is a national policy that strikes a reasonable balance between the promotion of diversity through cable and the preservation of an effective system of over-the-air broadcasting."

Easier said than done. For years, the F.C.C. has been promising to formulate such a policy and submit it to Congress. So has the White House. Congress, for that matter, has promised to come up with its own plan. Watergate slowed the effort; election-year politics has slowed it further. Still, there has been some movement, however glacial.

The Justice Department has filed a number of briefs in behalf of the cable industry, and has warned the F.C.C. that its efforts toward shielding the broadcast business could lead to a "dismal swamp of protectionism." In the Senate, Edward Kennedy and Philip Hart are sponsoring a "competition improvements act" designed to ease broadcasting's stranglehold over cable. The Senate Judiciary Committee, meanwhile, has completed its proposed revision of the Copyright Act of 1909. Its bill, S.22, calls for a statutory schedule of fees for cable operators based on gross receipts: one-half of one percent of the first $40,000 would be paid to the Register of Copyrights tor distribution to copyright holders; 1 percent of the next $40,000; and so on to a top fee of 2½ percent on gross receipts of $160,000 and over.

A House Judiciary subcommittee is also moving toward copyright legislation, and it is weighing the Senate approach as well as a couple of other, more complex ones. Thoughtful cable executives agree that without a revamped copyright law to cover their business, there is not likely to be an effective overall measure. "The most urgent need is a resolution of the copyright issue," said a congressional aide who is sympathetic to the cable industry. "The cable operators have got to be made to pay for the material that is the foundation of their whole industry." But as the House subcommittee is learning, finding a formula that everyone can live with is devilishly difficult.

There are other thorny issues. Exclusivity, for instance. If a cable system is allowed to pipe a great number of signals to its subscribers from stations near and far, how can a local station prevent duplication of its own programming? And if broadcast television is weakened, will the poor be penalized because they cannot afford to pay the $10-a-month fee that prevails in some places?

Clearly, any legislation that is produced in the next year or so will have to deal with some nigh-insoluble problems—problems of competition versus protectionism, the role of the marketplace, the question of reasonable profits, the whole direction of electronic communications, the social impact of cable.

Beyond all that is perhaps an even tougher issue than any of these. "People are limited in the amount of information they can absorb," the C.E.D. noted in its 1975 report. "If the move from scarcity to abundance in communications does not guarantee better or more complete information, if it only guarantees *more,* then it may well serve no constructive purpose."

For all its promise, the fact is that cable is still a long way from guaranteeing anything much more than—well, more.

RADIO '76: MOVING IN MANY DIRECTIONS

by MARC KIRKEBY

In this article from Record World, Marc Kirkeby gives an overview of the state of radio at the end of 1976. He notes that programming has changed, primarily because of demographic shifts. As is the case with so many other media, the radio audience, says Kirkeby, is "certainly more fragmented in its tastes than ever before."

New York—In other years, the changes in radio have seemed volcanic; in 1976, radio was also moving, but slowly, in many directions at once, like a glacier that may not reach its destination tomorrow, but will get there eventually no matter what.

The biggest trends in radio did not begin in 1976, but were apparent throughout the year: an increasing reliance on research in almost every musical format; an inexorable movement of such formats from AM to FM; and an intensifying competition among all stations for the adult audience.

Distinctions between formats were blurring: FM rock radio, once a monolith of loudness and drug lyrics in the minds of many advertisers, was noticeably broken into at least three groups, progressive, "album-oriented rock" and soft rock; and the differences between top 40, adult contemporary and traditional MOR* were also lessened by the increasing reliance of all three on softer pop sounds.

The American Research Bureau released a study in August that confirmed what most observers had been predicting since the start of the decade: FM penetration in the nation's largest markets is increasing at a rapid rate, with more people now listening to FM than AM in such markets as

Radio '76: Moving in Many Directions: From *Record World* (December 25, 1976). Reprinted by permission of *Record World*.

* MOR: middle of the road.

Dallas-Fort Worth and Washington, D.C. In six years, FM's share has grown by 100%.

Move to FM

The most powerful format on the FM band in 1976 remained beautiful music, but there were signs that it would have some strong competition for an ever-wider audience. Top 40, for years the dominant factor (edging out MOR and all-news) on the AM side nationally, was moving speedily to frequency modulation. More than a dozen major top 40s on FM now report to the RW [*Record World*] Singles Chart, double the number reporting a year ago. And in some markets, the departure of a leading AM top 40 station was seen to re-orient the thinking of the entire market. In some cities, including Chicago, one was hard pressed to find a station in the same circumstances as at this time a year ago.

Music formats won some sort of victory with the apparent cresting of the all-news trend; the dismemberment of NBC's News and Information Service seemed to indicate that all-news is a powerful format in big cities, but not in secondaries, where it was often more popular with advertisers than with listeners.

Demographic Shifts

For top 40, or mass-appeal radio, as many stations are now labeling themselves, it was population data that signalled the need for change. Studies showed that the age breakdown of the radio audience was moving steadily toward the older groupings, and likely to continue to do so, making reliance on teens alone a probable path to failure. But it was still teens that were accounting for the bulk of singles sales, long the basis for top 40 research, and programmers saw the need for new techniques to ferret out the likes and dislikes of an older audience.

The result was the rise of "passive research"—call-outs, questionnaires, and greater efforts to ascertain the age and tastes of those calling to request records. Rochelle Staab told the CBS convention last summer that the Bartell chain was moving to just such a reliance, and Neil McIntyre, program director of WPIX-FM in New York, revealed in an RW Dialogue (Oct. 30) that he was disregarding singles sales altogether and broadening his use of passive research.

There were still other signs that such research would become increasingly important in 1977. The growth patterns of a number of singles late in the year told the unsettling tale that the key indicator markets watched by programmers across the country were less and less accurate as predictors of how a given record would do in a given city, demographic similarities notwithstanding. While major stations continued to watch those markets, they evinced a self-reliance that might well become more and more necessary.

Country radio too was turning to research as never before, following the leads of WMAQ (Chicago) and WHN (New York), the format's biggest success stories of recent years. Playlists at big-city stations grew shorter and shorter, and it was hard for many not to follow suit. Still, country research developed its own wrinkles: country singles in general do not sell as heavily as pop singles; in some markets they hardly sell at all, and many country programmers were faced with an avid, adult audience who apparently listened constantly, but bought few if any records. Seeking them out was the program director's obvious task for the future.

As the movement from AM to FM took on the characteristics of a gold rush, some stations were, perhaps unavoidably, left behind, and it began to look as if only government action of some sort would save them. The AM "daytimer"—a station required to sign off at local sunset—looked like an endangered species in 1976, and although any number of interesting music formats were to be found on such stations, they were difficult to sell; ownership changes were frequent; and stability was often low. Similarly, a number of formats that might have had larger audiences in the past, but in any case were ill-suited for the commercial competition of a large market, were fighting off format changes with difficulty. An appellate court ruling said that in general a station could not abandon a format if that format was providing a unique service to the market, even though it might be highly unprofitable.The FCC, wanting no part in such regulation, pushed another, higher court test, the result of which is still pending. And listener groups, such as the ones that had saved WNCN's classical format and WRVR's jazz format in New York, were springing up in other cities to save small stations.

If there was a Slogan Of The Year in radio in 1976, it was "The MOR of Tomorrow." Just about every station in every format used the phrase, or one like it, to describe its goals for next year and the years to come. Only top 40 stations seemed to value teens as anything more than a segment of 12-49's, and emphasis on 18-49's seemed everyone's preoccupation.

Thus, the central question facing radio as 1976 ends is how so many stations will successfully compete for the same audience.

It is large enough, and certainly more fragmented in its tastes than ever before, but there is still much to be learned about programming radio for an audience that grew up on TV, and may be making different demands on radio stations than in the past. Many programmers enter 1977 looking for more information about the adult audience, and those looking most vigorously will likely be those with a competitive edge in 1977.

AMERICA'S OWN MUSIC

by PAUL ACKERMAN

Paul Ackerman, Editor Emeritus of Billboard magazine and a much honored historian of country music, shows the important impact that country music has on popular music today.

American pop music is many-faceted. It derives from many sources and represents a kaleidoscope of cultures—rural and urban. The richest of these sources may be called the Southern heritage. For it was in the South —or to use the phrase of a much beloved jazz piece, "Dear Old Southland" —that country music developed its wealth of song material and style of instrumentation. This developing was to prove so crucial to the ultimate maturity of the pop field.

While a big city music business thrived in the early decades of the century with its center in New York and its song forms reflecting considerable European influence, the Southern, rural areas remained largely unknown to important publishers and urban music markets. They were waiting . . . these folk oriented artists who wrote their own songs and sang them to local audiences. They were waiting for improved communications, for socio-economic changes occasioned by the war and a changing agriculture . . . changes which were to encourage an interchange of music cultures. In factories and urban centers, and at war bases during the 1940s, listeners heard the music of the Louisiana bayous, of the hills and hollers of Appalachia, of the bluegrass country of Kentucky, of the Mississippi delta, and even the so-called Tex-Mex strains and Western swing bands of the Texas lands near the Rio Grande.

All these areas and their artists contributed to what became country music. The late Frank Walker, pioneer record executive and a key figure in country music both at RCA Victor—where he trained Steve Sholes—and then as president of MGM Records where he maintained a close relationship with the immortal Hank Williams—said of country music in a Billboard interview late in 1963: "It is music which is distinctly our own. And just as other nations have become more nationalistic about their musical heritage, so have we Americans . . . and this is one reason why our native music is enjoying increasingly broad acceptance."

Walker noted that it is not possible to say just when the country music field started, even though some record collectors and historians arbitrarily say that the era crystallized at the time of Jimmie Rodgers, who died in 1933. According to Walker, the country field grew naturally, fusing many types of material into a distinctive culture. Natives of the Southern mountains contributed folk material derived from that area. In addition, there was an interchange of material indigenous to the white and black segments of the population.

Walker pointed out that the music of the Southern white also contained elements of song derived from the British Isles such as jigs and reels, or hoedowns and so-called "event songs" which are so similar in concept to the English broadside ballad and which were, of course, "transportation songs"—songs of the railroad, the canal and the open road.

Event songs, like the broadside ballad of a much earlier day, were not merely songs; they were a form of communication to the rural folk in the hills and hollers. Thus, when a dramatic or shocking event occurred such as the sinking of the Titantic or the murder of the child, Marion Parker, records were out telling of these events. Walker, while with Columbia Records in the 1920s, issued many disks of this type, including records about the Titantic and Marion Parker. "I had Carson Robison write event songs," Walker said.

But perhaps the greatest single body of country song material is what were called, in an earlier day, heart songs: songs of life and life and its tribulations, of love and tragedy, of happiness and pain. These songs differed from regulation Tin Pan Alley product in that they came from the heart; they lacked the fabricated quality of the Tin Pan Alley song. And whereas the Tin Pan Alley song of love was often an artificial, sugar-coated version of the relationship between a man and a woman, a country song on the same subject was often painfully truthful. The first lines of a Floyd Tillman song will suffice as an example: "Seems I always had to slip around to be with you, my dear. . . . Slippin' around. . . . Afraid we might be found."*

A song such as "Slippin' Around" tells the truth. Not only that, it also brings to the song a moral quality—in this case the element of retribution. For in the "answer song" the lover marries his paramour and shortly thereafter finds her slipping around again. He takes this philosophically, mentioning that he had it coming to him..There is, in other words, an awareness of guilt.

Both the Southern white and Southern black were, and in many cases still are, close to the Lord. And their music reflects this—the Southern white in his love of sacred material and the black, whose rhythm and blues is shot through with what is known as the "church sound." And both segments of the Southern heritage—black and white—understood.

There are countless examples of white and black Southern artists influencing each other. The late, great Red Foley, mentioning his youth in a Billboard story years ago, told how he always listened to the music emanating from black churches in his neighborhood. And he was proud of the fact that blacks bought his records and went to his concerts. They knew he was "for real."

Perhaps the most important example of the music of Southern blacks and whites influencing the vast body of American pop music—and finally the music of the Western world—was the fusion of blues and country which resulted in the rockabilly trend, culminating with Sam Phillips' development of Sun Records in the 1950s.

The story of the fusion of blues and country music is a long one. A milestone along the way was the career of Jimmie Rodgers, the Singing Brakeman, the father of country music.

Jimmie was born in 1897 in Meridian, Miss., the son of a railroad man, Aaron Rodgers. In his teens Jimmie started working for the railroad as flagman, baggageman and then brakeman. He absorbed the lore of the trains, but delicate health forced him to seek a less physically demanding occupation. So he became an entertainer—an occupation permitting him to use his knowledge of railroad musical lore. Rodgers' first group was known as the Jimmie Rodgers Entertainers and they performed over WWNG in North Carolina.

During a historic week in 1927, both Rodgers and the Carter Family were discovered by Ralph Peer, then a field recording man for RCA Victor. Peer, who later founded the Peer-Southern empire, had already made his mark in both black and white Southern music. For instance, he was the first to record Trixie Smith. But on that day in Bristol, Tenn., he really hit the jackpot—for he recognized the value of the talents who had shown up at his audition session.

Historians are of course familiar with the contribution of the Carter Family. But some tend to forget an important fact about the music of Rodgers. His song catalog is blues-drenched and contains a wealth of blues images constantly used by both black and white artists. Thus in "Jimmie's

Texas Blues," copyrighted by Peer-Southern, are the lines:

"Some like Chicago, Some like Memphis, Tennessee
(repeat)
Some like Sweet Dallas, Texas,
where the women think the world of me."*

Rodgers' blue yodels, "The Brakeman's Blues," and many others of his songs are distinctly in the blues tradition.

In 1933, in need of money and desperately ill of tuberculosis, Rodgers came to New York to record what were to be his last sides. They were cut at RCA's 24th Street studios. According to the late Bob Gilmore, a long-time official of the Peer-Southern organization, Rodgers had to be propped up in a cot while the sessions were cut. Shortly after, Rodgers died at Hotel Manger, now the Taft, and his body was shipped in a casket to Meridian, his home town.

One is struck, in recalling these early years of the country field and the Southern heritage in general, by the fact that so much was accomplished by commercial music men. Samuel B. Charters in his book, "The Country Blues," notes that Peer was a man of exceptional discrimination and taste "and he had the marked ability to bring out warm personal performances."

These commercial music men were also talented in virtually all facets of the Southern music field. Peer again is an example, for he did much pioneering among black bluesmen.

Another such rounded authority was the late and aforementioned Frank Walker. Early in the career of Hank Williams, Walker recognized his genius—terming him a "hillbilly Shakespeare." And this same man, who was so close to Hank Williams, also discovered the great blues singer, Bessie Smith. The event occurred early in Walker's career—in his pre-Columbia Records period. The place was Selma, Ala. The young executive was feeling lonesome and he went to a spot in the black section of town where he could hear some music. He sat at a table where he could listen to a girl singer and piano player. As Walker remarked in Billboard's "World Of Country Music" in 1963: "The songs were blues. . . . The girl was barefooted . . . and so gol-darn country!"

Walker said he never forgot that performance, and several years later when he had joined Columbia, he sent Clarence Williams South to find her and bring her to New York, where Walker found lodgings for her. He recorded most of her sides.

Another executive who understands the entire Southern musical heritage and fortunately is still with us is Sam Phillips, the founder of Sun Records and discoverer of Elvis Presley, Charley Rich, Johnny Cash and many others. Phillips' contribution was monumental, for he brought together the idioms of country, blues and religious music. Phillips, prior to working with white Southern artists, recorded Jackie Brenston, B.B. King, Howlin' Wolf and many fine bluesmen. His fusion of that idiom with country music was the most important development in American pop music in our time—for the ultimate product affected the music of the Western World.

Unlike the rhythm and blues field, where independent labels finally outpaced the majors, in the country field the majors never lost their dominant position. Important indie labels did come along—such as Syd Nathan's King operation in Cincinnati; Acuff-Rose's Hickory Records in Nashville, Starday in Nashville and others. But by and large it was the four traditional majors that built the great catalogs. Again, it was a case of commercial music men who proved they had vision and taste. In the country field, they had another element going for them: loyalty. Once a record artist made it, he was not likely to fall into limbo. Thus it is that during the important period when country was entering the pop field—the late 1940s, 1950s and on up to the present, the standard name artists constantly made the charts: Hank Williams, Ernest Tubb, Lefty Frizzell, Hank Snow, Kitty Wells, Loretta Lynn, George Jones, Bill Monroe, Bob Wills, Eddy Arnold and countless others who already are—or one day will be—counted among those in Hillbilly Heaven.

In addition to fostering loyalty on the part of the buying public, the country field also proved stable in other ways. All during the depression, and during the early days of radio, record sales generally diminished—but not country records. They continued to sell. And the artists & repertoire executives who produced these records had long tenures of duty with their various companies and with the artists of those labels.

These men—those who built the great catalogs, are legion. We can mention only some: Steve Sholes and Chet Atkins of RCA Victor; Don Law and Art Satherley of Columbia; Lee Gillette and Ken Nelson of Capitol; Dave Kapp, Paul Cohen and Owen Bradley of Decca.

The country field, too, always valued its music publishers. In the 1950s when publishers in the pop field had shrunk in stature in comparison to the record producer, the country field continued to venerate its great publishers: Fred Rose, father of Wesley and whose relationship with Hank Williams can only be termed providential; Roy Acuff, who persuaded Rose to join him in a publishing company; Jack Stapp, builder of Tree Music, Bill Denny of Cedarwood and the countless others who knew the value of a good song.

Country music was also fortunate in having dedicated people to foster and promote its interests. An example is the Country Music Assn. which serves every facet of the country music industry.

Country music is also favored in having a Museum and Hall of Fame which is one of the most successful operations of its type in the United States.

And, of course, country music and Nashville in general is blessed by being the home of WSM, the broadcasting service of the National Life and

Accident Co. The operation first went on the air Oct. 5, 1925. Among those attending was George D. Hay, "the Solemn Old Judge" who stayed on in Nashville as WSM's first director.

We have sketched in this story some of the broad outlines of the country field. What has it done for our culture?

Country music, our Southern heritage, has brought to American music a rich, indigenous wealth of song material. Once a self-contained cultural entity, country music now has entered the mainstream. It has made our musical culture more varied. It has given our pop culture honesty and a sense of history. As the first locomotives threaded their way into the hill towns, and as the strains of country music finally reached the urban centers, Americans learned how the people of the other half of their country lived, loved and died. Country music, then, is a unifying element.

In the words of Frank Walker: "It is distinctly our own."

MINI-CASE STUDY

Violence and the Electronic Media

News coverage of kidnapper with hostage as Indianapolis police officers attempt to negotiate the victim's release.

While several of the articles in this section discuss the effects of television on its audience (of whatever age), this mini-case study focuses on the much discussed subject of violence in the electronic media, particularly television. Criticism of television violence reached a peak in early 1977 when groups, such as the Parent-Teacher Association and the American Medical Association, began demanding that changes be made in programming and sponsors. Media experts like George Gerbner, Dean of the Annenberg School of Communications at the University of Pennsylvania, noted definite behavioral effects of excessive viewing of violence while the National Citizens Committee for Broadcasting began disseminating rankings of the most violent shows. Clearly, the time had come to take notice.

The following articles indicate the concerns that exist about violence in the media. In addition to the articles in the mini-case study, you will want to turn to Farber (pp. 281–289), Waters (pp. 122–133), and Larsen (pp. 451–455). For students interested in exploring the subject further, additional sources are listed in the bibliography at the end of this section.

FROM

TELEVISION AND GROWING UP

The Impact of Televised Violence

SUMMARY OF A REPORT BY THE SURGEON GENERAL'S SCIENTIFIC ADVISORY COMMITTEE ON TELEVISION AND SOCIAL BEHAVIOR

Violence on Television

Studies of media content show that violence is and has been a prominent component of all mass media in the United States. Television is no exception, and there can be no doubt that violence figures prominently in television entertainment. People are probably exposed to violence by television entertainment more than they are exposed by other media because they use television so much more.

In regard to dramatic entertainment on television, and with violence defined as "the overt expression of physical force against others or self, or the compelling of action against one's will on pain of being hurt or killed," an extensive analysis of content has found that:

—The general prevalence of violence did not change markedly between

From *Television and Growing Up: The Impact of Televised Violence,* Summary of a Report to the Surgeon General, United States Public Health Service, from the Surgeon General's Scientific Advisory Committee on Television and Social Behavior (Washington, D.C.: U.S. Government Printing Office, 1972), 4–9.

1967 and 1969. The rate of violent episodes remained constant at about eight per hour.

—The nature of violence did change. Fatalities declined, and the proportion of leading characters engaged in violence or killing declined. The former dropped from 73 to 64 percent; the latter, from 19 to 5 percent. The consequence is that as many violent incidents occurred in 1969 as in 1967, but a smaller proportion of characters were involved, and the violence was far less lethal.

—Violence increased from 1967 to 1969 in cartoons and in comedies, a category that included cartoons.

—Cartoons were the most violent type of program in these years.

Another study concluded that in 1971 Saturday morning programming, which includes both cartoons and material prepared for adults, approximately three out of ten dramatic segments were "saturated" with violence and that 71 percent involved at least one instance of human violence with or without the use of weapons.

There is also evidence that years high in violence also tend to be years high in overall ratings, and that the frequency of violent programs in a year is related to the popularity of this type of program the previous year. This suggests that televised violence fluctuates partly as a function of the efforts of commercial broadcasters to present what will be maximally popular.

Television's Effects

Television's popularity raises important questions about its social effects. There is interest and concern in regard to many segments of the population—ethnic minorities, religious groups, the old, the unwell, the poor. This committee has been principally concerned with one segment, children and youth, and in particular with the effects of televised violence on their tendencies toward aggressive behavior.

People ask behavioral scientists various questions about television and violence. In our opinion the questions are often far too narrowly drawn. For example:

(1) It is sometimes asked if watching violent fare on television *can* cause a young person to act aggressively. The answer is that, of course, under some circumstances it can. We did not need massive research to know that at least an occasional unstable individual might get sufficiently worked up by some show to act in an impetuous way. The question is faulty, for the real issue is how often it happens, what predispositional conditions have to be there, and what different undesirable, as well as benign, forms the aggressive reaction takes when it occurs.

(2) It is sometimes asked if the fact that children watch a steady fare

of violent material on television many hours a day from early childhood through adolescence causes our society to be more violent. Presumably the answer is, to some degree, "yes," but we consider the question misleading. We know that children imitate and learn from everything they see—parents, fellow children, schools, the media; it would be extraordinary, indeed, if they did not imitate and learn from what they see on television. We have some limited data that conform to our presumption. We have noted in the studies at hand a modest association between viewing of violence and aggression among at least some children, and we have noted some data which are consonant with the interpretation that violence viewing produces the aggression; this evidence is not conclusive, however, and some of the data are also consonant with other interpretations.

Yet, as we have said, the real issue is once again quantitative: how much contribution to the violence of our society is made by extensive violent television viewing by our youth? The evidence (or more accurately, the difficulty of finding evidence) suggests that the effect is small compared with many other possible causes, such as parental attitudes or knowledge of and experience with the real violence of our society.

The sheer amount of television violence may be unimportant compared with such subtle matters as what the medium says about it: is it approved or disapproved, committed by sympathetic or unsympathetic characters, shown to be effective or not, punished or unpunished? Social science today cannot say which aspects of the portrayal of violence make a major difference or in what way. It is entirely possible that some types of extensive portrayals of violence could reduce the propensity to violence in society and that some types might increase it. In our present state of knowledge, we are not able to specify what kinds of violence portrayal will have what net result on society.

What are the alternatives? If broadcasters simply changed the quantitative balance between violent and other kinds of shows, it is not clear what the net effect would be. People hunt and choose the kinds of stimulus material they want. Violent material is popular. If our society changed in no other way than changing the balance of television offerings, people, to some degree, would still seek out violent material. How much effect a modest quantitative change in television schedules would have is now quite unanswerable. More drastic changes, such as general censorship, would clearly have wide effects, but of many kinds, and some of them distinctly undesirable.

In our judgment, the key question that we should be asked is thus a complicated one concerning alternatives. The proper question is, "What kinds of changes, if any, in television content and practices could have a significant net effect in reducing the propensity to undesirable aggression among the audience, and what other effects, desirable and undesirable, would each such change have?"

"I don't know where he learned that. We don't even have a television set."

The state of our knowledge, unfortunately, is not such as to permit confident conclusions in answer to such a question. The readers of this report will find in it evidence relevant to answering such questions, but far short of an answer. The state of present knowledge does not permit an agreed answer.

. . .

THE SCARY WORLD OF TV'S HEAVY VIEWER

by GEORGE GERBNER
and LARRY GROSS

Many critics worry about violence on television, most out of fear that it stimulates viewers to violent or aggressive acts. Our research, however, indicates that the consequences of experiencing TV's symbolic world of violence may be much more far-reaching.

We feel that television dramatically demonstrates the power of authority in our society, and the risks involved in breaking society's rules. Violence-filled programs show who gets away with what, and against whom. It teaches the role of victim, and the acceptance of violence as a social reality we must learn to live with—or flee from.

We have found that people who watch a lot of TV see the real world as more dangerous and frightening than those who watch very little. Heavy viewers are less trustful of their fellow citizens, and more fearful of the real world.

Since most TV "action-adventure" dramas occur in urban settings, the fear they inspire may contribute to the current flight of the middle class from our cities. The fear may also bring increasing demands for police protection, and election of law-and-order politicians.

Those who doubt TV's influence might consider the impact of the automobile on American society. When the automobile burst upon the dusty highways about the turn of the century, most Americans saw it as a horseless carriage, not as a prime mover of a new way of life. Similarly, those of us who grew up before television tend to think of it as just another medium in a series of 20th-century mass-communications systems, such as movies and radio. But television is not just another medium.

TV: the Universal Curriculum

If you were born before 1950, television came into your life after your formative years. Even if you are now a TV addict, it will be difficult for you to comprehend the transformations it has wrought. For example, imagine spending six hours a day at the local movie house when you were 12 years old. No parent would have permitted it. Yet, in our sample of children, nearly half the 12-year-olds watch an average of six or more hours of television per day. For many of them the habit continues into adulthood. On the basis of our surveys, we estimate that about one third of all American adults watch an average of four or more hours of television per day.

Television is different from all other media. From cradle to grave it penetrates nearly every home in the land. Unlike newspapers and magazines, television does not require literacy. Unlike the movies, it runs continuously, and once purchased, costs almost nothing. Unlike radio, it can show as well as tell. Unlike the theater or movies, it does not require leaving your home. With virtually unlimited access, television both precedes literacy and, increasingly, preempts it.

Never before have such large and varied publics—from the nursery to the nursing home, from ghetto tenement to penthouse—shared so much of the same cultural system of messages and images, and the assumptions embedded in them. Television offers a universal curriculum that everyone can learn.

Imagine a hermit who lives in a cave linked to the outside world by a television set that functioned only during prime time. His knowledge of the world would be built exclusively out of the images and facts he could glean from the fictional events, persons, objects and places that appear on TV. His expectations and judgments about the ways of the world would follow the conventions of TV programs, with their predictable plots and outcomes. His view of human nature would be shaped by the shallow psychology of TV characters.

TV Hermits

While none of us is solely dependent upon television for our view of the world, neither have many of us had the opportunity to observe the reality of police stations, courtrooms, corporate board rooms, or hospital operating rooms. Although critics complain about the stereotyped characters and plots of TV dramas, many viewers look on them as representative of the real world. Anyone who questions that assertion should read the 250,000 letters, most containing requests for medical advice, sent by viewers to "Marcus Welby, M.D." during the first five years of his practice on TV.

If adults can be so accepting of the reality of television, imagine its effect on children. By the time the average American child reaches public school, he has already spent several years in an electronic nursery school. At the age of 10 the average youngster spends more hours a week in front of the TV screen than in the classroom. Given continuous exposure to the world of TV, it's not surprising that the children we tested seemed to be more strongly influenced by TV than were the adults.

At the other end of the life cycle, television becomes the steady and often the only companion of the elderly. As failing eyesight makes reading difficult, and getting around becomes a problem, the inhabitants at many nursing homes and retirement communities pass much of the day in the TV room, where the action of fictional drama helps make up for the inaction of their lives.

To learn what they and other Americans have been watching we have been studying the facts of life in the world of evening network television drama—what that world looks like, what happens in it, who lives in it, and who does what to whom in it. We have explored this world by analyzing the content of the situation comedies, dramatic series, and movies that appear in prime time, between eight and 11 P.M.

The Simple World of TV Plots

Night after night, week after week, stock characters and dramatic patterns convey supposed truths about people, power and issues. About three fourths of all leading characters on prime-time network TV are male, mostly single, middle and upper-class white Americans in their 20s or 30s. Most of the women represent romantic or family interests. While only one out of every three male leads intends to or has ever been married, two out of every three female leads are either married, expected to marry, or involved in some romantic relationship.

Unlike the real world, where personalities are complex, motives unclear, and outcomes ambiguous, television presents a world of clarity and simplicity. In show after show, rewards and punishments follow quickly and logically. Crises are resolved, problems are solved, and justice, or at least authority, always triumphs. The central characters in these dramas are clearly defined: dedicated or corrupt; selfless or ambitious; efficient or ineffectual. To insure the widest acceptability, (or greatest potential profitability) the plot lines follow the most commonly accepted notions of morality and justice, whether or not those notions bear much resemblance to reality.

In order to complete a story entertainingly in only an hour or even a half hour, conflicts on TV are usually personal and solved by action. Since violence is dramatic, and relatively simple to produce, much of the action tends to be violent. As a result, the stars of prime-time network TV have for years been cowboys, detectives, and others whose lives permit unrestrained action. Except in comic roles, one rarely sees a leading man burdened by real-life constraints, such as family, that inhibit freewheeling activity.

For the past four years, we have been conducting surveys to discover how people are affected by watching the world of television. We ask them questions about aspects of real life that are portrayed very differently on TV from the way they exist in the real world. We then compare the responses of light and heavy viewers, controlling for sex, education, and other factors.

Anyone trying to isolate the effects of television viewing has the problem of separating it from other cultural influences. In fact, it is difficult to find a sufficiently large sample of nonviewers for comparison. For this article we have compared the responses of light viewers, who watch an average of two hours or less per day, and heavy viewers, who watch an average of four or more hours per day. We also surveyed 300 teenagers in the 6th, 7th, and 8th grades, among whom the heavy viewers watched six hours or more per day.

The Heavy Viewer

Since the leading characters in American television programs are nearly always American, we asked our respondents: "About what percent of the world's population live in the United States?" The correct answer is six percent. The respondents were given a choice of three percent or nine percent, which obliged them either to underestimate or overestimate the correct percentage. Heavy viewers were 19 percent more likely to pick the higher figure than were the light viewers.

We next took up the subject of occupations, since the occupational census in prime time bears little resemblance to the real economy. Professional and managerial roles make up about twice as large a proportion of the labor force on TV as they do in the real world. To find out if this distortion had any effect on viewers, we asked: "About what percent of Americans who have jobs are either professionals or managers—like doctors, lawyers, teachers, proprietors, or other executives?" When forced to make a choice between either 10 or 30 percent (the correct figure is 20 percent), the heavy viewers were 36 percent more likely to overestimate.

One might argue, correctly, that heavy viewing of television tends to be associated with lower education and other socioeconomic factors that limit or distort one's knowledge about the real world. But when we controlled for such alternative sources of information as education and newspaper reading, we found that although they did have some influence, heavy television viewing still showed a significant effect. For example, while adult respondents who had some college education were less influenced by tele-

Drawing by C.E.M.; © 1976 The New Yorker Magazine, Inc.

vision than those who had never attended college, heavy viewers within both categories still showed the influence of television. We obtained similar results when we compared regular newspaper readers with occasional readers or nonreaders.

The only factor that seemed to have an independent effect on the responses was age. Regardless of newspaper reading, education, or even viewing habits, respondents under 30 consistently indicated by their responses that they were more influenced by TV than those over 30. This response difference seems especially noteworthy in that the under-30 group on the whole is better educated than its elders. But the under-30 group constitutes the first TV generation. Many of them grew up with it as teacher and babysitter, and have had lifelong exposure to its influence.

Diet of Violence

Anyone who watches evening network TV receives a heavy diet of violence. More than half of all characters on prime-time TV are involved in some violence, about one tenth in killing. To control this mayhem, the forces of law and order dominate prime time. Among those TV males with identifiable occupations, about 20 percent are engaged in law enforcement. In the real world, the proportion runs less than one percent. Heavy viewers of television were 18 percent more likely than light viewers to over-estimate the number of males employed in law enforcement, regardless of age, sex, education, or reading habits.

Violence on television leads viewers to perceive the real world as more dangerous than it really is, which must also influence the way people behave. When asked, "Can most people be trusted?" the heavy viewers were 35 percent more likely to check "Can't be too careful."

When we asked viewers to estimate their own chances of being involved in some type of violence during any given week, they provided further evidence that television can induce fear. The heavy viewers were 33 percent more likely than light viewers to pick such fearful estimates as 50-50 or one in 10, instead of a more plausible one in 100.

While television may not directly cause the results that have turned up in our studies, it certainly can confirm or encourage certain views of the world. The effect of TV should be measured not just in terms of immediate change in behavior, but also by the extent to which it cultivates certain views of life. The very repetitive and predictable nature of most TV drama programs helps to reinforce these notions.

Victims, like criminals, must learn their proper roles, and televised violence may perform the teaching function all too well [see "A Nation of Willing Victims," *pt,* April 1975]. Instead of worrying only about whether television violence causes individual displays of aggression in the real world, we should also be concerned about the way such symbolic violence influences our assumptions about social reality. Acceptance of violence and passivity in the face of injustice may be consequences of far greater social concern than occasional displays of individual aggression.

Throughout history, once a ruling class has established its rule, the primary function of its cultural media has been the legitimization and maintenance of its authority. Folk tales and other traditional dramatic stories have always reinforced established authority, teaching that when society's rules are broken retribution is visited upon the violators. The importance of the existing social order is always explicit in such stories.

We have found that violence on prime-time network TV cultivates exaggerated assumptions about the threat of danger in the real world. Fear is a universal emotion, and easy to exploit. The exaggerated sense of risk and insecurity may lead to increasing demands for protection, and to increasing pressure for the use of force by established authority. Instead of threatening the social order, television may have become our chief instrument of social control.

FROM

a psychiatrist LOOKS at television and violence

by NER LITTNER

. . .

I can summarize my own views of the effects of television violence as follows:

1. I believe that the vast amount of violence on television is *basically a reflection of the violent interests of the viewers;* it is a symptom, not a cause; it graphically portrays the violence in our souls. I doubt that it is a serious cause of much of it.

2. I do not believe that television violence, when *honestly portrayed,* engenders violence in viewers of any age who were not violent already; and I do not believe that it raises violent impulses to an uncontrollable pitch in those who are already violent. (I will discuss later what I mean by "honest" television.)

3. I do think, however, that for some who are already violently disposed, TV violence may provide a model, a *modus operandi,* when they choose to discharge their violent urges. However, a book, a newspaper, or a radio program may provide a violent person with the same type of detailed plan for the expression of his violence.

4. As far as *dishonest* television violence is concerned, I do think that exposure to repeated doses may possibly interfere, to a degree unmeasurable at present, with the normal development of impulse control in normal or disturbed children; but I do not think that "dishonest" television violence has any marked pathological impact on the average adult.

5. Instead of wasting their efforts on such red herrings as censorship,

A Psychiatrist Looks at Television and Violence: From *Television Quarterly* (Fall, 1969). Reprinted by permission.

violence, sex, or nudity, I think that both the viewing public and the television industry would be far better off if the television industry would devote its considerable talents and energies to creating conditions that would make it possible to develop and screen television shows specializing in such qualities as excellence, artistic value, creativity, originality, honesty, and integrity. If *these* were the hallmark of our television shows, we would not have to worry about possible censorship of their violence, sex, or nudity.

. . .

. . . let me discuss for a moment the whole subject of violence on television. There has been until recently an increasing trend to violence on television. I think that this is due to a variety of reasons:

1. We are, and always have been a violent nation. We live in an age of violence. Therefore, to a large degree the violence on television accurately reflects the violence of our times.

2. We are increasingly freer in our acceptance of freedom of expression. The public and the courts are showing greater tolerance of, and are more

"Keep your shirts on! I'll find you some violence."

Drawing by Whitney Darrow, Jr.; © 1969 The New Yorker Magazine, Inc.

liberal towards, what can be shown. In a similar way we are far more relaxed about displays of sex and morality. Therefore, more violence is being shown as part of this relaxation of censorship.

3. For some program directors and moviemakers, the showing of violence is a cheap way of producing something that may make money. Instead of relying on art, talent, or creativity, reliance is placed on violence for the sake of violence, of shock for the sake of shock. The shock effect of the violence is being used to sell the movie or the program.

4. Because the portrayal of obscenity is against the law, this sets a limit on the amount of sex that can be safely sneaked in. The portrayal of violence is not against the law and therefore can be used to the extent that audiences will accept it.

These are four reasons (there probably are many more) for the great use of violence on television programs. This is not to say that the showing of violence on television is necessarily bad. Actually, it can have decidedly positive effects on the viewing public, and particularly children. These *positive effects* include the following:

1. An appropriate display of violence tends to present the world as it really is, rather than as we wistfully wish it would be. It is unrealistic to leave it out when it is part of the scene. Therefore, when shown in appropriate amounts it can be of *educational* value.

2. It can also be of *mental health* value, if appropriately done. Like watching a bullfight or boxing match, it can help discharge indirectly various violent feelings of the viewer. This tends to keep the viewer's violent feelings from boiling over in more dangerous ways. Therefore, in appropriate amounts it can provide a safe catharsis.

On the other hand, the *negative effects* of viewing television include the following:

1. The child or adolescent has not yet settled on his typical behavior patterns for functioning. If exposed to a repetitive display of *violence as a television-approved method for solving problems,* the child may be encouraged in that direction, particularly if he already comes from a family setting where violence also is the way of settling difficulties. Therefore, there may be an encouragement towards immature methods of problem solving. When, in an attempt to show that crime does not pay, there is violent retribution, its main effect is still to teach violence as the way to solve problems.

2. The individual, whether child or adult, who already uses violent behavior as a solution, may find worked out for him on television a detailed *modus operandi.* Therefore, the violent viewer may use the detail of the television programs as a way of expressing his violence. Television does not cause juvenile delinquency, but it can contribute techniques for a child already delinquent.

3. If excessive doses of violence are presented on television, it may have sufficient of a shock effect to prevent it being used for catharsis. There is

a limit to how much viewing of violence can be used for a safe discharge.

The impact of repeated exposure to excessive violence depends on at least three factors: (a) the age of the viewer; (b) the maturity of the viewer; and (c) the way in which the violence is presented and packaged.

The Age of the Viewer

As I have already mentioned, the mature adult will be offended and disgusted by excessive or inappropriate displays of violence. Therefore he can ignore it or turn it off. The *normal adolescent* (*or the immature adult*) is in a different situation. The excessive display of violence may cause a sympathetic resonance of inner violent feelings in the adolescent to a degree that he cannot handle it. There is no socially acceptable way of discharging excessive violent feelings. Therefore the adolescent may have his normal attempts to come to peace with his violent and rebellious feeling jeopardized. The normal adolescent, unlike the normal adult, will also tend to be attracted to the violence rather than repelled. The *normal preadolescent child* may also be disturbed by excessive and inappropriate displays of violence. However, he probably will be less upset than the adolescent because he is not as concerned, as is the adolescent, with problems of violent rebellion against authority.

The Maturity of the Viewer

The more emotionally disturbed the viewer is, the more likely it is that he will have difficulty in managing stirred-up violent feelings.

Let us consider an extreme situation where an adolescent, immediately after seeing a TV program in which a juvenile delinquent violently rapes a girl, leaves the TV set and violently rapes the first girl he meets. For such a sequence of events to have occurred, one would have to say that the adolescent probably was seriously disturbed emotionally *before* he saw the TV program. It is highly unlikely that any program, no matter how violent, could have such an effect on a normal adolescent.

One also could not say that it was the viewing of the TV program that "caused" the adolescent to rape the girl. One could only say that the program had two effects. Its first was to *trigger* a previously existing emotional disorder. The traumatic effect of the program was but one of the many etiological factors which, coming together, resulted in the adolescent's violent action. The second effect would be to provide the disturbed adolescent with a *blueprint* for discharging his violent tensions. These violent tensions, of course, would probably have originated in violent problems within his own family, completely predating his ever seeing the TV program.

Violent television does not make children aggressive; rather, *the aggressive child turns to violent TV*. And, for that matter, TV does not make a child passive; rather, it is the passive child who chooses the TV.

The Way in Which the Violence Is Presented and Packaged

I. The television violence will be least traumatic if it is completely appropriate and realistic to the story in which it is contained;

II. The television violence will be most traumatic if it is presented dishonestly, if it is being used to sell the program, if it is contrived and inappropriate, if it is unrealistically focused on, if it is presented out of context—in other words, if it is violence for the sake of violence and if the television show is deliberately using violence and brutality to attract and hold a larger audience.

The reason why *dishonest* television violence can be traumatic to the normal child or adolescent is because he feels exploited and used. *He senses he is being taken advantage of*. This tends to reactivate any conflictual feelings he may have about being exploited by his own parents. These reactivated feelings add an additional traumatic impact. In addition, the inappropriateness of the violence makes it harder for the child to deal with it mentally.

. . .

FROM

MASS MEDIA AND VIOLENCE

Report to the National Commission on the Causes and Prevention of Violence

The Two Worlds of Violence: Television and Reality

. . .

The norms for violence contained in the television world of violence are in stark contrast to the norms espoused by a majority of Americans.[1] The most notable contrasts bear upon the criteria which distinguish between approved and disapproved violence. Legality is a primary criterion of approved violence for the majority of adults and teens, while it is not in the television world of violence. In the television world, violence is used almost without restriction as successful means to individual ends. The majority of adult and teenage Americans place severe restrictions on the use of violence in such a manner. For example, low-level violence is approved as a means of punishment and control when a person is in a position of authority or when he is sufficiently provoked. Severe violence, on the other hand, can only be used as a means to law enforcement, or defense of self, others, or property, when the situation clearly necessitates its use.

The norms for violence espoused by a majority of Americans are virtually at polar opposites with those contained in the television world of violence. There is an even greater disparity between the minority of adults and teens who espouse norms of non-violence (persons who very rarely or never approve of violence in any situation) and the television world's norms for violence.

The least disparity between the television world and real world in norms

From *Mass Media and Violence,* a Report to the National Commission on the Causes and Prevention of Violence (Washington, D.C.: U.S. Government Printing Office, November, 1969).

[1] References to television programming or the TV world of violence are based on the programs broadcast during the weeks of October 1–7 in 1967 and 1968 during prime-time hours 4 p.m. to 10 p.m. Monday through Friday and Sunday, and 8 a.m. to 11 a.m. and 7 p.m. to 10 p.m. on Saturday.

"But first this message. Any and all acts of violence in the following program are not to be construed as an advocacy of violence by this station."

for violence is found between the sizable minority of adults and teenagers who have been called the "violents." Their norms for violence are *less* restrictive than the majority of Americans', but are still *more* restrictive than implied norms in the television world.

The television world of violence does not accurately reflect the real world in many significant respects. The vast majority of all levels of violence experienced by adult and teenage Americans as victims, observers, and assailants occurs with persons who are friends or family members of the respondents.[2] In the television world, the majority of violence occurs between strangers. The most prevalent type of violence in the television world involves the use of a weapon; the great majority of adults and teenagers have never experienced this type of severe violence. The most common role in the television world of violence is the assailant, while the least common is the role of observer; in the actual world, the observer is most common and the assailant is the least common role.

The television world of violence is often set in a time and place other than contemporary America. Television may or may not inaccurately reflect the actual world of violence in the American past or in foreign countries; there is no evidence from present research which can prove or disprove this statement.

When comparing the actual and television worlds of violence, our concern lies with the kinds of implied norms that are projected by television. What can or do audiences, especially children, learn from short- and long-term exposure to the television world of violence and what are the behavioral implications of such learning?

[2] The great majority of homicides (94 percent) occur within racial groups and in only twelve percent of all homicides were the assailant and the victim strangers. One-quarter of all homicides involve family members, and twenty-eight percent involve close friends. For further information, see Marvin Wolfgang, *Patterns in Criminal Homicide,* Philadelphia, Pa.: University of Pennsylvania Press, 1948.

The Relationship of the Two Worlds of Violence

The viewing habits and preferences of American audiences are a vital link between the actual and television worlds of violence. One method of assessing the relationship between the two worlds is to compare the characteristics of those in our study sample who have been identified as "violents" with the characteristics of persons who use television as their primary mode of media entertainment. Characteristics of adult and teenage "violents" can also be compared with the characteristics of those who have strong preferences for media violence, especially on television.

Users of TV for Entertainment

Adults and teenagers were presented with a list of mass media (radio, newspapers, magazines, television, books, movies) and asked which one, if any, they most frequently chose when they wanted to relax and get away from daily tensions. The responses are presented in Table 1.

Table 1 Adult and teen media choices for entertainment or relaxation (in percent)

	ADULT	TEEN
Television	43	32
Books	19	22
Radio	12	26
Magazines	9	6
Newspapers	9	4
Movies	5	9
Other	1	1
None	2	
Total	100	100

Teenagers, in general, choose the electronic media (radio, television, and movies) more than adults. A larger percentage of adults choose television as the mass medium most frequently used for relaxation. Note that these figures do not represent all television users, but only those who prefer television as a method of relaxation.

The same demographic characteristics which best distinguished "violents" in norms for and experience with violence were used to describe groups who choose television.

The demographic subgroup of adults with the highest proportion of its members choosing television for relaxation is composed of adults (no difference between males and females) between the ages of eighteen and thirty-five having less than a college education. Age and education characteristics are the same both for this subgroup and the group of adult "violents."

The demographic group of teenagers with the highest proportion of its members choosing television for relaxation consists of males, between the ages of thirteen and fifteen, who are black. Common characteristics between this subgroup and the teenage "violents" are sex, race, and, to some extent, age.

The Approvers of Television Violence

Twenty-eight percent of the adults said they approved of the kind of violence portrayed on television. The group with the largest proportion approving of television violence is composed of males, from eighteen to thirty-five years of age, residing in metropolitan areas, and having less than a college education. This group contains the largest proportion of adult "violents" in terms of norms and experience with violence.

Fifty-three percent of the teenage respondents approved of the kind of violence portrayed on television. The group with the greatest proportion of approvers is made up of males, between the ages of thirteen and fifteen, living in metropolitan areas, who are black.

There is almost a complete overlap between this group of approvers and teenage "violents" both in terms of norms and experience with violence. Common characteristics are sex, race, and, to a large extent, age and residence.

Persons with a Strong Preference for Media Violence

Adult and teenage respondents were given a series of six paired alternatives, with each pair containing one violent media content choice and one nonviolent choice. For each pair, the respondents were asked to pick the one that they would prefer. An analysis of the choices can be summarized into an index of overall preference for media violence.

Fifteen percent of the adult respondents express high media violence preference.[3] The demographic group with the largest proportion of its members having a high media violence preference consists of males, eighteen to thirty-five years of age, who have less than a college education. This group overlaps with adult "violents" in all respects except residence.

Thirty-three percent of the teenagers have a high media violence preference. The demographic group with the largest proportion of its membership having a high media violence preference consists of males between the ages of thirteen and fifteen. This group overlaps with teen "violents" with regard to sex and, to some extent, age, but not in terms of residence and race.

. . .

[3] A high media violence preference is defined as those persons who select four or more violent alternatives out of the six paired alternatives.

THE ELECTRONIC MEDIA

STUDY QUESTIONS

1. Boorstin says that "the television set has democratized experience." One cannot disagree, in view of the fact that 99 percent of American homes have at least one TV set. But with so many people watching the same few television channels, how can Boorstin claim that television causes segregation and isolation? How does this claim relate to Marshall McLuhan's concept that television has made the world a "global village"?

2. Both Boorstin and Johnson would like television to present individual and personal views, to break audiences into specialized interest groups, or, as Johnson says, to present alternatives to the conspicuous consumption life-style." Is this feasible? What steps have been taken in this direction? What can you as a viewer do to "talk back to your television set," as Johnson suggested in 1970?

3. What are the implications of television's being second only to parents as the most important shaper of the child if, as was reported in **Newsweek,** "the overwhelming body of evidence . . . is decidedly negative"?

4. Why have women been depicted in films as they have been throughout the years? What are some facets of human experience which seem not to have been portrayed on film? Can you give reasons why certain subjects and/or ideas have not been developed in the film medium?

5. One of the concerns Kriss cites is the social impact of cable TV. What problems do you foresee in this regard?

6. What changes or developments does Kirkeby point out as necessary if radio is to be competitive in a media market of "fragmented tastes"?

7. What elements of the America you know do you recognize in country music? Is your America more recognizable in country music than in rock music?

8. What are the implications of the vastness of the common pool of messages and images which television audiences share when one considers the amount and kind of violence depicted on television?

BIBLIOGRAPHY FOR FURTHER STUDY

Arons, Stephen, and Ethan Katch. "How TV Cops Flout the Law." *Saturday Review* (March 19, 1977), 10–18.

Barnouw, Erik. *A History of Broadcasting in the United States: A Tower in Babel, The Golden Web, The Image Empire, Tube of Plenty.* 4 vols. New York: Oxford University Press, 1966, 1968, 1970, 1975.

Bawden, Liz-Anne, ed. *The Oxford Companion to Film.* New York: Oxford University Press, 1976.

Bogart, Leo. *The Age of Television.* 3rd ed. New York: Frederick Ungar Publishing Co., 1972.

Bower, Robert T. *Television and the Public.* New York: Holt, Rinehart and Winston, 1973.

Bright, Hazel V. "TV Versus Black Survival." *Black World* (December, 1973), 30–42.

Brown, Les. *Television: The Business Behind the Box.* New York: Harcourt Brace Jovanovich, 1971.

Casty, Alan. *Development of the Film: An Interpretive History.* New York: Harcourt Brace Jovanovich, 1973.

Cater, Douglass, and Michael J. Nyhan, eds. *The Future of Public Broadcasting.* New York: Praeger Publishers, 1976.

Cooper, B. Lee. "Exploring the Future Through Contemporary Music." *Media & Methods* (April, 1976), 32ff.

Cripps, Thomas. *Slow Fade to Black: The Negro in American Film, 1900–1942.* New York: Oxford University Press, 1977.

Davis, Douglas, and Allison Simmons, eds. *The New Television: A Public/Private Art.* Cambridge, Mass.: The MIT Press, 1977.

Eisen, Jonathan, ed. *The Age of Rock.* New York: Vintage Books, 1969.

Gerbner, G. "Cultural Indicators: The Case of Violence in Television Drama." *Annals of the American Academy of Political and Social Science* 388 (March, 1970), 69–81.

Gross, Larry. "The 'Real' World of Television." *Today's Education* (January/February, 1974), 86ff.

Head, Sydney W. *Broadcasting in America: A Survey of Television and Radio.* Boston: Houghton Mifflin, 1976.

Hendrick, Grant H. "When Television Is a School for Criminals." *TV Guide* (January 29, 1977), 4–10.

Henninger, Daniel. "Violence on Television." *The National Observer* (February 12, 1977), 1, 12.

Hollister, Bernard. "Old-Time Radio: Recapturing Images of the Past." *Media & Methods* (February, 1976), 26ff.

"Image of Women on Television: A Dialogue." *Journal of Broadcasting* (Summer, 1975), 259–309.

Jaffe, David L. "CATV: History and Law." *Educational Broadcasting* (July/August, 1974), 15–17, 34–35.

Johnson, Nicholas. *How to Talk Back to Your Television Set.* New York: Bantam Books, 1970.

———. *Test Pattern for Living.* New York: Bantam Books, 1972.

Jowett, Garth. *Film: The Democratic Art.* Boston: Little, Brown, 1976.

Kauffmann, Stanley. "Blood on the Screen." *The New Republic* (December 25, 1976), 20–21.

Mast, Gerald. *A Short History of the Movies.* 2nd ed. Indianapolis: Bobbs-Merrill, 1976.

McCluskey, Paul. *Movies: Conversations with Peter Bogdanovich.* New York: Harcourt Brace Jovanovich, 1974.

Moody, Kathryn. "Growing Up on TV." *MediaCenter* (October, 1975), 21–23.
"A Nation of Videots: David Sohn Interviews Jerzy Kosinski." *Media & Methods* (April, 1975), 24ff.
Newcomb, Horace, ed. *Television: The Critical View.* New York: Oxford University Press, 1976.
Schillaci, Peter. " 'Roots' on TV: It Touched Us All." *Media & Methods* (April, 1977), 22ff.
Schmidt, Carol. "No Freeze on Radio's Growth." *Educational Broadcasting* (January/February, 1977), 29–32.
Schramm, Wilbur, and Lyle Nelson. "Financing Public TV." *Columbia Journalism Review* 12 (January/February, 1973), 31–38.
"Studies of Five Children's Programs on the CBS Television Network." (1976) Available from: CBS Office of Social Research, 51 West 52 Street, New York, New York 10019.
Tate, Charles, ed. *Cable Television in the Cities: Community Control, Public Access, and Minority Ownership.* Washington, D.C.: The Urban Institute, 1971.
Wagoner, Gary. "The Trouble Is in Your Set: The TV As Homunculus." *Phi Delta Kappan* (November, 1975), 179–84.
Warnock, Thomas. "Public Radio: Taking Off at Last?" *Public Telecommunications Review* (January/February, 1976), 27–31.
Winn, Marie. *The Plug-In Drug.* New York: Grossman/Viking, 1977.
Wood, Michael. "Hollywood's Last Picture Show." *Harper's* (January, 1976), 79–82.

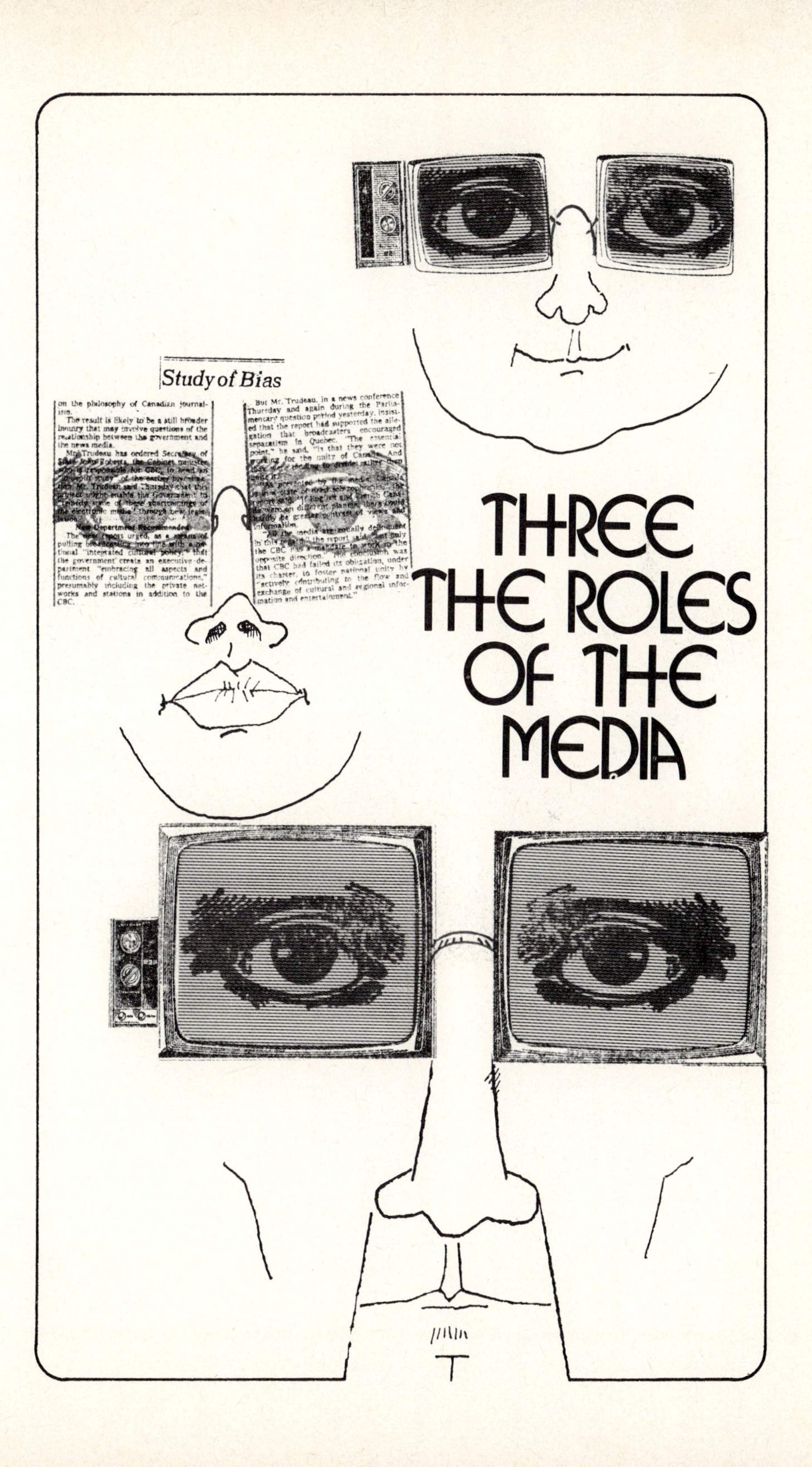

THREE
THE ROLES OF THE MEDIA

While Part 2 looked at the media from the point of view of their technical and physical potential, Part 3 examines them as they perform their basic roles as informers, entertainers, and persuaders. We have a great dependence on the media. C. Wright Mills, a media critic, has claimed: "Very little of what we think we know of the social realities of the world have we found out firsthand. Most of 'the pictures in our heads' we have gained from these media."*

The three media roles are not isolated from one another. Although we will attempt to distinguish the roles for purposes of analysis, they are rarely fully separate. Nor should they be. For instance, without the persuasive function of advertising, many of the media that inform and entertain would cease to exist. This interdependence causes problems, for readers and listeners often fail to differentiate between editorial and advertising content. Pauline Kael has noted: "Television is blurring the distinction for all of us; we don't know what we're reacting to anymore, and, beyond that, it's becoming just about impossible to sort out the con from the truth because a successful con makes its lies come true."†

Any element of a medium may be playing a hidden role as well as its obvious one. While advertising is readily understood to be persuasive, the media content, while on the surface appearing to be entertaining or informative, may also be persuasive. Consider the sports magazine. Some readers would claim that the magazine's role is to entertain, just as the sport itself entertains. Others would maintain that the magazine's most important role is to inform us about amateur and professional sports, which often occupy significant economic and cultural positions in our lives. Both views are legitimate. However, it should be noted that the content of the magazine, while informing and entertaining the reader, is also promoting sports.

The newspaper also illustrates how the three roles are blended. More and more newspapers today present human interest features, leisure time ideas, community action lines, food and decorating hints, some in separate entertainment sections and some alongside the hard news. Perhaps this indicates our desire to be entertained as well as informed. In addition, one can find the generally acknowledged persuasive devices—editorials, columns, and letters—on the editorial page. However, it should be noted that persuasion may also appear in the guise of news. Front-page news stories often advocate a cause or a point of view. For example, an account of the conditions of a minority group may be intended to stimulate corrective measures by a legislative body, or a news story about the President may be the result of his deliberate generation of news in an attempt to change public opinion about a certain issue.

To educated, responsible members of a free society, the media's role as informers is perhaps their most significant one. It is essential that there be

* C. Wright Mills, **The Power Elite** (New York: Oxford University Press, 1956), p. 311.
† Pauline Kael, "Numbing the Audience," **The New Yorker**, XLV (October 3, 1970), 74.

objective reporting of all issues and events. In 1947 the Commission on Freedom of the Press declared:

> Today our society needs, first, a truthful, comprehensive, and intelligent account of the day's events in a context which gives them meaning; second, a forum for the exchange of comment and criticism; third, a means of projecting the opinions and attitudes of the groups in the society to one another; fourth, a method of presenting and clarifying the goals and values of the society; and fifth, a way of reaching every member of the society by the currents of information, thought, and feeling which the press supplies.*

In our present pluralistic society, these ideals are a challenge to the media. Representing the majority is not enough; blacks, radicals, reactionaries, youth, the aged, the poor—all must find their world represented accurately. ABC Correspondent Harry Reasoner has said that we are the best informed mass citizenry in the history of the world†; yet many feel that the media are not successful in informing us about all segments of society.

Because of the variety of media, we are at least well informed in the sense that we are able to obtain many different kinds of information. The type of information provided by a medium is largely determined by its primary function and by the size and nature of its audience. For example, the size of television's audience—55 million viewers for network news shows—requires that it present the news in a broader perspective than that of William Buckley's **National Review** or Jann Wenner's **Rolling Stone.** The media also differ in degree of immediacy. Radio and television can give live coverage of an event, while newspapers can at best reach the public a few hours after the event. Days or weeks intervene between an event and a magazine's reporting of it; yet this delay enables the magazine to present more background information than radio, TV, and newspapers can. However, all media, regardless of their functions and their audience, attempt to provide more than just reports of events.

If a poll were taken, we would probably find that most people think the chief role of the mass media is entertainment. We are a nation of people who want to be entertained. In fact, we generally like to be informed in an entertaining way, as in the magazine format of television news programs like **Sixty Minutes** and in the increasing number of "light touches" on the evening news and even the weather report.

All media entertain to some extent—and entertainment in the media can be anything. It can be reality or fantasy. It can deepen our awareness or it can insulate us from the real world; it can expand our understanding of our fellow

* **A Free and Responsible Press,** Report of the Commission on Freedom of the Press (Chicago. 1947), pp. 20–21.

† Neil Hickey, "An Anchor Man Answers Some Questions," **TV Guide** (March 20, 1971), 7.

humans or it can reinforce our stereotyped opinions. It can be a Marvel comic book or Reed Whitmore's "The Newspeak Generation" in **Harper's** magazine, the "Top 40" or **La Bohème,** Norman Lear's **Mary Hartman, Mary Hartman** or Ingmar Bergman's **Scenes from a Marriage.**

The more homogeneous the audience of a medium is, the greater are the medium's chances of satisfying all members of that audience. Perhaps the central problem faced by the mass media in their role as entertainers is that it is almost impossible to satisfy the tastes of a wide audience. Television, in attempting to make its programs accessible to large masses, is less likely to provide culturally rich experiences than, say, an FM radio station. Moreover, media that are designed for mass audiences are less likely to satisfy the needs of segments of their audience than is, say, **New York** magazine (with its primarily local appeal) or the rock-oriented magazine **Circus** or an underground film.

The final role to consider is that of the media as persuaders. On the one hand, the media can be used to move an audience to a particular belief or action by a persuasive editorial or advertisement. On the other hand, if we think of "persuasion" in its broadest sense, the media can be used to persuade an audience to accept new information. (Here the role of persuasion overlaps the role of "informing through entertainment.") A good illustration of the latter is **Sesame Street,** which uses the persuasive techniques of the television commercial to educate preschool children.

Persuasion can take two forms. The message can be obvious, open, and forceful, as in political speeches or hard-sell advertising for detergents and headache remedies. More important, the persuasive message can be subtle, as in the more sophisticated political commercials or the deliberate use of an inner-city setting on **Sesame Street** to suggest a point of view. Attitudes about such matters as families, morality, religion, technology, work, drugs, minorities, youth, women, politicians, and "cops" are greatly influenced by the way they are treated in the media. Thus it is especially important that any media treatment of such subjects be viewed in the context of the interrelated roles played by the media.

THE INFORMERS

What it's like to broadcast news

by WALTER CRONKITE

CBS anchorman Walter Cronkite defends his profession by citing the unique elements that make up a TV newscast and the difficult demands made on the newscaster's judgment. He holds that TV news reporting has largely positive effects on society and argues for the TV journalist's freedom to report all the news "and let the chips fall where they may."

When Vice President Agnew, in November 1969, unleashed his attack upon the news media, he was following, albeit with unique linguistic and philosophic departures, a long line of predecessors. Somewhere in the history of our Republic there may have been a high government official who said he had been treated fairly by the press, but for the life of me, however, I can't think of one.

Mr. Agnew's attacks, of course, were particularly alarming because of their sustained virulence and intimidating nature. But the Vice President was simply joining the chorus (or, seeing political opportunity, attempting to lead it) of those who have appointed themselves critics of the television medium. Well, I don't like everything I see on television either, but I am frank to say I'm somewhat sick and mighty tired of broadcast journalism being constantly dragged into the operating room and dissected, probed, swabbed, and needled to see what makes it tick.

I'm tired of sociologists, psychologists, pathologists, educators, parents, bureaucrats, politicians, and other special interest groups presuming to tell us what is news or where our responsibilities lie.

Or perhaps I'm phrasing this wrong. It is not those who squeeze us between their slides and hold us under their microscopes with whom my patience has grown short. The society *should* understand the impact of television upon it. There are aspects of it that need study so that the people can cope with an entirely revolutionary means of communication. Those who disagree with our news coverage have every right to criticize. We can hardly claim rights to a free press and free speech while begrudging those rights to our critics. Indeed, that would seem to be what some of them would like to do to us. So believing, it clearly cannot be the responsible critics or serious students of the TV phenomenon with whom I quarrel. I am provoked more by those in our craft who, like wide-eyed country yokels before the pitchman, are losing sight of the pea under the shell.

We must expose the demagogues who would undermine this nation's free media for personal or partisan political gain. That is news. And we should not withhold our cooperation from serious studies of the medium. But we must not permit these matters to divert us from our task, or confuse us as to what that task is.

I don't think it is any of our business what the moral, political, social, or economic effect of our reporting is. I say let's get on with the job of reporting the news—and let the chips fall where they may. I suggest we concentrate on doing our job of telling it like it is and not be diverted from that exalted task by the apoplectic apostles of alliteration.

Now, a fair portion of what we do is not done well. There are things we are not doing that we ought to do. There are challenges that we have not yet fully met. We are a long way from perfection. Our problems are immense, and they are new and unique.

A major problem is imposed by the clock. In an entire half-hour news broadcast we speak only as many words as there are on two-thirds of one page of a standard newspaper. Clearly, the stricture demands tightness of writing and editing, and selection, unknown in any other form of journalism. But look what we do with that time. There are twenty items in an average newscast—some but a paragraph long, true, but all with the essential information to provide at least a guide to our world that day.

"That's the trouble with a truly *enlightened electorate."*

Film clips that, in a way available to no other daily medium, introduce our viewers to the people and the places that make the news; investigative reports (pocket documentaries) that expose weakness in our democratic fabric (not enough of these, but we're coming along), feature film reports that explore the byways of America and assure us that the whole world hasn't turned topsy-turvy; graphics that in a few seconds communicate a great deal of information; clearly identified analysis, or commentary, on the news—I think that is quite a package.

The transient, evanescent quality of our medium—the appearance and disappearance of our words and pictures at almost the same instant—imposes another of our severe problems. Most of us would agree that television's greatest asset is the ability to take the public to the scene—the launch of a spaceship, a Congressional hearing, a political convention, or a disaster (in some cases these are not mutually exclusive). Live coverage of such continuing, developing events presents the radio-television newsman with a challenge unlike any faced by the print reporter. The newspaper legman, rewrite man, and editor meet the pressure of deadlines and must make hard decisions fast and accurately. But multiply their problems and decisions a thousandfold and you scarcely have touched on the problems of the electronic journalist broadcasting live. Even with the most intensive coverage it still is difficult and frequently impossible to get all the facts and get all of them straight as a complex and occasionally violent story is breaking all around. We do have to fill in additional material on subsequent broadcasts, and there is the danger that not all the original audience is there for the fuller explanation.

When a television reporter, in the midst of the riot or the floor demonstration or the disaster, dictates his story, he is not talking to a rewrite man but directly to the audience. There is no editor standing between him and the reader. He will make mistakes, but his quotient for accuracy must be high or he is not long for this world of electronic journalism. We demand a lot of these on-the-scene television reporters. I for one think they are delivering in magnificent fashion.

Directors of an actuality broadcast, like newspaper photo editors, have several pictures displayed on the monitors before them. But they, unlike their print counterparts, do not have ten minutes, or five, or even one minute to select the picture their audience will see. Their decision is made in seconds. Theirs is a totally new craft in journalism, but they have imbued it with all the professionalism and sense of responsibility and integrity of the men of print. Of course we make mistakes, but how few are the errors compared to the fielding chances!

Our profession is encumbered, even as it is liberated, by the tools of our trade. It is a miracle—this transmission of pictures and voices through the air, the ability to take the whole world to the scene of a single event.

But our tools still are somewhat gross. Miniaturization and other developments eventually will solve our problem, but for the moment our cameras and our lights and our tape trucks and even our microphones are obtrusive. It is probably true that their presence can alter an event, and it probably also is true that they alter it even more than the presence of reporters with pad and pencil, although we try to minimize our visibility. But I think we should not be too hasty in adjudging this as always a bad thing. Is it not salutary that the government servant, the politician, the rioter, the miscreant knows that he is operating in the full glare of publicity, that the whole world is watching?

Consider political conventions. They have been a shambles of democratic malfunction since their inception, and printed reports through the years haven't had much effect in reforming them. But now that the voters have been taken to them by television, have sat through the sessions with the delegates and seen the political establishment operate to suppress rather than develop the democratic dialogue, there is a stronger reform movement than ever before, and the chances of success seem brighter.

I would suggest that the same is true of the race rioters and the student demonstrators, whatever the justice of the point they are trying to make. Of course they use television. Hasn't that always been the point of the demonstrator—to attract attention to his cause? But the *excesses* of the militants on ghetto streets and the nation's campuses, shown by television with almost boring repetition, tend to repel rather than enlist support, and this is a lesson I hope and *believe* that rational leaders are learning.

Scarcely anyone would doubt that television news has expanded to an immeasurable degree the knowledge of many people who either cannot or do not read. We have broadened the interests of another sizable group whose newspaper reading is confined to the headlines, sports, and comics. We are going into homes of the untutored, teaching underprivileged and disadvantaged who have never known a book. We are exposing them to a world they scarcely knew existed, and while advertisements and entertainment programming whet their thirst for a way of life they believe beyond them, we show them that there are people and movements, inside and outside the Establishment, that are trying to put the good things within their reach.

Without any intent to foster revolution, by simply doing our job as journalists with ordinary diligence and an extraordinary new medium, we have awakened a sleeping giant. No wonder we have simultaneously aroused the ire of those who are comfortable with the status quo. Many viewers happily settled in their easy chairs under picture windows that frame leafy boughs and flowering bushes and green grass resent our parading the black and bearded, the hungry and unwashed through their living rooms, reminding them that there is another side of America that demands their attention. It is human nature to avoid confronting the unpleasant. No one *wants* to hear that "our boys" are capable of war crimes, that our elected officials are capable of deceit or worse. I think I can safely say that there are few of us who want to report such things. But as professional journalists we have no more discretion in whether to report or not to report when confronted with the facts than does a doctor in deciding to remove a gangrenous limb.

If it *happened,* the people are entitled to know. There is no condition that can be imposed on that dictum without placing a barrier (censorship) between the people and the truth—at once as fallible and corrupt as only self-serving men can make it. The barrier can be built by government—overtly by dictatorship or covertly with propaganda on the political stump, harassment by subpoena, or abuse of the licensing power. Or the barrier can be built by the news media themselves. If we permit our news judgment to be colored by godlike decisions as to what is good for our readers, listeners, or viewers, we are building a barrier—no matter how pure our motives. If we permit friendship with sources to slow our natural reflexes, we also build a barrier. If we lack courage to face the criticism and consequences of our reporting, we build barriers.

But of all barriers that we might put between the people and the truth, the most ill-considered is the one that some would erect to protect their profits. In all media, under our precious free enterprise system, there are those who believe performance can only be measured by circulation or ratings. The newspaper business had its believers long before we were on the scene. They practiced editing by readership survey. Weak-willed but greedy publishers found out what their readers *wanted* to read and gave it to them—a clear abdication of their duties as journalists and, I would submit, a nail in the coffin of newspaper believability.

Today, before the drumfire assault of the hysterical Establishment and the painful complaints of a frightened populace, there are many in our business who believe we should tailor our news reports to console our critics. They would have us report more good news and play down the war, revolution, social disturbance. There certainly is nothing wrong with good news. In fact, by some people's lights we report quite a lot of it: an anti-pollution bill through Congress, a report that the cost of living isn't going up as fast as it was last month, settlement of a labor dispute, the announcement of a medical breakthrough, plans for a new downtown building. There isn't anything wrong either with the stories that tell us what is right about America, that remind us that the virtues that made this nation strong still exist and prosper despite the turmoil of change.

But when "give us the good news" becomes a euphemism for "don't give us so much of that bad news"—and in our business one frequently means the other—the danger signal must be hoisted.

It is possible that some news editors have enough time allotted by their managements to cover all the significant news of their areas—much of it, presumably, in the "bad" category—and still have time left over for a "good news" item or two. But for many and certainly those at the network level, that is not the case. To crowd in the "happy" stories would mean crowding out material of significance. Some good-news advocates know this, and it is precisely what they want: to suppress the story of our changing society in the hope that if one ignores evil it will go away.

Others simply are tired of the constant strife. They would like a little relief from the daily budget of trouble that reminds them of the hard decisions they as citizens must face. But can't they see that pandering to the innocent seeking relief is to yield to those who would twist public opinion to control our destiny?

It is no coincidence that these manipulative methods parallel those adopted half a century ago by Russian revolutionaries also seeking the surest means to bend the population to their will. You will not find bad news in Russian newspapers or on broadcast media. There are no reports of riots, disturbances of public order, muggings or murders, train, plane, or auto wrecks. There are no manifestations of race prejudice, disciplinary problems in army ranks. There is no exposure of malfeasance in public office—other than that which the government chooses to exploit for its own political purposes. There is no dissent over national policy, no argument about the latest weapons system.

There is a lot of good news—factories making their quotas, happy life on the collective farm, successes of Soviet diplomacy, difficulties in the United States. The system works. Without free media—acerbic, muckraking, irreverent—the Soviet people are placid drones and the Soviet Establishment runs the country the way it wants it run.

Since it is hard to know the real motives in others' minds—indeed, it is hard sometimes to know our own motives—and since few are likely to admit that they would seek to suppress dissent from Establishment norms, it would be wrong to ascribe such Machiavellian connivance to the good-news advocates. The only trouble is that the other, more likely motive—profiting from the news by pandering to public taste—is almost as frightening. To seek the public's favor by presenting the news it wants to hear is to fail to understand the function of the media in a democracy. We are not in the business of winning popularity contests, and we are not in the entertainment business. It is not our job to please anyone except Diogenes.

The newsman's purpose is contrary to the goal of almost everyone else who shares the airwaves with us, and perhaps we should not be too harsh with those executives with the ultimate responsibility for station and network management. We are asking a great deal of them. For seventeen of the eighteen hours during an average broadcast day their job is to win friends and audience. They and we live on how successfully they do this difficult job.

But then we ask them to turn a deaf ear to the complaints of those dissatisfied with what we present in the remaining minutes of the day. We ask them to be professionally schizoid—and that would seem to be a lot to ask. But is it, really? After all, in another sense, as journalists we live this life of dual personality. There is not a man who can truthfully say that he does not harbor in his breast prejudice, bias, strong sentiments pro and con on some if not all the issues of the day.

Yet it is the distinguishing mark of the professional journalist that he can set aside these personal opinions in reporting the day's news. None of us succeeds in this task in all instances, but we know the assignment and the pitfalls, and we succeed far more often than we fail or than our critics would acknowledge. We have a missionary duty to try to teach this basic precept of our craft to those of our bosses who have not yet learned it. We in broadcasting, at least, cannot survive as a major news medium if we fail.

We were well on the way before the current wave of politically inspired criticism. In my twenty years in broadcasting I have seen more and more station owners taking courage from their news editors, tasting the heady fruit of respect that can be won by the fearless conveyer of the truth. Some years ago William Allen White wrote that "nothing fails so miserably as a cowardly newspaper." I suspect he spoke not only of commercial failure but of the greater failure: not winning the confidence of the people. A radio or television station also can fail this test of courage, and when it does its owner wins not a community's respect and gratitude but its contempt.

Broadcast management is going to need a stiff backbone in the days ahead—not only for its own well-being but for the good of us all. We are teetering on the brink of a communications crisis that could undermine the foundation of our democracy that is a free and responsible press. We all know the present economic background. We in radio and television with our greater impact and our numerous outlets have forced many of our print competitors out of business. It is a rare American city today that has more than one newspaper. And yet I think most of us will acknowledge that we are not an adequate substitute for the newspapers whose demise we have hastened. We cannot supply the wealth of detail the informed citizen needs to judge the performance of his city, county, or state. If we do our jobs thoroughly, however, we can be a superb monitor over the monopoly newspaper, assuring that it does not by plot, caprice, or inadvertence miss a major story.

We *can* be, that is, if we are left alone to perform that essential journalistic function. The trouble is that broadcast media are not free; they are government licensed. The power to make us conform is too great to lie forever dormant. The ax lies there temptingly for use by any enraged administration, Republican, Democrat, or Wallaceite. We are at the mercy of the whim of politicians and bureaucrats, and whether they choose to chop us down or not, the mere existence of their power is an intimidating and constraining threat.

So on one side there is a monopoly press that may or may not choose to present views other than those of the domineering majority, on the other side a vigorously competitive but federally regulated broadcast industry, most of whose time is spent currying popular—that is, majority—favor. This scarcely could be called a healthy situation. There is a real danger that the free flow of ideas, the vitality of minority views, even the dissent of recognized authorities could be stifled in such an atmosphere.

We newsmen, dedicated as we are to freedom of press and speech and the presentation of all viewpoints no matter how unpopular, must work together, regardless of our medium, to clear the air while there is still time. We must resist every new attempt at government control, intimidation, or harassment. And we must fight tenaciously to win through Congress and the courts guarantees that will free us forever from the present restrictions. We must stand together and bring the power of our professional organizations to bear against those publishers and broadcast managers who fail to understand the function of a free press. We must keep our own escutcheons so clean that no one who would challenge our integrity could hope to succeed.

If we do these things, we can preserve, and re-establish where it has faded, the confidence of the people whose freedom is so indivisibly linked with ours.

Trends in Attitudes Toward Television and Other Media: An Eighteen-Year Review

by BURNS W. ROPER

This report, based on 2,000 interviews with Americans aged eighteen and older conducted in November-December 1976, considers shifts over an eighteen-year period in the public's opinion about the various news media as sources of information.

This series of studies, begun in 1959, has shown television increasingly becoming the dominant medium in people's lives. From a secondary position in 1959, television moved almost steadily upward in public regard and approval of its programming. After assuming a leading position in 1963, television steadily increased its lead in successive years, reaching a record high in 1974. This 1976 study shows television essentially in a holding position on levels of approval in the various comparative measurements.

The progress shown for television has been made during a period of turbulence and change in all aspects of American life. Today's lifestyles, social mores and customs are far different from those of 1959—mostly because of upheavals that occurred during the sixties. The seventies presented problems in different areas. There was the trauma of ending the Vietnam War, quickly followed by Watergate and the resignation of President Nixon. Gerald Ford's ascendency to the Presidency brought a brief surge of optimism that was soon ended by increasing inflation and a recession that threatened to develop into a true depression. The public reacted with increasing cynicism and skepticism toward leadership and institutions, with increased demands for consumer protection and with increasing apprehension regarding the future.

Trends in Attitudes Toward Television and Other Media: An Eighteen-Year Review: From *Changing Public Attitudes Toward Television and Other Mass Media 1959–1976,* a report by the Television Information Office. Reprinted by permission.

Now, however, other of our current studies show the tide of public confidence sharply on the rise. With signs of economic recovery, the public is beginning to show a more favorable attitude towards the institutions of society and a measurably more hopeful attitude about the future.

During these years, television has proved itself successful not only in meeting the challenges presented by demands for keeping up with changing times, but in providing services and entertainment of a caliber recognized by the public as essential to modern life. Entering what may be a new era in America, television is in a unique position to be an effective force in meeting the needs of the future.

At the same time there appears to be a slight weakening of support for the commercial system on which television is based and heightened sentiment for government control of programs. But these changes should be assessed in the context of the fact that approval of the commercial system still heavily outweighs disapproval, and respondents who want less government control of programs substantially outnumber those who want more.

The current study was almost equally divided between trend questions asked in past studies and questions asked for the first time.

Analysis of the results shows television holding its leading position with the American public. The public continues to regard television as the number one source of news, and by a wide margin. Television also continues to be the most believable medium. And as mentioned earlier, the public still largely rejects government regulation of TV programming, generally approves of the programming it gets on TV, and endorses the commercial system. The current study, however, shows some signs that the public is beginning to reflect or share increased special interest group criticism of program content and of the commercials that support them. This is particularly true with regard to children's programs and the commercials in them, a frequent target in recent years.

Source of News

Since the first study in 1959, all questions comparing the various media have been asked ahead of those questions that specifically focus on television, in order to avoid bias.

The first question in each study has asked people where they get most of their news. Television, which has led all other media on this question since 1963, continues to hold a sizeable lead, 15 points, over the second place medium—the widest ever except in 1974.

"First, I'd like to ask you where you usually get most of your news about what's going on in the world today—from the newspapers or radio or television or magazines or talking to people or where?"

Source of most news:	12/59 %	11/61 %	11/63 %	11/64 %	1/67 %	11/68 %	1/71 %	11/72 %	11/74 %	11/76 %
Television	51	52	55	58	64	59	60	64	65	64
Newspapers	57	57	53	56	55	49	48	50	47	49
Radio	34	34	29	26	28	25	23	21	21	19
Magazines	8	9	6	8	7	7	5	6	4	7
People	4	5	4	5	4	5	4	4	4	5
All mentions	154	157	147	153	158	145	140	145	141	144
Don't know or no answer (DK/NA)	1	3	3	3	2	3	1	1	-	-

Until 1972, newspapers had led television as the main source of news among the college educated. Since then, the two media have been almost even, with newspapers ahead by 2 points in 1972, television ahead by one point in 1974, and newspapers ahead by one point this year—58% to 57%.

Analysis of multiple responses:	12/59 %	11/61 %	11/63 %	11/64 %	1/67 %	11/68 %	1/71 %	11/72 %	11/74 %	11/76 %
TV only	19	18	23	23	25	29	31	33	36	36
N'pers only	21	19	21	20	18	19	21	19	19	21
Both n'pers and TV (with or without other media)	26	27	24	28	30	25	22	26	23	23
N'pers and other media but not TV	10	11	8	8	7	6	5	5	4	4
TV and other media but not n'pers	6	7	8	6	8	5	7	5	6	5
Media other than TV or n'pers	17	15	13	12	10	13	13	12	12	11
DK/NA	1	3	3	3	2	3	1	-	-	-

In all studies multiple answers have been accepted when people have named more than one medium. Analysis of multiple responses showed television steadily increasing its lead as the single most-relied-upon medium up to 1974, with well over one-third mentioning only television in that year, and the same percentage again naming it alone this year.

The Relative Credibility of Media

Since 1961, television has led as the most believable news medium, and in 1968 reached a two-to-one advantage over newspapers. By 1974, it had widened its margin over newspapers to a two-and-a-half-to-one advantage. This study shows it holding that lead by almost the same margin.

"If you got conflicting or different reports of the same news story from radio, television, the magazines and the newspapers, which of the four versions would you be most inclined to believe—the one on radio or television or magazines or newspapers?"

Most believable:	12/59 %	11/61 %	11/63 %	11/64 %	1/67 %	11/68 %	1/71 %	11/72 %	11/74 %	11/76 %
Television	29	39	36	41	41	44	49	48	51	51
Newspapers	32	24	24	23	24	21	20	21	20	22
Radio	12	12	12	8	7	8	10	8	8	7
Magazines	10	10	10	10	8	11	9	10	8	9
DK/NA	17	17	18	18	20	16	12	13	13	11

Trends in Hours of Viewing

Television viewing increased steadily between 1961, when we first asked about the amount of time individuals spent viewing television, and 1974 when it reached 3:02 hours daily. This year, viewing for the total sample, but not all sub-samples, shows a drop-off from 1974, to 2:53 hours. However, it appears that respondent perceptions in 1974 may have been distorted by events in that year (Nixon resigning, Ford assuming the Presidency, etc.). If the progression in amount of viewing time is looked at omitting 1974, the 1976 figure appears to be in line with the more gradual rise in time spent with television reflected in more precise measurements of this dimension of television usage, e.g., the A.C. Nielsen Company's reports.

While answers to this question are subject to respondents' reporting error, the trend results are meaningful, even if the absolute responses may be somewhat off the mark.

"On an average day, about how many hours do you personally spend watching TV?"

	11/61	11/63	11/64	1/67	11/68	1/71	11/72	11/74	11/76
Median hours of viewing	2:17	2:34	2:38	2:41	2:47	2:50	2:50	3:02	2:53

Television viewing by the college educated, while consistently below the national average each year, has been steadily increasing since 1961, except for a drop-off in 1972. There was a marked increase in viewing in 1974, however, which has held up this year. Reported television viewing has shown a similar pattern among the upper economic groups, although there is lower reported viewing this year than in the abnormally high 1974 period.

Median reported hours of viewing by:	11/61	11/64	1/67	11/68	1/71	11/72	11/74	11/76
College educated	1:48	2:04	2:10	2:17	2:19	2:12	2:23	2:24
Upper economic levels	2:02	2:14	2:21	2:24	2:30	2:29	2:47	2:40

Jane Pauley

Marilyn Berger

Renée Pouissant

Lesley Stahl

A New Visibility for Women in Television News

ENG 'Live' news from almost anywhere

by PHILLIP O. KEIRSTEAD

ENG, Electronic News Gathering, although it may complicate the news reporter's routine, is a giant step forward in giving television news a currency which had previously been limited to radio.

The revolution in the nation's television newsrooms has nothing to do with labor disputes or the Bicentennial. The revolution is electronic. Film is out, electronic is in.

Portable videotape, long the erratic toy of the television industry, has come of age. All of a sudden the electronic studio camera has a little brother, wandering around town, providing nearly instant color coverage of the day's news. Portable videotape, small color cameras and microwave have been combined into a potent competitive package for television news coverage.

The revolution is called electronic newsgathering, or ENG. (The networks, to forge their own identities, have adopted their own terminology, such as electronic camera coverage or electronic journalism, but ENG is the generic term.)

ENG came into being partly through a basic dissatisfaction with film which was costly and slow in relation to the needs of modern television news departments. These stations chafed at being restricted to newspaper-like deadlines while radio stations were developing a highly flexible approach to covering up-to-the-minute news.

ENG: 'Live' News from Almost Anywhere: From *The Quill* (May 1976). Reprinted by permission of *The Quill,* published by The Society of Professional Journalists, Sigma Delta Chi.

In the early days, television stations simply adapted Hollywood film techniques. A smaller frame film (16mm) was adopted later to cut down on the bulk associated with Hollywood's 35mm equipment. Eventually, what is called reversal film was developed, eliminating any need for waiting to make a separate print.

But even in taking giant strides toward top quality in the manufacture of low-light-level film and the development of color, television stations still had to cope with an old bugaboo—artificial lighting. The need for added light meant more equipment, and more time consumed in setting up.

For many years news directors watched the production staff put together slick commercials using the studio videotape machine. And on weekends they would watch the miraculous live coverage of sporting events on network television. But how do you get the cumbersome equipment used by both groups to perform for news purposes?

You miniaturize it.

As the electronics industry moved further in this direction, various groups began experimenting with the newly developed miniature videotape recorder. Originally the marketing moguls thought their product would find its best reception for use in people's homes. But the new equipment, and some equally portable cameras, stimulated interest among media people who prepared materials for classrooms and business seminars. And then the educational TV folks began to experiment, doing some interesting work on machines inadequate for continuous broadcast use.

Commercial TV stations adapted some of the machines to specific applications, but for the most part the pictures weren't consistently up to broadcast standards. For a long time, the machines didn't even produce adequate color pictures.

But, ever on the mind of the broadcaster was a compelling force—the political conventions. All three major networks had been working at miniaturization of their convention equipment. The idea was to put a correspondent on the floor, backed up by a live television camera, without the problems of weight or being tied to heavy cables which were normal at the time.

New and sophisticated equipment was developed, including high-quality portable cameras. Videotape machines were brought up to standards, and ways were found to use lighter cables or totally eliminate cables by using short-range transmitters.

The switch to electronic news gathering began in earnest after the 1972 political season.

One of the leaders in the transition was KMOX-TV in St. Louis. As early as 1973 KMOX-TV was using portable cameras and videotape.

The original equipment did not meet the station's exacting demands. Newer components developed in conjunction with CBS engineers were brought into the system, and in September, 1974, KMOX-TV took a bold step into the total electronic age, abandoning the use of film for news coverage.

The first steps were faltering. Everyone concerned with the news operation had to learn how to deal with this new technology. The newsroom was completely remodeled to concentrate work areas around the various functions, such as a news coordinator's desk, the editing booths and the technical area where air-quality tapes were recorded and assembled.

Among the early problems was the fear of editing videotape, a tradition dating back to when editing videotape was a technician's nightmare.

With the preliminary kinks soon worked out, KMOX-TV was producing sophisticated news reports and even mini-documentaries on tape.

Around the country news directors are reporting significant changes in their operations as a result of electronic newsgathering. As story counts go up, old-fashioned deadlines go out the window. In fact, in some markets it's almost routine for stations to go on the air without having the newscast "locked up." Late-breaking stories can be inserted confidently.

Relieving the Pressures

ENG planners cite three reasons for the big switch: immediacy, productivity and economy. Immediacy is greatest when a station is equipped to go live. But even a station which uses only recording equipment can reduce deadlines. Productivity comes from the elimination of transportation and processing time for fully equipped stations, and elimination of processing time for less well-equipped stations. Even where a station does not have live capability, a reporter can review an interview while riding back to the station. More time is saved back at the newsroom.

A productive day in the newsroom can be leveled out. Normally things start slowly and accelerate until a total crunch hits in the late afternoon as everyone frantically tries to view, edit and write at the same time. With ENG, some of this deadline pressure is relieved.

It costs significantly more to set up a full-fledged ENG operation as opposed to moving into film. But from then on, ENG spells significant savings. Tape is vastly cheaper than film because it is reusable. Tape means there are no chemicals to be purchased. There are additional savings in labor costs. KMOX-TV finds that the cost of gathering, editing and broadcasting a single story using ENG is 57 per cent of the cost of producing the same story on film.

However, there are philosophic considerations at work. From the reporter's viewpoint there is now the spectre of big brother looking over one's shoulder during the newsgathering process. In the case of ENG stations which use microwave to transmit the television picture directly back to the newsroom, it is possible for anyone in the newsroom to watch an interview in progress, and make suggestions as to how it is conducted. On the positive side, this means when a camera angle doesn't look right, it can be corrected. And if there is some new information, or an added question to be asked, the reporter can be reached while he still has the interviewee available.

Of course, there is also the possibility that the reporter and the editor will disagree on how to conduct the interview. Some reporters decry this as interference when their editors do not know the details of the story.

Regardless of one's viewpoint, the inherent problems of centralized control will exist. A vindictive editor could easily destroy a reporter, and a lazy reporter could shift too much of the burden of reportorial judgment on the editor. There is no use lamenting the change wrought by technology. It is here, and must be dealt with responsibly.

Graphic Disaster Coverage

Another philosophic debate arose after the crash last year of an Eastern Airlines plane at New York's Kennedy Airport.

It was late afternoon. Ordinarily the distant location plus rush-hour traffic would have prevented transportation of film to Manhattan television studios in time for the early evening news. However, one metropolitan station had an ENG unit working fairly close to the airport. The crew was told to go there and set up for immediate live coverage. Within a few minutes the station was able to show live pictures of the burning aircraft as well as efforts to rescue the injured and remove the dead.

Some critics have felt that the live coverage of the burning aircraft and the rescue and recovery operation was just too graphic for a suppertime audience.

Such debate has gone on for some time, pointing up that the use of ENG can call for some tough, fast, editorial and managerial decisions—the type that are often tempered by community attitudes and the competitiveness of local media.

ENG is changing television news from a feature medium to a spot news medium. The evening news is becoming more than a summary of events which took place earlier in the day. It is now possible to be Johnny-on-the-spot, if the nature of a news event warrants, to break into regular programming live with minimal notice.

One station has even experimented with two-way audience participation within its newcasts. One evening, the station dispatched ENG mobile units to suburban locations. People gathered at these locations were given a chance to question a panel of experts seated in the station's studio.

Just how extensive is ENG? Some sources estimate there may be more than 400 ENG-equipped stations. That's a pretty impressive figure when one considers that ENG has only been moving full force since 1973 and the total number of commercial television stations in the country is just over 700. Relatively few educational stations make comparable use of ENG equipment, preferring to apply it to their documentary and public affairs programming.

Our City Council Is Meeting

You and I, hypothetically for the moment, are preparing for tonight's coverage.

"Do we want to be featured in a TV news segment about the collapse of the middle class?"

A public clash is anticipated at this evening's city council session between two council members who have widely divergent views on acceptance of a new elementary school building. A councilman in whose district the school is being built is anxious to see the building accepted, thus quieting pressure he's been feeling from parents whose children are currently being transported to a more distant school. A councilwoman says the school building should not be accepted because, in her view, the building has structural deficiencies which threaten the children's safety.

It's decided that our television station will do an advance piece for the

6 o'clock news and then follow with what happens at the meeting on the 11 o'clock news.

We've already secured appointments to interview the two council members. The councilwoman will be available at 11 this morning and the councilman at 2 this afternoon. So far, no one representing the construction company is willing to go on record, but we have secured permission to shoot visuals at the building site.

First, how might we handle this assignment as a film story? We'll go by the school and shoot some film of the structure, including parts of the building described to us as being hazardous or inadequate.

Then, on to the our first interview. We carry in the sound camera, tripod, equipment box and light box and set up. Of course the time needed varies with the individual setup, but let's say it takes us 10 to 15 minutes. The interview isn't very long, so we finish without having to stop to reload film. But once we get back to the mobile unit, we must pause and reload, because we can't afford to run out of film on the second interview. While we're reloading, the assignment editor radios us and says there's a demonstration under way on the plaza in front of City Hall. We drive over, shoot a little covering film and set up for a couple of quick interviews. But, we're helpless. There's no way we can get this story on the noon news. So we quickly radio back some basic details so a writer can insert into the newscast an accurate description of what is going on.

At this point it's 12:45. We clean up from the City Hall demonstration and reload. Now, we make a flying trip back to the station, drop off the morning film for processing and head for lunch and our next interview.

The second interview is routine and we're back at the newsroom by 3 o'clock. The second batch of film goes to the processing room. We view the first batch and begin scripting our story. The story is fairly well blocked out when the phone rings. A contact tells us that the contractor on the school job has capitulated and is going to agree to make certain modifications when he appears at tonight's meeting. We call the contractor and confirm the story. Again we're helpless. There's just too much film in the shop right now to bust out a crew and go shoot even a quick interview and try to get it onto the early news.

The ENG Way

What if we had been using electronic news gathering equipment? Rather than being film-oriented, our station has gone all the way and invested in equipment to relay a signal from the mobile van directly to the studios by microwave.

At the school site, we would take the camera and the portable videotape recorder and shoot exterior and interior shots of the building. We would activate a microwave dish on top of the van, open communications with the studio and adjust the microwave signal for best quality. Then the tape from the school site would be transmitted back to the station. Due to the nature of the school construction site, we used a camera with its recorder attached instead of running a cable back to the truck or using a low-power transmitter. The flexibility of ENG is already apparent.

As we feed, the executive news coordinator, the 6 o'clock news producer and a writer all view the incoming pictures.

We then go on to our morning interview.

We have two options: carry the portable videotape machine into the building or use a small electronic relay placed on an office windowsill and aimed at the van. We take the latter option. Our setup time, including focusing the electronic relay, is only five minutes.

If we had brought the videotape recorder, the setup time could have been as little as one minute. We work without lights because our camera is very sensitive, even at low light levels. In fact, we can shoot at night on some brightly lighted downtown streets.

We decide to do a direct relay from the van to the studios. As we're doing the interview, the news coordinator, producer and writer can see what's taking place. The whole interview is recorded on videotape at the studios so that editing can begin, using the school site tape and the first of the two interviews.

During the interview, the producer suggests a question we have overlooked and we tag it on the end. The news coordinator comments on our camera angle and fills us in on a recent comment made by the opposing council member.

Once we return to the mobile van, we're ready to move on. There's a quick conference with the newsroom to discuss the parts of the interview that seemed best to us. At this point better than half of the piece is done and has been roughly edited. It isn't yet noon.

We get the call about the City Hall demonstration. We pull up to a preselected spot we know is good for live transmissions, set up and do a live cut-in for the top of the noon news. We show scenes of the demonstration and do an interview with its leader. We scramble upstairs to the mayor's office, set up the window-ledge transmitter, and do a second cut-in toward the end of the news. The cut-in begins with a replay of scenes of the demonstration which we transmitted earlier, followed by an interview with the mayor in his office and an on-camera close by our reporter.

We then shoot a little more tape to make sure we can vary the visuals for tonight's 6 o'clock news. There's still time to talk with the newsroom more about this story. The demonstration is part of a long-running protest. No particular followup is needed right now, so a writer goes to work reediting the material we fed into a piece for the evening news.

We have lunch and do our second interview. We're back at the newsroom at 3 and can begin viewing the material immediately, including a rough cut of the opening portion already prepared by a writer. We have the whole story locked up and approved by the producer by 3:30. Then the phone rings and we get our tip about the contractor. Hit the intercom and ask the news coordinator if it's possible to do an interview. Yes, we have another crew on the road and if you'll just radio some questions to the reporter we can insert an interview with the contractor into the piece. By 5 o'clock everything is wrapped up and the segment is completed and transferred to standard tape for airing in the early news. We then go to an editing booth and rerun some of the tape from the construction site and set up a rough cut for the late news. We'll set up for live transmission from the council chambers this evening, but this way we'll have some covering visuals ready if we need them.

When it gets to covering the council meeting, ENG wins again. With film, we have to break out before the debate is over and rush back to the studios to process our film. With ENG, we feed the whole thing back live, including the reporter's open, close and narration. The piece is finished comfortably by 10:30 for our 11 p.m. show.

Toward Totally 'Live'

Reporters working with ENG find it a mixed blessing. They like being able to review interviews and plan cuts and scripting as the day goes on, rather than face a crushing deadline in late afternoon. Also, some of the limitations of film are removed, such as the frequent film changes that ordinarily must be made.

However, now there is a greater potential for "bugs" of other kinds. And the reporter must be more flexible than before. One may have to go from coverage of a city council dispute to a demonstration on very short notice, and be able to stand before a live camera and do a convincing professional presentation with no chance for retakes.

On balance, television news appears to be more than pleased to erase old frustrations. ENG is on its way to maximum acceptance.

Newspapers May One Day Let You

PICK THE NEWS YOU WANT

by MICHAEL T. MALLOY

In this **National Observer** article, Michael T. Malloy cites evidence that newspapers—in their attempt to serve the public and to secure a greater share of the print media audience—may have to follow the specialization trend of magazines. (See John Peter, pp. 35–44.)

One of these mornings the newspaper delivered to your doorstep may be different from the one that lands on your neighbor's. Both papers may roll off the same presses, call themselves the Daily Bugle, and be delivered by the same carrier. But your neighbor the tennis buff may get more tennis news than you do, the professor down the block may get more world affairs, and the housewife who shops but doesn't read may get just the advertising.

"I suspect [papers may distribute] maybe 5 or 6—or 20 or 25—different kinds of supplements on different subjects at different time intervals," speculates Ronald Semple, an executive with the Lee Enterprises chain of newspapers. "Most daily newspapers now throw away about 70 to 90 per cent of the information they receive. They have production capacity they never had before. And they have readers with tremendous interests they never served before, because the newspaper was a hybrid product of Everyman, and Everyman does not exist."

A newspaper custom-designed for Everyman's component parts could be the ultimate result of experiments by publishers who fear that Americans, especially young Americans, are being weaned from the newspaper habit. Though it grates on many an editor's ear, executive-suite conversation in some publishing empires is now laced with such Madison Avenue terms as "market segmentation" and "psychographics." They are "marketing a product" instead of "selling a newspaper."

"The trend is away from publishing newspapers for other journalists, to win prizes, and more toward publishing a newspaper for the readers," says Robert G. Marbut, president of the Harte-Hanks chain of newspapers, which some analysts consider among the most innovative in the business. "Somewhere along the line we've got to ask the question, What do consumers in my market want? If I can give it to them when they want it, the way they want it, I have found a niche."

This is a new kind of talk in the tradition-encrusted newspaper business. But it is becoming more common as more and more newspapermen begin to fear they are losing their grip on the reading audience.

Sales of daily newspapers have lagged well behind population growth since at least 1950. The American population has grown almost 40 per cent since then; newspaper circulation, only 15 per cent. More important, perhaps, the trend toward smaller families and "singles" living has increased the number of American households even faster than the population. And this suggests to some that newspapers are losing their edge as the best way for advertisers—who provide most newspaper profits—to saturate a community's homes with their messages. In 1950 more than 1.2 newspapers were sold for each household in the United States. By 1974 it was only 0.89 newspapers per household.

The relative decline in circulation of daily newspapers, and their absolute decline in "household penetration," has been accompanied by a growth of other printed media that duplicate one of the local daily's functions, but often better:

- Almost 20 million copies of TV Guide are sold each week, although newspapers run their own TV logs.
- Circulation of The Wall Street Journal rose to 1,406,000 from 888,000 in the last decade, although the dailies have their own business pages and stockmarket reports.
- Neighborhood and suburban papers flourish in the shadows of the big dailies, which cannot cover all the local events in their circulation areas.
- City magazines, such as New York and the Washingtonian, duplicate the dailies' where-to-go and what-to-do columns.
- The underground press apparently satisfies the young and the anti-Establishment better than some local dailies.
- People magazine and four celebrity-oriented tabloids headed by the National Enquirer have a combined circulation of around eight million, although daily newspapers also supposedly know that "names make news."
- And advertisers, trying to penetrate the growing number of households that dailies don't seem to reach, have given more business to an explosion of "shoppers" and advertising sheets, whose number has grown to 15,000 today from 6,000 in 1960.

Nonetheless, most of the nation's 1,768 daily newspapers are thriving. Some newspaper chains make a profit of 33 cents on the dollar; the pretax average reported for the industry through most of last year was 16 or 17 cents, much better than for American business in general.

Despite the recession, newspaper profits and advertising revenue continued to rise last year. And surveys dating back to 1957 show little change

THE WIZARD OF ID by permission of Johnny Hart and Field Enterprises, Inc.

in the proportion of adults—at least 70 per cent—who read a newspaper daily. "A look at major trends—economic, social, demographic, life-style, whatever—all point to a nice future for newspaper readers, advertisers, and stockholders," wrote Thurman R. Pierce, Jr., vice president for print media at the J. Walter Thompson advertising agency, in Advertising Age.

Deliberate Circulation Cuts

The circulation decline turned from relative to absolute in 1974, dropping to 61.9 million from 63.1 million in 1973. But so many newspapers sharply raised their prices in 1974 that the small size of this decline is considered by some to be a sign of reader loyalty. Indeed, newspapers engineered some of the decline themselves, to save newsprint and distribution costs by cutting off "ego circulation" in outlying areas of little interest to their advertisers.

The long-term decline in circulation-per-household may well be related to the competition of television and other leisure activities. But it is not as simple as the popular image of a "television oriented" generation abandoning the printed word.

On the contrary, sales of books and magazines have substantially increased over the years, and young people are heavy readers of both. A recent survey for the Newspaper Advertising Bureau found that newspaper readership was almost precisely the same among light, medium and heavy TV viewers. And the more persons watched TV news, the more likely they were to be regular newspaper readers. So rather than blaming television for the long-term circulation weakness, some analysts find its cause in two other areas.

'A Lot to Look Forward To'

First, much of the drop apparently is caused by families taking one newspaper instead of two. Second, the baby boom of the 1940s and '50s gave the American population a disproportionate "bulge" in the younger age groups. "I've been active here about 30 years, and we never have been big [among] young people, young singles, or even young marrieds," is the widely held view expressed by J. Robert Hudson, vice president for marketing at the Des Moines, Iowa, Register and Tribune. "We really come into the household about age 30; we're traditionally strongest between age 30 and 60. The postwar baby crop is just coming into that bracket. I think newspapers have a lot to look forward to."

But many newspapermen are not so sure that young people will follow the same road their parents did: establishing families, buying homes, putting down roots, and developing the interest in community affairs that translates into high newspaper readership. Economic trends may compel a high proportion of these people to remain apartment dwellers, which usually means high mobility and lack of involvement in community affairs. Marbut has noted that by 1973, multiple-unit dwellings had risen to 42 per cent of all housing starts.

'Segmented Marketing'

"The more people you have living in apartments, the harder it is to reach them with a sales message," says Robert Hudson. "Or collect from them. It's a nightmare for the carrier. At any one time, he'll probably not find more than 30 or 40 per cent of the people are home."

"To get those young readers, either they are going to have to change as they grow older, or we are going to have to do something different than we are doing today," says Edward H. Harte, publisher of the two Harte-Hanks newspapers located in Corpus Christi, Texas. "Maybe we will end up with a different product for people who live in apartments," says Marbut.

That would be what Don Nizen, the New York Times' director of circulation, calls "segmented marketing." Radio stations already do it, aiming at a rock, country, or news audience, and ignoring the rest of the market. The daily New York Times reaches only 11 per cent of the homes in New York City, but it reaches 40 per cent—and the Sunday Times 93 per cent —of the high-income, well-educated families that advertisers look for.

But segmentation is no answer for the typical daily newspaper, whose profits depend on its ability to bring an advertiser's message into the overwhelming majority of homes in his marketing area. The goal is to increase that "household penetration" by appealing to new audiences that don't now read newspapers, without turning off old audiences that do. The Harte-Hanks newspapers are trying at least three approaches to this.

One common method is to segment the audience geographically; in Massachusetts, Marbut says, his company's South Middlesex News is "zoned" into seven geographical editions that amount to community dailies.

In Corpus Christi, Harte-Hanks is trying a second approach: an effort to define its morning Caller and evening Times as two different "products" aimed at two different audiences. The Times doesn't try to compete with the TV evening news by warming up stories that already appeared in the morning paper, as many afternoon papers do. Instead it leans heavily on utilitarian articles of the how-to, where-to, what-it-means-to-you variety and entertainment news.

'A Middle Ground'

There may be a trend here. The afternoon Louisville (Ky.) Times and Huntington (W.Va.) Advertiser were recast along similar lines last year in the hope of broadening their audiences. The Louisville paper built on a more audacious experiment made five years ago, when just the Saturday edition was redesigned for people who don't usually read newspapers.

The editors dropped the editorial page and slashed news content. They added astrology and car columns, a "where-to-go-and-what-to-do" magazine, and packaged it with the television logs. Sales of the Saturday edition now outsell the weekday Times, which is unusual. A spokesman says it is reaching people who don't buy newspapers any other day of the week and is "a middle ground between television and people who don't read at all."

In a third approach, the Corpus Christi papers have also broadened their advertising reach into a new market segment with a "Pennysaver" advertising supplement. It is enclosed in the daily newspaper and also distributed free to other homes along the carriers' routes. A similar shopper rides piggy back on the Harte-Hanks twice-weekly paper in Chula Vista, Calif. "It allows us to reach everybody in the market for the mass advertiser, and emphasizes the editorial product for those who are willing to pay," says Marbut.

Right on Target

The next step beyond this could be a newspaper with content segmented according to readers' life-styles. This kind of segmentation has already been pioneered by the monthly Tuesday, and Tuesday at Home supplements. They are distributed in almost 30 major newspapers but only in predominantly black neighborhoods. There is a lot of talk in the publishing business of similar special-interest supplements.

Technological advances have already given newspapers the capability to print and distribute more "products" than they do now. Soaring postal rates are already making newspapers vehicles for advertising brochures that used to go by mail. Shake some Sunday newspapers and a blizzard of "junk mail" falls out. Newspapers can target this advertising on smaller and smaller markets too. "If you just want 40th to 50th street, we can give you that," says the Times' Nizen.

Postal rates for magazines are going up so fast that some publishers fear they will be driven out of business unless they find alternative delivery methods. To some observers this suggests a happy marriage between newspapers' mass-distribution systems and their need to serve the kaleidoscopic needs and interests of Everyman.

"It may be the newspapers are going to supplant some specialty magazines," says Ron Semple of Lee Enterprises. "Let's say you're a rather sophisticated executive from New York, and you move to East Nowhere, Nebraska. The paper there tells you more than you really want to know about what's happening in East Nowhere, but not enough about what's happening in Europe. The key question is, are you ready to pay extra for a weekly supplement that tells you what's happening in national and international affairs? It may be you can build, off the base of the local daily newspaper, a range of supplements . . . to take the Sunday Times and sell its component parts."

The big thing among newspapers now is market research. Newspapers have always surveyed their readers, and often ignored the results. Now they are also surveying the people who *don't* read newspapers, trying to find a way of appealing to them.

Newspaper consultant Joe Belden of Dallas says 80 per cent of his 40 or 50 clients are trying to apply market research to the editorial content of their newspapers. The changes in the three afternoon newspapers mentioned earlier were undertaken after careful soundings of the potential audience.

"If we were selling breakfast cereal, we'd know we have to do research, that we've got to keep an eye on the market and change the product as things go along," says Marbut. "A lot of editors think this is not right. . . . If we tried this two years ago, I don't think we'd get as much cooperation from our own publishers. But more and more they are getting comfortable with this kind of thing.

Pleasing the Consumer

"Why not look at other consumer-product industries and see if any principles can be adopted? One is, *it all starts with the consumer,* and that's one we missed. We edited newspapers for other journalists."

This emphasis disturbs some newsmen to whom journalistic integrity means giving the readers the news that editors, not readers, think is important. Too often, Belden says, this means using the front page to repeat stories that readers already learned about from television.

Ed Harte now wonders if his Corpus Christi papers didn't "waste tons of newsprint" on front-page Vietnam War stories that confused the reader without enlightening him. Marbut says it may be more important to tell the reader how stories affect him, rather than repeat the facts he already heard on his car radio. Joe Belden sometimes holds up the "magazine" style used by The National Observer as an alternative.

Says Marbut: "If it is true that there are certain subjects and certain reasons people buy a newspaper, and if we can find out what subjects will turn on the largest number of people, and then what subjects will turn on the next largest number of people, we could build the product horizontally. If we knew what 12 or 16 subjects would satisfy these different subgroups every day, we could also tell editors what items to tear off [news agency Teletype machines] every day, and tell the picture editors which pictures to choose; then we can have a custom-designed product for the local audience.

"I think everybody is going to win on this. It will help us find a niche as an industry and give readers a better choice of product."

Notes on the New Journalism

by MICHAEL J. ARLEN

Critic Michael J. Arlen outlines the development of "the New Journalism," which, by its personal, nonfiction-narrative style, offers an alternative to traditional, objective journalistic reporting. Arlen concludes that the New Journalist is "less a journalist than an impresario," presenting the audience with only his or her personal views of people and events.

It's probably easier than it should be to dismiss the articles which appeared recently in *New York* magazine on the subject of "The New Journalism." In the first place, the articles, which were by Tom Wolfe (himself a founding member of *New York* and author of *The Kandy-Kolored Tangerine-Flake Streamline Baby*), had most of the defects of the form he was extolling—the pop sociology, the easy cultural generalities—with few of the compensating attractions—the dramatic scene-setting, the impressionistic color (such as had made, for instance, his own piece on the stock-car racer Junior Johnson so vivid and fascinating to read). "The voice of the narrator, in fact, was one of the great problems in non-fiction writing," Dr. Wolfe now intoned. Also: "The modern notion of art is an essentially religious or magical one . . ." etc. Also: "Queen Victoria's childhood diaries are, in fact, quite readable." Also: "Literary people were oblivious to this side of the New Journalism, because it is one of the unconscious

Notes on the New Journalism: From *Atlantic Monthly* (May, 1972). Reprinted by permission of the author.

assumptions of modern criticism that the raw material is simply 'there.' " And so forth. In the second place, although it must have been fun to work at the *Herald Tribune* in its last few years of existence—when and where, according to Wolfe, the birth of New Journalism mostly occurred—he manages to describe this great moment in Western cultural life with a school-boy reverence which somehow doesn't leave anyone else much breathing room, a combination of Stalky & Co. and The Day That Curie Discovered Radium. In Tom Wolfe's world, in fact (as he might say), there is perpetual struggle between a large and snooty army of crumbs, known as the Literary People, who are the bad guys, and Tom's own band of good guys: rough-and-tumble fellows like Jimmy Breslin, dashing reporters such as Dick Schaap, the savvy nonintellectuals, the aces, the journalistic guerrilla fighters, the good old boys who "never guessed for a minute that the work they would do over the next ten years, as journalists, would wipe out the novel as literature's main event."

It's easy enough to fault this sort of treatment of a complicated subject. A bit too simpleminded. Too in-groupish. Me and My Pals Forge History Together. All the same, it seems to me that beneath, or despite, the blather, Tom Wolfe is right about a lot of it. And very wrong too. And journalism is perhaps in the kind of muddle it's in today not, lord knows, because Tom Wolfe sat down at his bench one day and invented a new art form, but because people in general, editors as well as writers as well as readers, have had trouble figuring out how to deal with this terrain that he and many, many other journalists have steadily been pushing their way into over a period of a good many years.

To begin with, of course, one can say that the New Journalism *isn't* new. That's a favorite put-down: the New Journalist prances down the street, grabbing innocent bystanders by the lapels, and breathlessly (or worse, earnestly) declaiming about his "new fictional techniques," or his "neo-Jamesian point of view," or his "seeing the world in novelistic terms" and all the rest of it, while the Old Literary Person gazes out his window and mutters: "New Journalism, indeed! What about Addison and Steele, eh? What about Defoe? What about Mencken? Joe Mitchell? Hemingway? Mark Twain?" That's right in a sense, but not, I think, in the most meaningful sense. It's right, at any rate, that there's been a vein of personal journalism in English and American writing for a very long time. For example, Defoe in his *Journal of the Plague Year* developed for *his* subject the same sort of new techniques that the New Journalists discovered yesterday—namely, he wrote it in the manner of a personal autobiographical narrative, and made up the narrative (although not the details, which he got from records and interviews) since he was about five years old when the incident took place. For example, Joseph Mitchell published a remarkable series of pieces in *The New Yorker* in the early 1940s on New York fish-market life—full of impressionistic detail, and centering on a man whom he had also invented: Mr. Flood. In a prefatory note to the first piece, Mitchell wrote: "Mr. Flood is not one man; combined in him are aspects of several men who work or hang out in Fulton Fish Market, or who did in the past. I wanted these stories to be truthful rather than factual, but they are solidly based on facts."

Here, by the way, is the opening passage from "Old Mr. Flood":

A tough Scotch-Irishman I know, Mr. Hugh G. Flood, a retired house-wrecking contractor, aged ninety-three, often tells people that he is dead set and determined to live until the afternoon of July 27, 1965, when he will be a hundred and fifteen years old. "I don't ask much here below," he says. "I just want to hit a hundred and fifteen. That'll hold me." Mr. Flood is small and wizened. His eyes are watchful and icy blue, and his face is . . .

Here is the opening to *The Earl of Louisiana,* by A. J. Liebling:

Southern political personalities, like sweet corn, travel badly. They lose flavor with every hundred yards away from the patch. By the time they reach New York, they are like Golden Bantam that has been trucked up from Texas—stale and unprofitable. The consumer forgets that the corn tastes different where it grows. That, I suppose, is why for twenty-five years I underrated Huey Pierce Long . . .

Here is the opening to *Homage to Catalonia,* by George Orwell, published in 1938:

In the Lenin Barracks in Barcelona, the day before I joined the militia, I saw an Italian militiaman standing in front of the officers' table. He was a tough-looking youth of twenty-five or six, with reddish-yellow hair and powerful shoulders. His peaked leather cap was pulled fiercely over one eye. He was standing in profile to me, his chin on his breast, gazing with a puzzled frown at a map which one of the officers had opened on the table. Something in his face deeply moved me. It was the face of a man who would commit murder and throw away his life for a friend . . .

And here is the opening of Tom Wolfe's piece on Phil Spector, the rock music figure:

All these raindrops are *high* or something. They don't roll down the window, they come straight back, toward the tail, wobbling, like all those Mr. Cool snowheads walking on mattresses. The plane is taxiing out toward the runway to take off, and this stupid infarcted water wobbles, sideways, across the window. Phil Spector, 23 years old, the rock and roll magnate, producer of Philles Records, America's first teen-age tycoon, watches . . . this watery pathology . . . it is sick, fatal . . .

According to Tom Wolfe and the various unofficial histories of New Journalism, something marvelous, exciting, dramatic—a light of revelation—happened to Old Journalism in the hands of the young hotshots at *Esquire* and the *Herald Tribune*. Since then, the novel has never been the same. A new art form was created. And so forth.

I wonder if what happened wasn't more like this: that, despite the periodic appearance of an Addison, or Defoe, or Twain, standard newspaper journalism remained a considerably constricted branch of writing, both in England and America, well into the nineteen twenties. It's true that the English had this agreeable, essayist, public-school-prose tradition of personal observation, which filtered down into their newspapers. *"As I chanced to take leave of my café on Tuesday, or Wednesday, of last week, and finding myself sauntering toward the interesting square in Sarajevo,"* the English correspondent would write, *"I happened to observe an unusual, if not a striking, occurrence . . ."* Even so, in spite of the "I," and the saunterings, and the meanderings, and the Chancellor-Schmidlap-informed-me-in-private business, English journalism was for the most part as inhibited, and official, and focused as was the society which paid for it and read it.

In America there was much of the same thing—some of it better, a lot of it worse. The American daily press didn't go in as strongly for the sauntering *I,* except for the snobbier Eastern papers, which presumably were keen to imitate the English style. The American press rested its weight upon the simple declarative sentence. The no-nonsense approach. Who-What-Where-When. Clean English, it was later called when people started teaching it at college. Lean prose. Actually, it was two things at once. It was the prose of a Europe-oriented nation trying to put aside somebody else's fancy ways and speak in its own voice. But it was also the prose of the first true technological people—Who? What? Where? When? Just give us the facts, ma'am—the prose of an enormously diverse nation that was caught up with the task (as with the building of the railroads) of bridging, of diminishing this diversity.

In those days, when something happened, an event—a hotel fire, for example—newspapers generally gave you certain facts, embedded in an official view. No matter that the reporter himself, personally, was a hotshot, a drinker, a roarer, an admirer of Yeats, a swashbuckler of the city room; in most instances he gave you the official view of the fire. Where it was. How many people got burned. How much property got damaged. What Fire Commissioner Snooks said of the performance of his men. And so forth.

Then, after the First World War, especially after the literary resurgence in the nineteen twenties—the *writers'* world of Paris, Hemingway, Fitzgerald, etc.—into the relatively straitlaced, rectilinear, dutiful world of conventional journalism appeared an assortment of young men who wanted to do it differently. Alva Johnson. John McNulty. St. Clair McKelway.

Vincent Sheean. Mitchell. Liebling. And god knows who else. A lot of them worked for the old *Herald Tribune*. Later, many of them connected in one way or another with *The New Yorker*. What they did to journalism I think was this: first, they made it somehow *respectable* to write journalism. A reporter was no longer a crude fellow in a fedora. He was a widely informed traveler (like Sheean), or had an elegant prose style (like McKelway), or a gusto for listening and finding out things (like Mitchell or Liebling). Second, when they looked at this same hotel fire, and how it had been covered by their predecessors and colleagues, they noted that, at the Fire Commissioner's briefing, for the most part no one started his camera, or pencil, until the Fire Commissioner came into the room, and walked to the lectern, and opened his Bible, and began to speak. One imagines that these young men saw things otherwise. Movies were already by then a part of the culture, although admittedly a lowly part of the culture. Motion was a part of the new vocabulary. And total deference to the Fire Commissioner, or to the General, or to the Admiral, had already begun its twentieth-century erosion. The *new* thing, it seems to me, that the writer-journalists of the nineteen thirties and forties brought to the craft was a sense, an interest, in what went on before (and after) the Fire Commissioner came into the room. What did he do when he got on the elevator downstairs? Did he drop a quarter on the floor? What were his *movements?* For the first time in conventional reporting people began to move. They had a journalistic existence on either side of the event. Not only that, but the focus itself shifted away from the Fire Commissioner or the man who owned the hotel, and perhaps in the direction of the man who pumped the water, or the night clerk at the hotel across the way. Thus: reduced deference to official figures. (For example: James Agee's *Let Us Now Praise Famous Men.*) Personal touches. Dialogue—in fact, real speech faithfully recorded. When you read a McKelway piece on Walter Winchell, for example, you found a public hero taken to task, you found out what Winchell did when he wasn't in the public view, and you heard him speak—not quotes for the press, but what he said when he was ordering a ham on rye. "I'll have a ham on rye." Few reporters had done that before. Newspapers hadn't had the space. And besides (editors said), who wants to know what Bismarck had for breakfast, or what his ordinary comments sound like.

Then time passes. The scene shifts—everybody shifts. The nineteen fifties. The nineteen sixties. Tom Wolfe writes that he came out of college, or graduate school, burdened like the rest of his generation with the obligation to write a novel—only to discover suddenly that the time of the novel was past. I don't know whom Tom Wolfe was talking to in graduate school, or what he was reading, but back in the early nineteen fifties you didn't have to read every magazine on the newsstand to realize that a fairly profound change was already taking place in the nation's reading habits. Whether it was *Collier's, The Saturday Evening Post,* or

The New Yorker, most magazines, which had been preponderantly devoted to fiction, were now increasingly devoted to nonfiction. It was also true, even then, that the novel itself was changing—changing, to be sure, as it had been since Henry James first gazed upward and noticed that the roof was off the cathedral. It was becoming easier, possibly, and more profitable, to become a novelist-disguised-as-screenwriter; but harder, perhaps, to become, and stay, a novelist of imagination and interior truth, which is what people increasingly seemed to be wanting of them. Mostly, in fact, one hears about the Death of the Novel from journalists, or from novelists-turned-journalists. And although there is only one *Painted Bird,* or *Separate Peace,* or *Play It As It Lays* produced in every twenty thousand books, people, the audience, still seem to be looking for *that* one; and the impress of each of those few books, I suspect, is still stronger and more lasting than nearly all the rest.

This brings us to the present state of the craft: the New Journalism. There is no getting around the point, I think, that a number of writers in the last dozen years have been exerting a steady (and often a self-dramatizing) push at the already-pushed boundaries of conventional journalism. I think of Gay Talese in many of his *Esquire* pieces, and especially in his last book, *Honor Thy Father.* I think of Terry Southern's magazine pieces, also for the most part in *Esquire.* Norman Mailer writing in *Harper's* about the peace march to the Pentagon, and the presidential campaign of 1968, and then in *Life* on the moon shot. Tom Wolfe and Breslin and Gail Sheehy and a whole lot of people who write for *New York.* Dan Wakefield in *The Atlantic.* John McPhee and Truman Capote in *The New Yorker.* A whole lot of people—sometimes they all seem to be the same person—who write in *The Village Voice.* Also: Nicholas von Hoffman, David Halberstam, Marshall Frady, Barry Farrell; and obviously a great many others. My guess is that anyone who denies that the best work of these writers has considerably expanded the possibilities of journalism—of looking at the world we're living in—is hanging on to something a bit too tightly in his own past. And on the other hand, that anyone who feels a need to assert that the work, especially the whole work, of these men composes a new art form, and a total blessing, is by and large talking through his hat.

Consider the mythic hotel fire we were talking about. Today, when a New Journalist tells it, there is likely to be *no* deference to an official version—if anything, perhaps a semiautomatic disdain of one. There is virtually no interest in the traditional touchstone facts, the *numbers*—the number of people dead, or saved, or staying at the hotel, the worth of the jewelry, or the cost of damage to the building. Instead, there are attempts to catch the heat of the flames, the *feel* of the fire. We get snatches of dialogue—dialogue overheard. A stranger passes by, says something to another stranger, both disappear. Rapid motion. Attempts to translate the paraphernalia of photography—the zoom lens, film-cutting. Disconnection. And nearly always the presence of the journalist, the writer—*his* voice. Our event, in fact—the fire—has seemingly changed in the course of time from (once) existing solely as an official rectilinear fact, to (later) a more skeptically official, looser, more written, human account, to (now) its present incarnation in New Journalism as a virtually antiofficial, impressionist, nonfactual, totally personal account of a happening—which often now is only permitted to exist for us within the journalist's personality.

The chief merits and demerits of New Journalism seem then as basic as these: the merit is—who really wants to read about this fire as it is likely to be presented in the New York *Times* or in a standard newspaper report? For those who *do* want to, the standard newspaper will give you the traditional facts: the number of people in the hotel, the number of people killed, who owns the hotel, etc. The standard newspaper considers these facts important, because (apparently) the standard newspaper for the last seventy-five years or more has considered these facts important. Here is the beginning of a front-page story in the New York *Times* on the controversial and emotional subject of housing in Forest Hills:

> A compromise plan to end the fight over the Forest Hills low-income housing project has been worked out by top aides of Mayor Lindsay, including former Deputy Mayor Richard R. Aurelio, and has been discussed privately with leaders of blacks and Jews and with high-ranking officials. The plan would call for a scaling-down of the Forest Hills project by about a third and the revival of the project for the Lindenwood section of Queens that was recently killed by the Board of Estimate. The Lindenwood project, however, would be smaller than the earlier one . . .

If this is the voice of conventional journalism speaking to us about our world, it is likely to find an increasingly restless, disconnected audience. The voice speaks too thin a language. The world it tells us about so assiduously seems but a small part of the world that is actually outside the window—seems a dead world, peopled largely by official figures, and by procedural facts, and written about in a fashion which is doubtless intended to be clear, and clean, and easy to understand, but which instead is usually flat, and inhuman, and nearly impossible to connect to.

If then the merit of New Journalism is that it affords us the possibility of a wider view of the world, a glimpse of the variousness and disorder of life, its demerits, I think, are that these possibilities are so seldom realized, or at such cost to the reality-mechanism of the reader. For instance, in the matter of our hotel fire; there is no need, it seems to me, for a journalist today to relate all the traditional facts (especially since most of them, in this sort of story, are basically concerned with Property); but if he is to tell it as a *real* story, an account of an event that actually happened, I think there is a very deep requirement on the part of the reader (usually not expressed, or not expressed at the time) that the objects in the account be real objects. If the fire took place at the Hotel Edgewater, probably one ought to know that much, and certainly not be told that it was the Hotel Bridgewater. "But what does it matter?" says the New Journalist. "That's not the important thing, is it?" In many ways it isn't, but in serious ways it is. It's a commonplace by now that contemporary life doesn't provide us with many stable navigational fixes on reality; and that we need them, and have trouble, privately and publicly, when we are too long without. Families. Schools. The Government. Movies. Television. None of these contribute much anymore to informing us of the actual objects in the actual room we move about in. Journalism *should* materially help us with this, but all too rarely does—is either too conventionally timid, or, with the New Journalist, too often (I think) gives up the task of telling us of the actual arrangement of the objects, or at any rate of trying to find out, get close to it, in favor of the journalist's *own* imposed ordering of these objects.

By no means all New Journalism is careless. Talese, for example, seems to be remarkably meticulous as to detail. Mailer's account of the march on the Pentagon seems to have been extremely faithful to what happened. There are other examples, although not, I suspect, all that many. *A careful writer*. That was Joe Liebling's way of praising a fellow journalist, his highest praise. There are probably few careful writers around anymore. And few careful editors. Few careful generals. Few careful stockbrokers. Few careful *readers*. This doesn't seem to be a very careful period we are living in. Relationships seem to break apart . . . carelessly. Wars are waged . . . carelessly. Harmful drugs are put on the market . . . carelessly. A soldier kills ("wastes") two hundred unarmed civilians . . . carelessly; and his countrymen, when told of this, first don't want to hear, then turn away . . . carelessly. The point is not that it is a better or worse era than Liebling's, nor that there is any sure way of measuring it—but it is different.

And swirling all about us—still swirling, although the motion has somewhat abated—has been the great sexual lather of the nineteen sixties. It was in the sixties, wasn't it, that we first had the miniskirt. Wife-swapping. Sex clubs. Swinging. The Pill. The sexuality of Kennedy politics. The new dances. Grove Press best sellers. *I Am Curious, Yellow*—and showing at a chic theater. The sexual emancipation of women. Kaffeeklatsches about the clitoral orgasm. All those strident sexy costumes—the cutout clothes, the glaring colors, the *threads* that lawyers started to wear on weekends, the big wide ties, the sideburns. Esalen. Touch therapy. Everybody (it seemed) committed to being sexy, or at any rate aware of it, or at any rate trying to deal with it. Since then, some of the stridency has quieted down a bit. Sex in writing, for instance, seems to be less insistent and obligatory. We've just had *Love Story,* haven't we? Fashion magazines have started muttering about a Return to Elegance, whatever that may mean. But it was back in the sixties the New Journalism made its big push —a debut which Tom Wolfe seems to think derived from some magic confluence of the stars, or at least from some solemn discovery of the Death of the Novel. I wouldn't say that it wasn't *at all* the way he says it was—but my guess is that a lot of what's happened in New Journalism has as much to do with the New Carelessness of the times, and the sexual stridency of writers (and of nearly everyone else), as it has to do with attempts to evolve freer journalistic techniques.

At any rate, the new journalistic techniques have produced a mightily uneven body of work. Some of it is as good as, for instance, Wolfe's own *Electric Kool-Aid Acid Test*—but much of it—for example a recent piece in *Rolling Stone* by Hunter Thompson on the New Hampshire primaries—is slipshod and self-serving. Partly this is because of the times we live in, and how both writers and readers respond to the times. Partly, too, it's because—with one, or two, or two-and-a-half exceptions—there are virtually no prose editors anymore. Already in reporting, one notes that what used to be called a reporter is now called an "investigative reporter"; the reporter is presumably the fellow who informs us that the President is now standing in the doorway of the plane. And in editing, the person who deals with the bloody manuscript is now somebody called the "copy" or "text" editor, and works in a small office behind the broom closet; while the Editor, of course, is the man having lunch with Clifford Irving. Editors today lunch, and make deals, and assign subjects—"concepts"—and discourse airily on the "new freedom" which they now provide writers; which in fact means that the Editor can remain at lunch, and not be much bothered on his return by a responsibility to his writer's story, or to his writer's subject, because he usually has none, claims none. And writers, for their part, are just as keen to escape the strictures of traditional editing—as indeed are so many others in our society to escape the traditional strictures of *their* lives, marriages, families, jobs; and possibly for the same sort of reasons.

Writers. Writer-journalists. It is clearly a splendid thing, a sexy thing, to be a writer-journalist these days. Admirals, aviators, bishops—everyone has his day. Today it is the journalist (and some others). He declaims about the end-of-the-novel while he hitchhikes on the novel. He has small patience for the dreary conventions of the Old Journalism, although he rides upon its credibility, on the fact that most people will buy and read his work on the assumption (built up by his predecessors) that when he writes: "Startled, the Pope awoke to find the Hotel Bridgewater in flames," it was indeed the Bridgewater, not the Edgewater, and that it was, in fact, the Pope. Even so, this is not the worst of crimes. When people complain too much about inaccuracy, or inattention to detail, it seems to me they are usually talking about something else, perhaps a larger, muddled conflict of life-views.

Where I find the real failure in New Journalism, or in much of it anyway, is in the New Journalist's determination and insistence that we shall see life largely on *his* terms. Granted one knows, by now, the pitfalls of conventional "objectivity." One is aware of the inaccuracies and timidities which so often have resulted from on-the-one-hand . . . on-the-other-hand reporting. Still, there is something troubling and askew in the arrogance—and perhaps especially in the personal unease—that so often seems to compel the New Journalist to present us our reality embedded in his own ego. A classic example of this, I thought, was Mailer's *Of a Fire on the Moon,* with its generalities about engineers and scientists—generalities which seemed less concerned with what scientists or engineers might be, even if one could generalize about them, than in the ego-ability of the writer to generalize about them. Lesser talents and egos than Mailer are less noticeable, although it seems to me that much, if not most, routine New Journalism—I am thinking of the dozens of pieces about movie stars and politicians that appear in magazines each year—consists in exercises by writers (admittedly often charming, or funny, or dramatically written exercises) in gripping and controlling and confining a subject within the journalist's own temperament. Presumably, this is the "novelistic technique." But in fact Madame Bovary is a creature of Flaubert's—regardless of whether Flaubert once spent a summer in Innsbruck with a lady who looked vaguely like her, and who expressed dissatisfaction with her husband. Whereas Phil Spector, for example, in the Tom Wolfe piece, or Bill Bonanno in *Honor Thy Father,* or George Meany in a *Harper's* piece by John Corry all are real people, *nobody's* creatures, certainly not a journalist's creatures—real people whose real lives exist on either side of the journalist's column of print. The New Journalist is in the end, I think, less a journalist than an impresario. Tom Wolfe presents . . . Phil Spector! Jack Newfield presents . . . Nelson Rockefeller! Norman Mailer presents . . . the Moon Shot! And the complaint is not that the New Journalist doesn't present the totality of someone's life, because nobody can do that —but that, with his ego, he rules such thick lines down the edges of his own column of print. Nothing appears to exist outside the lines—except that, of course, it does. As readers, as *audience,* despite our modern bravado, I don't think we show much more willingness, let alone eagerness, than we ever did to come to terms with this disorder—the actuality, the nonstorybook element in life. And it seems to me that, on the whole, the New Journalist (despite *his* bravado) hasn't risked much in this direction either; and if you think none of it matters, my guess is you're wrong.

by JAMES D. WILLIAMS

In this article from **Black Enterprise,** James D. Williams analyzes problems faced by black newspapers since the 1960s when the other media began covering black affairs. He points to the need for a black press and shows how it can thrive when it serves its community.

Something happened to black newspapers in the years between 1949 and 1976; something that has generally gone unrecognized by the vast majority of blacks, but something that offers a grim lesson of how power, once possessed, can slip away almost unnoticed.

In less than three decades, black newspapers—once the most powerful secular institution of the black community—have seen their circulations decline and their power slowly vanish, leaving behind a leadership vacuum at a time when blacks can ill-afford to lose any power base.

To understand the implications of this major loss of black power, it is first necessary to understand the dimensions of the power possessed by black newspapers during their "Golden Years," running roughly from World War II to the early 60s. Their prestige was then at its highest, their importance without question, their circulation at record levels, their ranks filled with talented people, and their voices powerful factors in the decision-making processes affecting black communities. They did not get that way by chance. There were factors at work to make it possible, including a retention of the readers picked up during World War II when black papers reported extensively on black servicemen and the burgeoning black awareness. They were not only centers of influence in their cities, but as a 1949 *Ebony* article reported, "a powerful economic force."

There was a special flavor to the black newspapers of the "Golden Years"; something unique. Almost without exception they were crusaders, differing, if at all, only in the intensity of their militancy—some more, some less. Their favorite and most consistent object of attack was the albatross of racism that America had draped about the necks of blacks. The newspapers consistently supported causes and yelled and screamed in print about the ills inflicted on black folk, even when it was not yet a popular subject. Along with their crusading they gave readers news that was available from no other source. And they presented news from a black perspective.

From the vantage point of the 1970s, it is difficult to realize just how important the papers were to black readers. But as historian John Hope Franklin has written in *From Slavery to Freedom:* "They became the medium through which the yearnings of the race were expressed, the platform from which Negro leaders could speak, the coordinator of mass action which Negroes felt compelled to take, and the instrument by which many Negroes were educated with respect to public affairs."

Much of black newspaper vigor was derived from black publishers of the period, a remarkable group of superbly gifted people who were conscious of the power they possessed and not reluctant to exert it. They were automatically marked as leaders by their communities and by the white power apparatus as well. While the establishment might not have approved of black newspaper policies, it had to accept the inescapable fact that the black publisher was in a position to exert more influence within the black community than anyone else. He had a weapon that no one else had, a weapon that could mold and influence public opinion, a weapon that could spread information—a newspaper.

If any one publisher of the "Golden Years" can be considered as the foremost among his peers, it is probably the late Carl Murphy. After graduating from Harvard, Murphy took graduate work at the University of Jena in Austria and taught German at Howard University. Then he returned to his native Baltimore, and took over leadership of the *Afro-American Newspaper*—a publication started by his father toward the end of the 19th century. Murphy built the *Afro* into a profitable and highly influential chain with a combined weekly circulation of over 250,000 copies and several hundred full-time employees.

Not very much happened in black Baltimore without Murphy having a hand in it. He worked behind the scenes, shunning the spotlight, playing the role of power broker to the hilt, never sharing his power or making the mistake of using it for personal gain. Knowing that the *Afro*'s influence was so great, there were very few city or state office-seekers who did not visit Murphy hoping for his support.

Murphy was not alone in his role as a black newspaper publisher with power. Others from that period include: C. B. Powell of the *Amsterdam News;* E. Washington Rhodes of the *Philadelphia Tribune;* Cornelius A. Scott of the *Atlanta Daily World;* John Sengstacke of the *Chicago Daily Defender;* Frank Stanley of the *Louisville Defender;* William O. Walker of the *Cleveland Call & Post;* Carter W. Wesley of the *Houston Informer;* and Mrs. Robert L. Cann of the *Pittsburgh Courier.*

In the early 60s, however, several tides converged to severely diminish the power of black publishers. With the heating up of the civil rights movement, white newspapers, magazines and television entered the picture and black newspapers lost their monopoly on black news.

In the black community itself, other blacks began to claim a share of the power—elected officials, civil rights and anti-poverty activists, business people, and clergymen who expanded the church's role in the secular world.

At the same time, the ranks of aging black publishers were reduced by the inexorable march of time. The young replacements lacked the power built up over the years by the old guards and, in some instances, their drive.

Concurrent with all this, white media discovered that they needed black journalists to report on black affairs; and they turned to the obvious source —black newspapers. The papers were caught in a crossfire. Just when they needed top talent the most, many of their best people were leaving for salaries they could not match. In one midwestern city, a black newspaper offered reporters a starting salary of $164 a week, while its rival white daily paid $288.

Soon, the newspages themselves began to reflect the exodus. In many instances, the quality and quantity of their news coverage began to deteriorate. Sadly, although the signs should have been clear that readers' tastes were changing, a number of papers clung to the old formula of playing up sensational news.

All these factors, combined with the fact that the circulation of black newspapers—with a few notable exceptions—is still steadily declining, attest to the very real possibility that unless this downward trend is halted, blacks may well witness, in the not too distant future, the demise of a valuable source of power that in the past has served them well.

Many of the problems faced by black newspapers today are attributable to their lack of financial resources. This, in turn, has a great deal to do with the limited advertising dollars they are able to capture. While the average daily with a 50,000 copy circulation derives 73 percent of its income from advertising sales, a recent survey showed that among nine leading black weeklies, advertising revenue represented only 31 to 61 percent of their incomes.

This places black newspapers at a competitive disadvantage because they cannot produce enough income to meet the competition, not only in the race for readers, but in the talent marketplaces as well. In such an unfavorable position, black newspapers cannot exercise the power they once had.

In the past, while the advertising dollar was important to black newspapers, it was not as important as it has become within recent years. This paradox is explained by the fact that for most of their existence, black newspapers have depended more heavily on circulation than on advertising for their primary source of income.

But the hard economic reality was that, even in the past, advertising dollars were hard to come by. As Roland E. Wolseley reported of the period prior to the mid-60s, "What advertising outside their own shopping areas they [the black press] were able to obtain was almost entirely from white companies and only a few of these were large accounts. Among these few were tobacco, soap, bread and motor car accounts."

This lack of total dependence on the advertising dollar was something of a blessing in that it freed the papers from the dominance of advertisers. The papers had to please their readers; the more readers pleased, the more papers the publisher sold and the more powerful he became.

Conversely, heavy reliance on circulation often led to the publication of sensational and sometimes lurid stories. The practice was not universally applauded by blacks, but it sold papers, and selling papers kept the publishers in business.

When pushed to defend the practice, as they often were, the publishers could always cite the classic case of Mr. and Mrs. V. P. Bourne-Vanneck, the English couple who bought the *New York Age,* a Harlem newspaper. When they toned down the paper's sensational approach to news, sales plummeted downhill. By the time the *Chicago Daily Defender* took over in 1952, the chastened couple and other investors were reported to have lost a considerable sum in the ill-starred venture.

The advertising dollar, however, has become increasingly important over the past few years. While black newspapers are still not receiving their fair share of advertising revenue, many of them have made breakthroughs in wake of the civil rights movement and the growing attractiveness of the black market. There have been additional national accounts and new local advertisers, most notably, department stores and supermarkets.

To a large degree, the limited advances on the advertising front have been negated by the presence of four factors. Two of these—declining circulations and loss of personnel—have already been noted. The third is the tremendous increase in production costs for all newspapers, regardless of size.

For just newsprint—that indispensable ingredient of a newspaper—the price has tripled in the last decade. In 1973, newsprint was selling for $185 a ton; by the end of 1975, it was up to $260 a ton; and on January 1, 1977, the price was $305 a ton. The rise in gasoline prices also adversely affected newspapers by increasing the cost of delivering papers and the price of petroleum-based products like ink. Frederick Howard, vice president in charge of production at the *Afro-American Newspaper,* estimated that overall production costs have risen by at least 30 percent within the past five years.

One obvious answer to escalated production expenses would be to raise the selling price of papers. But here, the fourth factor comes into play. Most newspapers already sell for 20 to 30 cents. It is reasonable to suppose that if they increase their prices any further, there will be a substantial drop in sales.

A more realistic answer would involve increased advertising revenue, yet despite spirited efforts by the National Newspaper Publishers Association and Black Media Inc.—a new group of black publishers—along such lines, the future does not look promising.

In 1975, *Advertising Age* reported that out of the $1.2 billion spent by national advertisers in newspapers, only $15 million found its way into the coffers of the black press.

In criticizing advertisers for not spending more in black media, Vernon E. Jordan Jr., executive director of the National Urban League, said, "This neglect [on the part of white advertisers] is often rationalized by statements to the effect that blacks are part of the general media audience and thus no special effort need be made to reach them."

That the advertisers' reasoning is at best specious is implicit in a survey by the Chicago-based research firm, Behavioral Systems Inc. In 1975, they concluded, on the basis of a 16-city study, that blacks—who constitute a national $80 billion annual market—are more highly motivated by ads appearing in black publications than in white ones, and that their reasons are "pride, progress, support of people and helping black business."

It is, therefore, evident that if black newspapers are going to approach anything like their former state of power, they must develop new formulae to increase their advertising revenues as well as their circulations.

This is not impossible. Witness the examples offered by two newspapers, at opposite ends of the country—the *Sacramento Observer* and the *Richmond Afro-American.*

The somewhat sedate capital of California is hardly the setting where one would reasonably expect to find a thriving black newspaper; but thriving indeed is the *Observer* and its spin-off projects.

First, there is the *Sacramento Observer*'s 37,000 circulation in a marketing area where the black population is only 80,000. Then there is the

Observer Newspaper, its sister in the San Francisco Bay area. That edition claims a circulation of 35,000 copies after just less than six months of publication. Add to this an entertainment supplement, *The Happenings,* distributed in the two newspapers and sold on newsstands as a separate item, with a combined reported circulation of 100,000 copies; the winning within a four year period of two Russwurm Awards, the highest accolade that can be bestowed by the National Newspaper Publishers Association; plus heavy advertising lineage in all its publications, and the sweet smell of success hangs heavy in the air over Sacramento.

The national importance of what *Observer* Publisher William Lee has accomplished lies in its promise of what a fresh approach to black newspapering can produce in terms of serving the public interest, making money and establishing a power base. As Lee has demonstrated, the three are not necessarily incompatible.

Lee's guiding principle is that "It's important to get away from subjective journalism and into a community journalism that reflects community thinking and concerns." He achieves this by deliberately playing down sensational news. "If anyone can show me that a headline about a crime will lower the crime rate, then I'll run it," Lee says, making evident his distaste for what he describes as "an over abundance of negative reporting that puts things out of proportion."

The *Observer* has used its clout to have rewritten a California law that barred all weekly papers from operating a news bureau in the state capital. The *Observer* also used its influence to get black newspapers a share of the $4 million spent by the state each year on legal notices.

Several years ago, when Mervyn M. Dymally, the black lieutenant governor of California, was under attack by white Los Angeles media, the *Observer* took the lead in lashing back at his detractors, and the attacks ceased shortly thereafter. The newspaper is widely quoted throughout the state by other media and consistently receives requests for permission to reprint its editorials and news stories.

Under a different set of circumstances, Raymond H. Boone at the *Richmond Afro-American* is proving that there is still life left in black newspapers. Unlike Lee, Boone took over a well-established newspaper that was part of Carl Murphy's chain operation. The *Afro* is still headquartered in Baltimore, where it publishes 113 papers, including Boone's Richmond, Va., edition, which traces its lineage back some 94 years.

When Boone assumed editorship of the Richmond newspaper 11 years ago, circulation was about 7,000 copies. It has increased to 15,000 copies and revenues have gone up by 500 percent. According to Boone, this is due to an increase in the *Afro*'s advertising dollar—an upswing primarily due to the *Afro*'s demonstration of its high acceptance within black Richmond.

"We are dealing with issues that touch the lives of people; and they can see concrete results," is the way Boone sums up his philosophy in the running of a black newspaper. Typical of this approach was the *Afro*'s attack last fall on Richmond's 27-year-old "Tobacco Festival" for its virtual exclusion of blacks, and the assignment of those permitted to participate to "demeaning roles." Over a period of several weeks, the *Afro* kicked up such a storm that one of the large tobacco companies rushed several top New York executives down to confer with local officials.

Other indications of the *Afro*'s power are its successful campaign waged in 1975 to have black judges named to Virginia courts and its ongoing battle to slow up efforts to annex surrounding areas to Richmond and thereby dilute the black vote.

"We not only cover the news," says Boone, "but we make news by putting pressure on people who have the power to make social change. The black press must always be committed to the black cause. And keeping faith with black people can be profitable."

In recognition of Boone's success in Richmond, the *Afro* recently named him vice president in charge of editorial development, with a mandate to further upgrade the publication's news content.

Ironically, the approaches of Lee and Boone bring into sharp focus the failure of many other black papers to meet the changing needs and desires of blacks, especially young black readers.

Too many of the papers continue to act as if time has stood still, as if a product that sold well 20 years ago, should still sell well unchanged. One result has been that many blacks have turned to other sources of information. This has given rise to a school of thought which argues that these alternate sources are sufficient and black newspapers no longer needed.

Nothing could be more mistaken. The interest of white media in black affairs cannot be depended upon for either consistency or sensitivity. When there is a crisis, or when some spectacular news occurs in the black community, then white media pays attention. But there is little or no interest in the bulk of news that is so important to the life of black people, on a day-to-day basis.

Black interests are much better represented by another source of information—the black magazine. These magazines have become extremely valuable transmitters of information and an integral part of black America. Their concerns, however, are generally national in scope or focused on a particular area. They cannot adequately serve as a total replacement for black newspapers whose primary concerns are local people and local issues. It should be noted that black magazines and black newspapers should never be in competition with each other. Each fills a different role and each is needed.

Without black newspapers, blacks would be left without a means of mass communication controlled by blacks, capable of not only informing them of the events that make up the lives of their communities, but also capable of fighting their battles and exerting pressure, when needed, on their behalf.

Without black newspapers, blacks would have to depend on others to speak for them—a situation found intolerable by John Russwurm as long ago as 1827, when he established the *Freedom Journal*. To use his words, "Too long have others spoken for us." And the degree that they have—that we have allowed it—is the degree to which we lose our power.

That blacks themselves want their own newspapers is clearly indicated by the previously cited Behavioral Systems survey which concluded that "black newspaper readers show an increasing desire and need for their own community newspapers." The survey also reported that the black consumer will go out of his way to buy a black paper and is willing to pay a higher price for it than a daily.

Underscoring reader interest in the papers, the report said: "While one out of two persons discards daily newspapers after reading them, one out of three regular readers of black newspapers leaves the paper at home, and almost one out of five gives it to someone else."

Such interest gives the lie to the notion that black newspapers have no role in today's society. The need for them obviously continues.

Perhaps black newspapers can never again assume the commanding positions they once held in their communities. Perhaps, too, the time is past for the emergence of any all powerful publisher along the lines of the "Golden Years" greats.

But the past is only a prologue, and under today's conditions it is not as important to yearn for a return to past days of glory, as it is to recognize that there exists a demonstrable need for black newspapers—and that they can be successful, as the *Sacramento Observer* and the *Richmond Afro* have shown.

The black community—which has the principle stake in the survival of the papers and in the growth of black media in general—has an opportunity to make its power felt, whether individually or collectively, by insisting that the businesses garnering dollars from blacks spend a fair share of their advertising dollars in black media.

The black businessperson can likewise become a powerful force by channeling his own advertising dollars into black media, and by insisting that those white businesses, which he deals with or on which he can exert influence, do the same.

At the bottom line, however, what makes a newspaper grow and prosper is its leadership, and as the examples of Boone and Lee so clearly demonstrate, such leadership depends for its effectiveness not only on the possession of business skills, but also on its ability to provide proper editorial guidance. Newspapers are a unique institution and not every businessperson—no matter how gifted he or she may be in cutting costs and increasing production—is possessed of the peculiar genius it takes to make the right editorial decisions that result in a good newspaper.

There are strong editorial leaders in the black press. The trouble is that there are just not enough of them with the power to establish and implement strong and modern editorial policies that attract and retain readers.

This year marks the 150th anniversary of the black press and while it may not be what it once was, there is every reason to believe that its usefulness is far from over, and that with the proper type of support and internal reform, it can continue to serve the public which has looked to it for leadership and guidance for so many years.

MINI–CASE STUDY

THE MEDIA– HOW FREE AND ACCESSIBLE ARE THEY?

Still Freedom's Bulwark

Roy Justus, The Minneapolis Star

Congress shall make no law respecting an establishment of religion, or prohibiting the free exercise thereof; or abridging the freedom of speech, or of the press; or the right of the people peaceably to assemble, and to petition the Government for a redress of grievances.

—The First Amendment to the Constitution of the United States of America

As we move into the later years of the 1970s, debate continues among various segments of society about the measure of freedom that is given to our news media as they strive to keep the public informed of the goings on in our democracy. Likewise, the public continues to be concerned about the accessibility of the press that serves them.

Quill, a magazine published by the Society of Professional Journalists, Sigma Delta Chi, devoted its September, 1976, issue to a discussion of the First Amendment. Articles from **Quill** by William Small, a former president of Sigma Delta Chi and vice president and director of news for CBS, and Ben Bagdikian, considered to be one of America's major press critics, are included.

The variety of concerns of print and broadcast journalists as they seek to preserve media freedom and accessibility is illustrated in the selections in this mini-case study. Additional articles related to this topic can be found in the mini-case study in Part 2, The Print Media.

from The Twentieth Century Fund
Task Force Report,
A Free and Responsive Press

The Media Under Attack

The 1960s were a decade of harsh discovery for Americans—discovery that social and governmental institutions, long taken for granted, no longer responded adequately to the needs and demands of a society under stress. And the nation's newspapers, news magazines, television, and radio—the media that communicated the assaults on established values and beliefs to the American public—found that they themselves had become targets of mounting accusation.

The press and broadcasting have never been beyond criticism, nor should they be. But there is abundant evidence that the criticism they now draw differs significantly in degree and kind from that of earlier periods.

One indication is the frequency and zeal with which the nation's highest public officials disparage the news media. Concurrently the government has taken a series of actions which would have been unthinkable a decade ago: "blanket" subpoenas of journalists' notes, photographs, and film and videotape "out-takes"; phone calls and letters to media executives from White House officials and the chairman of the Federal Communications Commission to inquire into planned or already disseminated comment; and, perhaps most dramatic, the Justice Department effort in the Pentagon Papers case to censor by prior restraint some of the nation's oldest and most respected newspapers.

There are other signs of disaffection. Criticism of the press has been the harshest in years—some of it the vulgar poison from racist and ethnic prejudice that editors recognize as symptomatic of deep frustration and often dangerous discontent. After two of Vice-president Agnew's attacks

The Media Under Attack: From *A Free and Responsive Press:* The Twentieth Century Fund Task Force Report for a National News Council. [Background Paper by Alfred Balk.]

on the media, Norman E. Isaacs, then president of the American Society of Newspaper Editors, reported a flood of "vicious" and "venomous" remarks; Robert Donovan of *The Los Angeles Times* noted that "yahoos are telephoning obscenities to television stations." The situation described by Ken Berg, editor of the Mankato, Minnesota, *Free Press,* probably is typical of that in many communities: "I'm getting twice the volume of mail I used to get, a lot of it from people who used to keep silent but are secretly pleased to see the media taking a licking."

United States Senator Jack Miller of Iowa told a New York County Lawyers Association in 1971 that in his opinion journalists should be licensed, with each subject to "having his privilege . . . to practice his profession revoked for unethical conduct." Dr. Walter W. Menninger expressed similar sentiments in a 1970 speech to the National Press Club in Washington. Government-sponsored "watchdog" councils have been proposed (though the proposals have not been acted upon) in both the Washington and Minnesota legislatures, among others; and at the 1970 Iowa American Legion convention a resolution called for a federal agency to deal with complaints against the press. The proposal ultimately was amended to request a media-established complaints agency.

Growing concern is being expressed about the difficulties of gaining access to newspaper columns or broadcast time—to the point that some legal theorists assert that a "right of access" to communications media exists and should be defined. In 1967, Jerome A. Barron, a professor at the George Washington University Law School, urged in a *Harvard Law Review* article an "interpretation of the First Amendment . . . focused on the idea that restraining the hand of government is quite useless in assuring free speech if a restraint on access is effectively secured by private groups." Not long afterwards, United States Representative Farbstein of New York introduced bills to require newspapers to present conflicting views on issues of public importance and to empower the Federal Communications Commission to enforce the Fairness Doctrine on newspapers. Another bill, introduced in 1970 by Representative Michael Feighan of Ohio, would require newspapers to print all advertisements submitted and create a right of reply for any organization or individual that has been the subject of editorial comment by a newspaper.

In addition, citizen organizations have sprung up to monitor media performance, challenge media practices in hiring of minority groups and related matters, and in some instances, to contest the renewal of local broadcast franchises.[1]

[1] These range from a right-wing organization with one professional staff member—Accuracy in Media (AIM) in Washington—to the more widely based Action for Children's Television (ACT) and the Office of Communication of the United Church of Christ, which has been prominent in reducing abuses of the Fairness Doctrine and in broadening employment and programming practices at several stations and station groups.

These developments scarcely have passed unnoticed by the nation's newsmen. Katharine Graham, president of the Washington Post Company, told a Southern California Distinguished Achievement Awards Dinner in 1969:

> The American people do not seem at all happy with their press. The fact itself . . . is beyond dispute and the nation's publishers are acutely aware of the general indictment. . . . It would be easy—and I think it would be foolish—to try to minimize the importance of this critical clamor. . . . All . . . in so large a chorus are hardly likely to be wrong.

And the Associated Press Managing Editors' publication, *APME News,* stated in August 1969 that "a 'credibility gap exists' for the press without question. . . . This is widely acknowledged both by editors and by public officials replying to a questionnaire."

Other observers tend to agree. A 1970 staff report for the National Commission on the Causes and Prevention of Violence declared:

> [The press] . . . has improved immeasurably since the beginning of the century. But the changes in American society have been more than measurable; they have been radical. . . . A crisis of confidence exists today between the American people and their news media.

However, the extent to which the public has lost confidence in the news media may have been exaggerated. In June 1971, for example, public opinion pollster Louis Harris wrote:

> Much of the alleged public unhappiness with news coverage in newspapers and on television appears to be overstated by critics of the media. Charges ranging from the news media being "too liberal" to "too conservative" as well as "too full of violence" or "too easy on protesters" simply have not gained majority acceptance among the readers and viewers themselves.

Even so, the time has clearly come to reexamine the dynamics of journalism in the United States today. How valid are the assumptions on which the media now operate? What is the relationship between these assumptions and the way in which the job of communicating is being done? In what ways is media performance failing to respond to the pressures of a changing society? What can be done to improve that performance and thereby strengthen the confidence of the public in the communications media?

One of the innovations most frequently suggested is a press, or media, council—a citizen-journalist group which, among other functions, could receive and act on specific complaints about news media performance and also defend freedom of the press. Such councils could be organized on a local, regional, or national basis. They have been established in Europe, and significant experiments with them already are under way in this country.

. . .

Treated Like... Distant Cousins

by WILLIAM SMALL

It was almost as if those fine fellows, our Founding Fathers, had sat down with quill pen in hand and Walter Cronkite in mind to frame the First Amendment thusly: "Congress shall make no law . . . abridging the freedom of speech, or of the press except, of course, on radio and television. There, Congress shall feel free to set government standards on fairness in news, bureaucratic definitions on what constitutes a need to reply, and slide-rule obligations on the care and treatment of political candidates."

If they didn't indicate such foresight, the Founding Fathers should be here today to see their political descendants do it for them. Jefferson and Madison and all those other fellows might find it hard to hide a smile as they see political figures and federal appointees and even Supreme Court justices rationalize why certain parts of the press can be fully free but some others free some of the time, partly so, in most cases.

The late Justice Hugo Black felt the First Amendment was absolute, it meant just what it said. The prevailing belief in most quarters is that this isn't quite so in the case of broadcasting.

Had broadcast journalism not emerged in recent times as the source for most of the people to get most of their news, this might be wryly amusing. It is not.

There are cliches to defend the bend-the-amendment position. One is that "the airwaves belong to the people." Former Secretary of State Dean Rusk, who has little patience with that one, has noted that the North Star and gravity also "belong to the people."

It has been noted that the government's right to regulate content because it is delivered over publicly owned airwaves means, with equal logic, that the government can regulate newspapers and magazines which are delivered over publicly owned streets or through the publicly owned post office.

Regardless of who owns the airwaves, the more important question is how they are used and, in terms of a free press, is the government's hand going to have a grip on that usage.

Treated Like Distant Cousins: From *The Quill* (September 1976). Reprinted by permission of *The Quill,* published by The Society of Professional Journalists, Sigma Delta Chi.

There is the scarcity argument. It states that government must license radio and television because the broadcast spectrum is limited. This is true; however, "limited" and "scarce" are not the same thing. As many have pointed out, there are several times as many radio and TV stations broadcasting daily as there are daily newspapers in America. Not everyone can own a television station, but very few of us can start a daily newspaper either.

Scarcity was the core of the so-called Red Lion decision by the Supreme Court in 1969. This was a definitive high-court ruling on the question of how far the Federal Communications Commission can go in imposing a "fairness doctrine." The Court, in fact, ruled that the FCC can go all the way, that the First Amendment was *not* fully applicable to the broadcaster.

The Court said in Red Lion, "Just as the Government may limit the use of sound-amplifying equipment potentially so noisy that it drowns out civilized private speech, so may the Government limit the use of broadcast equipment." Agreed. That is exactly what the original legislation of radio was meant to do, to control the broadcast spectrum so that—as happened in the 1920s—one broadcaster does not infringe on the broadcast channel of the next. It is quite a different thing to extend that concept to the insertion of government into what is being said.

The Red Lion ruling also said, "It is the right of the viewers and listeners, not the right of the broadcasters, which is paramount." That, too, is a common argument in favor of a controlled broadcast press. It assumes, somehow, that broadcasters are oblivious or callous towards their viewers. A strong argument can be made that that is not the case.

Take the Fairness Doctrine. William S. Paley, the chairman of CBS, noted that "we in broadcasting have no quarrel with fair coverage of news and public issues. We insisted on it, and lived by it, as the record shows, before the Fairness Doctrine came into being. What we object to is setting up the government as the arbiter of the fairness of our coverage—usurping the function of those directly responsible for news and public affairs broadcasts."

"Fairness" has such a marvelous ring. How can one oppose it? Paley noted, "Whenever I hear the misnomer, 'Fairness Doctrine,' I am reminded of Voltaire's remark about the Holy Roman Empire—that it was neither holy, nor Roman, nor an empire."

Paley called the Fairness Doctrine "an open defiance of the First Amendment. We all would be outraged if the government were allowed to impose standards of fairness on the contents of newspapers or magazines . . . Yet, under the Fairness Doctrine, we are enduring a situation where government—through an administrative agency—can impose such standards on the contents of broadcast journalism. Thus, we find full First Amendment protection denied to the very media—radio and television—that have become the primary source of news and information for the American public."

The irony of the Fairness Doctrine is that broadcasters can fulfill it by tucking away an interview or a contrary viewpoint somewhere in the schedule. NBC found the FCC insisting that it do so after it produced a first-rate documentary called "Pensions: The Broken Promise" in September 1972. On the same day that "Pensions" won a Peabody Award as a "shining example of constructive and superlative investigative reporting," the FCC ruled that it should have presented more material on those pension plans that were sound and reliable. NBC could have had someone on the "Today" show or elsewhere to placate the Washington bureaucrats. Instead, it went to court to fight the ruling.

Up through the courts it went, and the FCC was reversed. Finally, the Court of Appeals ruled for "Pensions" and the Supreme Court rejected a request to review. Julian Goodman, chairman of NBC, two and a half tedious years later, noted that "over those months, as NBC's legal expenses mounted and lawyers' time burned away, there were those who said, 'Why don't you give them five minutes and talk about good pension plans and get rid of it? What can it cost?' I suspect that Samuel Adams in 1773 heard someone say, 'Come on, Sam. Pay the tax on the tea. What difference does a few dollars make?' The cost, quite simply, is our freedom."

Goodman concluded, "It is easier for broadcasters to steer clear of controversial issues because of the high price tag that can be placed on freedom of expression. It *is* easier to give in. But it is not in the public interest."

It means lawyers and money to fight and only five minutes of air time to give in. Give in enough, however, and you have the most damaging impact of government in the newsroom, the so-called "chilling" effect of the "Fairness Doctrine." Richard Salant, president of CBS News, once noted that FCC inquiries result in reporters, producers, executives stopping and spending days "to dig out stuff and try to reconstruct why they did what they did." You don't have to do that often before your enthusiasm for taking on controversy slows down.

The Supreme Court, in Red Lion, did not find this persuasive. In a critical review of that decision in the *Texas Law Review* (April, 1974), P. M. Schenkkan wrote, "The Court approved an entire system of direct government intervention in broadcasting upon a mere hypothesis of public injury and dismissed the possible chilling effect as mere speculation."

There are those who argue that the government imposition of "fairness" means many voices will be heard. There are others who contend that not more voices but fewer will be heard and those opinions will be bland and safe.

Americans don't lack exposure to ideas if they seek them out. One estimate is that the average American probably has access to at least eight radio stations, two newspapers, all the magazines he can afford, and six or seven television channels. The danger in the information flow is not the scarcity of voices but hearing some who have nothing to say.

Fed Up

If all of this has the ring of a broadcast journalist who is sick and tired of intrusions into the daily work of editorial judgments by the need to worry about and respond to the specter of the bureaucrat in the newsroom, it is just that. Let editors edit, reporters report. The public will, as it should, be the proper judge.

In the political arena, the equal time provisions of Section 315 create similar problems. You can't set up debates between candidates. You can't do documentaries involving candidates except when they are incidental to the main subject which, therefore, can't be "them." One presidential election ago, before candidate George Wallace was shot, CBS had to kill an hour-long documentary about the Wallace movement. It was an important political phenomenon and deserved better than death in the cutting room.

Under the political equal-time provisions, a violation of Section 315 means equal time for lots of candidates (maybe as many as 100 declared or would-be candidates in 1976), ranging from Lar (America First) Daly, who has run for president seven times going back to 1948 and for the Senate seven and the House thrice and three times for governor of Illinois, to Merril Riddick, an 80-year-old Montana prospector who believes in the Puritan ethic and turning garbage into electricity. Giving time, and lots of it, to these minor figures, no matter how pure their motives, is what keeps us from a repetition of broadcasts like the Kennedy-Nixon debates of 1960.

Broadcasters have found few sympathizers to their problems. One came, unsolicited, last October when the chairman of the Federal Trade Commission, Lewis A. Engman, gave an eloquent speech to the UCLA law school on the Fairness Doctrine. He spoke to the traditional arguments from scarcity of channels to multiplicity of voices and finally addressed the question of the intent of the framers of the First Amendment, saying, of the contention that they would have excluded broadcasting from its protection, "That is literalism requiring suspension of reason to accept."

Chairman Engman asks us to "Recall [that] the 18th Century philosophical underpinning for the First Amendment was that no one had the right to control the speech of anyone else. Freedom to express one's opinion was deemed an inalienable right which could not be abrogated by government.

"The fashionable mid-20th-Century explanation that the First Amendment is a legal expression of our conviction that if everyone were allowed to speak his mind, the truth would somehow emerge, may be correct. But it was not the reason the First Amendment was adopted.

"It is crucial that this be understood. For, to suggest that freedom of speech is merely a privilege granted by the government in the belief that it will lead to truth—which some have done in embracing the Fairness Doctrine—is to suggest that freedom of speech is no more than a political expedient. Government might as easily decide the opposite—that uninhibited speech was a nuisance, that it resulted in rumor, gossip, lies and self-serving half-truths; that it was not, therefore, in the public interest. More than a few governments around the world have reached precisely that conclusion."

The Principle Stands

Broadcasters have tried again and again to show that they belong under the full protection of the First Amendment. Few in government, hardly any in the courts, and not many in the general public hear them. In the case of *CBS v. the Democratic National Committee,* Justice William O. Douglas, was one of the few.

He wrote, "My conclusion is that the TV and radio stand in the same protected position under the First Amendment as do newspapers and magazines. The philosophy of the First Amendment requires that result, for the fear that Madison and Jefferson had of government intrusion is perhaps even more relevant to TV and radio than it is to newspapers and other like publications."

Said Douglas, "One hard and fast principle which it announces is that government should keep its hands off the press. That principle has served us through days of calm and eras of strife and I would abide by it . . ."

A Free and Accessible Press

by JULIUS DUSCHA

One day last fall *The Los Angeles Times* ran an unusual editorial. Prosaically headed "Some Changes in the Editorial Pages," it reported the decision of Publisher Otis Chandler to end the *Times'* editorial endorsements of candidates for major offices. The editorial went on to announce that the drawings of the *Times'* brilliant cartoonist, Paul Conrad, would henceforth appear on the page opposite the editorial page because "he works in black and white [while] the editorial writers work in shades of gray."

The editorial was unusual not only because just ten years ago the *Times* was a strident voice for a virulently conservative brand of do-nothing Republicanism that often spilled off the editorial pages into its news columns, but also because of the mere fact that the newspaper took space to explain itself.

The *Times* noted that readers "find it hard to believe that this newspaper's editorial page endorsements really don't affect the news columns . . . especially so when this paper endorses a candidate in those elections that arouse the sharpest political passions—for President, for Governor,

A Free and Accessible Press: From *The Progressive* (January, 1974). Reprinted by permission.

for Senator," and that "the wide public exposure of the candidates for the top partisan offices makes our judgment on these dispensable; our readers have more than ample information on which to make up their own minds."

In discussing the decision to move the cartoon off the editorial page, the *Times* said: "It will come as no surprise to our readers to hear that sometimes Paul Conrad speaks for the *Times,* and sometimes not . . . Nuances in a point of view can destroy a cartoon's effectiveness, but they are essential to an expression of opinion based on the spirit of moderation."

These two actions by *The Los Angeles Times,* which in the last decade has become one of the better newspapers in the country, are part of a developing trend in the press to try to meet one of the principal complaints of readers and critics of the media—the helplessness often felt by readers confronted with monopoly newspapers.

The Long Island newspaper *Newsday* announced in the fall of 1972 that it would no longer endorse political candidates on any level of government. And only last October—a week before the New Jersey gubernatorial election—*The Newark Star-Ledger* took a similar stand, declaring that its editorials would discuss issues but let readers "draw their own conclusions" on candidates.

The St. Petersburg Times now runs long pro-and-con editorial-page articles on a major issue on the day the paper itself takes a stand on that issue. The St. Petersburg paper also maintains a twenty-four-hour-a-day telephone line for readers who want to register complaints over the way the paper is reporting or not reporting news events.

The key question of access to ever-shrinking media outlets held in the hands of fewer and fewer people is likely to be a more important press issue in the years immediately ahead than the skirmishing that continues between the press and the White House or even than the freedom-of-the-press cases now finding their way into the courts with disturbing frequency.

At a Washington Journalism Center Conference on the Media last fall [1973], the access problem kept coming up, from both the left and the right, from speakers representing the media and from such leading critics as Ben Bagdikian and Victor Gold, the former press secretary to Vice President Agnew and newly-minted syndicated columnist.

The New York Times' op-ed page is the best-known example of recent efforts to open up newspapers to a wide range of views. Since it began more than three years ago, the page, which appears opposite the *Times*' editorial page, has run a wide variety of articles and commentary, much of it in disagreement with *Times* editorials and news coverage. Recently the *Times* also hired its only avowedly conservative columnist, William L. Safire, a former Nixon White House aide.

The Washington Post has expanded its letters-to-the-editor column and has also opened up its editorial page to views opposed to its own. The result at both the *Times* and the *Post* has been better, more imaginative journalism, as well as a demonstration to readers that the papers are hospitable to a variety of views.

The *Post* has also had an "ombudsman" for the last few years. He writes occasional columns on news coverage and other problems facing the press and deals directly with individual readers' complaints about news stories. *The Louisville Courier-Journal and Times* and a few other newspapers around the country have ombudsmen, too.

The CBS radio program "Spectrum" is the best example of efforts by broadcasters to open up the air waves to more diversity. The commentators who present their views on these five-minute programs range from Nicholas von Hoffman on the left to James J. Kilpatrick on the right.

Former Vice President Agnew's attacks on the media unquestionably have had much to do with these recent efforts by publishers and broadcasters. White House aide Patrick Buchanan, who wrote Agnew's speeches and has been orchestrating the Nixon Administration's campaign against the media, claims credit, for example, for goading CBS into starting the "Spectrum" programs. CBS denies this, but Buchanan may be right. It really does not matter, because "Spectrum" is good journalism.

Access to a diminishing number of channels of information is a problem that concerns both the left and the right. During the 1960s it was as difficult for the New Left to get its views a fair hearing in the nation's press as it often has been for the far right to break into daily newspapers and radio and television. Thomas R. Asher, a Washington lawyer who heads up the Media Access Project, told the Journalism Center's conference he thought that the media were most hostile to right-wing views, and Asher's own political orientation is to the political left.

Charles Morgan, Jr., director of the Washington office of the American Civil Liberties Union, told the conference he believes that there is an Eastern Establishment press, highly articulate and often out of touch with readers and viewers. He cited a CBS News television account this fall of a major automobile race at Darlington, South Carolina, which he said emphasized "male chauvinistic piggery, bathing beauties and the 'good old boys' who drink their way through the day and then pour water over the head of the winner of the race.

"If I were part of the sub-world of auto racing and had seen that on television," Morgan added, "I would know that I had just been put down. Yet auto racing is as important a sub-world as rock music, which gets far different treatment on television. And the winner of the auto race represented all of the traditional American values—he got over $30,000 for winning, he lives in a nice mansion eight miles from the racetrack, and his winnings so far this year have gone over a million dollars."

Marquis Childs, the Pulitzer Prize-winning columnist and a liberal, has been looking into the question of press freedom for the Ford Foundation and has concluded that the lack of diversity of voices in the media and the feeling among people that they have no access to the media are two of the major problems facing publishers and broadcasters today.

"There are two principal attitudes toward the press," Childs told the conference. "One views the press as a public service that had better be delivered like water or light, and the other view is of the media as an entrenched monopoly concerned only for profits.

"There is no good in preaching the First Amendment," Childs added. "It's futile. Most people don't know what the First Amendment is. You have to prove that the newspaper is a service to the reader. As a result of Watergate, the reaction on the right is that the sole purpose of the press is to destroy elected officials, a reaction that has been abetted by President Nixon's criticism of the media at his press conferences."

Clay T. Whitehead, director of the White House Office of Telecommunications Policy and the man tapped by Nixon to keep broadcasters on their toes, emphasized in his remarks to the conference that much of his criticism of radio and television has been aimed at bringing more voices to the airwaves. Conceding that the Administration's own voice "got a little loud, a bit strident" in its appraisal of the media, Whitehead maintained that all he and other Administration critics of television have been trying to do is make sure that the nation has "a television system that provides adequate diversity for the American people."

Whitehead and other conference speakers saw considerable hope in cable television for the development of a greater diversity of views over the airwaves, since cable will make it possible to provide 100 or more channels in any community. But the realization of this potential is still a long way off, and like all broadcasting it will be expensive.

In the meantime, there is radio, which, despite the large number of stations on the air, remains a neglected and largely untapped communications resource. Since the demise of network radio programs following the rise of television in the early 1950s, radio has become largely a medium for music interspersed with frequent and often ear-shattering commercials. Radio talk shows were popular in the 1960s, and for a time offered considerably more diversity than listeners had ever before been accustomed to on radio. In more recent years all-news radio has developed, but with only a few exceptions it is in the staccato, bulletin tradition of American news broadcasting.

One possibility discussed by Asher of the Media Access Project was the suspension of the Federal Communications Commission's Fairness Doctrine, which requires broadcasters to present all sides of controversial issues. Asher suggested that with the fairly large number of radio stations operating in major metropolitan areas, considerable diversity might be developed among the stations. One station, for example, might present a conservative viewpoint, another a liberal position, and so on across the political spectrum, in the manner of opinion magazines. And there would be still other stations adhering to efforts to be strictly "objective."

Media critic Ben Bagdikian pointed out to the reporters and editors attending the conference that the development of new, less expensive printing techniques ought to make it easier to establish more newspapers for specialized audiences. Most of the underground papers that sprang up in the middle 1960s were printed cheaply on offset presses. Much of the underground press represented shoddy journalism, and the movement has long since passed its peak. Nevertheless, the underground papers filled a need, and the movement has spawned a national publication like *Rolling Stone,* which produced some of the best political reporting in the country in 1972.

No discussion of the media today can go for long without mention of Watergate and its effect on the press, and the Nixon Administration's extraordinary efforts both to intimidate reporters and to make ordinary Americans feel that the press is their enemy.

"To the Editor:
I was amused to read the opinion expressed in . . ."

Benjamin C. Bradlee, executive editor of *The Washington Post,* which won a Pulitzer Prize for its uncovering of the Watergate scandal, told the conference he thought that the Watergate exposures lifted the Nixon Administration's siege of the press and that "the next President would have to run a more open shop." But neither Bradlee nor other speakers at the conference felt that Watergate had suddenly and miraculously vindicated the press in the minds of the general public or of government officials. Cited again and again were the frequent court cases calling into question basic First Amendment rights long taken for granted by the press.

Discussing the legal problems confronting the media today, Washington lawyer E. Barrett Prettyman, Jr., who has represented reporters in subpoena cases, pointed out:

"There are two misunderstandings that seriously affect the media. One is a misunderstanding by the courts of the media and their proper role. A newsman is treated just like another person by the courts. The second is a misunderstanding by the press of what is going on in the courts. I would love to stand on First Amendment rights, but the First Amendment is what the courts say it is, and that is a far different thing today from what we were all taught about the First Amendment. Cases are coming along that will put reporters in real trouble."

Two of the cases were mentioned by Jack Landau of the Newhouse Newspapers Washington bureau, one of the founders of the Reporters Committee for Freedom of the Press, an organization set up to help reporters fight back when their rights appear to be threatened by the courts.

One case involved a hearing in a civil rights case in Baton Rouge, Louisiana, where a Federal judge told two reporters that they could sit in on the hearing but not write about it because he feared that newspaper articles would prejudice the defendant's rights in a pending criminal trial. When the reporters did write about the hearing, the judge found them in contempt of court. The contempt citations were reversed by the U.S. Court of Appeals in New Orleans but the court said that even an invalid contempt citation must be obeyed until it is reviewed. The case is now before the U.S. Supreme Court.

The other case cited by Landau involved an attempt by the judge in the Gainesville Eight case to prevent an artist not only from sketching in the courtroom but from sketching the courtroom from memory. This decision, too, is being appealed.

The conference sessions indicated that other pressures on the press will continue. The National News Council, the first effort to set up an American press council on the twenty-year-old British model, is just getting under way in New York under the direction of former *Look* magazine editor William Arthur. It will monitor the performance of the national media. And in Washington a small, right-wing oriented group called Accuracy in Media headed by a former USIA employee, Abraham Kalish, is also having some impact, despite the obvious political bias of most of its complaints.

Much of this ferment could merely persuade an already excessively timid American press to take refuge in still more blandness. But the chances are just as good that government attacks on the media and nagging criticism from private individuals and organizations may result in a healthier press receptive to more ideas.

The late Bill Baggs, who was editor of the *Miami News,* once said that if Jesus Christ reappeared and walked down Flagler Street in Miami proclaiming the Second Coming, he would probably not get space in the papers unless he hired a press agent and had his publicity man call a press conference to proclaim the glad tidings.

And, the editor continued, to get the story out of Miami and onto the wire services, it would be necessary for one of the Miami papers to get a special angle so it could copyright its story and thus make the wire services take notice of it as something obviously extraordinary. And that, if you'll pardon the expression, is a hell of a way to have to get access to a press which claims it reflects the community it serves.

Media Access: Romance and Reality

by WILLIAM FRANCOIS

Once upon a time, not many years ago, there were citizens who thought they had a right of access to the mass media. Mostly, these people were from public interest and minority groups who wanted to get their ideas before the American people. And there were some theorists who likewise argued that the First Amendment was intended to ensure that the citizenry received a diversity of viewpoints about important matters. For a brief time, there even appeared the glimmering prospect that the Federal Communications Commission and the U.S. Supreme Court also were becoming "access-minded." Now, however, consumer groups, minorities, environmental protectionists and others probably know better, having suffered a severe setback at the hands of the FCC and the highest court in the land.

Let's go back and trace some of the developments that led to the concept of a public's right of access to the media since, as most of us believed, the First Amendment basically was intended to protect mass communications from governmental interference. In 1919, Supreme Court Justice Oliver Wendell Holmes uttered his famous "marketplace of ideas"

Media Access: Romance and Reality: From *America* (September 22, 1973). Reprinted with permission of *America*.

concept of the First Amendment, that is, that the "ultimate good is better reached by free trade in ideas," and "the best test of truth is the power of thought to get itself accepted in the competition of the market."

A beautiful idea. But according to Prof. Jerome A. Barron, of George Washington University Law School, such an idea is pure romanticism. If there ever was such a marketplace where citizens could go and choose from among competing ideas, it long since has ceased to exist, says Prof. Barron, because of monopolistic conditions in mass communications and the media's penchant for blandness in content so as not to offend mass audiences. In place of this outmoded concept, the law professor called upon Congress, the courts or the regulatory agencies to advance the public's right of access through a reinterpretation of the First Amendment so that "meaningful expression" is produced despite repressive effects of the mass media.

In support, Prof. Barron cited the First Amendment concept of the late Prof. Alexander Meiklejohn, who had argued that "political speech," as distinct from "commercial speech," should be fully protected by the Constitution so that everything worth saying would be said.

The Meiklejohn concept of the First Amendment was influenced by, and in turn influenced, the ideas that undergird the Fairness Doctrine. This doctrine applies only to radio and television, and took the form of a Congressional amendment, in 1959, of the Communications Act of 1934.

Other than news and news-type shows, which are exempt, the amendment imposes an obligation upon licensees "to operate in the public interest and to afford reasonable opportunity for discussion of conflicting views on issues of public importance." Language similar to this had been used by the FCC as far back as 1929, when the federal agency declared that "public interest requires ample play for the free and fair competition of opposing views and the commission believes that the principle applies . . . to all discussion of issues of public importance. . . ."

There are considerable problems involving interpretation of the Fairness Doctrine, so let's turn instead to the formalization of the doctrine into specific rules. In 1967, the FCC issued rules governing personal attack and political editorializing. The personal attack rule states that when an identifiable person or group is attacked, the broadcast station which permitted the attack must, within one week, notify the attacked party, provide a script or summary of the attack and offer a reasonable opportunity to respond over the licensee's facilities. Similarly, a right of access is assured a political candidate who is opposed by a radio or TV editorial. News and news-type programs are exempt from the personal attack rule which, along with the question of constitutionality of the Fairness Doctrine, led to a famous U.S. Supreme Court decision in 1969.

In *Red Lion,* as the case is called, the Court unanimously upheld the FCC's rule-making authority and the constitutionality of the Fairness Doctrine. Justice Byron R. White wrote for the Court that there is a public's right of access insofar as radio and television are concerned because they have characteristics that make them more subject to regulation than other media.

But Justice White also made it clear that this right of access is abridgeable. "Where there are substantially more individuals who want to broadcast than there are frequencies to allocate, it is idle to posit an unabridgeable First Amendment right to broadcast comparable to the right of every individual to speak, write or publish."

Despite this limitation, much of what the Court had to say was access-oriented. For example: "As far as the First Amendment is concerned," Justice White stated, "those who are licensed stand no better than those to whom licenses are refused. A license permits broadcasting, but the licensee has no constitutional right . . . to monopolize a radio frequency to the exclusion of his fellow citizens. There is nothing in the First Amendment which prevents the government from requiring a licensee to share his frequency with others and to conduct himself as a proxy or fiduciary with obligations to present those views and voices which are representative of his community and which would otherwise, by necessity, be barred from the airwaves."

And Justice White included this intriguing statement: "It is the right of the viewers and listeners, not the right of the broadcasters, which is paramount."

Here, then, is the language of access. The public has a right of access to the broadcast media, and the federal government can require licensees to share their frequencies with others, as in the case of personal attack or political editorializing. Exactly who may appear on television or speak on radio is abridgeable, because of the scarcity of channels. But that which remains unabridgeable "is the right of the public to receive suitable access to social, political, esthetic, moral and other ideas and experiences." And it is this right, according to *Red Lion,* that cannot "constitutionally be abridged by Congress or by the FCC."

This unabridgeable right is a mix of the Holmesian marketplace concept and the Meiklejohn protection for "political speech." Thus, *Red Lion* beautifully—and romantically, as it turns out—fits our popular notions of democracy for it allows truth and falsehood to grapple for public support. And whoever heard of truth being put to the worst by such an encounter?

Prof. Barron hailed *Red Lion* as launching the Supreme Court "on the path of an affirmative approach to freedom of expression that emphasizes the positive dimension of the First Amendment." And he contended that "the new First Amendment right of access" in *Red Lion* did not apply just to broadcasting. *Red Lion* is a media case, he said.

"I'm with the Federal Communications Commission. Do you have a license?"

Wall Street Journal

A crucial intersection, therefore, had been reached between old and new interpretation of the First Amendment—the older view being that freedom of press was intended to keep government from interfering in the operation of the media; the newer, that the First Amendment was intended to assure the public of access to important ideas.

Reality seems to have a way of catching up with romance. And out of *Red Lion* came a range of difficulties indicated to some extent by the following questions:

Since access is idea-oriented, what ideas must be aired? Must "voices" of the public be permitted to use radio-TV facilities, apart from the requirements laid down by the personal attack and political editorializing rules? How will the FCC decide if the licensee has met his fiduciary obligation to the public since there are more than 7,000 such licenses in all, and a case-by-case determination would be impossible? Can the FCC administratively cope with a right of access? Does *Red Lion*'s access language apply to the print medium, or only to radio-TV?

Such difficulties have led the FCC to increasingly pull back from the concept of public access to the broadcast medium. And so, when the Democratic National Committee (DNC) and a Vietnam antiwar group, Business Executives' Move for Vietnam Peace (BEM), sought to force broadcasters to accept paid editorial advertisements, the FCC upheld the right of the broadcasters to refuse. DNC and BEM appealed, and the outcome was a complicated Supreme Court decision last May 29 that has seriously undermined any push for access by public interest or minority groups.

Writing for a majority of the Court, Chief Justice Warren E. Burger said: "As we have seen, Congress has time and again rejected various legislative attempts that would have mandated a variety of forms of individual access. That is not to say that Congress' rejection of such proposals must be taken to mean that Congress is opposed to private rights of access under all circumstances. Rather the point is that Congress has chosen to leave such questions with the [FCC] commission, to which it has given the flexibility to experiment with new ideas as changing conditions require. In this case, the commission has decided that on balance the undesirable effects of the right of access . . . would outweigh the asserted benefits."

The Chief Justice argued that any government-supervised right of access, such as proposed by DNC and BEM, would run counter to the Congressional prohibition against censorship of program content by the FCC (a prohibition contained in Section 326 of the Communications Act of 1934). Such supervision on a day-to-day basis would result in more, not less, government intervention in programming. In addition, the Chief Justice concluded that licensees must be given considerable journalistic discretion in meeting their obligations to the public, and that their performance should be judged on overall programming, not by isolated actions.

Justice William J. Brennan Jr., joined by Justice Thurgood Marshall, dissented vigorously: ". . . in the light of the current dominance of the electronic media as the most effective means of reaching the public," wrote Justice Brennan, "any policy that *absolutely* denies citizens access to the airwaves necessarily renders even the concept of 'full and free discussion' practically meaningless." Regrettably, added Mr. Brennan, "it is precisely such a policy that the Court upholds today."

If the Court's opinion in DNC and BEM is coupled to the current mood of a majority of FCC commissioners, then not only the concept of access (except for personal attack and political editorializing) is administratively and judicially dead, but the Fairness Doctrine itself may be gasping for life. With Nicholas Johnson, the foremost advocate of access on the FCC, due to leave as soon as his successor is appointed, this regulatory agency now seems bent on diminishing the sole vestige of access. The name may remain, but not the substance of fairness. In fact, the chairman of the FCC, Dean Burch, recently confessed "to a growing perplexity about the foundations of the Fairness Doctrine and its role in the regulatory scheme." This change of heart seems to have been brought about, in large part, by the complexities of administering the doctrine.

The trend in the FCC and among a majority of the U.S. Supreme Court seems to have taken a turn toward making the broadcaster into a journalist (at least in theory), with the journalist's traditional First Amendment right to determine what he will or will not print or broadcast. Instead of *Red Lion* being applied as an access case to the print medium, as Prof. Barron believed might happen, it now is beginning to look as if the tradition of print journalism is going to be applied to broadcasting (much to the delight of broadcasters).

Whatever the merits of such a change, and there are some, access to the media appears to have been administered a severe setback. This public's right seems now to be regarded as a merely romantic ideal.

Big-Time Pressures, Small-Town Press

by ROBERT J. BOYLE
Editor of the Pottstown (Pa.) *Mercury*

The bee stings in Washington and the pain is felt in Pottstown, too. The government clamps Les Whitten, Jack Anderson's aide, in jail for eight hours, and the clanking jail door is heard round the world. The Pottstown Council holds a secret meeting, and when it's uncovered, the news about it is confined to Pottstown.

Censorship, government controls and secrecy aren't limited to people like Anderson. The small-town newsman is also feeling the sting.

Certainly officials in Washington aren't telling officials in Pottstown not to cooperate with the press. But when the government hides things from the national press, and when government officials make snide remarks against the press, small-town politicians feel that they, too, should follow the leader, and they institute roadblocks to limit freedom.

The label a politician or an official wears doesn't matter. Pottstown is a swing community in a solid Republican county. But Democrats and Republicans alike have started attacking the press.

Small-town police departments suddenly are setting themselves up as censors. They become "unavailable" when the press calls them. Justices of the peace are starting to determine what cases to give to the press and what cases to hold back.

One Pottstown justice of the peace tried to stop a Mercury reporter from using a pencil and notebook at a hearing because they were "recording devices." Use of a recording device is banned in justice-of-the-peace courts. It took a ruling from the county solicitor before the reporter could use his pencil and notebook again.

School boards have been using the "executive sessions" ploy more and more. The public and press are barred from executive sessions. Board members decide at those sessions what course of action to follow and then simply approve the action at a regular meeting.

The simple news story, too, is getting more difficult to come by. Recently there was a small fire in the Army officers' club of Valley Forge General Hospital. Damage amounted to $750. The Mercury tried to get an item on the fire, and the story would have amounted to a paragraph or two.

But the Army refused to give any information until the "news release cleared the channels."

In Pottstown, a community of 28,000 about 35 miles from Philadelphia, the Council meetings always have been open and above-board. But late last year the Council held a secret meeting. It wasn't advertised, the press wasn't alerted and those who attended were told to keep it secret. The action taken at the meeting affected the entire community.

The Council voted, in secret, to get rid of the police chief, Dick Tracy. As God is my judge, that's his name. A group from the Council, including the mayor, was selected to tell the chief, secretly, to look elsewhere for a job. He was told it would be in his best interest to keep the decision secret.

"Keep your mouth shut and we'll make it seem as if it is your choice to leave," he was told. "Open it and it'll make it rougher for you to get another job."

He kept his mouth shut.

But one of the participants of the secret meeting discussed it at a local bar. He was overheard, and the newspaper, the Mercury, was tipped.

Tracy was confronted with the story and confirmed that he had been told to leave. He eventually did. He wasn't a bad cop. With a name like that he couldn't be. But he was ousted because he refused to play small-town politics. He refused to fix parking tickets, he refused to let oldtime politicians run the department and he was strict. He got the ax because he wouldn't play ball.

The Mercury headlined the story of the secret meeting. And the community was disturbed for several weeks. Later the Mercury investigated and revealed conflict-of-interest possibilities on some Council proposals.

In nearby Collegeville, a community of 5,000, the newspaper there, the Independent, was creating a stir in a nine-part exposé on the Pennsylvania state prison at Graterford. The Independent doesn't make much of a splash statewide, but ripples from it reached the state capital at Harrisburg.

The word went out that no one from the state prison was to talk to the

Independent publisher, John Stewart. Because he uncovered and published some sordid facts about Graterford, he was put on the "no comment" list.

If you multiply the troubles the Mercury and the Independent are having in their small areas by the number of smaller papers across the country, then you must recognize the press is being hamstrung nationally and on all levels.

Remarks by the Vice-President and the President may be targeted at papers such as the Washington Post. But they're also hurting the smaller papers. By design or not, those officials in Washington who are anti-Anderson, anti-Times, anti-Post, are also anti-Mercury and Independent. They're anti-press. Anti-freedom.

THE INFORMERS

STUDY QUESTIONS

1. What does Walter Cronkite give as some of the major problems in presenting the news on television? How would you rate television's success today in its role as informer?

2. Although Cronkite calls his article "What It's Like to Broadcast News," he also makes several statements about television's effect upon our society. What are the restrictive forces controlling television that he is concerned about?

3. Irving Fang attacks Cronkite's assertion that news broadcasters are not responsible for the effects of their reporting. He cites riot news as one example of news that has a strong effect on viewers, including rioters. Which do you consider to be more important, the right of broadcasters to broadcast the news or their responsibility for the possible effects of that news?

4. Compare the way your newspaper reports a certain event with the way it is reported on television. Do the two versions differ greatly in depth of coverage? Do both report the same facts?

5. Cronkite emphasizes the need for objectivity in news reporting. Do you think the journalist should remain uninvolved? Why or why not?

6. Again compare the coverage of one event in your newspaper with its coverage on television. Does one report seem more objective than the other? Is one medium more **able** to be objective?

7. What were the chief findings of the Roper survey? What implications do the findings have for the theories of Cronkite and Fang?

8. Arlen says that if "the merit of New Journalism is that it affords us the possibility of a wider view of the world, a glimpse of the variousness and

The Child in Jeopardy

by BEN H. BAGDIKIAN

There are many reasons why freedom of the press and expression are in danger, and one of them is the behavior of the news media themselves. Let me begin the sermon with readings from secular scriptures:

(1) The citizens of the Union of Socialist Soviet Republics are guaranteed by law (a) freedom of speech; (b) freedom of the press. . .
—Article 125, Constitution of the U.S.S.R.

(2) Question: Would the nation be better off, in your opinion, if every news article sent out of Washington was checked by a government agency to see that the facts are correct?
Answer: Yes, 63 per cent.
—Gallup Poll of American high school juniors and seniors, 1974.

Freedom of the press engraved in the First Amendment is simply a birth certificate. Nothing written on paper alone guarantees that the infant will survive. That is up to the American population and its leaders. If most surveys asking basic questions are correct, the child is in jeopardy.

Like any edict, the First Amendment will survive only if it is a living principle in the minds of its constituents and there is doubt that this is true in the United States today. An appalling number of Americans, including judges, legislators, doctors and some of the most powerful leaders in our society, give lip service to the Bill of Rights but are hostile or indifferent to the actual exercise of those freedoms. Lip service, like Article 125 of the Soviet Constitution, is not enough.

Any freedom always is in danger because that is the nature of freedom. If it means anything, then anyone is free to argue against freedom and this argument may be persuasive. It is the risk we take by saying anyone can say anything without prior restraint.

But there is another way a people may decide against freedom—by failing to experience it in their lives. And this is the reason some of our failure can be laid on the news media themselves.

Most of the press and broadcasting have accepted a narrow definition of what are legitimate political, economic and social subjects for news and commentary. As a result, they have, by their own publications and broadcasts, conditioned the public to accept as legitimate only the limited spectrum they see and hear.

Insular Majority

I am not talking about the small minority of the major media which regularly stimulate and display a broad spectrum of vigorous events and ideas. I am talking about the broad mass of daily papers and broadcasts whose content reflects a microscopic range of the real world of events and ideas, to whom maoist communism is not a legitimate subject, nor fascist totalitarianism, nor democratic socialism, nor syndicalism, nor a number of policies concerning the practical problems of society that simply lie outside the conventions of the mass media, but which exist as realities in the world and within the United States. If anyone doubts it, look at a random selection of 100 dailies or watch prime time for five week nights in a row. This is what two-thirds of the American population absorbs as the product of its mass communication (read "educational") system.

Our news media, with minor exceptions, accept the legitimacy of national security censorship by government, or unaccountability in corporate life, and either do not disturb or actively cooperate in the silence of local policy-making bodies doing public business. The minority that regularly does break through these barriers creates a sensation because it is so unusual.

Where they display historical events, or influence them, our news media do not stress the real reasons for freedom of the press and of expression. They seldom remind the public that one person's truth is another's anathema. We learn in school that Tom Paine was a great patriot whose writing helped win the Revolution. We don't teach perhaps the most important meaning of Paine's life, namely that he died broken and despised by his own society because he was considered a soiled-shirt radical by those who, with his help, rose to power. It is an important lesson: freedom of the press is revered in words by those in authority, but the desire to practice it is strongest among those without formal power. One of the corruptions of power is the desire to suppress information "for the public good."

Unless persons are taught the true evolution of freedom of the press, they cannot understand its importance. But teaching the truth about it is imprudent, because any honest lesson shows that the desire for suppression, for Star-Chamber proceedings, for official control of public information, for privacy in public matters exists today and always will.

The conflict between the desire for free expression and the desire for restriction reflects the problem in society as a whole, and schools alone will not reverse tides of popular passion or ignorance. But if schools are not to be divorced from learning, then they must make their students think about their own society.

Education in the nature of freedom has to begin with education of teachers, who come out of colleges, are hired by school boards, and are subject to social pressures as anyone else. Here, again, the local community media are important. If the media support the effective teaching of intellectual freedom, they will be a powerful force in breaking the present cycle of morbidity in the Bill of Rights that continues largely through silence.

Teachers need to know that if they do their instruction well in the matter of the Bill of Rights they will be supported by media operators in their community. School boards, like Supreme Court justices, read the papers.

Should Dissidents Speak?

Then let teachers do with students what pollsters have done periodically with adults—ask if they believe in the Constitution and then ask if they believe that a Communist or a fascist should be allowed to speak in their community. Ask the students if they believe that a pro-Communist magazine or a pro-fascist newspaper should be permitted in the town's newsracks. If they say they believe in the Constitution but do not think people with ideas they dislike should be free to speak and publish, let this be the beginning of a serious discussion of what the Bill of Rights really means.

Reprinted by permission of the Chicago Tribune—New York News Syndicate, Inc.

In high schools, for example, speakers on serious controversial and conflicting ideas should appear before civic classes—speakers who argue against capitalism and the free enterprise system, libertarians, democrats, republicans, socialists, John Birchers, and any other variety of points of view that exist; and by that program itself demonstrate the reality and legitimacy of free speech.

How often do we teach what happens in a society where the aggrieved are not free to complain and to have their media make their grievances heard? Do we put the First Amendment in the context of the need—today, not just in 1776—to complain, to protest, to agitate, to react as a necessary part of a decent and viable society?

Do we also teach the effect on the individual human psyche of repression of spontaneous ideas and emotions, and therefore the importance for individuals to have the constitutional freedoms?

James Madison was a conservative against the Bill of Rights. I don't agree with his position, but there is a powerful insight in what he said against it (another proof that it is better to let people with disagreeable ideas speak out). Madison said in the *Federalist Papers:*

"What signifies a declaration that 'the Liberty of the press shall be inviolably preserved?' What is the Liberty of the Press? Who can give any definition which does not leave the utmost latitude for evasion? I hold it to be impracticable; and from this I infer that its security, whatever fine declarations may be inserted in any Constitution respecting it, must altogether depend on public opinion and on the general spirit of the people and of the Government."

What is American "public opinion" on press freedom?

On Feb. 28, 1973, Richard Nixon, then President, said to John Dean, then Nixon's faithful servant, speaking about their plans to bring the disobedient portion of the American press to heel: "One hell of a lot of people don't give one damn about this issue of suppression of the press."

One way or another, Nixon's judgment has been echoed over the years by a disturbing portion of the American public.

In May of 1961 Gallup found that 31 per cent of American adults would approve of "placing greater curbs, or controls, on what newspapers print." Another 14 per cent had no opinion. Forty-five per cent hostile or indifferent to uncontrolled publication is not a national commitment. Of those who approved greater controls, most thought it should be with national defense information.

Apparently, this attitude has not changed much since 1961. In 1973 Gallup asked, "Do you think that freedom of the press is endangered in this country or not?" Fifty-five per cent said no and 13 per cent didn't know.

Almost all of these people studied the Constitution in school but obviously as a piety rather than a living practice. Most read newspapers and watch television but they, like all Americans, see little in their mass media that reminds them of the full range of economic and social ideas in the world. Not seeing something on authoritative channels implies absence because of non-existence or illegitimacy.

The fact that Archie Bunker and "Mary Hartman, Mary Hartman" could cause sensations in the media world is a sign of the stereotyped and constricted display of human emotions and ideas ordinarily disseminated.

Our media are only a narrow crack in the fence around the real world. Papers that carry a "conservative" and a "liberal" columnist, with George Will on one side and Jack Anderson on the other, are hardly displaying the real range of ideas available in society. Some think that Nicholas von Hoffman on the left and William Safire on the right are at the farthest possible extremes; but they are, in fact, moderate and pale reflections of the richness and variety of human thinking on public affairs. If one looks systematically at the kinds of people and life situations portrayed in newspapers and broadcasts, there, too, is the constricted view of human variety that leads consumers to a similar view of what is normal or legitimate.

The mass media are a major socializing influence on American citizens. What they display and comment upon becomes a powerful influence on the priorities and the values of the population. What is in the media becomes legitimate subject matter in society. The converse is true: what is not included becomes illegitimate. Disagreement is inevitable in any mix of ideas, but outrage at the existence of an expression should not be.

I once asked the leading political columnist in the Soviet Union how it was that the Soviet Constitution guaranteed freedom of the press and yet so many writers were imprisoned. He replied, "Freedom of the press means freedom to print the truth, to be accurate and responsible." A few years ago at a lunch, former presidential aide John Ehrlichman condemned the "liberal press" as violating the First Amendment. I asked what he understood to be the meaning of the First Amendment. His answer was almost precisely the same as the columnist from *Pravda.* This is not an invidious comparison of Ehrlichman and the Soviet functionary. I think most of the people in the United States unfortunately hold the same view: freedom of the press applies only if they think the press is being "responsible." Yet, they seldom learn in a convincing way that what may be considered "irresponsible" at one time (Richard Nixon on the idea of normalizing relations with China in 1952) may become official policy at another time (Richard Nixon in 1972). And what is "wrong" for some people (gun control for members of the National Rifle Association) is "right" for others. And that society at its peril chokes off any idea at its point of expression.

When the newspaper trade magazine, *Editor & Publisher,* condemns Daniel Schorr as irresponsible for releasing information because the House of Representatives had voted to keep it secret, what are we to expect the lay public to think about the legitimacy of censorship?

In the Heart

Being against censorship is like being against sin—if it's merely verbal it is meaningless. Freedom of the press is never going to survive by ritual but by its rigorous demonstration in the daily product of our publications and our broadcasts. If the public continues to get a limited diet of social and economic information it will soon hate and forbid anything else.

Judge Learned Hand said, "Liberty lives in the hearts of men; if it dies there, no law, no courts, no Constitution can keep it alive."

Judge Hand almost certainly meant his word "men" to include women —and children. If freedom of expression becomes merely an empty slogan in the minds of enough children, it will be dead by the time they become adults.

THE INFORMERS

STUDY QUESTIONS

1. What does Walter Cronkite give as some of the major problems in presenting the news on television? How would you rate television's success today in its role as informer?

2. Although Cronkite calls his article "What It's Like to Broadcast News," he also makes several statements about television's effect upon our society. What are the restrictive forces controlling television (and thus its effect on the public) that he is concerned about?

3. In light of what Cronkite says, what difficulties do you foresee for broadcasters whose staff relies on ENG?

4. If what Malloy says about specialization of newspapers comes to pass, what are the political and social implications?

5. Compare the way your newspaper reports a certain event with the way it is reported on television. Do the two versions differ greatly in depth of coverage? Do both report the same facts?

6. Williams says that without black newspapers blacks would have to depend on others to speak for them. Why is having their own voice important?

7. Again compare the coverage of one event in your newspaper with its coverage on television. Does either report seem to be objective? Fair? Is objectivity more easily attainable in one medium than the other? Would fairness in reporting be more attainable (or desirable) than objectivity?

8. What were the chief findings of the Roper survey? What implications do the findings have for the theories of Cronkite? Of Malloy? Of the use of ENG?

9. Arlen says that if "the merit of New Journalism is that it affords us the possibility of a wider view of the world, a glimpse of the variousness and disorder of life, its demerits, I think, are that these possibilities are so seldom realized. . . ." What difficulties does Arlen see in the New Journalism? By what techniques do the New Journalists enable their readers to feel the reality of an event?

10. Is there danger in the inclusion of the writer's own voice and viewpoint in the New Journalism? What is the difference between the New Journalism and the advocacy of a cause such as Williams suggests?

11. Does the New Journalism succeed on its own merits, or might its success be at least partly the result of the reader's being accustomed to experiencing events through the more immediate electronic media?

12. Distinctions have been made between electronic and print journalism and the responsibility of each to present all sides of an issue. Should there be a "fairness doctrine" for print as well as for television and radio? Or should the "fairness doctrine" be abolished?

BIBLIOGRAPHY FOR FURTHER STUDY

Bagdikian, Ben H. *The Effete Conspiracy and Other Crimes by the Press.* New York: Harper & Row, 1972.

Barron, Jerome A. *Freedom of the Press for Whom? The Right of Access to Mass Media.* Bloomington: Indiana University Press, 1973.

Berns, Walter. *The First Amendment and the Future of American Democracy.* New York: Basic Books, 1976.

Cirino, Robert. *Power to Persuade: Mass Media and the News.* New York: Bantam Books, 1974.

Deutsch, Linda. "The Hearst Epic, or Telling the Tale of an Enigmatic Sleeping Beauty." *AP World* (October, 1976), 16–24.

Devol, Kenneth S., ed. *Mass Media and the Supreme Court.* 2nd ed. New York: Hastings House, 1976.

Dickerson, Nancy. *Among Those Present.* New York: Random House, 1977.

Downie, Leonard, Jr. *The New Muckrakers.* Washington, D.C.: New Republic Book Co., 1976.

Emery, Edwin. *The Press and America: An Interpretative History of the Mass Media.* Englewood Cliffs, N.J.: Prentice-Hall, 1972.

Fang, Irving E. "It *Is* Your Business, Mr. Cronkite." *Saturday Review* (January 9, 1971), 46, 54.

Friendly, Fred W. "The Campaign to Politicize Broadcasting." *Columbia Journalism Review* 11 (March/April, 1973), 9–18.

———. *The Good Guys, The Bad Guys and the First Amendment: Free Speech vs. Fairness in Broadcasting.* New York: Random House, 1976.

Gelfman, Judith S. *Women in Television News.* New York: Columbia University Press, 1976.

Gilmor, Donald M. *Free Press and Fair Trial.* Washington, D.C.: Public Affairs Press, 1966.

———, and Jerome A. Barron. *Mass Communications Law: Cases and Comments*. St. Paul: West Publishing Company, 1974.

Goldman, Elaine. "ABC Passes 'Go.' But Will It Continue to Collect?" *The Quill* (November, 1976), 21–22.

Hofstetter, C. Richard. *Bias in the News*. Columbus: Ohio State University Press, 1976.

Jennings, Max. "The Murder of a Newsman." *The Quill* (July/August, 1976), 12–18.

Johnson, Michael L. *The New Journalism*. Lawrence: The University Press of Kansas, 1971.

Johnstone, John W. C., Edward J. Slawski and William W. Bowman. *The News People: A Sociological Portrait of American Journalists and Their Work*. Urbana: University of Illinois Press, 1976.

Knightley, Phillip. *The First Casualty*. New York: Harcourt Brace Jovanovich, 1975.

MacDougall, Curtis D. *Interpretative Reporting*. New York: Macmillan, 1972.

McCartney, James. "The Washington 'Post' and Watergate: How Two Davids Slew Goliath." *Columbia Journalism Review* 12 (July/August, 1973), 8–22.

Marbut, Robert G. "Our Media Environment—How It May Change." Speech at Abilene, Texas, Christian University (April 22, 1976). Available from Harte-Hanks Newspapers, Inc., P.O. Box 269, San Antonio, Texas 78291.

Mears, Walter. "Databank or How AP Kept Book on the Candidates." *AP World* 34 (April, 1977), 13–15.

Mott, Frank Luther. *American Journalism: A History 1690–1960*. New York: Macmillan, 1962.

"150th Anniversary of Black Press in United States." Six separate articles. *Editor & Publisher* (March 12, 1977), 14–22.

Porter, William E. *Assault on the Media*. Ann Arbor: University of Michigan Press, 1976.

Powers, Ron, and Jerrold Oppenheim. "The Failed Promise of All-News Radio." *Columbia Journalism Review* 12 (September/October, 1973), 21–28.

Reston, James. *The Artillery of the Press*. New York: Harper & Row, 1967.

Rivers, William L. *The Adversaries: Politics and the Press*. Boston: Beacon Press, 1970.

Rooms With No View. Compiled by the Media Women's Association, Ethel Strainchamps, ed. New York: Harper & Row, 1974.

Schmidt, Benno C., Jr. *Freedom of the Press vs. Public Access*. New York: Praeger, 1976.

Sevareid, Eric. "What's Right with Sight-and-Sound Journalism." *Saturday Review* (October 2, 1976), 18–21.

Shapiro, Fred C. "Shrinking the News." *Columbia Journalism Review* 15 (November/December, 1976), 23–26.

Wolfe, Tom. "The New Journalism." *The New Journalism*, Tom Wolfe and E. W. Johnson, eds. New York: Harper & Row, 1973.

"Women: A Special Issue." *Journalism History* 1, no. 4 (Winter, 1974–75).

Woodward, Bob, and Carl Bernstein. *All the President's Men*. New York: Simon and Schuster, 1974.

———. *The Final Days*. New York: Simon and Schuster, 1976.

The Entertainers

SAME TIME, SAME STATION, SAME SEXISM

by GAIL ROCK

Author and critic Gail Rock looks at the depiction of women in television series. She concludes that few leading roles are available to women, and of those few, most portray women merely "as appendages to men, who are the center of the TV universe."

It's no secret that TV is the single most influential medium of communication in American society. American children spend more time in front of the TV set than they do in the classroom. More people watch TV than read books or magazines, or go to the movies. More people get their news from TV than from newspapers.

The television industry, however, is dominated by white, middle-class men, and the information dispensed and the social attitudes presented cannot help but be part of that group's own self-aggrandizing view of the world.

Consider the statistics. During prime evening hours on the three networks, there are 62 shows which have regularly appearing leading performers. Of those 62 shows, 48 have only male protagonists, 8 shows have men and women sharing the leads, and a mere 6 shows have only female protagonists. (This total of 62 does not include news shows which are always anchored by men, or "anthology" series which have no continuing characters. And there is not one woman on a regularly scheduled sports show, not one woman hosting a game show, and not one woman as an evening talk-show host.)

Of the six shows (9½ percent of

Same Time, Same Station, Same Sexism: From *Ms.* (December, 1973).

the TV schedule) which do star women (51 percent of the population), four—"Here's Lucy," "Diana," "The Mary Tyler Moore Show," and "Maude"—are situation comedy; one —"The Carol Burnett Show"—is musical comedy; and one—"The Snoop Sisters"—is adventure comedy. Ha ha. Aren't we women funny? Well, we're sure as hell not serious —at least not on TV. There are 34 "serious" shows (adventure, drama, and so on) on the tube this season, and not one has a solo woman star. The only one that even has a woman sharing the lead is "The Waltons." But then, "The Waltons" has been an exception to every rule, so one might not be surprised to see it treating women with respect.

Lucille Ball ("Here's Lucy" on CBS) pretty much wrote the rule book for the standard "dumb broad" format that has dominated the TV image of women. Now in her twenty-third TV season, she is still playing the same character: the birdbrained redhead who gets into ridiculous trouble, draws everyone else in with her, and finally gets out by some equally birdbrained scheme. In the old days the plots hinged on her driving Desi Arnaz crazy with her antics and fearfully waiting for his exploding temper. He would scold and discipline her like a child, and finally forgive her. Now she drives Gale Gordon crazy.

The Lucille Ball situation comedy model is a zany child-woman who is dumb and innocent and who has to be patronizingly disciplined by the husband/father/boss. (In situation comedies starring women, there is always a dominant male. Women are never independently in charge of their own lives.) This format depends for much of its comedy on the woman manipulating the man: tricking, deceiving, flirting, coddling, finally admitting she's doing wrong and being forgiven. It is, thankfully, going out of style, though remnants of it still persist in even the most updated shows.

"The Mary Tyler Moore Show," now in its fourth year on CBS, is probably the best example of how things have changed. Mary is over 30, unmarried and not the least in a panic about it, actually appears to have a sex life, and is neither stupid nor helpless. Her show is the most consistently well-written comedy on the air because the people are funny, not the situation, and that's what makes a sitcom work. The comedy evolves from characterization, and not from strained sight gags or unbelievable twists of plot. Moore is the superb straight woman for a terrific bunch of second bananas, and she remains the most realistic and identifiable "heroine" of all the women on the tube. Still, she has her problems.

Mary is supposedly the associate producer, which would make her second in command on her evening news show. Yet she addresses the producer (the dominant male) as Mr. Grant, and he calls her Mary. She takes dictation from him and answers his phone. Would a male associate producer play secretary? No way. It is also interesting to note that though she is second in command and refers to him as Mr. Grant, mere writers on the show call him Lou. They, of course, are men, so it's okay. (Never let a woman get familiar with you; she's in a lower caste.)

There is another character on this show of particular interest to women, and that is Mary's friend Rhoda (played by the excellent Valerie Harper). Rhoda's character began as a rather frumpy, overweight, wise-cracking man-chaser. Then at the beginning of last season, Valerie Harper returned, weight off, looking gorgeous, and they had to rewrite her part. She became the very attractive, wisecracking Rhoda who now makes jokes about all the men who are chasing her instead of those who got away. She's just as funny now that she's an attractive woman. (In fact, there is talk of spinning off a new series based on Rhoda herself.) You see? And they said it couldn't be done.

"Diana," on NBC, is producer-director Leonard Stern's attempt to do a ripoff of "The Mary Tyler Moore Show," and he at least had the good sense to get a terrific actress for the part. Diana Rigg is probably the most talented woman any sitcom has to offer, but Stern's brain seems to have turned to mush once he had her sign the contract. He forgot to get a concept for a show and then forgot to get good writers. So we have a very tired "cute" idea about a 30-year-old British designer who comes to New York to work in a department store full of cute sexist men, and she sublets her bachelor brother's cute apartment, not knowing that he has loaned keys to a lot of other cute sexist men.

Any woman with a brain in her head would: (a) get a job where men didn't treat her like a piece of meat, and (b) change the lock on the apartment door. But then Leonard Stern wouldn't have a series, which shows you that he doesn't really have a series in the first place. Rigg plays a divorcée who is, in her words, "not untouched by human hands." Score one for reality, but it ends there. The result is a lot of smirky sex from her boss (the dominant male) and from the assorted creeps who have apartment keys. If this series makes it, it will be only because Rigg is able to inject some of her own wit and intelligence into this dated idiocy. She deserves better, as reruns of "The Avengers" will prove.

"Maude" is back on CBS for her second year, and we are promised an answer this year to that age-old question, "What does she do all day?" She has no outside job; she has only a five-room house with a maid who comes in to clean and cook, but we never see Maude do anything except yell at everyone. No wonder she's testy; she's bored to death. But she's also very funny. Bea Arthur can get a laugh from just about any old line. Happily, she has a lot to work with, as this is one of the best-written sitcoms on the air.

There is, of course, the dominant male, her husband, who gets the best of her by being calm while she blows up, but once in a while she wins one. Maude is over 40, four times married, and has an apparently happy sex life. She is a sassy, brainy, knee-jerk liberal who now and then mouths a few things about women's rights, but shows no evidence of it in her own lifestyle. The show has had the guts to tackle subjects like abortion and alcoholism head-on, and for that, one must be grateful. Whether the series will reconcile Maude's intelligence and independence of spirit with the life she lives remains to be seen. It's a problem a lot of women have in real life, and ought to be worth a provocative episode or two.

"The Snoop Sisters," on NBC, is a new 90-minute show that appears once every four weeks in rotation with other series. It stars the top-notch Helen Hayes and Mildred Natwick as two sisters who live in luxury in a Gramercy Park town house in New York and meddle in their nephew's police detective work. They, of course, solve all the crimes because Hayes is a mystery writer.

Alan Shayne, the creator of the series, had intended the pair to be two anachronistic characters, one a tweedy anthropology buff (à la Margaret Mead) and the other an elegant diplomat's widow, determined above all else to live life with style and grace. Leonard Stern strikes again. He is producing the series and has watered the characters down, at least in the pilot episode, into cute old ladies doing a lot of shtick that doesn't fit their characters, and bogged down by phony plot details. If the series survives, it will be due, again, to the power of two strong, superb actresses to overcome their material.

Carol Burnett, now in her seventh season on CBS, has a show that seems to improve with age. Burnett is quick to proclaim her admiration for Lucille Ball, but, though Ball has obviously influenced some of her work, she reminds me much more of the great Imogene Coca. Burnett, like Coca, is at her best in sketch comedy, and will do anything for a laugh, which is what endears her to her audiences. The running-gag characters she plays on her show are almost always funny because they are ugly, ridiculous, stupid, haggy, or in some other way grotesque; unfortunately, Burnett's humor epitomizes the idea that a woman can't be attractive while she's being funny. Wit has little to do with it except in Burnett's own ability to kid what she's doing even while she's doing it, a subtlety that is not lost on those of us who have loved her over the years. She is also blessed with the greatest second banana in the business, Harvey Korman, and writers who are able to come up to her talent about 75 percent of the time. For TV, that's not bad.

In addition to the six shows mentioned above, in which women star on their own, there are eight more shows in which they star with men. Half a dozen of them are situation comedies: "Adam's Rib," "Room 222," "The Girl with Something Extra," "Bob & Carol & Ted & Alice," "The Partridge Family," and "The Brady Bunch." The other two shows are a musical comedy, "Sonny and Cher," and the previously mentioned drama "The Waltons."

The most promising of the sitcoms was "Adam's Rib," based on the Tracy-Hepburn movie, and starring as the husband-and-wife lawyers two delightful actors, Blythe Danner and Ken Howard. The scripts seen at this writing did not live up to the promise. The other sitcoms have to do with cute domestic situations between hubby and wife and kids, except for "Room 222," in which Denise Nicholas has the only leading black woman's role in all of prime-time TV, that of a school counselor.

In the 48 remaining shows on the schedule, dominated by male stars, the women's roles are almost all those of housewives, secretaries, nurses, or the male star's girlfriend, mother, child, or ex-wife; women who exist not on their own character contributions to the show, but as appendages to men, who are the center of the TV universe.

It matters not that some women have "star" billing in these 48 series. They are not the protagonists. Hope Lange, for instance, who "stars" as Dick Van Dyke's wife, is leaving even if the show is renewed, because all she does is "pour coffee." On "Ironside," the policewoman, played by Elizabeth Baur, has so little to do that one woman who watched two whole episodes thought she was Ironside's secretary.

But then, the "crime drama" format is not very sympathetic to women, and there are 26 of those shows on the tube this season—almost half the schedule. None of them have women protagonists, and what's worse, a recent study at the University of Pennsylvania shows that not only is violence on TV on the increase again, but that women and minorities are increasingly being shown as the victims of that violence. Further, the study shows that this repeated victimization of women and minorities adds to their own feelings of insecurity and to a reduced self-image. Could it be that it's backlash time from all those white middle-class men over there on Broadcast Boulevard?

If what you see on the tube isn't enough to convince you, consider this: there is not one woman executive producer on any of those 62 shows. There is only one woman producer (Cleo Smith, an old friend of Lucille Ball's and producer of her show) and not one regularly scheduled woman director. Out of all 62 shows, there is only one woman script consultant or story editor and only three regularly retained women writers, two of them teamed with their husbands.

If the three commercial networks aren't guilty of discrimination against women, I don't know who is.

BLACK MOVIES AND SHADES OF GRAY

by MARTIN MITCHELL

In this article Martin Mitchell asserts that the term "black movies" connotes "less about the movies themselves than about the audience for which these movies have been designed." Mitchell looks forward to the day when a film's label will be less important than its quality.

Theoretically, at least, the word *black* would seem to pertain even less to the word *movies* than when used in phrases, such as "black athlete" or "black salesman," in which color has only a temporary statistical significance. And the category of films to which the term "black movies" has been applied is so broad as to make it hopelessly ambiguous. Is a black film one that has been directed by a black man? One that features black actors? For a film to qualify for the label, do at least half of those responsible for its production have to be black? Taken literally, it's an expression that prompts as much silliness as considerations of color as applied to people in most cases probably should.

When writers and critics refer to "black movies," they are really talking less about the movies themselves than about the audience for which these movies have been designed. The term is useful only insofar as it helps define that large group of viewers toward which a great number of recent motion pictures have been geared.

At the end of the 1960's, when the popularity of the youth-oriented films spawned by the enormous, unexpected success of *Easy Rider* had waned to the point where such films were losing money or were not even being released, the larger film companies, which tie their production

Black Movies and Shades of Gray: From *After Dark* (January, 1974). Reprinted courtesy of *After Dark* Magazine.

schedules closely to what they see as moviegoers' habits, were briefly without a trend to guide their box-office aims. They did not have long to wait. Melvin Van Peebles, who had directed one low-budget, personal film (*Story of a Three-Day Pass*) and one studio-supported comedy (*Watermelon Man*), came up with *Sweet Sweetback's Baaadass Song,* a now-legendary work of such unsparing militancy and innovative partisanship as to appeal almost exclusively to blacks. After a slow start it became a smash hit, and the big companies had, unequivocally, found a new audience.

The rest, as they say, is history. M-G-M, immediately thereafter, did very well with *Shaft* (though, of course, not well enough to save themselves for long), and other studios and film-makers followed the lead, often with barely disguised imitations of, or variations on, the original money-makers or with sequels of them. In time these pictures had given rise to a new breed of screen hero, in many ways the black equivalent of the tough individualists—the Bogarts, the Cagneys, and the Alan Ladds—of many Hollywood films of the 1930's and 40's. Indeed some of these pictures—like *Hit Man,* which had the same plot as the English *Get Carter,* issued in the late sixties when the British went on a brief, Hollywood-inspired action-flick binge—owed their origins to characters devised by the post-Depression, pre–World War II screenwriters.

Naturally enough, however, while acknowledging a link to the past (sometimes through the backgrounds of their white scenarists), these black movies have displayed more often than not a singleminded concern for the harsh realities of today. Even the most escapist of them have paid at least lip service to the kind of problems that are likely to be most familiar to the underprivileged as black agents, crusaders, and other supermen go after drug pushers, exploiters, and the representatives of organized crime. Sometimes, with a little wit and inventiveness, these films (and I am speaking now of financially successful, run-of-the-mill examples of the action genre, not of the exceptional ones, such as *Buck and the Preacher*) have—like *Cleopatra Jones* or *Cotton Comes to Harlem* and its successor, *Come Back, Charleston Blue*—provided good entertainment and can stand beside any other species of film on their own merits. Others, accentuating the violence and bloodletting that have lately proved so lucrative at the box office and combining this with an exaggerated form of the sexism from which James Bond figures derive their *macho* appeal, have brought charges of "blaxploitation." *Trouble Man, Hit Man,* and the Shaft sequels are among the worst offenders. Whatever the virtues or weaknesses of individual examples, the drawing power of black movies continues into the present, only slightly abated by the new interest in kung fu pictures, a fad that has already affected, and been partly absorbed into, longer-term trends, including that of black films.

Not long ago, on New York's public-service TV station, a panel was convened to discuss the phenomenon known as the black movie. The participants didn't cover much ground, partly because several of them were black film-makers with their own products to plug but primarily because the program was one of those shows where listeners call in to make long statements or to ask questions that have already been answered. But when it could, the conversation focused on the interesting problem of whether the black film-maker, especially, has a responsibility to his potentially wide audience in terms of providing something more substantial than the usually escapist, and often perhaps brutalizing, fare of action dramas populated by the Shafts, the Slaughters, and all the other superheroes. Should they, in other words, provide more suitable, realistic models for younger viewers, as well as handling subjects with which audiences can more closely identify and sympathize? The point was argued from various aspects with equal conviction until, addressing himself to the predicament of the many blacks who work on properties in which they can voice little pride, Ossie Davis, whose *Gordon's War* was about to open, brought up the simple matter of economics. Only when blacks can gain full control over a production, starting with financial backing and continuing all the way through distribution, he said, can they begin to talk about serving the aspirations of their public and themselves. Because at least one phase of every black film has been in the hands of whites, nearly always including the backing, he suggested, the results have been unsatisfactory.

Thus Ossie Davis offers a modified definition of "black movies." In his (and in many others') view, they would, ideally, be produced and created entirely by blacks, who would then be able to accept full credit—or blame, as the case might be—for their work. Besides incidentally providing a solid instance of a situation in which the director does not have the omnipotence that he is often given credit for (there are many black directors now, but few with sufficient clout), Davis does have a point, to the degree that blacks will be able to gain this degree of independence in film production. But this point is somewhat (and *only* somewhat) weakened by the lessons of experience. So far, those films in whose making blacks have had a dominant role (*The Spook Who Sat by the Door* and *Five on the Black Hand Side,* to cite two current examples) haven't always been among the best (though some, like *Black Girl,* have). And, as corollary, the most integrious movies about black people (such as *Sounder* and the early, pioneering *Nothing but a Man*) have been made by whites (who, again, have also made the worst: look at the callous brutality of *Hit!*). Of course, these facts are in part just a reflection of prevailing, and therefore changeable conditions.

As for the future, black control is one possibility, particularly in the direction suggested by both *Black Girl* and *Five on the Black Hand Side,* which were adapted from plays by black authors. There is a great deal of promising material to be found in the work of such authors as Ed

Bullins and Ron Milner, who might be more favorably disposed toward writing directly for the screen were the inducement to come from black enterprise.

It is more likely, though, that the superior films, as they always have been, will be those that transcend category. These will be made, possibly, in a day when a less fragmented society will respond to pictures more in terms of quality than specialized appeal, and the label "black movies" will refer to a transitional period in the history of the American cinema. However quaint the notion might seem now, pictures of the future—good and bad—are likely to be made by black and white working together, as a means of expression for their common interests. In any event, the so-called black movies have produced a crop of immensely talented black actors, directors, and technicians for whom the future looks very bright.

While many media critics have been focusing on the excessive display of violence on television, Stephen Farber, film critic for **New West** magazine and author of "Where Has All the Protest Gone? To Television," (see pp. 312–15) has turned his attention to the many reasons movies are becoming more violent.

by STEPHEN FARBER

Many of the women waiting in line claimed that they had not really wanted to see *Two-Minute Warning,* the bloody new movie about a sniper going on the rampage in a crowded football stadium; they protested that they had been dragged there by their husbands or boyfriends. A European woman shrugged helplessly. "Aren't all movies violent these days?" A young man in his twenties was irritated when I tried to question him about violence in films. "I don't see anything wrong with it," he snapped. "I see all the violent movies." His mother, a woman in her sixties, smiled benignly.

In a trailer for a new movie called *Shoot*—about a band of hunters who start killing people instead of animals—a booming voice announces that the film is "in the great tradition of American violence." The audience howled with laughter, but they probably went back to see the movie. Most of the successful films of the last few years have been violent action pieces or grotesque horror stories, and the depiction of violence is more graphic than at any time in film history. Some recent high points: Robert De Niro shooting off a man's hand in the bloody, phantasmagoric climax of *Taxi Driver;* a sharp piece of plate glass slicing David Warner's head off in *The Omen;* Laurence Olivier torturing Dustin Hoffman in *Marathon Man* by drilling into the nerve of his front tooth; football fans trampling each other to escape from a sniper in *Two-Minute Warning*. In the upcoming *Rolling Thunder,* written by *Taxi Driver*'s Paul Schrader, a Vietnam veteran has his hand ground off in a garbage disposal, and when he recovers, he goes after his attackers wielding his razor-sharp hook as a weapon.

Critics regularly deplore this kind of violence, but the simple fact is that audiences seem to enjoy it. During a recent showing of *Marathon Man* that I attended, a few people did walk out during the scenes of dental torture. One nauseated young man who was recovering in the lobby asked, "Can you believe only four people walked out?" Many other people whom I questioned afterward admitted that they had not known the film would be so violent, but if there is any negative word around, it doesn't seem to have hurt the film too severely at the box office; *Marathon Man* is one of the few hits of the fall.

Dextor York, a young hairdresser who fancies himself a connoisseur of violent movies, must speak for a lot of movie fans when he says, "I get a kick out of seeing violence. I've never fought in a war. I've never even been in a fight. Violence is a fantasy release for me. We need that release. Man has become so sophisticated. Nobody gets to fight anymore. During the sixties I was part of the peace-and-love movement, and I was very frustrated. We have to get those feelings out somehow. The big turning point for me was when I saw *Jaws*. I just ate it up, and I realized that I needed that kind of violence. It may be a cheap thrill, but these days how often do you get anything cheap?"

Before we get too moralistic, it is worth remembering that ours is not the first society to merchandise violence as a form of entertainment. Violence has always been a part of art, from Greek tragedy through Shakespearean drama and up to modern times; when Dickens gave public readings late in his career, he took special pleasure in reading the murder of Nancy from *Oliver Twist* and watching the ladies in the audience faint. Since the earliest two-reel Mack Sennett comedies, violence has been a staple of movies, though it has expressed different attitudes and different social values over the years. In the gangster movies of the thirties, for example, the violence reflected some of the anger, irreverence, and disaffection that many Americans felt during the Depression. In World War II movies the violence was an expression of a belligerent jingoism and xenophobia, with strong racist undercurrents. And the police movies of the early seventies represented a response to the rabid law-and-order ethic of the Nixon era.

The manner in which violence is portrayed has also changed radically, chiefly because of the dissolution of censorship restrictions that once inhibited filmmakers. The Production Code, which regulated movies until the mid-sixties, placed rigid constraints on the content of violent movies. For example, the code specified that crimes against the law "shall never be presented in such a way as to throw sympathy with the crime as against law and justice or to inspire others with a desire for imitation. . . . The technique of murder must be presented in a way that will not inspire imitation. Brutal killings are not to be presented in detail. Revenge in modern times shall not be justified."

In forbidding a realistic portrayal of crime and its consequences, the code had an insidious effect on our perception of violence. Movies made under the code suggested that murder was bloodless and painless. This dishonest approach to violence is still characteristic of much television fare, and it can be argued that this kind of "tasteful," antiseptic violence is in the long run more dangerous than the graphic brand of violence on movie screens today. In any case, one of the impulses behind the new movies is the filmmakers' desire to record the real impact of violence, without the beautification that falsified scenes of violence in the past. Serious filmmakers claim that they want to portray murder and mayhem in bloody detail in order to take the glamour out of violence. Sam Peckinpah has always insisted that he intends to dramatize the horror of violence, though anyone seeing his movies can tell that he also responds passionately to the "blood ballets" that he choreographs so lovingly.

Lawrence Gordon, the producer of *Hard Times* and *Rolling Thunder,* defends the violence in current films as valid in terms of the characters represented: "Of course there are some filmmakers who include violent scenes purely for shock value. But I think most filmmakers include violence because that is where the character takes you. People like Dirty Harry and *Taxi Driver*'s Travis Bickle exist, and audiences want to get inside those characters. They don't want to be cheated. And I think most people who see these violent films will be so horrified that they wouldn't think of going near a knife or a gun. The people who see *Taxi Driver* are going to be revolted by violence."

Unfortunately, the effect of violence on audiences is never so simple. While the filmmaker may well intend to repel viewers, there are always some people who are excited and aroused by the most ghastly images. Responses to violence are incredibly difficult to gauge and control. A great many people seeing *Taxi Driver* are undoubtedly appalled, sickened, terrified by the violence, which is what director Martin Scorsese intended; other viewers laugh and cheer when Travis goes on his murderous rampage. Scorsese looks back on the film and says, "The movie provoked different reactions from what I anticipated. When I was filming it, I never thought there would be such strong responses to the violence. But then I never thought *Taxi Driver* would be a hit. You can never anticipate those reactions, and you shouldn't try."

Responses to these films seem to become more volatile and unpredictable as the violence becomes more graphic. There were always graphic moments of violence in film—like the famous scene of the razor slitting an eyeball in the Buñuel-Dali classic, *Un Chien Andalou.* Then in 1960 *Psycho*'s shower scene startled audiences accustomed to seeing the camera turn

"Fifty per cent sex and fifty per cent violence. That's the balance we've been looking for!"

Drawing by J. Mirachi; © 1969 The New Yorker Magazine, Inc.

discreetly away from violence. Over the next several years the camera turned away less and less: Violence began to escalate in the James Bond films and in more realistic movies like Roman Polanski's *Repulsion.* But *Bonnie and Clyde,* produced in 1967, was probably the first movie to become a major source of controversy because of its violence. Arthur Penn's explicit close-ups of bloody faces and bodies twitching with bullets were more grisly images than some viewers wanted to see. Perhaps the most unsettling thing about the movie was that Penn asked us to identify with two killers; it was the film's sympathetic portrayal of two attractive criminals that represented the most subversive blow to the orthodox depiction of violence onscreen.

Sam Peckinpah continued this assault on audience complacency in *The Wild Bunch* by asking us to sympathize with killers who were even more hardened and depraved. Peckinpah perfected the use of the realistic blood squib, and the climactic massacre in *The Wild Bunch* remains one of the most shocking bits of orgiastic violence ever committed to celluloid. But Peckinpah's *Straw Dogs* may have had an even stronger impact, because it brought that same level of violence into the contemporary world, and asked us to identify with a meek intellectual who came to recognize a deep sexual satisfaction to be derived from murder.

Peckinpah's violent credo was appropriated by less talented filmmakers, and a good many reactionary action movies—*Dirty Harry, Walking Tall, Death Wish,* and dozens of sleazier imitators—celebrated revenge and vigilante justice in contemporary urban settings. These popular movies encouraged audiences to accept and applaud the most savage forms of violence. The next stage was ushered in by *The Exorcist,* which combined sex and violence in a peculiarly unsavory fashion, assaulting the audience with images more grotesque than any seen on the screen before. Since then, it seems, filmmakers have been competing in a sensationalism sweepstakes, restlessly searching for ever more horrible sights and sounds. *The Towering Inferno* featured close-ups of burning bodies; *Jaws* boasted an amputated leg and a man being gobbled whole by a shark; the climax of *Lipstick* showed a rapist shot in the genitals. David Seltzer, the skillful, unpretentious writer of *The Omen,* admits that in writing it, "I was very conscious of including the most repulsive scenes I could imagine. I wanted to write a commercial movie."

In addition to these expensive major-studio films, there are dozens of low-budget exploitation movies—revenge melodramas, tales of the occult, demolition derbies—that aim to capture the undemanding popcorn crowd with violent chills and spills. Roger Corman, the head of New World Pictures—a company that specializes in car-crash movies like *Death Race 2000, Eat My Dust,* and *Cannonball*—says, "Violence is going to escalate because the public always demands more than what they saw the last time out. Our films are not the most violent produced today. We make action pictures, but we try to stay away from extreme person-to-person violence, like heads being cut off. But even in our car-chase pictures we are conscious of putting more crashes in each movie than in the last one. The public always demands more."

Martin Scorsese reflects, "There seems to be a roller-coaster effect. Violence just keeps increasing. We seem to be heading toward that scene in *Satyricon* where a man's hand was actually cut off as part of a play. Hopefully, in about four or five years things will balance out. Eventually audiences will get tired of excessive violence."

In the meantime today's filmmakers speculate on the reason for this proliferation of violence. Robert Evans, the producer of *Marathon Man,* insists, "Violence is not the only criterion for a successful movie. In fact, I think audiences are turned off by excessive violence. We cut several minutes from *Marathon Man* because preview audiences were repelled by the violence. But you do need scenes that people will remember—like the scene where Roman Polanski cuts Jack Nicholson's nose in *Chinatown.* When we previewed *Rosemary's Baby* in Palo Alto, a woman came up to me afterward and said, 'You should be ashamed of yourselves.' At that moment I knew we had a hit. You have to have a movie people will talk about; even if they say it's terrible, at least they remember they saw it."

Producer Lawrence Gordon believes that the competition from television is the major factor encouraging violence in films. "Television has become much more violent," he points out. "Therefore your violence must be even more graphic. Audiences for action pictures expect it. Your film has to be more violent than *Starsky and Hutch*."

There are less obvious reasons for the surge of violence. In a provocative article in the November *Harper's* novelist Stephen Koch discusses a recent violent exploitation picture, *The Texas Chainsaw Massacre,* which was praised by many film buffs and even shown at the Museum of Modern Art; as a result of this exposure, the makers of the movie were signed to a five-picture contract by Universal. Koch argues that film buffs have begun to praise sadistic trash, and he contends that "the buffs form a quite coherent and by no means powerless subculture of the general intelligentsia, and they have played a very real role in the formation of modern taste." That may be overstating the point, but the film buffs certainly have a greater influence on the media than they did ten years ago. Today many buffs have critical posts with major publications, and they have a regular forum for their orgasmic reviews. Buffs evaluate movies purely in sensory terms, and they exalt the brutal movies made by the American action directors. This kind of critical acceptance certainly helps violent movies to flourish.

Besides, many former film buffs are now filmmakers active in the industry. And many of these new filmmakers regard the humanism and the social concern of the last generation of filmmakers as hopelessly old-fashioned. They want to reproduce the violent genre pictures that they loved as children. To them violence is part of the magic of movies, and they are unconcerned about the effect these movies may have on audiences.

A veteran director once told me that he has observed that some of the new filmmakers specializing in violence are meek, frail, and sickly in reality. Obviously the savage violence they work into their movies is some kind of fantasy fulfillment. For them, and perhaps for the audiences as well, testing oneself against extremes of violence is a verification of masculinity. Steve Shagan, the author of *Save the Tiger* and *Hustle,* suggests that violence comes from "the failure of American films to be sensual. The only sensuality in our movies is in violence."

Along these lines, consider the studies of sociologist Marvin Wolfgang, who has found that the great majority of murders are committed by the victim's family or close friends. In reality, murder is an intimate act; in movies like *Two-Minute Warning* and *Taxi Driver,* the murders are committed by strangers. American movies are terrified of intimacy—sexual intimacy, or even the intimacy of a crime of passion.

Obviously, there is no single explanation for the craving for violence. Moviemakers commonly justify their preoccupation by arguing that violent films only reflect reality. "The United States is the most violent country in the world," Roger Corman asserts. "We have the most murders and assaults. We have been called the rape capital of the world. I think the function of the artist is to reflect the times."

Violence in America is not limited to crime on the streets. The success ethic that dominates American life is savagely violent. Battles in the boardroom may be relatively bloodless, but they leave some of the ugliest scars. The movie industry is one of the most ruthless of all the businesses in America. The studio chiefs who produce ultra-violent movies may be expressing their own fantasies and experiences in the sadistic melodramas they peddle.

Yet their fantasies undoubtedly have wide appeal. Psychologist Seymour Feshbach contends, "Many people today feel powerless in controlling their lives. That feeling of impotence makes them susceptible to the substitute offered by movies." One of the functions of popular art has always been to give people some notion of experiences denied them in reality—a taste of romance, glamour, adventure, danger. But perhaps as everyday life becomes more smoothly homogenized, people need splashier, more grotesque vicarious thrills. Today, most people have their only contact with danger second-hand—at professional hockey and football games, at high-powered rock concerts, or at the movies. Violence as spectacle is integral to modern life.

Violence begets violence in films. Writers who want to break into the industry know that violent scripts are the easiest to sell, and so there is an unspoken pressure on them to keep the cycle going. Steve Shagan points out, "There are 4,000 members of the Writers Guild, and there were only about 55 films made by the major studios last year. Writers know that if you write a soft, introspective character study, it's a gamble. *Save the Tiger* took me three years to sell. *Hustle* came together in two weeks."

Once writers have acquired some standing in the industry, they may be in a position to say no. Shagan was offered the script of *Two-Minute Warning,* but he turned it down because, he says, "There was no attempt to explore the motivation of the sniper. I think a writer has a responsibility to define the causes and roots of violence. Otherwise you are pandering to the lowest element in the country. I wouldn't want some kid with a gun to climb up above the scoreboard at a high school football game because of a movie I wrote."

This question about the actual influence of brutal movies is one of the trickiest in the debate over violence in films. Key researchers commissioned by the surgeon general feel that they have shown how violent shows inspire violent behavior, but they have literally been in fistfights with each other over interpretation of their data. Psychologist Feshbach admits that most clinical studies have focused on TV violence rather than film violence. Nevertheless, he believes, "A steady diet of heavy, graphic violence in films does tend to make people indifferent to real-life violence. In the long run people will become inured to violence." In doing the federal index on TV violence, psychologist George Gerbner found this year that heavy TV viewers live in greater terror—feeling themselves more likely to be mugged in the streets—than do light viewers. Gerbner believes that brutal fantasies on TV have become an instrument for keeping the population scared and submissive.

One writer who is concerned about the impact of violence is Brian Garfield, who wrote the novel *Death Wish*. He intended the novel as a cautionary tale about the dangers of the vigilante mentality; the hero began by killing muggers and ended by killing children. Garfield explains, "I wanted to show that when you begin to act as a vigilante, it quickly goes out of control. The movie changed the novel to show vigilantism as a heroic act. And I was alarmed by the effect the movie had. I saw it on Times Square, and the audience reaction was terrifying. People stood up and cheered, 'Kill that mother!' " Garfield points to cases where real-life killers imitated the hero of *Death Wish,* and he says, "I feel a degree of responsibility for the victims of the violence." Recently, Garfield tried to stop CBS from showing *Death Wish* in prime time; he failed.

At the same time, however, Garfield raises another caution: "As a writer I resent censorship in any form. If people get too carried away with this antiviolence crusade, we could find ourselves in a position where violent acts are proscribed, which would mean that certain valid stories simply could not be told. That is censorship, and it is as great a danger as violence."

Edward Anhalt, the Academy Award–winning screenwriter of *Becket,* has had some direct experience with the controversy regarding violence in films. A movie that he worked on back in 1952, *The Sniper,* was caught up in a court case in Canada. A boy in Ottawa saw the movie and went out and shot eleven women. A lawsuit was brought against the filmmakers on behalf of one of the victims, but the Canadian Supreme Court decided that the filmmakers did not bear responsibility for the violence. Anhalt believes, "Most people release their aggressions and hostilities by seeing a violent film. There will always be a few neurotic, disturbed people who may be stimulated by the violence. But whatever the dangers of violence, I think censorship is a far greater danger."

Many of the best American films have always been violent. *Bonnie and Clyde, The Wild Bunch, The Godfather I* and *II, Deliverance, Mean Streets, Taxi Driver,* and the new *Carrie* are among the best movies made in this country during the last decade. Some of the worst American movies made during the same period—low-budget melodramas like *The Texas Chainsaw Massacre,* as well as big-budget productions like *Drum* and *Two-Minute Warning*—are also extremely violent. But I think we will always have to tolerate the trash for the sake of the achievements of artists like Penn, Coppola, Peckinpah, and Scorsese. The escalation of violence in films is troubling, but there are no easy solutions.

Has the saturation point been reached in the new wave of cinematic gore? The fate of violence in films rests with the moviegoing public. Some people feel that the trend toward increasing violence has already peaked.

After that recent showing of *Two-Minute Warning* I attended, a lot of people walking out admitted that the film had disappointed or disgusted them. An articulate black couple spoke for quite a few others when they said, "We feel ripped off. We'd like to get our money back. The movie was really sick, and we didn't enjoy it. But it had been advertised so heavily on television that we wanted to see what it was all about. If there were different kinds of movies around, we wouldn't be going to see junk like this." If their dissatisfaction begins to spread, maybe the situation will finally change. The only message that Hollywood understands is the ring of the cash register.

ROCK: Mirror to the World?

by EDWIN MILLER

Edwin Miller, entertainment editor of **Seventeen** magazine, sketches the history of rock music, noting how changes in rock have mirrored changes in society.

The joyous wail of an electric guitar in the night has replaced the lonesome sound of a train whistle that for generations symbolized the expanse of America. Ankle deep in the Woodstock mud, a half-million rock fans scream for more as Sly and the Family Stone sing *Higher*. Shoulder to shoulder in the Sheep Meadow in New York's Central Park, seventy thousand strong, they warm to Carole King singing *You've Got a Friend,* while overhead a crane-held cameraman films the scene. Six hundred thousand young people swarm into Watkins Glen, New York, for the biggest "Summer Jam" ever. Around the country thousands pack arenas like Manhattan's Madison Square Garden and Southern California's Hollywood Bowl watching guitar and bass players circling each other in a musical mating dance; exuberant ticket-holders swarm through the aisles in a never-ending chain with firecrackers, sparklers and Frisbees livening the scene.

In a small club in Cambridge, Massachusetts, or San Diego, California, in a cellar halfway round the world where Moscow teens duplicate smuggled rock singles on X-ray plates, it's all the same. Rock is the great leveler. No social distinctions. If you wear jeans and long hair, curly, frizzy or straight, and have a habit of occasionally questioning established values in a way that makes some older folk uneasy, you belong to the rock generation. Inside, communication is universal. Any auditorium where a group like the Allman Brothers plugs in its high-watt amplifiers becomes your living room. Groove in your seats. Jump up and shout, you're among your own people. The music is often exhilarating, sometimes deafening, because that's one way to achieve complete involvement. Few teens worry about their eardrums.

Rock, more than just another way to say pop music, is a word that underlines the vitality of a sound which suckles you, gives you comfort in loneliness and insecurity. Ex-Beatle George Harrison sings of *Living in the Material World;* Arlo Guthrie reminisces about *Alice's Restaurant* in a search for identity. There is no one dominant form; rock is a musical mosaic. In an earlier day, a song heard on a first date, on a jukebox or car radio at some meaningful moment, shaped taste for life. That time came to be encased, mummylike, in nostalgic memories. Now groups survive or founder as they vibrate to society's shock waves, mirroring images of changes everyone is going through. Hard rock, raunch rock, psychedelic rock. Soft, country, folk, transvestite or glitter rock. Jesus rock. Live in concert, on records, radio and TV, its hearers are put into direct contact with those who create it on a scale no other popular art form has ever achieved.

It's a long cry from the year 1955, when bandleader Bill Haley's version of a primitive chant, *Rock Around the Clock,* shook up the (then) older generation in a movie called *Blackboard Jungle*. But in a way, rock and roll really arrived a year later, in an explosion sparked by Elvis Presley. If you were born in '56, both you and rock would be seventeen this year. Search your growth grooves; what's your earliest subliminal memory? Elvis singing *Blue Suede Shoes*!

That growl of raw excitement was compounded of country music and rhythm-and-blues—black pop music—which most white people never heard. On tour Elvis had to be locked into the basement of a school gym between shows, the doors secured by chains that were marked with blood where girls tore their hands on the locks. Girls prowling the building were after him in their need for a souvenir of an overwhelming experience. Teens in starched Sunday dresses were turned into a raging force by his vocals, to which he kept time with swiveling hips. Adults denounced Elvis as obscene, a six-month fad. Now they applaud him in palatial Las Vegas hotels.

Rock has always urged its listeners to have fun. Somewhere in your makeup is a memory of the Beach Boys singing the American dream—surfin' in the California sun. You learned how to do the twist. A couple of years later, Mick Jagger, live, was singing *Paint It Black,* with the violence and sexual power that were to become the Rolling Stones' trademark. Older girls in his audience leaping at the stage would be hurled back into the orchestra by security guards. Always, it has been the girls trying to break out from an emotional doll's house through the explosive force of music, seeking physical release in a male-dominated society.

Millions of you wanted to see Liverpool when the Beatles appealingly sang *I Want To Hold Your Hand.* English groups fell in love with American rhythm-and-blues music on records, digested the black experience, then gave it back to us with their own changes. The Beatles paid homage to black musician Bo Diddley, the Rolling Stones studied Chuck Berry before most white Americans had ever heard of either. English rock spurred tourism and London became a big European attraction to youthful travelers.

Growing up, you were stirred by human rights, antiwar protests. Pete Seeger, Joan Baez, Peter, Paul and Mary sang in a tradition that stretched back hundreds of years to Anglo-Saxon balladeers and the political-broadside singers who sang of dissolute lords in England, coal-mine disasters in the United States. The spirit of Woody Guthrie, the daddy of protest songs, flowered in Bob Dylan, whose *Blowin' in the Wind* called the tune for civil rights activity. 1962. That was the year Bob said he would never desert his Greenwich Village haunts to roam uptown Manhattan again, after being stopped by the police one midday in Times Square. Palms out and up against the wall while they searched him for something illegal. Long-haired in jeans, he didn't, they said, look as if he belonged there! Ironically, as white teens took to jeans in the late sixties like the music-makers they followed (partially in protest against middle-class origins) musicians from the ghetto appeared in peacock splendor. Some groups were integrated. But audiences were affected by the same polarization that marred the country. Diana Ross and the Supremes performed *Stop! In the Name of Love* for white audiences, but few blacks went to white rock concerts. Blacks preferred their own singers like Aretha Franklin or James Brown. Marked by the blues, inflected by gospel harmonies, distilled from emotions that went with slavery and ghetto poverty, their music had a quality that came to be known as soul. Something white singers imitate but rarely originate. In the ghetto, many kids couldn't afford musical instruments, many didn't read very well—but they talked. Street rap. Verbal textures became all important and black groups emphasized intricate vocal harmony.

In rock, as in the larger society, negative forces thrive in a welter of one-night stands and ego trips, side by side with the positive need to communicate the hunger for mutual affection and hope for the world to become a better place to live in. Drugs have been openly opposed since the days when Jefferson Airplane's Grace Slick regularly belted out the ironic message in *White Rabbit:* "Feed your head! Feed your head!"—the first major counterculture hit.

The flower generation bloomed briefly as bands played acid rock at the San Francisco Fillmore while audiences danced amid the flashing light shows. At Fillmore East in New York, Janis Joplin bawled out the blues in a hoarse frenzy, only to die of an overdose of heroin four years later. As rock became a billion-dollar business, outstripping television and the movies, pressures on companies and performers alike kept getting heavier to produce profitable records. A modestly successful performer cutting an album every six months, playing two or three dozen concerts a year might make up to a hundred thousand dollars; a superstar could pull in five million.

By the time you reached your teens in the late sixties, rock was drawing upon every musical form, past or present. Teens may look alike, with blue jeans and long hair, but they don't listen alike, just as they don't think alike. In your mid-teens, you're at home anywhere, here or abroad, as is Paul Simon; he draws upon such sources as South American Indian rhythms and the Caribbean "reggae" beat for his eclectic ballads, sings the joy, sadness and despair of life in *American Tune*. Country music with its perennial themes of heartbreak, religion and patriotism, has become more sophisticated, as wandering Kris Kristofferson sings *Me and Bobby McGee*. Bluegrass with its fiddles and banjos and steel guitars, the Indian sitar, classical, electronic—all music is fused into rock. Short-sighted critics debate whether or not rock is dead or dying, failing to see that the living essence of rock is continuous change. No one knows which new variation some musical messiah will expand upon next year, except that it will reflect the world around you.

Rock. The music of the young. It's made you what you are.

NATALIE COLE:
Producers' Puppet, Father's Daughter, or the New Queen of R&B?

by JOHN STORM ROBERTS

The record industry is illustrated here by Natalie Cole, daughter of the late Nat "King" Cole, and winner of Grammy awards in 1975 and 1976 for Rhythm and Blues. She is, as John Storm Roberts says in High Fidelity, "as new as her audience. Black middle of the road. . . ." The emphasis is on personality as much as on music, with the question: "Who is the real Natalie Cole?" The question is pertinent since commercial success is dependent on the "package" being marketed by her producers.

The skeptical may attribute her success to her father's fame and the fact that 1975 was an off year for pop. But the achievement of winning two Grammy awards with her first album, at the age of twenty-five, remains remarkable. Still more remarkable, it came only five years after her first public performance, and to cap it all, she hadn't—she claims—intended to go into music at all.

In fact, Natalie Cole says she got very little musical prodding from her father, Nat "King" Cole: "That was his life, and I think he wanted us to know and be interested in what he was doing, but he never encouraged or discouraged any of his children to become involved in music."

She did appear with him when she was eleven, in a summer theater production of a black variation on the *Gigi* story called *I'm with You.* She was also involved in a teenage group with Carmen Dragon's and Nelson Riddle's sons. "We took piano lessons from the same teacher, and we formed a little combo, doing Ella and things like that."

But Natalie was neither aimed at a professional career, nor inclined to one. "I took piano lessons for two years, and it was just a drag for me," she says. "If I'd taken the kind of music my father played, I probably would have enjoyed it a lot more!"

All that changed in her junior year at the University of Massachusetts, Amherst, where Natalie took a degree in psychology. She got a job working as a waitress at a local club in 1971 and was soon singing with the band there on weekends. Within two years she was working the East Coast cir-

Natalie Cole: Producers' Puppet, Father's Daughter, or the New Queen of R & B?: From *High Fidelity* (February 1977). Reprinted by permission of High Fidelity.

cuit—New York, Miami, the Bahamas, TV's Mike Douglas and Jack Paar shows. Then, in late 1974, she met her present producers, Chuck Jackson and Marvin Yancy, who had had a string of gold albums with the Independents on the small r&b label Scepter.

"We went into the studio in December and did some demos with full orchestra," she says. "We didn't sign with a record company until the following year, so we really were taking a chance. But I believed in them that much—I liked what they did for me, I liked the way I sounded singing their material, and they liked the way I sounded, so when I went to sign with Capitol, I said, 'I want Jackson and Yancy with me.' "

That was a decision nobody was to regret. A year later, Natalie Cole had carried off two Grammies with her first Capitol album, "Inseparable," for Best New Artist and Best Female R&B Vocal Performance on the soul-style single *This Will Be*. Within a few months she was headlining on the supper-club circuit, on even terms with the likes of Debbie Reynolds, Manhattan Transfer, Liza Minnelli, Gladys Knight and the Pips, B. B. King and Bobby "Blue" Bland, the Spinners, and Roy Clark. And getting over musically: When she first appeared at New York's Beacon Theater, the prevailing judgment of a hip and musician-heavy audience was favorably summed up by a woman sitting next to me: "How bad is ba-a-a-d?"

These two poles—the supper clubs and the "ba-a-a-d" Beacon performance—pretty much bracket Natalie's style as well as her public. When talking influences, she tends to dwell on "singer" singers, mostly from jazz, mostly from the past. Ella Fitzgerald: "The big influence on me, the voice and the style." Carmen McRae: "A little bit of Sarah Vaughan." Judy Garland: "She was very emotional, and I liked that. Whatever Judy Garland was singing about, she just had to know what she was talking about, because she sang it with so much conviction."

But the main thrust of Natalie's singing comes from none of these. Her repertoire is given breadth by jazz-tinged ballads like *Inseparable* and *Joey* on the first album, "Inseparable"; *Good Morning Heartache* on the second, "Natalie"; and occasional scatting, in a song from "Natalie," *Mr. Melody*. But always the core, both in quantity and quality, is a joyous pop-soul singing: The sound of early Motown soul, Marvin Gaye, the Supremes, and above all, the early Aretha Franklin. Sometimes slow, like *Touch Me,* which she turns into a tour de force in concert; but mostly in uptempo numbers like the Grammy-winning *This Will Be,* in which her lead, extraordinarily like a lighter-voiced mid-'60s Franklin, tosses like spray over the jagged gospel-backup harmonies as the bluesy piano struts beneath.

Nor is Natalie about to argue with success. Her new album is "basically similar to my last two—probably more like 'Inseparable' than the second one," she says. "It's a little more r&b. I'm taking advantage of my youth right now. I like the commercial music, most of it—I've always been a Stevie Wonder and Marvin Gaye fan, and I was very much into r&b just recently. I don't want to wear that out, and that's why even on a so-called

r&b album of mine you'll hear several ballads and maybe something like *Mr. Melody,* with some scatting in it. But you have to think of the market, and my market now is young people and r&b.

"I do plan on doing a jazz album, probably in about two years. The one after this is going to be a live album, and I'd like to do an album of my father's songs. But right now, having established myself doing what I'm doing, I think it would be a mistake for me to try to go back to any standards."

Given where Natalie Cole came from, how far she has come and how fast, two questions hover constantly in the wings: Did she make it on her father's name, and, in an era of producer-domination, is she a product of her producers?

Without a doubt, her father's name got her the first club dates. She didn't much care for that, even though it saved her the years of dues paying that face almost any singer: "It was only natural that I should resent it, because I wanted to be recognized for my own talent, but at the same time it made me realize just how famous my father was. And I guess if I had been Ann Smith, I'd probably still be struggling and maybe just now being able to get ahead. . . ."

It's equally plain that Jackson and Yancy were crucial in her move from potential to success. In her own understatement, "I would say that we have formed as close a producer-artist relationship as anybody could have in a very short time." They not only produced but wrote virtually everything on her first two albums, though the new one has two of her own songs on it: *Peaceful Living* and *Your Eyes*.

But to see her as a puppet dancing on their strings would be an oversimplification. First, she was well launched before they came along. Second, whereas producer-dominated artists normally come off feebly in concert, Natalie is better on stage than on record—quite as tight, and more varied and spontaneous. Moreover, Jackson and Yancy simply aren't Gene Page. Unlike too many "creative" producers who are the bad news of the mid-'70s, they avoid both the retread lushness and the Funkzak discoplast in which the times are awash.

While they obviously understand "the market," they also do what producers are supposed to do: bring out the quality of the artist they are producing. Few of their songs have much distinction, and most are vaguely reminiscent of something else, but they suit Natalie's range admirably. As producers, they use the current commercial "sound"—the disco-soul beat of *Sophisticated Lady,* the syrupy strings of the ballads—but they also have the taste to keep things simple, framing her best young-Aretha moments with a fine backup duo, bluesy piano, and jazz-based rhythm all in vintage gospel-soul vein. In all, it's a partnership that obviously can't be faulted commercially; but it also works well musically, never dominating her or giving the impression that she is being jammed art-first into some unsuitable sack marked, "What's happening."

That's important. Part of Natalie's strength, artistically as well as commercially, is that in a period of decadence, fatigue, and gimmicks she returns to the central issues of voice, tune, and spirit. To reinterpret the ethos of the young Aretha, to keep it all clean and tight and youthful, to back herself with classically joyous, shouting gospel-soul chorus and jumping musicians, is to return to what classic r&b was all about.

Yet, for all the help her father and producers have given, Natalie's talent is her own. So are its limitations—most obviously its derivativeness, which goes beyond general similarities. Her scatting isn't simply pop-bop scatting, it specifically sounds like Ella Fitzgerald's personal style; her soul singing isn't just vintage soul, but a lighter alter ego of Aretha Franklin. Nor is she really up to her models. Her scatting is engaging but has little of Ella's breathtaking rhythmic legerdemain. Though she has something of the marvelous warm/cool jazz-ballad tone, she comes off as singing notes rather than sharing experience—perhaps because she is young and relatively sheltered. Though it is what she does best, she isn't a particularly heavy rhythm-and-blues singer, compared with (to stick to newcomers) the eccentric but marvelous Chaka Khan. She swings and bounces, but she lacks that church-bred ability to shake the foundations.

In reality Natalie Cole is, I believe, an interpretive show or club singer with an almost perfect command of the current hip-pop middle ground. She doesn't excel at any one of the styles in her repertoire, but she does well by them all. Compared even with rather similar contemporaries like

Melba Moore, her voice isn't outstanding, but she uses it with flair. Her emotions aren't deep, but her timing is beautiful. Like all the best show singers, in fact, the whole is more than the sum of its parts.

It becomes obvious when you see her on stage, in a muted long cocktail dress and necklace, moving comfortably and not much, her only prop a little silver goblet out of which she drinks rarely. She is a lifestyle away from the flash and filigree of even the more staid r&b groups, let alone the dry ice and high jinks, the constant capering of, say, Earth, Wind & Fire.

This at least is a legacy from Nat "King" Cole: "I never needed much polishing on stage. Watching my father on stage helped me a lot, even though I never thought that I'd be doing the same thing. It was just something that really impressed me, the way he worked."

Natalie Cole is, in fact, an entertainer in one of the classic American pop veins. But she is also a black singer, of an emphatically contemporary sort. Whether deliberately or by instinct, Natalie as interpreter and Jackson and Yancy as writers and producers talk primarily to a world very different from either "the streets" or the sophistication of Harlem in its flower—a world typified by her appearance last fall at the Latin Casino in Cherry Hill, New Jersey.

From outside, the Casino looks like a consumer-product factory, which, in a way, it is. Inside, space enough for a Boeing 747 is set up as an intimate bistro seating—surely—three thousand on terrace upon terrace of cramped tables and serving fair and pricey food. For Natalie's show, three-fourths of the audience was professional-class blacks from Philadelphia and Camden's ample suburbs, dressed semi-hip-casual, eating well and feeling good—an audience that the white supper club circuit has known for years but that black music has acquired only in the last five or six.

Like Melba Moore, like Ben Vereen, Natalie Cole's style is as new as her audience. Black middle of the road, you might call it, not simply all-American middle of the road sung by black singers, but m.o.r. with specifically black references: hip but slightly deodorized rhythm and blues, gospel-soul, the jazz-ballad tradition, and a nostalgia for the great period of soul when its audience was kids.

If anything, Jackson and Yancy's lyrics cater more obviously to this new audience than their music. Whereas Ellington's *Sophisticated Lady* exuded a big city world-weariness, theirs is more like an upwardly mobile black executive's dream wife: "She's a different lady with a different style/She stands tall and steady like the Eiffel Tower/She is hip to politics but loves her jazz/She's got lots of rhythm, she's got lots of class." But her man needn't feel threatened, because "She talks quiet and gentle, she acts very cool/She stays close to her lover, she obeys God's rule."*

This hip conservatism, which is, I believe, a very 1970s suburban ethos, becomes quite remarkably sexist in their ballad, *No Plans for the Future:* "Let the dishes wait, no need of dusting/No reason to clean the dirty floors/Cause I'm sure it doesn't matter now that he's gone away/I've got no plans for the future, 'cause he's not here today."

Later the question. "Why should I comb my hair when I know I'm not going anywhere?"* And nowhere the answer that the young Aretha gave a decade ago,.in her classic *Respect.*

In the long run, of course, the key question is whether she can keep this audience. And the question on which *that* ultimately depends is, behind the skill and the charm and the influences, who is the Real Natalie Cole? It's a question that her phenomenally rapid success may make hard to answer, even though age is on her side, because it's difficult to develop a personal style in the limelight, and the years of dues paying that she has missed are usually also years of growth and focus. If she pulls it off, those Grammies will have been justified, even though 1975 was an off year.

The Game's The Thing:

A Defense of Sports as Ritual

by MICHAEL NOVAK

The following article is adapted from Michael Novak's book, **The Joy of Sports: End Zones, Bases, Baskets, Balls, and The Consecration of American Spirits.** Novak, who understands that sports have assumed an importance equal to liturgy and drama for many Americans, touches briefly on radio and television sports announcers; more important, though, are the sportswriters, whom Novak calls "guardians of important treasures of the human spirit."

Years ago, the sports pages were the best-written, liveliest, and most informative about the many cultures of this nation of all the pages in the paper. The writers, or at least a good share of them, were poets, lyricists, modest craftsmen. They delighted in the nation and its variety; they loved their beat. Such love is at the heart of any form of art. It forms a secret bond between the artist and his audience. Behind the words in newsprint on the page lay a secret bond of understanding. Readers met the writers in their hearts.

Back then, one waited for terse accounts of great games or great fights by teletype. Line by line they came—bare, stark, to the point. Knowing the games and how the players looked and moved, the men gathered around the local teletype, animation rising and falling, as in their heads they recreated every action, every deed.

On the radio in the past, hearing the play-by-play, one learned to love the basic accuracy and the single bare detail that lifted the imagination. Latc for a football game at Notre Dame, I once heard the first half on the car radio. The terse verbal images, the cadences of mounting excitement, the use of the half-minute between plays to feed the imagination with details about the substitutions, tempo, and mood, reminded me of how objective and to the point sports broadcasting used to be—still is, where television is not watched. There was no pretense that sports is entertainment. One got the basic liturgy, the essential drama.

The Game's the Thing: A Defense of Sports as Ritual: Reprinted from the *Columbia Journalism Review* (May/June 1976). Excerpted from Chapter 14 of *The Joy of Sports: End Zones, Bases, Baskets, Balls, and the Consecration of the American Spirit,* by Michael Novak, © 1976 by Michael Novak, Basic Books, Inc., Publishers, New York. This excerpt first appeared in the *Columbia Journalism Review*. All rights are controlled by Basic Books, Inc.

That one received it through an eyewitness whose skills and perception one had some reason to doubt, no two witnesses being the same, did not detract from the essential focus of the experience: on the game itself. Perhaps things never happened on the field exactly as Bill Stern, or Rosie Rosewell, used to call them. Carrying a portable radio to the game, one could see with one's own eyes that "racing back on the warning track" might, or might not, threaten the outfielder with the crash into the wall that the broadcaster seemed to suggest. But excitement in the voice of the broadcaster also helped one to *see* even what in the park one's own eyes "saw"—added form, added consistency, supplied a context for comparison. All the more so when one wasn't present. Not for nothing have millions of men had fantasies of broadcasters' voices in their ears as they practiced shooting baskets, or even weaving through traffic: ". . . *three seconds left to play, one point behind, Bradley shoots, it's up, it's good! . . . He's to the thirty, gets one block, sidesteps the safety man, he's to the twenty, only one man has a shot at him now, the ten, the five, he's over! Touchdown, Olivieri! . . .*" Even the great Bill Bradley, practicing his shots "around the horn," hour by hour, disciplining himself to make ten out of thirteen from every spot before he moved to another, broadcast his own game with his own lips, cheering himself on, in isolation, in Crystal River, Missouri.

The advent of television has made cowards out of many sportswriters, mere chatty, fatuous, and complacent entertainers out of many broadcasters, and a shambles out of the religion of sports. It is true that television has given us enormous pleasures, and taught us to watch the games with new eyes. The "instant replay" has helped us to freeze the instantaneous ballet of a runner's moves; but it has also rendered the unaided eye weak and undisciplined at a real game. It is harder to concentrate in the stadium. The game looks totally different there. One regains one's peripheral vision. One doesn't have to peer through the limits of the television box, subject to the judgments of a producer about which camera angle shows which portion of the play. One sees the whole. How large it is!

One feels, in a stadium, present at a liturgy, at a kind of worship service where delight and fun are proper decorum. There is a sense of presence. Smells, touches, discomforts, the sweat and heaving of one's fellow spectators give one the sense of flesh, humanity, and actuality. At home, pleased as one is to settle back and watch the vivid color in contemplative enjoyment, there is, rather, the feeling of being a *voyeur;* one feels a kind of distance and detachment. To be sure, the power of the drama itself is often so intense that one is drawn "into" the game. One's living room, hotel room, or bar becomes an arena of its own. One cheers, yells, groans, gets up and walks around, whoops, hollers.

Between the moments of high drama, however, the broadcasters go back to being entertainers. The game is not allowed to speak for itself. Instead of the steady beat of the radio voice, there is the mindless chatter of a late-night talk show, a Johnny Carson in a jock. Everything one loathes about the entertainment ethic now obtrudes itself in places where respect is called for. Blessed are they who can listen to the radio while watching the plays on silent television. I seldom find a television broadcaster suited to the demands of sport. The tolerable voices among them would be Frank Gifford, who understands and has accurate sympathies for the ritual he is faithful to; Vince Scully when he is covering the Dodgers (but not at other times); and Curt Gowdy, who is endurable when he does not overpraise or gild or give us pieties. What I admire is a workmanlike performance that allows the game to come to me itself. The announcers are far too conscious of themselves, watching Liz Taylor and Doris Day gaining on them over their shoulders, thinking they have to please us with their (God forbid) personalities. *I do not want to be entertained.* I want to experience the event.

Howard Cosell, on the other hand, stresses the primacy of entertainment. In *Like It Is,* he explains that ABC had to attract thirty million viewers and that each paragraph he spoke needed to earn back "$100,000 a minute." Covering sports on television was big business, a risk; it had to compete, and it had to succeed. Cosell's reply to his critics was: "ABC will not be like the others. We'll be number one because we make football entertaining."

Because they establish a level of patter—and what Cosell calls the "chemistry" of interaction—the sportscasters trap themselves in banality; they cannot rise to the level of the high drama right before their eyes. When nothing is happening, they chatter on. When something happens, they can't escape their chatter. Their voices may get louder. Their exclamations are not different from our own. Where the radio broadcaster must describe what happened, carrying its inherent dramatic power, the television broadcaster says: "Did you see that! Did you see that!" They have a naive faith in the human eye. Among the millions of bombardments the eye receives each second, it needs to know *which* to fasten on. The function of a broadcaster is to give us form. But the television people have forgotten form. They do not trust the power of the word.

Television has brought millions participation, but it has also distorted what we share. The fault lies not in the technology, but in the conception of many of the sports directors, producers, and sportscasters. They boast endlessly about their skills. The self-hawking of television is revolting. A particularly disgusting point was reached in 1975 when ABC used sports shows to shill for Howard Cosell's extracurricular career as the emcee of a variety show. Nothing better showed the corruption of sports by entertainment than this transition of Cosell's; having turned football into television entertainment, he moved by inexorable logic to what he may have really wanted all along. To argue, as Cosell does, that this shilling is made necessary by money already invested and by the pressures of competition is the oldest excuse for corruption known to history.

Were television to govern its approach to sports by the nature of sports, rather than by the canons of entertainment, the technology available could do the job. For dozens of years, sports did not bore Americans. Television sports have begun to bore. Iron laws of entertainment so decree.

The most damaging effect of television has been its enervation of newspaper writers and their editors. On occasion, one cannot see the televised game. Then it is almost impossible to find out in the papers the drama of the game itself. The writers take for granted that their readers have seen the game; they write about everything else. They have lost their faith in the power of the written word. For even when one *has* seen a game, either in the flesh or on the tube, the desire to read about it the next day is undiminished. Words direct the eye and heart. Words sort out diffuse impressions. Words contrive a permanent form for life.

The power of words is vaster than that of television. We need the sports pages to nudge the word back to the center of our culture. The time would seem to be right. The novelty of the silver screen is wearing off. One wearies of the parade of athletes, celebrities, and multiple broadcasters on the tube, just as one has long since grown weary of the faces of anchormen, experts, and politicians, who all begin to resemble one another. One hungers for words to sink one's imagination into. The game's the thing. One craves words about it.

A television sportscast is too close to the event to render an account of it as a single form. A contest is a drama, whose meaning is not clear until beginning, middle, and end are seen as one. The writer can bring back a portrait, complete, whole, whose end is included in its beginning, whose unfolding he can clearly see. The live camera cannot. And sportscasters are merely guessing in advance, or from the press box, precisely what will work, or is working on the field. The writer has a better opportunity to find out, and to make the conscious strategy part of his story.

On September 8, 1975, for example, Alabama met Missouri in a televised game. I was reading a biography of coach Bear Bryant that week-

DOONESBURY by Garry Trudeau

do at Alabama and what his traditions at the school meant. The spring before, I had visited Missouri and had sharp images in my mind both of the campus on the plains, the relatively humble stadium there, and the faces of Missouri students. I knew a little of the function of the Missouri team in the state, and a little of its struggles toward greatness. For the first time in my life, my sympathies were very strongly with Alabama, which Bear seemed to hope might become his best team ever. One former Alabama player, now a coach in another league, said before the game that the Alabama team included the greatest talent ever assembled on one team in the South. Yet Missouri totally mastered Alabama. The frustrations of obviously excellent players were tangible; one wanted, almost, to reach out and help. I couldn't figure out exactly how Missouri was doing it. Two or three offensive plays they used seemed extraordinarily interesting; they worked with such brilliance I wanted to know the secret.

The next day, I looked in vain in the relatively long accounts of the game in *The New York Times* and *Newsday* for an account of those plays, and of the defensive formations that kept Alabama contained as they had not been in five years. Gladly would I have exchanged a dozen articles on trades, analyses of financial conflicts, and organizational chit-chat about players' unions and corporate bosses, for intelligence about the strategic insights that dominated the actual play. A friend of mine in Alabama, blessedly, mailed me the sports page of the Anniston *Star*. There, precisely diagrammed, were the plays I wanted to know about. That is the sort of intelligent reporting one longs for in the press. Football is delightful because it bears such study. More is always happening than meets the eye. The players and the coaches, appearing for television interviews, have been intimidated by the entertainment format; they seldom get a chance to say abstractly and technically what we need to know—what they would tell their own observers in the booths above. Television, in its hunger to personalize the game, seldom deals with its abstract strategy, its formal design, its team execution. It gossips.

Yet not all the failings of sports reporters today are due to cowardice in the face of television. In at least two ways the writers, some of them at least, undercut themselves. Some of them believe that they are superior to those they cover; they believe it is their function to prick the bubble of illusion surrounding sports. One could therefore call them pricks. But Jimmy Cannon's gentler term, "chipmunks," from a singing group that specialized in mixing electronic sounds, is the one that has stuck. Some "chipmunks" would prefer to be working on some other section of the paper, covering financial or business news, or investigating politics. There is some plausibility to their new conception of sports reporting: the growth of sports as a plaything of millionaires, for example, badly needs to be investigated. Still, it seems astonishing to read writers who seem not to love their subject.

In early 1975, David Shaw of the *Los Angeles Times* wrote a page-one article of 129 column inches on the new sportswriting, praising his own paper's sports page as the best in the country, and lavishly commending its publisher and editors. He had warm enthusiasm for the new breed of sportswriters. He praised the "quality of their writing," their "questioning minds" and "master's degrees." According to Shaw, the movement started with Larry Merchant, Joe McGinniss, Jack McKinney, and George Kiseda at the *Philadelphia Daily News* in 1957. It has spread to the *Los Angeles Times*—but not to its opposition (Shaw emphasizes), the *Herald-Examiner*—to *Newsday, The Boston Globe, The Philadelphia Inquirer,* and "only a few other sports sections in the United States now actively moving toward the level of those already mentioned": *The Washington Post,* the *New York Post,* the *Chicago Tribune,* the *Chicago Sun-Times, The Miami Herald,* and *The New York Times.* The new sportswriters have a "litmus test" for their side: how a writer covered Muhammad Ali, Joe Namath, and the early New York Mets. The good writers dealt with such men "on their own terms, as representatives of a new independence and self-awareness." The good guys saw that the early Mets weren't serious but a diversion, and the good guys "laughed sympathetically" with them. The way you laugh is important nowadays, even in sports.

It is astonishing to read Shaw's description of earlier sportswriting: " 'Meat and potatoes' sportswriting, it was called, and it consisted almost solely of scores and statistics—batting averages, shooting percentages, earned-run averages, running yardage, passing percentages . . ." Shaw must not have gained his master's degrees in sportswriting history, or dipped into anthologies; for the older sportswriting was some of the most sociologically acute, colorful, lyrical, and biting in the history of journalism. What pleasure it affords to read collections of old clippings.

Shaw, however, was deeply moved by "the socio-political upheavals of the 1960s." He writes:

> The times—and the nation's sports pages—they are a changin', and it is now no longer sufficient to write sports stories by the numbers . . . or by the clichés. The more sophisticated and literate reader of today's sports page wants to know more than what happened on the field. He also wants to know how it happened and why (or why not), as well as what may have happened before (or after) the event, in the locker room, the courtroom, the boardroom, and the bedroom.
>
> Racism, drugs, sex, religion, gambling, exploitation, psychology, cheating, feminism, dress styles, violence, antitrust legislation—all these subjects, and many more, have been explored in detail on the sports pages in recent months.

Shaw lists several ways in which the new sportswriters are better than the old; to me, his claims sound either untrue or dismaying. The athlete is not romanticized, but "analyzed, criticized, and even condemned." The sporting event is not "treated as seriously as a holy crusade" but dealt with "lightly, humorously, sarcastically or scornfully." We now probe "the athlete's development as an individual, his relations with others (on and off the field) and his attitude toward a whole range of personal, political, and psycho-social issues." In addition, "Where once the sports pages contained some of the worst writing in the newspaper, now—on any given day—the best piece of pure writing in some very good newspapers might well be found on the sports page." Also, "the rooter as writer is a vanishing breed." Finally, "the biggest single change in sportswriting has been the coming of sociology to the sports page."

Shaw, above all, exalts his own group's new intellectual status. The sports department is no longer "the toy department . . . a sandbox peopled by the idiot children of journalism." The "new-breed sportswriter" is "socially and politically aware, motivated more by his own curiosity and need to write than by a love of sports for sports' sake." The greatest impetus to the new sportswriting, Shaw admits, however, is television. The "good" papers no longer re-create or analyze games; they look for "soft angles" not covered by television.

The new sportswriters do not actually write very well; only Roger Kahn —and he is not really one of them—writes with distinction. The late Leonard Shechter wrote with bite and wit, however, and his book is the fullest statement of the chipmunks' position to date. The title of his delightful, wry, and astringent book is itself an insult: *The Jocks*. He describes it as "a sports book by a man who hates sports." Hate, of course, is next to love, and infinitely to be preferred to indifference. Many a good book has had its origin in hate. Passionate attack is at least as important in writing as in football. What Shechter adds to hate are arrogance and contempt.

There is a virulent passion for debunking in the land, one of the consequences of the horrors of Vietnam, the sudden visibility of the depth of racism, and Watergate. In Shechter, as in others, however, the rage against sports seems overwrought, disproportionate, and off the mark. Sports are symbolic realities, but somehow in these writers sports begin to symbolize *political* evils. It is as though their rage against the nation, and perhaps against themselves, is misdirected into sports. They do not, by and large, distinguish clearly enough between the realm of the spirit acted out in sports and the impact of mass communications and commercial interests.

"Nowhere else in the world," Shechter writes, "is such a large portion of the population so consistently engaged in sports and games." One wonders. It is estimated that two billion persons saw the World Cup Championships in soccer in 1973, outside the United States. It offends him that 228 million Americans paid to attend major sports events in 1967. The figure sounds impressive until we average it out for a population of 210 million: paid attendance is approximately one per person every year. In 1973, by comparison, 112 million Americans visited a zoo. Only 35.9

million attended football games in 1967, according to Shechter; 34.7 million, baseball games; 22 million, basketball games. (These figures are for professional or college games.) Another 67.8 million went to the races. It dismays Shechter that sports have become "a monster, a sprawling five-billion-dollar-a-year industry." This is a large sum. Yet many industries are larger, including the print and broadcast media, the pet industry, and cosmetics. Out of a gross national product of almost $3 trillion, $5 billion does not seem disproportionate.

Shechter devotes most of his energy in *The Jocks* to every example of "the dump, the fix, the thrown game, the shaved points" he can find in the history of American sports. He adds little new evidence to familiar allegations, and lists few episodes that are not well known. His point is a good one. Wherever money is involved, it is best to be on guard. From his point of view, however, the public gets pitifully little from the hoopla. Sports yield, in his judgment, "a marvelous sense of the importance of the unimportant." His prose is passionate:

> Around the simplicity which most of us want out of sports has grown a monster . . . which pretends to cater to our love for games but instead has evolved into that one great American institution: big business. Winning, losing, playing the game, all count far less than counting the money. The result is cynicism of the highest order. There is no business in the country which operates so cynically to make enormous profits on the one hand, while demanding to be treated as a public service on the other. . . . What we get, as opposed to what we think we get, is what this book is about. . . . It's about the cynicism of American sports. . . . It's about the newspapers and the newspapermen who shill for sports. It's about television, the conscienceless and ruthless partner of sports. It's about the spoiled heroes of sports, shiny on the outside, decaying with meanness underneath. It's about the greedy professionals and posturing amateurs, the crooks, the thieves, the knaves and the fools. These are not trivial things. Sports have a great and continuous impact on American life.

Shechter's passion for purity is a useful contribution. But how will it be executed? If it means that sportswriters will now become investigative reporters whose mission is to prove that men in sports are as venal as men outside of sports, we shall not learn much we don't already know.

The main business of a sportswriter is to describe what happened in athletic events. The contests themselves are the forms of his craft. Everything else is secondary, instrumental, and to be judged in that light. The business side of sports smells of rot; but the business side of sports should be reported on the business pages. The politics of sports are rotting, too; but the politics of sports belongs on the national or the city desk. Many of the stories about big money in sports—money made by teams or paid to individual players—are not true; they are exaggerated as part of the hype to attract attention. Nothing should be hidden; everything should be reported. *But not in the sports pages.*

When I read the sports page, I'm not interested in big business, wheeling and dealing, money; all that is part of the mundane world of everyday and belongs on the other, boring pages of the paper, to be read from a sense of duty. On the sports page, I seek clear images of *what happened,* or, in advance, *what is likely to happen* in athletic contests. I expect guidance in learning afterwards exactly *how it happened.* I would like sports reporters to be, in this sense, better newsmen. I would like them to give probing, intelligent, and artistic accounts of the one world that here interests me: the events on the field. The essential craft of the sportswriter is mimetic: to recreate events, to imitate and to reveal their form, to catch new sides to their significance. The craft is more like that of the novelist or dramatist than like that of the investigative reporter.

It is important to our kind of civilization to keep sports as insulated as we can from business, entertainment, politics, and even gossip. Naturally, sports involve all these elements. But none of them should be permitted to obscure the struggle of body and spirit that is their center. The athletic contest has too much meaning for the human spirit to be treated with contempt. Our civilization needs sports, and it needs as well the skillful exercise of the sportswriter's craft. The narrative forms that recount athletic struggles supply millions with a sense of form. These forms express implicitly realities of law, fairness, effort, and spirit. Each of our major sports dramatizes a different myth. Each dramatizes forms of art and beauty and excellence precious to the human race.

Who, watching the sixth game of the World Series of 1975 in Boston's ancient and angular Fenway Park, as first the Cincinnati Reds and then the Boston Red Sox fought their way back from three-run deficits and battled for four hours with brilliant play after brilliant play—Lynn of Boston lying immobile after crashing his spine into the centerfield wall; Foster of Cincinnati throwing sharply from left field to make a bases-loaded double-play at the plate; Evans of Boston racing back to the seats in right in the eleventh to take away a certain home run; Fisk fighting the night breeze with his hands to pull his twelfth-inning homer far enough inbounds to hit the foul-line pole and give Boston the victory 7-6—who, watching this game, could not detect some of the main sources of our civilization's strength, acted out in ritual form? It is ponderous to put it this way; best if one drinks in the pleasure, imitates the attitudes, without too many words. But it is precisely in tacit and unspoken ritual forms that all religions have most effectively taught their hidden mysteries. The account of these rituals, in narrative form, is the main business of the sports page. It is being seriously neglected.

Without narrative forms, a culture flies apart; sorting out the relevant from the irrelevant becomes impossible; living loses zest. Life in its multiplicity overwhelms the brain. The function of religion, art—and sports—is to gird up perception with *form*: to show those in the midst of struggle what to look for. The opera, the play, the cinema, the short story, the ballet, the modern dance, wrest form from chaos. The forms of play *constitute* civilization; the forms of the free ("liberal" arts) give it shape. Without them, there is no civilization. Work alone does not give form; neither does politics. More radical than either, at the basis of culture, is play.

The forms of play, including the narrative forms crafted by sportswriters, are absorbed into the psyche, become *its* forms. They become forms through which other forms may be perceived. That is why games are so important. They expand, or limit, future possibilities. For this reason, above all, it is important to be vigilant over the corruptions and the range of sports. Standards of fair play, honesty, courage, scrappiness, law-abidingness, excellence, perfect execution, are dramatized in a baseball game, in football, and in basketball. These are standards difficult to meet in the contests themselves, in the industry that brings them to the public, and in the rest of life. As we have seen, these standards belong not to the players, who may not embody them, but to the inherent structure of the game. Without such standards in its ritual structure, a game could not be played; it would be meaningless. Without such standards in a culture, human beings could not complain of corruption or incompetence.

Sports are not a sufficient vocabulary of forms for a whole human life; but they are a fundament, a basic vocabulary, around which it is possible to build an ampler human structure. I have heard artists say, "Poetry is my whole life!" or, "Acting is my whole life!" Similarly, some athletes or coaches have said, "Football is my whole life." Such sentences are not to be taken literally; ordinarily they mean that every life has its finite work around which the rest of life centers. In choosing the centerpiece for one's life, one wants to choose a form that allows growth in other dimensions. A high proportion of athletic interest lies in self-knowledge and in insight into the psyches of others: many with the same skills do not play as well as others; inner struggles differ dramatically. So, too, do attitudes. Thus, many athletes and coaches find their work of absorbing interest. For others, athletics are just a job for a certain time in their lives. For most of us, they are part of our mythic world—nourishment for body, soul, and imagination.

They dramatize our sense of order. They show how the experience of defeat is a kind of death. They feed our lust for unfaked excellence. Sports are our nation's strongest forms of natural religion, inculcating discipline, a taste for perfection, and the experience of beautiful and perfect acts.

Writers on the sports page need to know that they are guardians of important treasures of the human spirit. Most of what Americans know about the humanistic traditions—about excellence in act, about discipline, about community, about the unity of body and will and spirit, etc.—they learn first-hand from their experiences in sport. More about the nature of reality is conveyed on the sports pages than in the smoke and puffery of the front pages. Sportswriters ply a craft indispensable to the human spirit. They should try to grasp the heart of the dramatic conflict in each game (each game being different), to report the shifts in strategy and tactics, and to render in accurate poetic fashion the great acts of every game. The human spirit in our time is starved for good reporting of strong narrative forms. Sportswriters are story tellers. They should tell truthful yarns. Leave the gossip to the Suzies and the Earls and the Ronas of the land. Be Lardners, Hemingways, Saroyans. Be themselves.

MINI-CASE STUDY

CURRENT SOCIAL ISSUES AND THE ENTERTAINMENT MEDIA

The ability of the media to present ideas, both overtly and subtly, is discussed in articles throughout this book. The subject takes on an added dimension, however, when dealing with the media presentation of controversial issues in an entertainment format.

The entertainment media—always hungry for subject matter—attempt to deal with social issues of the day, such as women's liberation, homosexuality, race relations, drugs, divorce. All too often, however, they merely exploit a social issue or treat it superficially. Although audiences will watch critically acclaimed programs—the television dramatization of Alex Haley's **Roots** drew the largest audience in television history—overall most people seem to prefer light escapist fare. Since commercial success is usually uppermost in the minds of the entertainers, the media will more often provide a show like **Good Times** than like **Roots.**

The following selections discuss the difficulties inherent in attempting to treat controversial social issues in a mass entertainment format.

Where Has All the Protest Gone?

TO TELEVISION

by STEPHEN FARBER

Although most American movies have always been designed as escapist fantasies, Hollywood has also produced a substantial number of hard-hitting, topical films dealing with controversial social issues. This muckraking tradition goes back to early Warners exposés like "I Am a Fugitive From a Chain Gang," and continues through such films as "Fury," "You Only Live Once," "The Grapes of Wrath," "The Snake Pit," "On the Waterfront," "Rebel Without a Cause," "Blackboard Jungle," "Twelve Angry Men," "I Want to Live," right up to "Easy Rider" and "Medium Cool." Many of these social dramas have dated badly, but over the years they gave American movies a measure of urgency, and a vital connection with the world outside the theater.

In the last couple of years, however, with only a few exceptions, our movies have nervously avoided social themes. Among the latest films only "Serpico" has tried to attack the failures of American society, and it had to be financed by an *Italian* producer. Of the films due out in the next year, it is hard to find more than one or two that sound even mildly controversial. The irony is that television, traditionally the medium for safe, frivolous entertainment, has been growing bolder while features have become more cautious and evasive.

Recent TV movies with a strong social consciousness include the highly praised "Autobiography of Miss Jane Pittman," "The Marcus-Nelson Murders" (about the police Gestapo tactics that led to the Supreme Court's Miranda decision), Stanley Kramer's "The Trial of Julius and Ethel Rosenberg," Tennessee Williams's "The Migrants," "I Love You . . . Goodbye" (about a married woman awakening to new possibilities and leaving her family), "A Case of Rape," and "The Execution of Private Slovik."

These TV films, like Hollywood's

old "social problem" pictures, vary widely in quality. Regardless of the merit of individual films, this change in the content of movies and television is a very significant development, worth examining in some detail. The movie studios essentially stopped making topical films after the box-office failure of the post–"Easy Rider" youth movies ("The Strawberry Statement," "The Revolutionary," "Dealing," etc.)

However, their cowardice can ultimately be traced to the Vietnam war. With the country polarized by Vietnam, Hollywood did not want to take a chance on alienating part of the audience by making either pro-war or anti-war movies. As a result, the only fictional movie about Vietnam ever made in this country was John Wayne's "The Green Berets."

Since the beginning of the Vietnam War, the studios' growing fear of controversy has affected other subjects as well. A film like Costa-Gavras's "State of Siege," which depicted U.S. support of military dictatorships in Latin America, could never have been financed by a major studio. Even "Executive Action," the clumsy, evasive film about the assassination of President Kennedy, had difficulty finding backers and was finally produced with independent financing.

And although black action movies have proliferated in the last few years, no dramatic film has touched on the civil rights protests or the black revolutionary movements of the sixties. I think one of the reasons "The Autobiography of Miss Jane Pittman" had such a strong impact was that the background to the civil rights movement had never before been explicitly dramatized in a fictional film. Watching that TV movie, set in 1962, one had the sense that films were finally catching up with recent American history.

The women's liberation movement is another subject that has terrified movie producers—so much so that most recent American films have dispensed with women altogether. Although modest in scope, the TV movie "I Love You . . . Goodbye" (written by Diana Gould and directed by Sam O'Steen) explored a contemporary woman's struggle for self-respect with more courage and honesty than any current Hollywood feature. And Fay Kanin's "Tell Me Where It Hurts" (directed by Paul Bogart) dealt perceptively with a consciousness-raising group organized by several middle-aged housewives.

In explaining their refusal to make films about controversial subjects, industry spokesmen often argue that Americans could not possibly want to see a feature film on any subject exhaustively covered by the news media. Yet fictional fllms can probe beneath the headlines to illuminate the human implications of abstract issues, and deepen our understanding of social problems. The powerful TV movie "A Case of Rape" (intelligently written by Robert E. Thompson, incisively directed by Boris Sagal) was more meaningful than any news story.

As a result of Elizabeth Montgomery's searing performance, we could *feel* the humiliation and impotent rage of a woman fighting vicious prejudices and archaic laws on rape. In one night, this movie probably did more to alter men's consciousness of the experience of rape than several thousand radical manifestoes.

Movie and television producers might insist that television is today a more appropriate medium for topical subjects than feature films.

For one thing, television can reach more people. For another, a TV movie can be on the air two or three months after the script is completed, whereas a feature may take as long as two years to reach the screen. With that long a time lapse, studios are very reluctant to invest in social dramas that may be out of date when they are released.

The television industry is actually comparable to the movie industry of the thirties and forties, when films could be turned out very quickly, and when each studio produced so many films that a few provocative, serious pictures did not represent much of a risk. Similarly, television gobbles up so much material in a single week that it can absorb an occasional social protest drama along with the sitcoms and cop shows and damsel-in-distress melodramas.

In today's movie industry, on the other hand, so few films are made each year that almost every one must be perfectly safe. The studios no longer feel they can afford the luxury of unconventional or controversial material; they are more insecure and therefore less adventurous than at any time in their history.

There is another, more disturbing reason for the increasing blandness of American movies: Whereas the last generation of important American filmmakers (including Arthur Penn, Sidney Lumet, John Frankenheimer and Martin Ritt) had and continue to have strong social concerns, many younger writers and directors have little or no interest in social issues. Peter Bogdanovich and William Friedkin have set the example for the new breed of filmmakers, who champion old-fashioned "entertainment" movies without the slightest social significance. Some of them come from film schools in which the auteur theory has been enshrined as gospel, and where courses of study concentrate on arcane meanings in the melodramas of Alfred Hitchcock, Howard Hawks, Don Siegel and Douglas Sirk. When they enter the industry, these young filmmakers want to remake the simple-minded genre movies that they loved as children and that the academics have finally made respectable.

Among these young filmmakers, and among some critics, "social consciousness" has become a term of mockery and abuse, synonymous with a creaky effort by Stanley Kramer, or a graceless piece of thirties agitprop. People forget that many of the most talented filmmakers outside America—De Sica, Godard, Bertolucci, Bellocchio, Rosi, Costa-Gavras, Satyajit Ray, Lindsay Anderson—have made strong social and political films that transcend didacticism. Only in Hollywood is the film of social criticism scorned.

The indifference of American movies to social realities is symptomatic of a radical failure of purpose. More and more movies are set in the past, and even the best movies set in the present ("Mean Streets" or "The Long Goodbye," for example) do not seem quite contemporary, for they concern characters with the sensibility of an earlier time.

The few films that do make some attempt at social criticism are hopelessly out of date. For example, Martin Ritt's "Conrack," about a young white idealist who comes to teach some black schoolchildren on an island off the coast of South Carolina, is a well-meaning liberal film; but in celebrating the teacher's swift, triumphant transformation of the illiterate kids into eager young scholars, the film denies the true challenge of teaching the underprivileged. A romantic glamorization of poverty, full of "heartwarming" movie clichés, "Conrack" seems painfully diluted next to television's "Miss Jane Pittman."

In comparing recent films and television, I am not trying to suggest that television is enjoying a sudden renaissance. It is worth remembering that the great bulk of TV fare remains moronic, and even the best TV drama is still a little too contrived and mechanical. Each scene is there to make a simple point; every character can be summed up in a single sentence; the story has to be kept straightforward and perfectly lucid.

Nevertheless, television has made giant improvements in the last year, and the fact is that the great majority of features are now substantially below the level of the best TV movies. Given a choice between staying home to watch "Miss Jane Pittman" or "A Case of Rape," and going out to see "Conrack," "McQ," "Busting" or "Blazing Saddles," the sensible decision would be to stay home. If television continues to take more chances while movies take fewer, even the most loyal moviegoers will surrender to the small screen.

There will always be a place for a variety of movies, including fantasy and escapism. But if movies ignore all social realities, and lose touch with the issue that concerns us, they will no longer matter; they will be just another enervated form of lightweight entertainment, comparable to roller derbies or flower shows.

'FUNNY—ONCE I START A SOLZHENITSYN NOVEL I CAN'T PUT IT DOWN UNTILL I FINISH IT,....'

O Maude, Poor Maude

by RICHARD A. BLAKE

How the tears flowed for CBS and its stellar producer Norman Lear when all the sponsors and 36 of 189 affiliates dropped the reruns of "Maude's Dilemma," August 14 and 21, as though they were tainted with plague bacilli.

Instrumental in the quarantine were the efforts of Bishop James S. Rausch, secretary of the U.S. Catholic Conference, and Robert Beusse of the USCC's Office of Film and Broadcasting in New York. Bishop Rausch sent a letter to 160 dioceses asking that local bishops contact CBS affiliate stations in their area; Mr. Beusse's efforts with CBS management resulted in a warning that flashed on the screen at the start of the program: "You may wish to refrain from watching it, if you believe the broadcast may disturb you or others in your family."

Because their actions were effective, the press was horrified. "Catholic Heat," claimed *Variety;* "Pressure," tsk-tsked *Broadcasting;* "Alien to the American concept of free speech," pontificated the New York *Times.* Most remarkably of all, Dr. Everett Parker, of the United Church of Christ Communications Office, accused his Catholic counterparts of returning "to the blackest days of the Legion of Decency when Catholic pressure reduced motion pictures to bland escape themes devoid of social or moral content." Take that, you Catholic repressionists!

It is a sad fact of life that, in the world of communications, Catholic spokesmen always speak in the shadow of the Index of Forbidden Books, the Inquisition and zealous denunciations and boycotts of Rossellini's *The Miracle* (1951) and Kazan's *Baby Doll* (1956). Little wonder that all these psychological skeletons were piously dragged from the closets of memory. The Deuteronomic historians were right: "The iniquity of the fathers will be visited upon their children to the third and fourth generation."

The scenario, then, was all too predictable: once a protest is labeled "Catholic," the issue switches from a discussion of the objectionable content of a program to an outcry against the horrors of Catholic thought-control. Ironically, the very day *Maude* was shown, CBS announced that 96 stations had rejected Joseph Papp's production of *Sticks and Bones,* rescheduled from last March. All the sponsors likewise dropped out. As yet I have seen nothing in the press questioning the kinds of pressures exerted or the groups who may have been active in taking more than half the affiliates out of the network for this prize winning drama.

Will a successful protest by one religious group encourage other pressure groups and eventually lead to a wasteland of "bland escape themes," as Dr. Parker fears? It is a question worth pondering, for in a nation of 200 million people, it is impossible to say anything significant without offending someone, and it doesn't take too many offended parties to become an organized protest. Since such continual pressure could become stifling, organized protest of this kind should be used rarely and selectively. Realizing that many of the most vocal groups do not reflect responsible opinion, the industry has the added burden of weighing each protest on its own merits.

What about "Maude's Dilemma"? The problem is not controversial content, but the mode of treatment; there are distinctions among the different genres. *Maude* is a comedy; it does not present a discussion of abortion by experts, offer the editorial position of a station, which by law must be identified as editorial and which may be answered by an opposing view under the equal time provision of the Fairness Doctrine, nor, finally, does it present a serious dramatic conflict in which a woman faces a tragic decision. Unless I am very much mistaken, any of these formats would meet only marginal objection.

In "Maude's Dilemma," abortion is not a matter of life and death; it is a joke with a deadly message: the divorced daughter tells Maude to outgrow her childhood hang-ups, since repugnance for abortion is a silly old-fashioned idea.

In comedy, taste is the all important criterion for acceptability. Some topics are agreed to be completely unacceptable for comedy: belief in God, homosexuality, drug addiction, genocide. Other delicate topics may or may not be treated in an acceptable style: Flip Wilson on race is tasteful but, by today's standards, *Amos 'n' Andy* is not.

Situation comedy presents its own special problems of taste since it presents approximations of real people as the basis of humor. Maude is such a character, and her joke involves contemplating, for laughs, what many people consider the murder of a human being. Her hesitations, and consequently the moral beliefs of many in her audience, are held up to ridicule. Her decision to go ahead with the abortion is more than black humor; it is grotesque.

Mr. Lear, whose success with *All in the Family* was built largely on his willingness to break the taboos of ethnic humor to arrive at a larger truth, is an effective social critic. But, in "Maude's Dilemma," he passed beyond social satire and became merely offensive to those of many faiths who oppose abortion. Like it or not, the Catholic hierarchy is the principal agent for voicing those beliefs.

Censorship is ugly, but telling a station or an advertiser that their presentation is offensive is another matter, especially when it is needlessly repeated after earlier protests. It is too bad that abortion and censorship always seem to provoke such strident rhetoric that stereotypes and acrimony generally replace dialogue and the expression of legitimate grievances.

new "permissiveness" TV in prime-time fare

by JOHN J. O'CONNOR

In any discussion of "permissiveness" on television, the favorite catchword of defenders is "contemporary." Second in popularity is "mature." Both words carry legitimate weight, but neither can obscure the fact that TV, as the most massive of mass mediums, is confronted with some very serious problems.

Permissiveness refers, of course, primarily to matters sexual. The public, ironically, is likely to be less concerned about such TV matters as violence or constant hucksterism. By now, those commodities are familiar on the small screen. The prime-time sex explosion is relatively recent.

Implied sex has long been a staple of cutely smarmy conversations on the late-night talk shows. More direct, but hardly explicit, treatments were incorporated into, of all places, some of the afternoon soap operas. In prime time, however, standard procedures had seemed curiously bound to the old movie code: A couple might be put in bed together, but at least one of the man's feet had to remain on the floor.

Now all has changed, and on all levels of TV programming. On "Gunsmoke," James Arness gets to indulge, quite tastefully, in an occasional but unmistakable dalliance. On "McCloud," the detective hero has a steady playmate. On "The Girl with Something Extra" and "Adam's Rib," the most prominent prop is a double bed on which the married couples cavort ingeniously.

Those are the basic, pervasive themes. Then there are the variations. On "Hawkins," James Stewart unblinkingly takes a tour through a Hollywood society of male homosexuals. On "Medical Center," Chad Everett discovers that the nurse he has been courting is a lesbian. And on "Police Story," vice-squad policemen become barely distinguished from the racially mixed ring of pimps and prostitutes they are investigating.

It's a long way from "The Many Loves of Dobie Gillis." And it leaves TV confronting those problems. One was pinpointed in a recent speech by Herbert S. Schlosser, president of the N.B.C. Television Network:

"This issue, in its basic terms, is how to balance a respect for creative freedom with an equal respect for television as a home medium, a medium that serves so wide a diversity of tastes and interests that it must observe certain limitations."

He added: "As a mass medium for home viewers, television will never lead any parade of permissiveness. But it should not lag so far behind the march of an audience of millions that it can be chained to the past by a few hundred letters of complaint."

That is the more noble and commendable aspect of the problem. Other aspects tend to be considerably more practical and perhaps more pressing. The pressures are coming from two directions.

One, very much in the present, involves advertisers who are assiduously courting urban "young adult" audiences, the more conspicuous of today's consumers. The other, still in the future, is the possibility of competition from pay-TV and video cassettes, both of which promise users more "mature" material than TV is currently able to provide.

Those young-adult audiences include a significant section of the population that has been entertainment-weaned on R-rated or X-rated movies. They have also contributed heavily to the success of such magazines as *Playboy*. They are partial to "contemporary" themes. They are unlikely to be turned on by the trials and tribulations of "The Brady Bunch."

The theory of community standards is dubious to begin with, but in TV it is impossible. The community is too vast, covering too many different standards. But for the moment, the urban, young adults are the TV-and-advertiser target. Some programs ("Hee-Haw" or "The Lawrence Welk Show") have been demonstrably popular but were dropped from network schedules because they appealed primarily to elderly or rural audiences.

The result is that the "certain limitations" on TV are being broadened. Another result is that, despite the injection of "contemporary" and "mature" situations, the mix of regular prime-time TV is no less banal or blatantly manipulative than it ever was. Contemporary, in most cases, has nothing to do with quality or intelligence.

"OUR STRUGGLE IS NOT TO BE WHITE MEN IN BLACK SKIN"

by
JOHN OLIVER KILLENS

There was a time not many years ago when 25 million Black Americans were invisible in the media of mass communications. A Black child could go to school and look into his school books and children's books and come home and stare at television and go to an occasional movie, and go through this routine from day to day, month to month and year to year, and hardly (if ever) see himself reflected in the "cultural" media. It was as if he had no real existence, as if he were a figment of his own imagination, or at best, if he had an existence it wasn't worth reflecting or reflection.

It was a time when my family and I lived in the Bedford-Stuyvesant section of Brooklyn, N.Y., in a brownstone, on the parlor floor and basement. Our television was in the living room on the parlor floor. At that time my daughter Barbara, who was 7 or 8 years old, was an incorrigible TV watcher. She stared at the little box hour upon hour, from program to program; she did not discriminate. She appeared to watch the commercials with as much interest as she did the programs, which was just as well when you think about it. We finally came to the conclusion that Barbara was looking for some reflection of her own identity, someone who looked like her or her mother or her brother or her father on the TV screen. When once in a month of Sundays she saw a Black man on television, she would run downstairs where we usually were, shouting: "Daddy! Mommy! Negro on TV!" And by the time we'd get upstairs, he would have done his little old thing and gone.

But Black men and women fought back, protested, demonstrated, wrote letters, threatened boycotts, played upon the White established conscience. P. J. Sidney walked a million miles in protest. And what have we to show for it? Progress, right? No more invisibility.

"What do you think of the progress we have made in TV?" I asked a lady.

"Just fabulous," Mrs. B. replied. "Tremendous. I mean we've really got it made." Mrs. B. is a middle-aged, middle-class, brown-skinned, pleasant-faced, exuberant woman. Her husband works in New York's transit system. Mrs. B. teaches school.

"What do you mean tremendous?" I asked her.

"I mean tremendous," she answered. "It's not like it used to be, when you could stare at TV all day and all night long and hardly ever see a Black face except in an athletic contest or clowning in the kitchen. But it's different now. You have to admit it's different now."

"Yes," I said. "I'll have to admit it's different. But I'm not sure about tremendous."

"Why," she said, "you can hardly look at a TV show without seeing a Black man or woman, and they're not domestic servants either. And if they are, they speak good English."

"Yes," I said reluctantly. "But—"

"Even the commercials got us in them."

"What is your favorite colored show?"

"I like **Julia** best of all. Diahann Carroll is such a lovely, charming lady, and that little boy just steals your heart away. What I like about **Julia,** it's a show that isn't about Negroes at all. It's universal. It doesn't stereotype the Negro. It's got no 'dis here' and 'dat dare' in it."

"That is apparently true," I had to admit reluctantly.

"I also like **Room 222** and **Sesame Street.** They're nice and easy—especially **Sesame Street**—and they're integrated. **Sesame Street** is especially good for children."

I posed the same question to Mrs. X., middle-class, middle-aged, nurse, socially-conscious, active in Black women's organizations. Her husband is a postal employee. Mrs. X. said she didn't watch much television. She usually listened to the talk programs over radio. "They're more informative." As to television, she shrugged it off with, "It's all right. **Julia** is OK and **Sesame Street.** Once in a while I watch **Mission: Impossible** and **Mod Squad** and **Julia.** My favorite show on television is **Sesame Street.** It's the best children's show they ever had." She said she liked to watch the variety shows in which Black people appear. She liked **Black Journal.** "On second thought," Mrs. X. said, "my favorite Black show is **Soul!** Did you see that wonderful show Ossie and Ruby did on Langston Hughes? That was truly soul. That's the kind of thing I'd like to see more of. And the one with LeRoi Jones and Abbey and Max and the Muslims. That was out of sight!"

"That was **Black Journal,"** I suggested.

"Yes, of course," Mrs. X. agreed.

Mr. A. is a working man on the waterfront. He stated matter-of-factly, "My favorite show is **The Name of the Game."**

"I mean Black TV shows."

Working man said, "Ain't no Black shows. They're just shows with Black people acting like they White. Excepting **Soul!** and **Like It Is** and **Black Journal.** They the only truly Black shows. I liked that Belafonte show a few years ago. Pigmeat Markham and Godfrey Cambridge and Diana Sands and the rest of them people. That was a Black show. One of the best shows

I used to like was **The Outcasts,** and it wasn't long before they cast it out and off the air. It had a feeling of truth to it somehow or other. I especially liked that time when Roscoe Browne was on that show and killed that **White** man. That was beautiful! I also like to watch the basketball games and stuff like that. The Black man really runs them games. It makes me feel so good to watch them."

I have a class in Black Culture at Columbia University. I asked the students what they thought about the strides Black folk were making in the television media. The response was almost unanimous.

Miss L. said, "Ain't nothing happening."

Mr. K. said, "All of them—**Julia,** Leslie Uggams, Della Reese, all those shows—are just White folks masquerading in Black skin."

Mr. F. said, "That cat in **Mission: Impossible** is the natural end. He's the White folk's handy man. They should call that show 'I was a Stooge for the CIA.' I mean, like what you're always talking about, Brother Killens, he puts you in the mind of good old Gunga Din."

From various and varied samplings of Black opinion, one gets a picture that only a very few people believe the millennium has come for colored people in television. There are some who believe that things are getting better, decidedly improving. Others agree, believing that it would **have** to be getting better, since it couldn't get any worse. "There is no way but up," they say. "Which is not saying very much."

How do I see it? I think that progress **has** been made, in that there are more actors employed in the medium, and that is good. The Black man is no longer invisible in the medium, and that is good. I mean a Black kid can see an image of himself on television, even though it is a false image. Is that good? The problem is that the television establishment is attempting to give to the world the image of an integrated society in all facets of American life, even in advertising and commercials, which is all well and good except that it is a colossal lie, because America is not an integrated society. It is a segregated society. A society in which the Black psyche and the White psyche are different altogether. So that the image is at the very best a false image, which is what some Blacks are realizing.

We also know that wishing or pretending will not make it so. The basic problem is, of course, that with all that "Black" exposure on television, there are damn few Black writers participating and the proof of the pudding is not only in eating but fundamentally in the ingredients. The play is the fundamental thing, not the players (as important as they certainly are). White writers, intentions notwithstanding, cannot write about the Black experience, cannot conjure up a true Black image, cannot evoke the wonderful—sometimes terrible—beauty of our Blackness. I have said it before and I say it again: only club members can sing the blues because we're the ones who have paid the dues—of membership in the Brotherhood of Blackness.

I am not one to attack Black actors like Diahann Carroll and Clarence Williams (in the first place, they are valued friends of mine) for appearing in **Julia, The Mod Squad,** etc. They are the **victims** of the establishment, not the culprits. They do not call the shots in television. It was clear in an interview in **TV Guide** that Diahann has no illusions about **Julia;** and, having spoken to Clarence, I know that he has none about **The Mod Squad.** It's a job. For Clarence it means employment and piling up some experience in the medium. For Diahann, and according to her, it is a means of getting into a position in which she **will** be able to do something truly of Black value. I hope her aspirations are realized, for all our sakes.

I would not be concerned with television at all but for the fact that millions of Blacks watch the damn thing every day. It is the great uncontested mass medium.

So what do I think Black people should work for in TV? The kind of television that reflects the Black experience and our special hopes and aspirations. I want to see some stories and programs on the screen that speak of the Black family, its trials and tribulations, its triumphs and defeats.

Life is a great, throbbing, dramatic thing in the Black community. Everything is there—life, death, laughter, tears, irony and paradox, tragic figures, heroes and heroines, living out their days in the Great American Tragedy. For, after all, the Great American Tragedy is the Black Experience. (The other Great American Tragedy is, of course, the experience of the Red men, the original Americans.) But what we see on TV is a very anemic imitation, acted out in pallid blackface.

For example, **Room 222** is a nice, liberal-oriented, interracial, innocuous show with handsome Lloyd Haynes and his beautiful love Denise Nicholas and Mike Constantine, all nice, wonderful people. The Black folk here are full of understanding and wisdom, sympathetic all the way. No basic problems between the races. All men are brothers. Right? An undramatic, middle-classish situation that hardly has anything to do with the Black experience.

I'm saying that Black people have an existence, a life's experience and a life style all their own in this segregated society. We did not segregate the society. The Whites did. We have an identity all our own. We have a peoplehood that shouts out for reflection and dramatization. As I have said before, our struggle is not to be White men in Black skin, but to be our own Black selves. This means, first of all, Black writers. But it also means Black producers, Black directors, Black cameramen, Black grips, Black set designers, all along the line. In a word, Black conceptualization.

But I try very hard to steer clear of illusions, so as not to become disillusioned. So I don't imagine that such Black television exposure will come to pass till we achieve some Black control.

I Am Woman

by HELEN REDDY

The women's liberation movement gained real momentum in the early 1970's, and this was duly reflected in the entertainment media. Helen Reddy's song "I Am Woman," a proud assertion of women's new self-image, was the first explicitly feminist recording to reach the top of the music charts.

Helen Reddy I Am Woman

I am woman, hear me roar
in numbers too big to ignore,
and I know too much to go back to pretend
'cause I've heard it all before
and I've been down there on the floor,
no one's ever gonna keep me down again.

Oh, yes, I am wise
but it's wisdom born of pain.
Yes, I paid the price
but look how much I gained.
If I have to I can do anything.
I am strong, I am invincible, I am woman.

You can bend but never break me
'cause it only serves to make me
more determined to achieve my final goal.
And I come back even stronger
not a novice any longer,
'cause you've deepened the conviction in my soul.

I am woman, watch me grow
see me standing toe to toe
as I spread my lovin' arms across the land.
But I'm still an embryo
with a long, long way to go
until I make my brother understand.
Oh, woman! I am woman! I am woman!

New Novels for Juniors

by JEAN A. SELIGMANN

Once upon a time, most books written for young people—aside from out-and-out adventure stories—were populated by cheerful white teen-agers whose biggest worries were how to get a date for the senior prom or whether the home team would win the Saturday-night game. Not any more. A pandemic of realism has invaded young people's fiction, and adults who haven't taken a look at this genre since the pre-Kennedy years are in for a shock. In books with titles like "Dinky Hocker Shoots Smack!," "Diary of a Frantic Kid Sister," "My Dad Lives in a Downtown Hotel" and "Mom, the Wolf-Man and Me," today's youthful heroes and heroines are smoking dope, swallowing diet pills, suffering mental breakdowns, worrying about homosexuality and masturbation, watching their parents squabble and split up, being battered by racial discrimination, confronting serious illness and even death. In short, they are doing things that real kids do.

Veracity

While the realistic novels have by no means completely replaced such old stand-bys as "The Secret Garden," "Junior Miss" and the Hardy Boys series, they are being read and purchased in ever larger numbers, according to librarians and booksellers across the country. The literary merit and psychological veracity in the new books are as varied as in the old ones. Francelia Butler, professor of children's literature at the University of Connecticut and editor of the first American scholarly journal of children's books, calls the realism offered by some of the new books "distorted," noting that they emphasize the physical aspects of sex, drugs and violence at the expense of the emotional context in which they are experienced. Other experts, such as Lillian Morrison, coordinator of the New York Public Library's Young Adult Services, contend that the old sweetness-and-light stories presented a much more spurious picture of life than the new books do.

But ultimately the best critics of children's fiction are the kids themselves, and they prefer books that speak to them in their own language, without condescending or trying to be superhip. One of the most popular new "junior novels" is M. E. Kerr's "Dinky Hocker Shoots Smack!" Dinky, who is a fat, sardonic 14-year-old girl, lives in Brooklyn Heights and doesn't shoot smack, but she does produce a splatter of Day-Glo graffiti to that effect in an effort to attract the attention of her do-gooding mother who keeps busy rehabilitating heroin addicts. The Los Angeles County Public Library has ordered some 70 copies of "Dinky," and the book is reported to be moving fast on the shelves of New York libraries as well.

Subtle

In "The Man Without a Face," Isabelle Holland treats an especially tricky subject with sensitivity and understanding. Her novel deals with one summer in the life of a fatherless 14-year-old boy who finds himself increasingly drawn to his tutor, a middle-aged man who gives him the affection he needs. The tutor, however, is a homosexual, and the relationship develops ambiguities and difficulties, which are short-circuited by the older man's death. Despite this convenient device, the book deals subtly and honestly with a subject that is not your run-of-the-mill fare for 13- to 16-year-olds.

"The realistic books encourage children to look forward much sooner to participation in the real world than they did ten or fifteen years ago," says Yolanda Federici, supervisor of children's services for the Chicago Public Library. For some young readers, however, the problems can seem overwhelming. Nicholasa Mohr's "Nilda," the highly realistic story of a young Puerto Rican girl growing up in New York's Spanish Harlem, is replete with hookers, junkies, cruel nuns, violent cops and angry street gangs. But for Karen Zich, 11, the worst part of "Nilda" is when a young girl becomes pregnant and has to leave school.

"When I found out Petra was pregnant," says Karen, "I had to put down the book, get myself a glass of milk, turn up the heat and cuddle up in my quilt." Karen likes many of the new realistic stories, but her all-time favorite remains Kathryn Forbes's "Mama's Bank Account" (1943). "You can dream and sort of drift away when you read it," says Karen. "It makes you so happy, you can shut everything else out."

Simplistic

"The realistic novels are probably here to stay," comments Cinda Graham, librarian at the City and Country School in New York, "and I just hope they start getting better." Too often, she says, the candor is only skin-deep; the stories and characters are really quite simplistic. But one of the best of the recent books is Norma Klein's "Mom, the Wolf-Man and Me," the story of an 11-year-old girl's attempt to keep her unwed mother from getting married.

Klein, 36, has published four children's books, dealing with such themes as abortion and divorce. Although some parents and librarians have called her books "dirty," Klein is an ardent crusader for realism in children's fiction. Occasionally, she's had to do battle with her editors who have cut some passages out of her books—a parent smoking dope, a widowed grandmother living with a new man. The mother of two daughters, Klein maintains that young people's fiction has an especially long way to go in portraying girls as real people. "There should be books in which girls are interested in sex," she says, "and books about girls wanting to do lots of things, like play chess. Books shouldn't teach," she concludes. "They should just describe life—real life."

THE ENTERTAINERS

STUDY QUESTIONS

1. Do you agree with Rock's criticism of women's image on TV? What sort of image do women have in other media—film, fiction, records?

2. How realistically have "black movies" portrayed black people? Have you observed any changes in recent years in the depiction of blacks in movies or in other entertainment media?

3. Miller says that rock music has "made you what you are." Would this statement apply to older people and other kinds of music? Which rock artists do you think have helped to shape you?

4. For what reasons does the recording industry rely so heavily on their artists' personalities? What characteristics does Natalie Cole possess that have made her a success at this time?

5. What are some of the major reasons why our movies not only contain more violence but also have changed its depiction from antiseptic to graphic?

6. What changes in sports reporting and sports appreciation have been brought about because of television? How have sports writers been affected by TV sports commentators?

7. Killens charges the media, especially television, with racial tokenism. How visible are minority-group members in media entertainment? How honestly are they presented? Are they exploited? Can any fictional portrayal of a character be honest if it has not been conceived and presented by people who have experienced the life-style that is being portrayed?

BIBLIOGRAPHY FOR FURTHER STUDY

Bluestone, George. *Novels into Film.* Berkeley: University of California Press, 1966.

Boeckman, Charles. *And the Beat Goes On.* New York: Robert B. Luce, 1972.

Bogle, Donald. "The First Black Movie Stars." *Saturday Review of the Arts* (February, 1973), 25–29.

Brown, Les. *Television: The Bu$iness Behind the Box.* New York: Harcourt Brace Jovanovich, 1971..

Canby, Vincent. "Should Movies Have Messages?" *The New York Times* (February 29, 1976), sec. 2, 15.

Christgau, Robert. *Any Old Way You Choose It: Rock and Other Pop Music, 1967–1973.* Baltimore: Penguin Books, 1973.

Crist, Judith. "Movies: Morals, Violence, Sex—Anything Goes." *The Private Eye, The Cowboy and the Very Naked Girl.* New York: Holt, Rinehart and Winston, 1967, pp. 262–71.

Cummings, R. "Double Play and Replay: 'Living Out There in Television Land.'" *Journal of Popular Culture* (Fall, 1974), 427–36.

Ellison, Harlan. "Writing for Television Today." *Writer's Digest* (July, 1976), 15–21.

Ewen, David. *Great Men of American Popular Songs.* Englewood Cliffs, N.J.: Prentice-Hall, 1970.

Farber, Stephen. "The Power of Movie Critics." *American Scholar* (Summer, 1976), 419–23.

Hammel, William M., ed. *The Popular Arts in America: A Reader.* 2nd ed. New York: Harcourt Brace Jovanovich, 1977.

Hedgepeth, William Bowling. "What Dylan Did." *Intellectual Digest* (February, 1973), 66ff.

Higgs, Jack, and Neil Isaacs, eds. *The Sporting Spirit: Athletes in Literature and Life.* New York: Harcourt Brace Jovanovich, 1977.

Jacobs, Lewis. *The Emergence of Film Art.* New York: Hopkinson and Blake, 1969.

Kauffmann, Stanley. *Figures of Light.* New York: Harper & Row, 1971.

———. "Film Negatives." *Saturday Review of the Arts,* (March, 1973), 37–40.

Koven, B. "Music: The Ragtime Revival." *Commentary* (March, 1976), 57–60.

Mariani, John. "The Missing American Hero." *New York* (August 13, 1973), 34–38.

Murray, J. P. "Black Movies/Black Theatre." *Drama Review* (December, 1972), 56–61.

Shalit, Gene. "Movies: What Makes You Flock to Flicks?" *Seventeen* (October, 1973), 90, 138.

Simon, John. "Wertmuller's 'Seven Beauties'—Call It a Masterpiece." *New York* (February 2, 1976), 24–31.

Stephenson, Ralph, and J. R. Debrix. *The Cinema as Art*. Rev. ed. Baltimore: Penguin Books, 1969.

Taylor, J. R. "Movies for a Small Screen." *Sight and Sound* (Spring, 1975), 113–15.

Winick, Charles, and Mariann Pezzella Winick. "Courtroom Drama on Television." *Journal of Communication* (Autumn, 1974), 67–73.

The Persuaders

Basic Research in Persuasion and Motivation: The Capability of Communications Media to Influence Opinions on New Issues

by JOSEPH T. KLAPPER

Joseph T. Klapper, Director of Social Research for the Columbia Broadcasting System, has studied mass communication for twenty years. The following is part of Klapper's testimony to the Subcommittee on International Organizations and Movements of the House Committee on Foreign Affairs on February 8, 1967. He discusses mass communication's tendency to reinforce already-held views and to create opinions on new issues, noting that people in developing countries are particularly susceptible to influence by the media.

. . .

I will devote myself for these few minutes to saying a few words about what research reveals about the effects of communication, particularly mass communication, here in the United States, and what this implies regarding the effects of mass communication in international persuasion. I would like to emphasize also that I am talking about effects on attitudes which are important to the individual; what I say cannot, therefore, be assumed to be true also of the effects of advertising, which is aimed at less basic attitudes.

Basic Research in Persuasion and Motivation: The Capability of Communications Media to Influence Opinions on New Issues. Testimony given at the Hearings before the Subcommittee on International Organizations and Movements of the Committee on Foreign Affairs, House of Representatives, 90th Congress (Washington, D.C.; U.S. Government Printing Office, 1967).

Here in the United States the effects of persuasive mass communication have been found to be in the main reinforcing. This is to say that mass communication seems in the main to buttress or reinforce the views already held by its audience. Rarely does it convert people from one point of view to another.

There are many factors which serve to produce this situation. In the first place, people tend to watch and listen to those mass communications which espouse views to which they are sympathetic and to avoid communications which preach opposing views. They remember material with which they are sympathetic better than they remember material with which they are unsympathetic. Other psychological factors, too complex to mention in these few minutes, are also at work.

People's social contacts, and the way they obtain information, also contribute to the tendency of mass communication to be reinforcive. For example, virtually all people belong to groups—family groups, peer groups, play groups, clubs, church groups, and the like. These groups are characterized by certain opinions, and are often the source, and also the guardian, of the individual's opinions. And these groups, through both formal and informal processes, serve to mediate the effects of mass communication on their members. For example, group discussion makes the member aware of communications with which both he and the group agree; the need for his being able to talk with the group prompts him to watch or listen to those communications; and if any communication threatens opinions which the group values, discussion among group members tends to find fault with and discount that communication. Thus groups are potent strainers in reference to mass communication, and they strain in such a way as to intensify the tendency of mass communication to serve as an agent of reinforcement.

This tendency of mass communication to reinforce is seen in many areas. In political campaigns, for example, people who are reinforced in their original vote intention have been found to outnumber those converted by about 10 to 1. Similar tendencies have been documented by research in reference to other important attitudes, and also in reference to less solemn modes of behavior.

Indeed, even conversion may be a kind of indirect reinforcement. We have noted in our research that in many cases of conversion, the convertee had become dissatisfied with his previous point of view before the communication converted him. He was already predisposed to some sort of change, and mass communication both reinforced that predisposition and pointed out a particular road of change. . . . I can give you many examples of this, if you desire them, and point out how the same factors that ordinarily make for reinforcement in these instances made for conversion.

But I have been talking up to now only about reinforcement or change of existing attitudes. There is another area in which mass communication is extremely effective, and that is in the creation of opinion on new issues.

By "new issues" I mean issues on which the individual has no opinion and on which his friends and fellow group members have no opinion. The reason for the effectiveness of mass communication in creating opinions on new issues is pretty obvious: The individual has no predisposition to defend, and so the communication falls, as it were, on defenseless soil. And once the opinion is created, then it is this new opinion which becomes easy to reinforce and hard to change. This process of opinion creation is strongest, by the way, when the person has no other source of information on the topic to use as a touchstone. He is therefore the more wholly dependent on the communication in question.

Now, what I have been saying is true in the United States and in Canada and in England and in other highly developed countries where mass communication reaches the masses and in sufficient variety for them to pick and choose which communications they will listen to and which they won't listen to. And I want to point out as my last point, that in many developing countries these conditions don't obtain in anything resembling the same degree. Where few people are literate, few can read the papers. Where there are few radios, few can hear them, and still fewer can choose what programs they want to hear. In such situations, mass communication reaches many individuals through intermediaries, that is, by word of mouth from those people who do have access to the media. These intermediaries therefore become particularly important in the communication process. Communication researchers call them gatekeepers or opinion leaders. . . .

Let me also point out, in closing, that in developing countries there is a far higher incidence of people who are unaware of various issues, who therefore have no opinions upon them, and who are thus, at least in theory, particularly susceptible to the influence of mass communication, whether from the media or through the intervening gatekeepers. In conclusion, then, the potential influence of mass communication in developing countries is vast, but the nature and limits of that potential must be clearly understood if the potential is to be realized.

. . .

Visual Persuasion in the Media

The following advertisements demonstrate various persuasive appeals used in advertising. The first ads illustrate the methods advertisers use in attempting to reach minority and ethnic groups. The Greyhound Corporation's soft-sell ad, which appeared in **Ebony** magazine, emphasizes human rights. Of course, underlying the message is the hope that blacks will go Greyhound. The Milk Foundation's billboard makes a more direct verbal appeal for its product while visually suggesting the theme of integration.

Philip Morris, in advertising its Virginia Slims brand of cigarettes, uses two basic ad campaigns, both of which are aimed exclusively at a female audience. One campaign, illustrated by the first ad shown here, emphasizes the progress that women have made in achieving equality with men. The other campaign, illustrated by the second ad, is fashion-oriented and stresses the point that Virginia Slims are made "especially for women."

The other advertisements for cigarettes are also intended to persuade particular segments of the market. Benson & Hedges uses a homey, down-to-earth appeal in its ad from **Intellectual Digest.** L & M cigarettes and Winchester little cigars use the sexy sell in their ads in **Playboy.**

Finally, the liquor advertisements, from **New York** and **Ms.**, reflect the sophistication that is expected of the readers of those magazines.

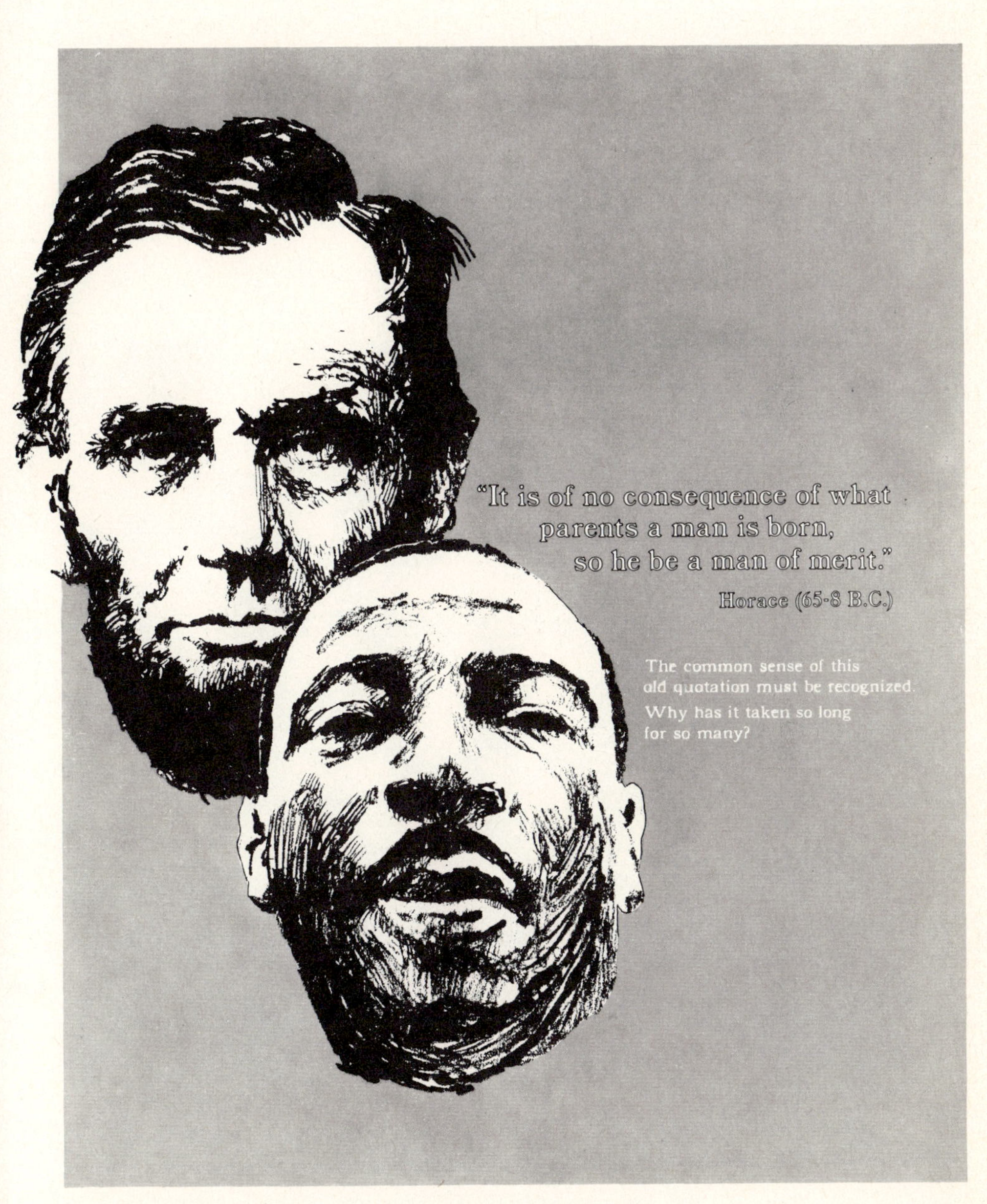
"It is of no consequence of what
parents a man is born,
so he be a man of merit."
Horace (65-8 B.C.)
The common sense of this
old quotation must be recognized.
Why has it taken so long
for so many?

The Milk Foundation

"The woman is neither sufficiently sensible nor sufficiently responsible to vote. Of politics and issues, she is, by nature, ignorant. Give a woman the right to vote and, by heavens, next thing you know, she'll want to smoke like a man." —Robt. D. Nolan

Philip Morris

Philip Morris

Philip Morris

Liggett & Myers, Inc.

The 9 Basic Winchester Positions. Try one on.

How you wear your Winchester has become the neatest new way to send messages since body language. Winchester's slim, sexy shape says you know what pleasure's all about. And the gleam in your eye says Winchester's taste delivers. Mild. Light. With a filtered smoothness and a come-hither aroma that tempts women to say, "I'll try anything once." And come back for more. So Winchester's not a cigarette. Not just another little cigar. It's a whole 'nother smoke. And how you wear your Winchester has suddenly become a whole 'nother way to send smoke signals. Try the 9 above. Then invent 9 more.

Winchester. It's a whole 'nother smoke.

R. J. Reynolds Tobacco Co.

First the agency people told me I could say anything I wanted to about scotch. Then they censored me.

BY TOMMY SMOTHERS

I'VE BEEN CENSORED one way or another practically all my life.

It all started when my mother used to stick a pacifier into my mouth anytime I opened it. Later, it was a bar of soap.

When Dick and I were kids, once Mother got him a dog and me a muzzle.

When I started taking guitar lessons, people would always steal my pick.

Even my dreams have snips cut out of them. Always the good parts, too.

That's the way it's always been with me.

So I wasn't surprised when one of the major networks joined the fun. It was annoying, I'll admit, but when it was all over all I could say was "et tu, CBS."

But all that is censorship under the bridge.

And speaking of censorship, it's certainly changed a lot since its beginning. Today, you can say anything as long as no one hears you. So probably the only way to steer clear of censors is to steer yourself into a closet and talk only to yourself.

Anyway, when the Teacher's advertising people heard I drink their scotch, they asked me to talk about it.

They gave me carte blanche, a yellow pad and a No. 2 pencil. Of course, the pencil had no point, but I got around that.

Well, first I wrote about how happy I was that everybody and his brother doesn't drink Teacher's. Which, in my case, is a definite plus.

No problems so far.

Then I started reminiscing about my experiences with scotch, pre-Teachers.

The first time I tasted scotch I tried to belt it down like they always do in the movies when the hero has just lost his girl.

Ecccch.

If this was what scotch tasted like, I vowed never to lose my girl or be a hero in a movie.

My stomach was the first casualty. Then my eyes started to water. And finally my tongue made itself heard. It gave me a severe tongue lashing.

However, I wasn't going to let myself be licked by a mere tongue, a pair of eyes and a stomach.

So I came back for less.

This time, I started with a Presbyterian. 2 parts this, 3 parts that, 4 parts something else and, if there's any room left over, scotch.

The trouble with that was I got tired of walking up to bars and ordering one Presbyterian only to have the bartender tell me I was in the wrong place and down the street at the church I could find all the Presbyterians I wanted.

So my conversion to Presbyterianism didn't last long.

Next I moved to scotch and soda. Or more accurately, scotch and soda, soda, soda and soda.

After that, it was the big time. Scotch on the rocks. Straight. At bars I'd order it out of the side of my mouth. I was tough. I started wearing black shirts white ties and woolen underwear. I even bought a hair piece for my chest. But again, secretly, I did such a terrific job of nursing my drink the Red Cross would have been proud of me.

All of which brings me to Teacher's. The first time I ever tasted it was the first time I ever finished my scotch on the rocks before it turned to water.

A scotch I liked. Teacher's, my tongue thanks you, my eyes thank you, my stomach thanks you. Even my sex life thanks you.

Once there was this girl and the back seat of this old DeSoto

Boy, those Teacher's people are great. They really let you say anything.

So anyway,

86 Proof Scotch Whisky Blended and Bottled in Scotland by Wm. Teacher & Sons, Ltd. © Schieffelin & Co., N.Y., Importers

Schieffelin & Co.

DEWAR'S PROFILES

(Pronounced Do-ers "White Label")

BLENDED SCOTCH WHISKY · 86.8 PROOF · © SCHENLEY IMPORTS CO., N.Y. N.Y.

SHEILA ANN T. LONG

HOME: Hampton, Virginia

AGE: 28

PROFESSION: Physicist

HOBBIES: Ballet, Sailing, Car Racing, Chess

LAST BOOK READ: "Beyond Freedom and Dignity"

LAST ACCOMPLISHMENT: Member of the team of international scientists who are mapping earth's electromagnetic field for the first time

QUOTE: "Scientific research in all fields has been a prime contributor to America's greatness. Let us not forget this in our concern for the dying environment, for Technology holds the very means to save it."

PROFILE: Brilliant, beautiful, in love with life. Involved, and unintimidated by difficult challenge. Saluted by *New Woman* magazine as one of the 26 women who "made it big in their twenties."

SCOTCH: Dewar's "White Label"

Authentic. Part of the great pleasure one gets from sipping Dewar's "White Label" Scotch is the reassuring knowledge that you have chosen something authentic.

Dewar's never varies.

Schenley Imports Co.

From an Interview with Alvin Toffler

Alvin Toffler, author of **Future Shock,** examines advertising's effect on American culture, in an interview that originally appeared in the J. Walter Thompson advertising agency's house organ, **JWT World.** Toffler states that effective advertising anticipates the future and that it has the moral responsibility of "educating people not simply about what or how to buy but, more important, how to cope with change."

. . .

JWT World Does advertising contribute to future shock?

Toffler You cannot watch television for an evening without being literally bombarded by advertisements to a point at which it really represents a tax on your nervous system and viscera. Much of the resistance to advertising, and the positive hatred for it in some sectors of the public, derives from this fact.

It's not the message, it's not even the medium. It's the sensory and cognitive over-stimulation that the medium and the message produce. Moreover, the ephemerality of campaigns, symbols, images, and the products themselves, intensify the sense of impermanence in life.

A few years ago someone computed that the average American is exposed to 560 advertising messages a day, ranging from the covers of matchbooks to TV commercials. Of these 560, he notices only 76. The individual must block out the rest. But the fact that he doesn't "notice" the other 484 doesn't mean they have no effect. They add to the general environ-

An Interview with Alvin Toffler: From *Advertising Age* (November 21, 1973). Reprinted by permission.

ment shrill. They raise the level of background noise and the viewer-reader-consumer twitches in response to them even though he may never pay an instant's attention to their formal appeals.

This has physiological as well as psychological significance, and it has more to do with the negative response to advertising than to all the familiar rhetoric about the manipulation of needs, economic waste, and so on.

JWT World Is this a consequence of what you call the "information-rich coded message?"

Toffler In part. Advertising is to the information-rich coded message what the Apollo project is to technology—a fantastic laboratory for the creation of new technology, linguistic technology, new symbolism. Advertising people are well paid for doing very systematically what poets used to starve doing.

In some ways, as I have said, the advertising industry has succeeded only too well, and the onset of future shock has curbed its efficiency in this respect. It's because you compress maximum message into minimum time that many recipients of the message feel as though they were having arrows shot into them. As I show in "Future Shock," we've gone from the handcrafted message to the engineered message, and this carries a heavy load of frequently unwanted information.

Advertising has a much more positive function as an adaptive aid. Like art, it makes possible a lot of "no trial" learning; it broadens the behavioral repertoires of people; but much of this valuable result is cancelled out by the information-enriched, perhaps over-enriched messages, that bombard us, endlessly forcing us to switch our attention and recategorize our imagery.

The development of specialized advertising media may be a partial solution to this problem. Between 1959 and 1969, for example, the number of American magazines offering special editions jumped from 126 to 235. People don't resent a limited number of ads that are aimed directly at them, or are relevant to their own interests. It's the irrelevant advertising pounding away constantly that drives them up the wall. This shift toward more specialized media, which I document in "Future Shock," is a shift to a much more sophisticated information system in the society. But, as I suggest elsewhere, it heralds a lot more conflict in the social order.

JWT World How will future shock affect the marketplace?

Toffler People have a feeling that things are getting out of control, that things are moving too fast, that they're being asked to cope with events that are running away from them. There is panic in the air. This is going to have an effect on the kinds of products we buy, the kinds of advertising we respond to, and the attitudes with which we approach the marketplace . . . Now we're beginning to see—with respect to many kinds of products—a growing consumer rebellion against change.

This reaction may grow stronger as the present generation begins to move into the marketplace. This is not an attack on change, *per se,* however. It is an attack on our cultural-pacing system, on the accelerating turnover rates in daily life.

What is involved here is a totally new consumer response to time. This will have obvious effects on manufacturers. And advertising designers—the people who write copy, and the ones who prepare the visuals, the ones who plan the strategy of an ad campaign—are all going to have to refocus themselves with respect to time.

For example, they will have to think especially carefully about the *duration* of a campaign, the duration of the symbols, slogans and phrases used. They're going to have to be very conscious of the distinction between those elements in a campaign that represent novel inputs; and they are going to have to learn to understand the links between transience, novelty and diversity, and to play on these factors like a piano.

For example, as "Future Shock" suggests, if we were to survey consumers, we would find significant differences between various cultural and economic groups in the marketplace with respect to time, to their durational relationships. Some people hold on to things longer than other people. If we made a similar analysis of the *duration* of place relationships, the duration of friendships and acquaintances, the duration of the individual's affiliations with organizations, and the duration of key values, we would find fascinating and useful patterns. This "transience index" could be invaluable to the advertiser and marketer because durational patterns are likely to correlate with consumer patterns.

In short, if we want to understand consumer behavior better, we are going to have to introduce much more serious analysis of the temporal factor, and make a much clearer distinction between routine and unroutine elements, *i.e.,* novelty.

JWT World Is what you call "psychologization of production" a function of the high rate of transience?

Toffler Partly, yes. But it is also linked to affluence. We're beginning to recognize that products have more than the obvious functions. A house houses many people—but it also does many other things. An automobile gets you from here to there—but it can pollute the sky at the same time, and also represent symbolic values for the individual, etc.

As a society gets richer, there are a number of different directions in which it can go. It can apply its new productivity to war, to space adventure, to foreign aid, to the creation of new products for ever more luxurious living, or to the psychologization of goods and services.

One of the things that we have done in America is to begin paying attention to the psychological overtones of our products and services, so that we engineer into them features which do not necessarily improve the basic performance, but which yield psychic payoffs to the consumer. There is nothing new or startling in this idea. But no one has examined the long-range significance of this trend very seriously. Yet this emphasis on psychology is beginning to take us beyond the traditional service economy toward what I call an "experiential economy."

In "Future Shock" I describe the move toward experiential industry. We've already seen the sudden rise of what might be called the sensitivity-training industry. The encounter group people are selling experiences. So is Club Mediterranée. The TV show "The Dating Game" is another example of people being paid off with psychic rewards instead of cold cash. The contestants compete for a date with a pretty girl, quite apart from whatever financial rewards there may be.

I see the possibility of our society pouring more and more of its resources into the provision of ever more refined psychological experiences which can be marketed or sold. This may be immoral in a world still struggling with belly-hunger. But it is a strong tendency that needs to be understood.

JWT World You think, then, that advertisements can perform cultural functions as well as selling products?

Toffler Not only can they, they already do, and can't avoid doing so. But we need a fresh definition of these functions. For example, certain ad campaigns are reassuring to the viewer or reader simply because they are repetitive over time. They are anchors in a sea of change. Of course, they may not sell the product, but they may serve as a kind of image prop, a bit of background continuity for the individual whose life is changing in so many other ways. This is—or may be—of crucial importance in a culture rocketing toward transience.

"The people know what they want, Garrard. Your job is to sell them something they don't *want."*

Drawn for Broadcasting by Sidney Harris

On the other hand, the constant shifting and changing of advertising themes, reflecting the repeated upheavals in the marketplace, generates a sense of discontinuity. These differences themselves affect different groups in society in different ways. Some groups are trapped in low-stimulation environments; others suffer from over-stimulation. Advertising forms a prominent part of everyone's environment, but it does not begin to do all it could to help people make the transition into super-industrial society. A carefully thought-out and future-conscious ad can help prepare the society for a more graceful entry into tomorrow, as well as sell more of the product than ever before.

JWT World Then the responsibility and relevance of advertising to lead us into the future with minimum shock is very great?

Toffler Right. The widespread interest in "Future Shock" by people in the advertising industry—the reason, I think, that it's been called a basic text for advertising and communications—has to do with the fact that ad people are among the groups in society who are most exposed to super-change. They are among the groups in society I call "people of the future."

People in advertising fight on the front lines of future shock because every day they confront the high rate of turnover, the rates of transience, and the necessity to make enormous and constantly changing kaleidoscopic adjustments on the job, with respect to consumer tastes, families, organizations, people, life styles. All the component elements of future shock, it seems to me, are raised to the *n*th degree in advertising and communications. I think this is why so many advertising and communications people have said, privately to me and even publicly on the air, that the book expressed what they have been feeling. A friend of mine got a letter from a well known advertising executive which said, "The book reads as though the author had been standing over my shoulder for the last six months."

In some sense, ad people are pre-tasting a possible and quite probable future, and they have some responsibility for either changing it or preparing us to cope with it better.

Advertising agencies can do a lot to help prepare society for the future —and also, of course, to keep their clients one step ahead of change. But they will need special resources to do so. They will have to draw on the new intellectual technologies being created by the people who are seriously studying the future. They will need direct ties with the futurist community worldwide. They will need to develop their own long-range planning operations. But not the old-style technocratic planning. They will need new, free-form post-technocratic planning—a style that takes into account all sorts of non-economic factors, that reaches beyond the 10- or 15-year horizon, and that taps into the feelings, wishes, hopes of people at all levels of the various social hierarchies.

Not only must advertising agencies move in this direction, if they are to survive the jolts that lie ahead, they ought to be educating their clients along these lines as well. Some of the best advertising agencies already are doing this, encouraging their clients to reexamine not only strategies, but even their most fundamental goals, drawing on the help of specially equipped outsiders.

You know, we've been talking about the rate of change and keeping an eye on the future. In "Future Shock," I quote a very pertinent article written by JWT's Henry Schachte in which he points out that in almost no major consumer goods category is there a brand on top today that was No. 1 ten years ago. Well, ten years ago those top brands must have had some good advertising to make them "top." But advertising is being reconceptualized, and what we regard as "good" today is already more than half obsolete.

If advertising is to be effective, its creators must continually anticipate the future. And if it is to be moral, they must assume a social responsibility that they have never accepted: The task of educating people not simply about what or how to buy but, more important, how to cope with change. And this means probing behind the "content" of advertising to its temporal connotations.

For society itself, I think it's time to ask very serious questions about advertising. More serious than the usual ones. It's time we dug deeper than the clichés about manipulation, economic waste, lack of veracity, and so on. These criticisms of advertising are important, no doubt, and ought by no means to be shrugged aside. But advertising is doing far more fundamental things to our culture than these arguments even begin to suggest.

JWT World In terms of "Future Shock's" analysis, what do you think of Marshall McLuhan's insight that the medium is the message?

Toffler The best thing that I heard anybody say about McLuhan came from Kenneth Boulding [the economist], who said that McLuhan had hit a very large nail not quite on the head. That is, in my opinion, very high praise, indeed. Not many books even come close to that.

There is more mysticism in McLuhan's work than I am comfortable with. But there is also more imagination than the media has been subjected to in 50 years of academic analysis. McLuhan has explosively enlarged our concept of the "content" of communications.

As I read him, McLuhan says that the analysts, until now, have been looking at what comes across the screen or the printed page, and examining it only on the most literal level. They have had a very limited notion of what actually happens between the receiver and the words, ideas, pictures or symbols reaching him. McLuhan has forced us to broaden our conception of "content" to include many of the side-effects—the effect of communication on the individual or cultural sense ratios, for example. And McLuhan has forced us to understand that these side-effects, all the events happening below the literal level, may be more important than the actual words coming across the screen and telling us to "Buy Widgets!" or "Vote Republican!" To the degree that he's got that message across—and that is only a small fraction of what he has to say—he has enormously expanded our understanding of what is happening to us.

What I have tried to do in "Future Shock" is to show that the "content" of change is also much bigger than we suspect. When we talk about change, we ordinarily confuse the directions of change with the content of change, just as the media analysts mistook what came across the screen for the whole content of communications. Change, too, has to be understood in terms of its secondary and tertiary consequences, some of which may well be more important than the so-called primary consequence.

For example, "Future Shock" argues that the *rate* at which change occurs is sometimes more important than the kind of change involved. The duration of an ad campaign may turn out to be more important than the specific sales message it projects.

Admen and market researchers have analyzed the consumer in terms of everything from Freudian drives to class position and color preference, but they—like most of the rest of us—have missed one of the most crucial elements in human behavior, the temporal dimension. They pay no attention to durational expectancies, although they act on them all the time. They seldom ask how people react to any stepup or slowdown in the pace of daily life.

More broadly, it is no longer possible for us to evaluate political changes, technological changes, social changes without an expanded definition of change, one that takes into account its less immediately evident results. We have got to understand that acceleration, the continual speedup of the rate of change, has consequences apart from, and possibly more significant than, the nature of the specific changes involved.

For advertisers, this means you have to begin asking how any specific ad or campaign affects the individual's transience level; how it raises or lowers the novelty ratio in his environment; and what it does to the number of choices he has to make in his daily life. Unless you begin asking questions like these, you may completely misunderstand the real content of change—and of your own behavior.

Super-change, and the decision crisis it is provoking in our culture, will compel us to think about change in totally new ways. Those who cannot will fall by the wayside—casualties of the accelerative thrust, victims of future shock.

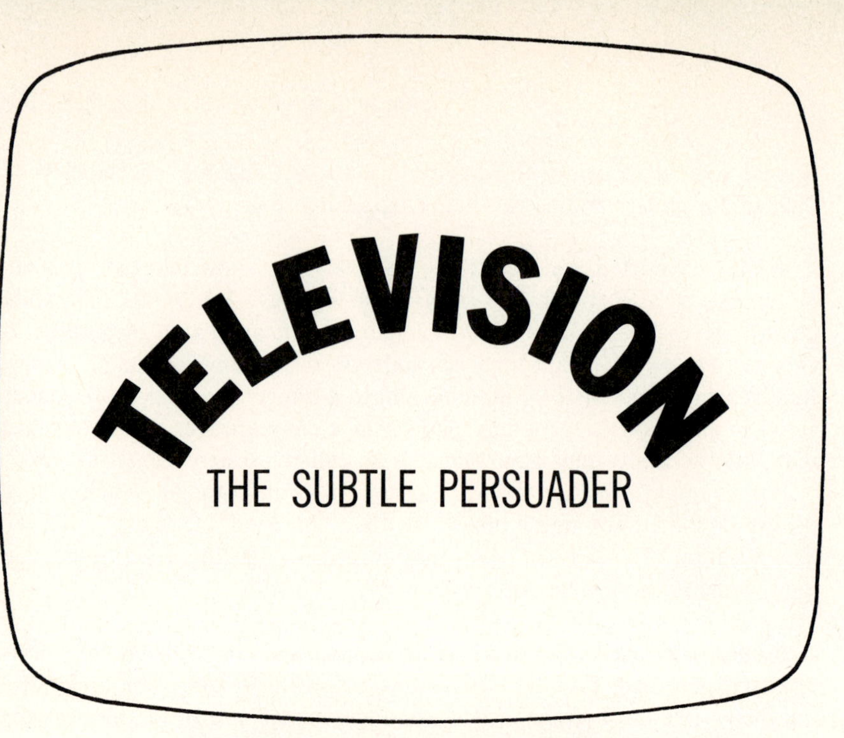

by RICHARD D. HEFFNER

Richard D. Heffner, Professor of Communication and Public Policy at Rutgers University, warns that the "less-than-conscious" level of content of television programs alters our values "subtly, without our even realizing it."

One evening, some years back, my sons and I were watching Chief of Detectives Robert Ironside become increasingly frustrated by his inability to get the goods on a suspect. Another character in the story—a key to Ironside's case—regularly used a certain public phone booth, however, and finally the Chief simply told his policeman side-kicks to "put a tap on it." Rising to the defense of privacy and personal liberties, I suggested that tapping telephones is illegal without judicial permission, and that Ironside should have known better; to which my boys replied, "Don't be silly, Daddy. If the Chief does it, it *must* be OK."

Now, Aristotle noted that "We believe good men more fully and readily than others." Ironside is Aristotle's good man incarnate. His actions spoke much louder than my feeble words—and my sons believed him, not me.

But why shouldn't they? Why shouldn't the values expressed by him loom so large and believable?

After all, I invite Ironside into my home each week, endowing him with an authority of friendship and familiarity that looms larger even than his official position. It would be strange indeed if the standards he embraces—even fleetingly—were not deeply influential.

Not that I believe that the creators of *Ironside* consciously intended to advocate wire tapping. The values they present in this area are probably inadvertent; the product more of rote than intent. Indeed, they may well have intended Ironside's staff to get an off-screen court order that authorized the wire tap. But what happened—what my sons and I saw and heard—was that our favorite law officer took the law into his own hands. And if this fictional chief of detectives were so free and easy with his wire taps, what about the livelier (and much more real) characters who work out of my precinct house—or yours?

Ironside's creators may not at all have wanted to take any side on this particularly bitter point of contention between hard-nosed law-and-order advocates and civil libertarians. Yet they did so, legitimizing, for my sons at least, one side of this highly contested public issue: "If the Chief does it, it *must* be OK."

There is much more to television than meets the eye. Understanding the medium requires not only a familiarity with the series plots that continue from week to week, but also an awareness of TV's less explicit levels: its offhanded comments, its modes of thought and action that we have come to take for granted. It is, you see, this *less-than-conscious* level of television's content that educates us, subtly, without our even realizing it.

The heroes and villains of fiction have long been considered influential in building character. From Simon Legree to John Galt, fictional characters have set the trends followed by the rest of us. Understandably, when movies came along they, too, influenced our thinking. Remember if you will, the panic that hit the undershirt industry when millions of American moviegoers discovered that under his shirt and tie, Clark Gable wore only bare chest. Why, then, don't we see equally as clearly that television, the newest and far more prevalent form of fiction, is even more profoundly influential on our lives—not in terms of the stories it tells, but, more importantly, the values it portrays.

Here is how television makes another kind of value statement: private-eye Joe Mannix's secretary, Peggy, becomes worried when his office is found empty yet his car is parked outside. Couldn't he have just stepped out for lunch? "He'd take his car!" she insists.

Gail Fisher, as Peggy, is a strong, friendly, familiar television figure. In her throwaway lines (". . . he'd be off and running—in his car . . ."), she underscores the medium's easy assumption that nearly everyone is on wheels. On television, mass transit is almost nonexistent. Yet Joe Mannix never suffers the consequences of all that driving around. There are few traffic jams and no choked highways on his show; there is no one searching desperately for a parking place. Indeed, if all we understood about the dangers of lead-laden smog derived from the values we saw on a show like *Mannix,* it would be impossible for environmentalists to convince viewers that the automobile is anything other than a harmless—and necessary—extension of the human body.

We have long recognized the impact that Horatio Alger's pluck-and-luck characters had upon the millions of Americans who read his novels in the last century. Can we doubt then, that week after week, Archie Bunker, Robert Ironside, Maude, Joe Mannix, Marcus Welby, Joe Gannon—all the video "best-sellers"—have any less influence on today's viewers?

Friendly family-practitioner Marcus Welby makes assumptions, expresses views and values that stay with his huge audience long after the details of any week's plot fade into oblivion. Welby's views on life have become so familiar to us that, indeed, one Midwestern medical school chose him to address this year's graduating class. Then there is Joe Gannon. His intricate operating-room procedures on *Medical Center* may be forgotten soon after the show flicks off, but Gannon's mod, hip philosophy of life won't.

Because television is so familiar to us—so much a totally integral part of our lives—it combines the traditional two steps of impactful communications: statement and reinforcement. Because, in fact, television mirrors us so well, it is its own agent of reinforcement—TV is so highly integrated in our lives that its characters create their own effective credibility, influencing us more than we realize with the life styles they portray.

Mass television is now just over a quarter-century old. And if we are ever to grasp its real significance, we must try to learn to recognize its symbolism—just as we read between the lines of our literature. Traditionally, we have tried to teach ourselves how to recognize and know the power of innuendo, implication and stereotype when it occurs in print. Isn't it time now to understand this new medium as well, to view it probingly and not absorb without thinking the values it so often thoughtlessly throws at us?

DOWN TO THE LAST DETAIL

by JEFF GREENFIELD

In this article, writer and political consultant Jeff Greenfield discusses the time and money involved in making commercials and their close attention to detail, which is not only an attempt to sell a product but also a message of "significant social consequence."

Why is Karl Malden wearing that hat? For months now, American Express has been running a series of commercials in which the dreams of vacationers are shattered through the loss or theft of their cash (one of them features a husband reassuring his wife that they can afford an expensive meal even as a thief is stealing his wallet from their car). In the last half of these ads, actor Karl Malden sternly warns us, "Don't carry cash!" and preaches the virtue of travelers' checks.

And in every one of these ads, Malden is wearing a hat. It makes no difference where he is: inside an imposing, high-ceilinged, old-fashioned bank, or standing by a desk in a contemporary office. That hat is planted firmly on Malden's head.

Why? A brief Socratic dialogue will answer that question. Who wears hats in this bare-everything day and age? Detectives and F.B.I. men, that's who. And what character has Karl Malden been playing on the ABC television network these last few years? Tough, crusty, but lovable Mike Stone, police lieutenant on *The Streets of San Francisco,* that's who. And what sort of figure would inspire confidence in the minds of prospective travelers, worried about the possible loss of their vacation money? A tough, crusty, but lovable police lieutenant, that's who.

Now you, as a viewer, are not supposed to notice this detail; you are not supposed to turn to your beloved and say, "Hey, Martha—what's that idiot doing with a hat on in the middle of a stuffy bank?" No, no, no.

Instead, you are supposed to absorb the general *impression* of the commercial: the sense that an authoritative figure with close ties to a law-enforcement agency is putting his word (and perhaps a few patrol cars) behind the promise of security through travelers' checks. Every detail of this thirty-second drama is designed to surround you with an aura of confidence in the rock-like strength of these travelers' checks. And Karl Malden's hat is one more detail. It is, in fact, a fine example of the *kind* of detailed planning that goes into the shaping of big-budget advertising: planning that has significant social consequences.

There are three things worth remembering about advertising: they are a) money, b) money, and c) money. According to *Advertising Age,* $26.7 *billion* was spent on advertising in 1974. Television alone accounted for $4.85 billion of that money. To bring it down to numbers that are (slightly) less staggering, if you want to sell something to the American people and want to reach tens of millions of them—once—it will cost you nearly $60,000 for thirty *seconds* of network TV time in the middle of a top-rated show such as *All in the Family*. If you want to reach the attention of one big city—New York, say—to introduce a new product or politician, then you had better be prepared to spend $50,000 or more a week to make a dent in the market.

And those numbers represent only the cost of *time*. They do not include the massive cost of writing, designing, and shooting a commercial. When you count the cost of lights, sets, costumes, talent fees (up to $250,000 in the case of a Laurence Olivier for Polaroid's SX-70 camera), market research, and the amortized cost of $50,000-a-year copywriters and art directors, the production cost of a single thirty-second commercial can exceed $200,000.

So what? Look at it this way. A two-hour movie that costs $6 million to shoot averages out to $50,000 a minute, or $833 a second. A television commercial, by contrast, can cost more than $6,000 a second, without even counting the far more expensive cost of time. Similarly, a network will pay a little less than $300,000 for a single one-hour episode of a television series—call it $5,000 a minute, or about $85 a second. Perhaps you begin to see the point: measured by money (which is the only sensible standard in such enterprises), the television commercial is by far the most valuable, and valued, production. And that is why so much attention can, and must, be paid to every single detail.

One former advertising agency employee, who worked on a major beer account, recalls the degree of preparation and detail involved in the shooting of one thirty-second comercial.

"The 'pour' shot is the key to a beer ad," he says. "How the beer looks going down the glass; whether the glass is completely clean and suggests ice-cold beer; how the bubbles look; whether the head on the beer is big enough, but not too big. Our standard order for a 'pour' shot was ten cases of beer—240 cans. And it wasn't overdoing it. I remember one pour shot which took 124 takes before the beer looked exactly right."

And it is not just the beer (or chicken, or car, or detergent, or soap) that must look exactly right. *Everything* must look exactly right. Are you selling to an "up-scale" audience (more affluent and educated)? Then make sure the furnishings, the home, the clothes, the haircuts, the accessories, the dishes, the books on the shelves, all look appealing to that audience. Are you trying to reach the blue-collar, lower-middle-class audience? Make sure the announcer has a tough, no-nonsense voice, and put a few people in the ad who look like they work with their hands. Are you selling Ajax dishwashing liquid with a "professional dishwasher" who can make the lowliest hausfrau feel superior? Don't take chances; black out one of the dishwasher's front teeth to strip him of any pretense of sophistication.

In its use of money and talent, the world of advertising resembles the process for making diamonds (I am here referring to process, *not* to the intrinsic value of the product). So much effort, so much money, so many minds, are focused on the development of thirty seconds of film or tape, that, like a piece of coal subjected to intense pressure over long periods of time, the commercial becomes crystallized into a miniature drama reflecting not just an attempt to sell a product, but an effort to harness attitudes, biases, tastes, life styles. It seems absurd to ascribe so much to so short a device as a commercial. But when thousands of dollars go into the planning of every second of what we see and hear, that effort becomes a lot less ludicrous, and a lot more feasible.

For the most remarkable fact about advertising is that it *works*. Call it offensive, puerile, insulting to the intelligence, barbarous, intrusive, antihumanistic, but the damn thing moves the goods. I have no doubt that the Charmin bathroom tissue commercials (they can't bear to call it toilet paper) will be a contributing factor to the fall of American civilization, should that happen. But those commercials carved out a substantial share of the market for a product that had nothing unusual to offer except a public impression formed from advertising. So compact are commercials, so frequently seen, that they can create not just new products but new personalities and folk figures within a few weeks: think of nature-loving Euell Gibbons and Post Grape Nuts; Alice Playton as the heartburn-inducing new bride in the Alka-Seltzer commercials. Think of the portly Southern sheriff in the Dodge Rebellion ads, Josephine the Plumber for Comet. These characters and situations, even more than the characters and TV shows of the networks, are the product of massive amounts of research, market testing, and above all, cold cash. And because advertisers can spend so much—so much talent, so much money, so much time—on every detail of every second, they can create a market by literally buying their way into our minds.

"VIABLE SOLUTIONS"

by EDWIN NEWMAN

Edwin Newman—NBC news correspondent and author of the best seller, **Strictly Speaking: Will America Be the Death of English?**—is in the forefront of those who are speaking out against "Doublespeak," a misuse of language that distorts the message and, he says, is in danger of destroying our language. His essay illustrates how complicated and obscure we have let our utterances become.

The day is not far off when someone about to join his family will excuse himself by saying that he does not want to keep his microcluster of structured role expectations waiting.

True, I came upon this gem of social-scientific jargon in London, but that only shows how far our influence has spread and how determined the British are to join the Americans at the kill when the English language finally is done to death. Asphyxiation will be the cause, with the lethal agent gas. This is the gas which, added to evidence, produces evidentiary material, and which, escaping from a Secret Service spokesman—how can you have a spokesman for a secret service?—turned President Ford and *his* microcluster of structured role expectations into protectees.

At that, protectee is better than a similar government word, escapee, which is used—misused—to mean somebody who escaped.

"To what do you attribute your escape?" (It is, by the way, becoming fashionable to say successful escape.)

"I am a fast runnee."

The chief current protectee of the Secret Service is not a gross offender —or offendee—against the language, and when he does offend, it is more often out of naïveté than self-importance. He has identified inflation as "the universal enemy of one hundred percent of our people" and has noted that in trying to deal with that enemy, we went through a "long process of economic summit." Others less fortunately placed were going through a long process of economic valley.

Mr. Ford is enthusiastic about the virtues of dialogue. He has called for a new dialogue with the nations of Latin America, though most of those

Viable Solutions: First published in *Esquire* Magazine (December 1975). Reprinted by permission of the author.

nations were not aware that the old dialogue had ended, or even begun. In one of his first speeches as President, Mr. Ford said he wanted to have "a deepening dialogue" with the nations of Latin America. Until then, I had thought that took place when two men talked to each other while digging a hole.

Last February, twelve Senators and seventy Representatives asked President Ford for a serious, unemotional dialogue on getting the United States out of Indochina. They should have asked for eighty-two dialogues.

It is curious, this devotion to dialogue. An Army officer involved in the amnesty program, Major General Eugene Forrester, was quoted as saying that he and his nineteen-year-old son had had an "extremely volatile dialogue over the war in Vietnam." He evidently meant that they shouted at each other.

General Forrester, the eighty-two members of Congress and President Ford, bent on dialogue though they may be, might well blanch at the prospect of engaging in one with Alan Greenspan, chairman of the Council of Economic Advisers. How would anyone hold up his end after hearing Greenspan say this:

"Thus, once the inflation genie has been let out of the bottle, it is a very tricky policy problem to find the particular calibration and timing that would be appropriate to stem the acceleration in risk premiums created by falling income without prematurely aborting the decline in the inflation-generated risk premiums. This is clearly not an easy policy path to traverse, but it is the path that we must follow."

If that is the path that we must follow, I hope we are able to find it before it (another Greenspanism) obsoletes.

Greenspan was speaking in Washington, a city where a scarcity of money is routinely referred to as a tight resource environment and where, after an experiment with fish in which all the fish died, the Atomic Energy Commission said that "The biota exhibited one hundred percent mortality response." There is a reason for this verbiage. In a tight resource environment, money is more likely to be forthcoming if whatever the money is wanted for can be made to sound abstruse and important. This is why money itself is rarely called money nowadays. It is called funding.

A reader sent me a report by the Youth Services Agency of the New York City Board of Education on the Board's summer program in 1974. The report concluded with the Y.S.A.'s opinion that the program should have more workers and more money, i.e., that it "should be considered for expanded allotments of enrollee personnel and more supportive measures from its own direct funding source."

The same report spoke of employees who had been held up after drawing their paychecks, listed precautions that had been taken, and concluded: "These precautions appeared to be quite successful in dissuading potential individuals with larcenous intent."

Now for a thrust:

"The major thrust of Y.S.A.'s recommendations to maximize the quality and efficiency of services rendered revolve around the necessity for more phone channels. Two additional phone channels would compensate greatly for both communicative and space difficulties and such implementation is strongly urged as an immediate necessity."

Revolve should be revolves, and such implementation also is urged as an immediate necessity, but no matter. A revolving major thrust is hard to match. Indeed, it is hard to find. However, the non-revolving species is spotted fairly often. It was seen at the 1975 convention of the American Booksellers Association, where a press release noted that the major thrust of the convention was (I ask myself whether this really happened) to "foster dialogue."

Major thrusts, unless met by major parries, may be fatal, but almost any thrust can be dangerous. A dean of a university department of home economics (no longer called home economics but family resources and consumer sciences) told an interviewer that in her previous job, in the Office of Education in Washington, most of her work had been in "conceptualizing new thrusts in programming." Beware the conceptualized thrust. There is a verified instance of one that went berserk. It took six strong men to hold it down.

Conceptualizing thrusts, or articulating them, is what we have come to expect from the social sciences. In that world, a sociologist will feel that he has advanced the cause of knowledge by classifying murder and assault as escalated interpersonal altercations; an applicant for a grant for technical training will write that "A quality void in technical capacity constrains achievement"; teachers who encourage children will be said to emit reinforcers; and an economist will be concerned about the adverse effect on the countercyclical dimension that would come from opening the Pandora's box of micro-goals.

It was a social scientist who wrote that knowledge that is transmitted from person to person *qua* knowledge is called intersubjectively transmissible knowledge or, for the sake of brevity, transmissible knowledge. Making knowledge something of a bridge over the river *qua*.

Words like funding, ongoing, constituency, thrust and viable can be worth millions in foundation grants. I received an appeal for money from an organization at Princeton University dedicated to finding viable solutions to international problems. We used to look for solutions and were pleasantly surprised on the rare occasions that we found them. Solutions are no longer sufficient. Viability is now required.

And if not viability, effectiveness. The Committee for Economic Development put out a statement of policy in which it said that a new generation of complex problems demanded fresh and effective solutions. A solution not effective would by definition not be a solution. Nor is there any reason that a solution must be fresh. Old solutions do the job and also have the advantage of experience.

But I stray. I recently came across a phrase that may be worth as much as funding, ongoing and viable put together. It was in a paper advocating the setting of behavioral objectives in schools. Behavioral objectives, so far as I can make out, mean nothing whatever, but it was claimed that they would enable teachers to "provide students with a pharmacy of learning alternatives matched to the objectives and tailored to the individual characteristics of each student." A pharmacy of learning alternatives. The proper reaction is wonder and veneration.

I do not wish to overlook the contribution of business to wrecking the language. B. Altman, in New York, has issued this invitation: "Sparkle your table with Cape Cod classic glassware." As it happened, I did not have time to sparkle my table because I was busy following instructions given in another advertisement and was accessorizing my spacious master bedroom with oil paintings and, in the words of another advertisement that appeared in *The New Yorker,* "making beautiful happen to [my] window treatments with Levolor Rivieras." Some days, I wish I could just make clean happen to my window treatments.

Saks Fifth Avenue, also in New York, has offered to sell men a magnificient—magnificient—glacé leather trench coat collared and lined with natural muskrat. Unnatural muskrat is a muskrat of doubtful sexual proclivities. An advertising executive I have been told of wrote to a client: "This will enable us to direct the most maximally impactful advertising toward the small and medium size dog owner."

I have seen advertisements for a recording of *Così Fan Tutte* that was "totally complete," and for a California Riesling that was "regretfully available only in very limited quantities." The latter is the hopefully disease spreading, though no variation is likely to approach the sheer majesty of the president of the Green Bay Packers saying, when discussing the hiring of a new coach, "We hope to have an announcement before the end of the week, hopefully before that." The wine is regretfully available only in limited quantities. You may have a vision of the Riesling sobbing itself to sleep over its inadequacy.

The Chesapeake and Potomac Telephone Company has something called a single payment gift plan. Under the plan, the customer may pay for a year in advance, and then he receives no other bills until the year is over. That's a gift. In Pompano Beach, Florida, condominium apartments have been offered in which the bedroom is a sleeping chamber, the kitchen is a culinary center, and the dining room is the place de dinner. That last would have been an appropriate place for a dish served at a book-and-author luncheon sponsored in the Athens of America by the *Boston Herald-American:* crepes a la seafood. Both the *Herald* and the condominium promoters may have received advice from the Biltmore Hotel in New York which, for the benefit of foreign visitors, has a sign outside a men's lavatory that reads not only "Gentlemen" but "Monsieurs."

Let us return to Britain, where the locals—quick learners—are having major confrontations, consulting in depth, satisfying targets, giving the score situation instead of the score, flaunting instead of flouting, making an effort to try, calling for legislation that will galvanize a new sense of opportunity and partnership, and describing the way people talk as their conversation culture, and swimming pools and playing fields as leisure complexes.

Remnants of Britain's sturdy conversation culture do survive. At a meeting of shareholders of the British Leyland Motor Corporation, the chairman, Lord Stokes, explaining the disasters that had befallen the company, found his explanation being drowned out by slow handclapping.

Said Lord Stokes, sarcastically, "Well, thank you for your support."

Said one of the shareholders, "There is only one support you want because you are a bloody big rupture all the way through."

It was a little too long to be ideal, but it undoubtedly enlivened the dialogue situation.

The British, in any case, are not as resourceful as the Americans when it comes to making language mushy and boneless. The playwright William Douglas-Home, writing to *The Times* of London, said that the Conservative party "should be plugging, day in, day out, the true facts about taxation." True facts are, of course, the only kind of facts available, but see what a press release for an American television program does with them: "The facts hew to actuality." True facts. The facts hew to actuality. No contest.

But don't cheer, folks.

Soon, also, no language.

What are we learning from television?

by NEWTON N. MINOW and NELL MINOW

Newton Minow, a former chairman of the Federal Communications Commission, and Nell Minow discuss the educational role of television. Noting that advertisers, followed by politicians, were the first to see the educational potential of television (see Greenfield, pp. 353–355), the authors see educators as finally realizing the potential of television as a teacher.

When most people speak of educational TV, they mean instructional programs on noncommercial television and documentaries on commercial channels. But in fact, as former Federal Communications Commissioner Nick Johnson has said, all television is educational. The real questions are, What are we learning from it? and Who are our teachers?

Advertisers were the first to understand the educational potential of television. They taught us that our marriages could be saved, our self-respect restored, and our families brought closer together if we bought Folger's coffee, Wisk detergent, Spic and Span cleaner, Downy fabric softener, and Coca-Cola.

Then came the politicians, seeking to sell themselves. They knew that television could persuade us to vote for them with appeals based on all the cleverness and depth of commercials for soapflakes. They could make a stronger impression in 10 seconds than in an hour-long debate. We learned their lessons, too.

The last group to understand how to use television has been professional

What Are We Learning from Television?: Reprinted with permission from *Change* Magazine (Vol. 8, No. 9), New Rochelle, New York.

educators. This is especially astonishing when one considers that by the time an average child has graduated from high school he will have spent some 11,000 hours in a classroom, but more than 15,000 hours in front of the TV.

After 25 years, however, teachers are finally waking up to the effectiveness of television and its power to do more than entertain. And they are beginning to lose their fear of television, perhaps because a new generation of teachers has grown up with it. It was, in any case, a fear based on a fallacy. Teachers worried that television would replace their own services and they conjured up images of roomfuls of schoolchildren watching a TV where once a teacher stood. It may be that when books were invented, teachers regarded them, too, with hostility, fearing they would eliminate the need for oral explanations.

Lloyd N. Morrisett, president of the Markle Foundation, has noted that one of the great paradoxes of our time is the acceptance and use of mass communications in daily life, and its absence within education. Hitherto based almost entirely on the technology of print, education, he believes, must now question not how to replace the old technology with the new, but how to integrate the new with the old. Many educators are beginning to examine the issue in Morrisett's terms. The challenge now is to define both television's unique possibilities and its special limitations.

The prime example, of course, is "Sesame Street." For years I served on the board of National Educational Television (NET)—now reincarnated as the Public Broadcasting System (PBS). A woman named Joan Ganz Cooney came to us with a proposal. Cooney had worked in Head Start but was discouraged because it reached so few children. She had worked in television but was discouraged by its neglect of children's programming. Her proposal was based on the following facts: that children learn from television; that no home in America is so poor it does not have television (in fact, the poorer the home, the more time the children spend watching television); and that the skills of filmmakers, entertainers, and educators had never really been effectively used in television to promote learning in an entertaining way.

Lloyd Morrisett had already backed Cooney, and we added NET's help; the big foundations and the government joined us. She had to buck the educational establishment every inch of the way. But James Earl Jones, Bill Cosby, and Big Bird have now taught the alphabet to more youngsters than any teachers in the history of the world.

"Sesame Street" has been well publicized, but there are dozens of other programs teaching us something we need to learn. "Villa Allegre" ("Happy Village") is a program in Spanish and English financed by the government and designed for 4- to 8-year-olds. The program deals with human relations, environment, food and nutrition, energy, and man-made objects. More low-key in its approach than "Sesame Street," it uses many of the same techniques: cartoons, live action, and a continuing population of characters, children and adults. Creators of some proposed new series hope the programs will be shown during school hours so that a teacher may answer questions, reinforce lessons, and plan his or her schedule accordingly. An organization called Prime Time Television (of which I am a director) publicizes excellent programs, prepares teacher study guides, and helps teach critical viewing habits to students.

Public television is not the only experimenter in the field of televised teaching. Commercial television is responding more effectively to the demands of groups such as Action for Children's Television. The Saturday morning lineup of violent and/or silly cartoons punctuated by blaring, hard-sell commercials for dolls and war toys has changed. The cartoons are less violent and there are fewer of them. Short spots such as "Multiplication Rock" and "In The News" match the best that public television has produced. Some of the programs ("Fat Albert and the Cosby Kids," for example), produced under the supervision of a large group of educators, deal with such problems as practical jokers, drugs, new babies in the family, and loyalty.

Commercial television has certain advantages. For one, it already has more of the children's attention. But there are also disadvantages. The largest is a tendency to go slowly and to stick with a lowest-common-denominator program, one that children will watch regardless of content. To paraphrase Mencken, no cereal or toy manufacturer ever lost money by underestimating the children of America.

Yet another obstacle to better educational programming has been the restrictions that educators have imposed upon themselves in the belief that educational television is only for children. This is evidenced by the new growth of excellent programs for children and a real lack of counterparts for teenagers, college students, and adults. This is changing, too, but far more slowly.

The Children's Television Workshop (CTW), for example, after the success of "Sesame Street" and "The Electric Company," created a program on health and nutrition for adults called "Feeling Good," using many of the techniques of the earlier shows. It was not successful because it tried to be too cute, and CTW had the courage and good judgment to pull it off the air for an emergency overhaul. The new version was much improved, dealing with the problems of mental health, stress, heart attacks, and eye problems in a more serious, coherent light. But the flaws were too deep. The show is no longer on the air.

The greatest potential for educational television for adults at this time is within the existing framework. "All in the Family" has given us programs on many previously taboo aspects of our lives and our society: aging, rape, menopause, impotence, and so on. Even medical programs have taught us, in a dramatic way, of sudden infant death syndrome, Tay-Sachs disease, VD, retardation, and many other medical problems. Occasionally they display an address at the end of the program where more information can be obtained; this should be done every week. Television productions of "Civilization," "The Forsyte Saga," "America," and "The Adams Chronicles," moreover, have turned people back to television's "competition"—books. They became best-sellers after the television series were on the air.

Most exciting was "The Ascent of Man," a soaring success in every possible light. Like "America," the book became a best-seller. More important, television became the world's largest classroom. The series was taken as a course by students across the country for college credit. Educators worked with the series narrator, the late Jacob Bronowski, in preparing the course, which included a booklist and study guide. Over 250 colleges and universities have already participated in the program, and it is estimated that over 23,000 students took the course. It is unlikely that even a dozen of those 23,000 would have otherwise had the chance to enjoy the personal teaching of Bronowski without television.

Why is there not more in good quality educational television? The major problem lies in the structure of commercial television. Three of the four networks are commercial. That means revenue depends on advertising, which depends on ratings. Perhaps the numbers will become more meaningful with an example.

In 1972 one of the networks presented a Joseph Papp production of Shakespeare's *Much Ado About Nothing*. It had been a critical and financial success on stage; but on television it had poor ratings, so poor that it has never been rebroadcast. And yet, even with poor ratings, more people saw the play that night than had seen it in the 350 years since the play had been written.

In the world of commercial television, and to a lesser extent, public television, the majority rules, with little place for minority perspectives. Programs are kept on the air until the public tires of them, and during that time there is little effort to improve the product.

Television's other great problem is, again, rooted in its very structure. The need for more creative programming simply cannot be met while the theory of television is a week of new shows at a time. If all of Shakespeare's plays were broadcast continuously, we would be out of material in less than three days. Television has more room for more material shown to a greater audience than anyone could have dreamed 50 years ago. But by its very enormity, it has created a need for material we have not yet learned how to fill.

But structural changes are coming. In many cities, cable television is removing television's most serious limitation, the number of channels. With cable television a city may have 30 or more stations, offering greater variety and scope. With so many channels, there will be more room for specialized programming. Already there are Spanish-language stations in areas with substantial Spanish-speaking populations. Someday there may be stations devoted entirely to children's programming, others to teenagers, hobbyists, sports fans, movie fans, and the aged. There could be all-news stations, like the ones on the radio. And, perhaps best of all, there will be much more room for community programming.

The next giant step in technology is the videocassette, which enables the viewer to catch and record the program, and see it at leisure. The viewer will even build a library of his own, just as he now records symphonies from his FM radio on an audiotape cassette. And the television set in the home will become infinitely more useful and important. We can hope that the teacher will get the message, not much later this time than advertisers and the politicians.

As new techniques of production evolve, teachers must learn how to use them. For the most part, public television has advanced in America without the support of intellectuals and academics, who were too busy looking down their noses at television as an inferior medium for the masses. If there were a limited number of printing presses in this country, intellectuals and academics would have vociferously insisted that at least one or two of them be set aside for noncommercial use for the advancement of knowledge and culture. But because the medium involves a technology other than familiar print, public television has had to win public support without the aid or support of the intellectual community.

A European friend visiting Los Angeles not long ago was riding along the freeways and noted that every house—rich, poor, grand, elegant, slum, cottage, whatever—had a television antenna on its roof. He saw those antennas as periscopes enabling the people inside to peer outside. What images should we send them?

Television can be, as Fred Allen said, chewing gum for the mind. Or it can be much more. As Edward R. Murrow once noted, "This instrument can teach, it can illuminate; yes, it can even inspire. But it can do so only to the extent that humans are determined to use it to those ends. Otherwise, it is merely lights and wires in a box."

NETWORK

Two Film Reviews

The following reviews of **Network,** Paddy Chayefsky's highly acclaimed movie about TV news shows, illustrate another form of persuasion: film criticism. Writing for their respective audiences, Daniel Henninger and Pauline Kael approach their criticism from different perspectives. Henninger, writing for **The National Observer,** a weekly newspaper with a news-oriented reader, after giving a brief resume of the plot, focuses primarily on the social effects of television. Kael, writing for the sophisticated readers of **The New Yorker** magazine, gives an involved review, which upon analysis becomes more a review of Chayefsky than of **Network.**

Although neither reviewer catches a major point in the movie, that entertainment is winning against news on network (and local) television, each has fit content and style to the publication the review was written for.

SHORT CIRCUIT IN THE WIRED CITY

by DANIEL HENNINGER

Prediction: Upheaval is imminent in the Wired City of television. The right hemisphere of my brain, that wholesale warehouse of the eye, is rumbling. Local network affiliates are telling the Wired City's fathers their programs are becoming too violent. A Federal judge has declared the Family Hour illegal. William S. Paley, chairman of CBS, high priest in the Wired City, has fired his company's president, not because the man failed to create revenue (of that, he made lots), but because the Delphic Nielsen told Paley that the city's citizens loved him (his programs, his videotaped children) less. A fighting-mad playwright, Paddy Chayefsky, has written an antitelevision movie, *Network* (MGM), playing soon in local movie theaters, the still-standing ruins of the ancient unwired cities. And *You Should See What You're Missing* is the title of a documentary to be seen on public television this Friday evening (Nov. 26, but check local listings), wherein writers tell mournful tales of esthetic corruption in the Wired City. I have heard them speak, I have seen *Network* by the mad Chayefsky. My dispatch:

The United Broadcasting System (UBS), Chayefsky's imaginary fourth network, is in the ratings basement. Told that he is being fired, Howard Beale (Peter Finch), the UBS evening-news anchorman, announces over the air that on his final broadcast he will take his life. Beale's ratings skyrocket. Instead of a suicide, viewers of Beale's last newscast see him go bonkers and deliver a crazed jeremiad against the general bullbleep, exhorting his audience to throw open their windows and scream: "I'm mad!" They do. Two powerful and ruthless UBS executives (Faye Dunaway and Robert Duvall) decide not to fire what one calls "this manifestly irresponsible man"; instead, they make the evening news a side show with Beale as prophet, abetted by a medium, Sybil the Soothsayer, who predicts the news. Beale's ratings enter outer space. Thus encouraged, programming chief Dunaway (a bravura performance, though some may cringe at this monstrous stereotype, a neurotically ambitious, castrating, amoral corporate female) creates *The Mao Tse-tung Hour,* featuring an authentic act of terror each week by a gang of radical crazies.

Short Circuit in the Wired City: From *The National Observer* (November 27, 1976).

Lowest Common Denominator

Chayefsky believes that the people who run television will do anything to make us watch their programs (revenues are directly related to audience size): distort life, replace reality with illusion, feed our worst instincts, reduce all to the rubble of banality. I am not giving my interpretation of *Network;* I'm reporting almost exactly the ideas expressed in several long speeches by Beale (the madman as truth-teller) and by the network's disillusioned news chief, well played by William Holden.

Chayefsky's clear intent is to make us see television for what he believes it to be—an uncontrolled money-making machine. His tone is hortatory and evangelistic. The long, exceedingly well written tirades Finch and Holden make against television might as well have been delivered by Billy Graham from an elevated stage in Yankee Stadium. If Chayefsky's Howard Beale actually were a real person, possessed of Graham's rhetorical power and Walter Cronkite's authoritative familiarity, he might indeed change minds with words alone. But he's Peter Finch, an excellent but not widely known actor. And Bill Holden is the guy who was in *Bridge on the River Kwai*. Can these men, actors, deprogram us with rhetoric? I think not.

Those who dislike television will find easy, eloquent confirmation of their beliefs in *Network*. Those who worry about television's influence without dismissing it will hear little new (if I must hear what I already know, I'm happy to get it from Chayefsky's high-voltage writing). But I think the people who I take to be Chayefsky's real target—moviegoers who watch a lot of television without giving it much thought one way or the other—may wonder what the ranting is all about.

A Cry in the Night

Chayefsky's harangue sounds like the cry of a desperate man, a last-ditch effort to rouse the citizenry after every alternatvie method of intellectual and moral persuasion has failed. In truth, alternatives to straight preachment have not been tried. Television is indeed guilty of most of the sins Chayefsky attributes to it, but the sad fact is that although television has become the central fact of our culture (President Ford named the new space shuttle after the Enterprise, the command ship in *Star Trek*), no American narrative artist—not one film maker, playwright, or novelist—has to my knowledge taken television and its effect on us (not its effect on network executives) as the sole subject of his art. There have been a couple of satirical films, *GrooveTube* and *Tunnelvision,* but they were just kidding the medium. An artist's gift is to show us how we appear at points in history, to identify clearly the changes we undergo as individuals and as a culture. Television has been changing us for 25 years, and artists, instead of showing us how, invariably have ridiculed us for watching it.

On *You Should See What You're Missing* a succession of TV writers who put words in the mouths of Kojak, Barney Miller, Archie Bunker, and others present their case against commercial television. Abby Mann (*Kojak, Judgment at Nuremburg, Medical Story*) explains why he writes for a medium that grinds imagination into cat food: "I do it because overnight something can become part of our culture." Yes. Crave it, hate it, belittle it, abandon it, but make no mistake about its essence: In the Wired City, TV is power.

HOT AIR

by PAULINE KAEL

In "Network," Paddy Chayefsky blitzes you with one idea after another. The ideas don't go together, but who knows which of them he believes, anyway? He's like a Village crazy bellowing at you: blacks are taking over, revolutionaries are taking over, women are taking over. He's got the New York City hatreds, and ranting makes him feel alive. There *is* something funny in this kind of rant—it was funny in Fred Wiseman's "Welfare," too; with the number of things that are going wrong in the city, it's a bottomless comedy to see people pinning their rage on some one object, person, or group, or a pet collection of them. Cabdrivers used to get it off on Mayor Lindsay, liberals on the moon landings, and now Chayefsky's getting it off on television. Television, he says, is turning us into morons and humanoids; people have lost the ability to love. Who—him? Oh, no, the blacks, the revolutionaries, and a power-hungry executive at the UBS network named Diana Christensen (Faye Dunaway). In Chayefsky's 1958 movie "The Goddess," the Marilyn Monroe-type heroine (Kim Stanley) sought movie stardom, fame, and adulation in order to compensate for her inability to love. This empty girl was supposed to symbolize our dreams; moviegoers were his morons then. Chayefsky said in 1958 that his heroine "represents an entire generation that came through the Depression with nothing left but a hope for comfort and security. Their tragedy lies in that they never learned to love, either their fellow humans or whatever god they have." God and love came together in his 1959 play "The Tenth Man," which ended with an old man saying of the hero, whose demon (of lovelessness) had been exorcised, "He still doesn't believe in God—he simply wants to love—and when you stop and think about it, gentlemen, is there any difference?" This mushy amalgam of God and love is Chayefsky's faith, and if you don't share it you're tragic. The new goddess, the unprincipled career girl Diana Christensen, is explained in "Network" in these terms: "She's television generation. She learned life from Bugs Bunny. The only reality she knows comes to her over the TV set." What Chayefsky is really complaining about is what barroom philosophers have always complained about: the soulless worshippers at false shrines—the younger generation.

In Chayefsky's last film, "The Hospital" (1971), the fiftyish Jewish chief of medicine (George C. Scott) has lost his potency, fails at suicide, and is disappointed in his children; he blows off steam about what's wrong with the society but ridicules the Puerto Rican community-action groups who march on the hospital. After an affair with a young Wasp (Diana Rigg), who urges him to leave with her, he decides that *somebody* has to be decent and responsible, and so, with his potency restored, he stays to make his stand for sanity. Youth-baiting played a strong part in "The Hospital," but Chayefsky's slapstick exaggeration of the chaos in a big-city institution had so much silly, likable crackpot verve that the diatribes against the disrespectful younger generation could be shrugged aside. "Network," however, is all baiting—youth, TV, the culture, the universe. The UBS network has been taken over by a conglomerate, and Howard Beale (Peter Finch), a veteran anchorman whose ratings have slipped, is given two weeks' notice by executives who want to jazz up the news to make it more entertaining. Angry at being dumped, Beale goes out of control, and his blasts on the air about "this demented slaughterhouse of a world we live in"—blasts sprinkled with cusswords—accomplish what his restrained behavior didn't: his ratings go up. His best friend, the head of the news division—the fiftyish hero, Max Schumacher (William Holden), who is Paddy Chayefsky in the guise of the unimpeachable Ed Murrow—loses his fight to keep the news independent. The chief of operations (Robert Duvall) fires him and turns the news division over to Diana Christensen, the vice-president in charge of programming. So when Beale begins to have visions (either he's having a breakdown or he's in a state of religious exaltation) and is advertised as "the Mad Prophet of the airwaves," Schumacher is on the sidelines, and has nothing to do but hang around Diana Christensen,

"We have some good news and some bad news, some mad news and some glad news, some sad news and some chase-away-the-blues news."

Drawing by S. Harris; © 1976 The New Yorker Magazine, Inc.

TV executive Diana Christenson (FAYE DUNAWAY) discusses the forthcoming year's programming with her staff, and plots to get the major audience share, in MGM's "Network," a United Artists release.

with whom he has an affair, and denounce her, television, and us soulless masses. The Mad Prophet and the sane prophet both deliver broadsides—enough to break a viewer's back. The screen seems to be plastered with bumper stickers.

The central gag in "Network"—Howard Beale becomes the first man killed because of lousy ratings—sounds like a good premise for a farce about TV, which has certainly earned farce status. (And, even if it hadn't, satire doesn't have to be fair to be funny.) But in the "Network" script Chayefsky isn't writing a farce: he's telling us a thing or two. And he writes directly to the audience—he soapboxes. He hardly bothers with the characters; the movie is a ventriloquial harangue. He thrashes around in messianic God-love booziness, driving each scene to an emotional peak. When Schumacher tells his wife (Beatrice Straight) that he's in love with Diana, his wife launches into a high-powered speech about "all the senseless pain that we've inflicted on each other," referring to his affair as "your last roar of passion before you settle into your menopausal years." It's a short, self-contained soap opera; she hits her peak—then she's invisible again. The director, Sidney Lumet, keeps the soliloquies going at a machine-gun pace. The movie might have been modelled on that earlier talk binge, Billy Wilder's "One, Two, Three;" Lumet is right—it's best not to let the words sink in. With Schumacher experiencing a "winter passion" and discussing his "primal doubts," you have to hurtle through to the next crisis. Lumet does Chayefsky straight, just as Chayefsky no doubt wanted. The film looks negligently made; the lighting bleaches the actors' faces, like color TV that needs tuning, and the New York views outside the office and apartment windows feel like blown-up photographs. The timing in most of the scenes is so careless that you may be aware of the laugh lines you're not responding to, and there's a confusing cut from Diana and Schumacher planning to go to bed together to Howard Beale in bed by himself. "Network" even fails to show the executives at meetings getting carried away by the infectiousness of Diana Christensen's ideas—getting high on power. But Lumet keeps it all moving.

Chayefsky is such a manic bard that I'm not sure if he ever decided whether Howard Beale's epiphanies were the result of a nervous breakdown or were actually inspired by God. Yet Beale's story has a fanciful, Frank Capra nuttiness that could be appealing. Peter Finch's sleepy-lion head suggests the bland, prosperous decay of an anchorman whose boredom is swathed in punditry. His gray aureole is perfect: the curly, thick hair, cropped short, is the only vigorous thing about him. (Does Finch, who is British-Australian, seem American? Not really, but then does Eric Sevareid, who comes from North Dakota?) If Chayefsky meant Beale to represent his idealized vision of the crusading mandarin journalists of an earlier day who are now being replaced by show-biz anchorpersons, Finch

Programming chief Diana Christenson (FAYE DUNAWAY) watches a power play develop between TV executives Frank Hackett (ROBERT DUVALL) and Max Schumacher (WILLIAM HOLDEN) in MGM's "Network," a United Artists release.

is miscast, but his fuzzy mildness is likable, and in a picture in which everybody seems to take turns at screaming (Robert Duvall screams the loudest) Finch's ability to seem reserved even when he's raving has its own satirical charm. Unfortunately, when Beale's wild-eyed ramblings are supposed to make his ratings zoom up, you can't believe it; he doesn't give off enough heat.

Beale the Prophet's big moment comes when he tells TV viewers to open their windows, stick out their heads, and yell, "I'm mad as hell and I'm not going to take this anymore!" But is the viewers' obedience proof of their sheeplike response to TV or is it evidence that the Prophet has struck a nerve—that the public is as fed up as he is? Considering that the entire picture is Chayefsky sticking his head out the window and yelling (in Chayefsky's world, that's how you prove that you're capable of love), it must be that Beale's message is supposed to be salutary. Yet there's no follow-through on this scene, and that's where the movie goes completely on the fritz. Chayefsky whirrs in other directions—Max's winter passion for Diana, and the Saudi Arabians taking over the conglomerate.

Early on, Howard Beale is awakened at night by the voice of the Lord or some Heavenly Messenger, who affectionately calls him "Dummy" and tells him what he must do on the air. The voice may be simply Beale's delusion, but how are we to interpret the turn of events when Beale is summoned to a meeting with the piggy-eyed master salesman Arthur Jensen (Ned Beatty), the head of the conglomerate, and Jensen addresses him as "Dummy"? Jensen, a corn-pone Grand Inquisitor, tells Beale that the multinational corporate state is the natural order of things now, and that he should embrace this one-business world, in which all men will be taken care of as humanoids. Converted, Beale asks the TV audience, "Is dehumanization such a bad word?" He preaches his new corporate faith—"The world is a business . . . one vast, ecumenical holding company." But people don't want to hear that their individual lives are valueless; he loses his ratings and is killed for it. Chayefsky, it seems, can be indignant about people becoming humanoids, and then turn a somersault and say it's inevitable and only a fool wouldn't recognize that. And he's wrong on both counts. There are a lot of changes in the society which can be laid at television's door, but soullessness isn't one of them. TV may have altered family life and social intercourse; it may have turned children at school into entertainment seekers. But it hasn't taken our souls, any more than movies did, or the theatre and novels before them. I don't know what's worse—Beale's denunciations of the illiterate public (Chayefsky apparently thinks that not reading is proof of soullessness) or Schumacher's pitying tone. When Schumacher tells Diana Christensen that she can feel nothing, while he's O.K. because he can feel pleasure and pain and love, you want to kick him. Doesn't Chayefsky realize that everybody can feel—even a kittycat?

The screw-up inside Chayefsky's message of kindness shows in the delight he takes in snide reactionary thrusts. Diana Christensen has no difficulty coöpting an Angela Davis-like activist (Marlene Warfield), the Communist central committee, and an extremist group that's a parody of the Symbionese Liberation Army and the Black Panthers. (Chayefsky can't even resist a sideswipe at Patty Hearst.) She propositions them to perform terrorist crimes—kidnappings, robberies, hijackings—on a weekly basis, in front of a camera crew, and their only quarrel is over money. Whatever one's disagreements with Angela Davis, she's hardly a sellout. Yet Chayefsky's venom is such an exuberant part of him that the best scene in the movie is the slapstick negotiating session in which the black revolutionaries, their agents, and the network attorneys haggle over residuals and syndication rights, and a revolutionary who wants to be heard fires his pistol to get some order. This is in the paranoid-comic-strip style of Norman Wexler, the scriptwriter for "Joe," "Serpico," and "Mandingo." Chayefsky's speeches may be about humanism, but baiting gets the old adrenalin going.

And what of Diana Christensen, the hopped-up *Cosmopolitan* doll with power on the brain? Look at her name: the goddess of the hunt, and some sort of essence of Christianity? In bed, on top of Schumacher, she talks ratings until orgasm. Chayefsky, in interviews, actually claims that he has created one of the few movie roles in which a woman is treated as an equal; this can be interpreted to mean that he thinks women who want equality are ditsey little twitches—ruthless, no-souled monsters who take men's jobs away from them. Diana Christensen is, Schumacher says, "television incarnate"—that is, she is symptomatic of what's spoiling our society. And, in case we don't get Chayefsky's drift, he presents us with that contrasting image of a loving woman who has the capacity for suffering —Max's wife, to whom he returns after he leaves rotten Diana.

As Schumacher, Holden is in good form, and now that he has stopped trying to conceal the aging process his sunken-cheeked, lined, craggy face takes the camera marvellously—he has a real face, like Gabin or Montand. He does a lot for the movie—he's an actor with authority and the gift of never being boring—but he can't energize the phoniness of a man who claims to be superior to his society. This hero is trampling out the vintage where the sour grapes are stored. Dunaway chatters as Kim Stanley did in "The Goddess" (Chayefsky must believe that women talk because of their tinny empty-headedness), and even when she's supposed to be reduced to a pitiful shell by Holden's exposing her "shrieking nothingness" she's ticky and amusingly greedy. She snarls at underlings and walks with a bounce and a wiggle. In the past, Dunaway hasn't had much humor or variety; her performances have usually been proficient yet uneventful—there's a certain heaviness, almost of depression, about them. It's that heaviness, probably, that has made some people think her Garboesque. A beautiful woman who's as self-conscious as Faye Dunaway has a special neurotic magnetism. (The far less proficient Kim Novak had it also.) In this stunt role, her usual self-consciousness is turned into comic rapport with the audience; she's not the remote, neurotic beauty—she's more of a clown. And though her Diana isn't remotely convincing—she's not a woman with a drive to power, she's just a dirty Mary Tyler Moore—it's a relief to see Dunaway being light. She puts us on the side of the humanoids.

The watered-down Freudianism that Chayefsky goes in for—i.e., people want fame or power because they're sick—seems to get by almost everywhere these days. It became popular with those analysts who, taking Hitler's crimes as evidence, deduced that he was sexually crippled; they really seemed to think they were explaining something. And it spread in TV drama and in movies as a form of vindictive, moralizing condescension. The trick in "Network," as in "The Goddess," is to use a woman's drive toward fame or success as the embodiment of the sickness in the society. What's implicit is that if she could love she wouldn't need anything more. You couldn't get by with this bulling if a man were television incarnate. "Network" starts in high gear and is so confidently brash that maybe people can really take it for muckraking. But it's no more than the kind of inside story that a lot of TV executives probably would secretly like to write. Chayefsky comes on like a patriarchal Jackie Susann, and he likes to frolic with the folksy occult. What happened to his once much-vaunted gift for the vernacular? Nothing exposes his claims to be defending the older values as much as the way he uses four-letter words for chortles. It's so cheap you may never want to say **** again. Chayefsky doesn't come right out and tell us why he thinks TV is *goyish,* but it must have something to do with his notion that all feeling is Jewish.

Guaranteed Effective All-Occasion Non-Slanderous Political Smear Speech

by BILL GARVIN

This speech does not refer to any specific political campaign; rather, through satire, it offers a comment on the entire political process, criticizing the intelligence of the electorate and the ethics of some candidates.

My fellow citizens, it is an honor and a pleasure to be here today. My opponent has openly admitted he feels an affinity toward your city, but I happen to **like** this area. It might be a salubrious place to him, but to me it is one of the nation's most delightful garden spots.

When I embarked upon this political campaign I hoped that it could be conducted on a high level and that my opponent would be willing to stick to the issues. Unfortunately, he has decided to be tractable instead—to indulge in unequivocal language, to eschew the use of outright lies in his speeches, and even to make repeated veracious statements about me.

At first I tried to ignore these scrupulous, unvarnished fidelities. Now I will do so no longer. **If my opponent wants a fight, he's going to get one!**

It might be instructive to start with his background. My friends, have you ever accidentally dislodged a rock on the ground and seen what was underneath? Well, exploring my opponent's background is dissimilar. All the slime and filth and corruption you can possibly imagine, even in your wildest dreams, are glaringly nonexistent in this man's life. And even during his childhood!

Let us take a very quick look at that childhood: It is a known fact that, on a number of occasions, he emulated older boys at a certain playground. It is also known that his parents not only permitted him to masticate excessively in their presence, but even urged him to do so. Most explicable of all, this man who poses as a paragon of virtue exacerbated his own sister when they were both teenagers!

I ask you, my fellow Americans: is this the kind of person we want in public office to set an example for our youth?

Of course, it's not surprising that he should have such a typically pristine background—no, not when you consider the other members of his family:

His female relatives put on a constant pose of purity and innocence, and claim they are inscrutable, yet every one of them has taken part in hortatory activities.

The men in the family are likewise completely amenable to moral suasion.

My opponent's second cousin is a Mormon.

His uncle was a flagrant heterosexual.

His sister, who has always been obsessed by sects, once worked as a proselyte outside a church.

His father was secretly chagrined at least a dozen times by matters of a pecuniary nature.

His youngest brother wrote an essay extolling the virtues of being a homo sapiens.

His great-aunt expired from a degenerative disease.

His nephew subscribes to a phonographic magazine.

His wife was a thespian before their marriage and even performed the act in front of paying customers.

And his own mother had to resign from a woman's organization in her later years because she was an admitted sexagenarian.

Now what shall we say of the man himself?

I can tell you in solemn truth that he is the very antithesis of political radicalism, economic irresponsibility and personal depravity. His own record **proves** that he has frequently discountenanced treasonable, un-American philosophies and has perpetrated many overt acts as well.

He perambulated his infant son on the street.

He practiced nepotism with his uncle and first cousin.

He attempted to interest a 13-year-old girl in philately.

He participated in a seance at a private residence where, among other odd goings-on, there was incense.

He has declared himself in favor of more homogeneity on college campuses.

He has advocated social intercourse in mixed company—and has taken part in such gatherings himself.

He has been deliberately averse to crime in our streets.

He has urged our Protestant and Jewish citizens to develop more catholic tastes.

Last summer he committed a piscatorial act on a boat that was flying the American flag.

Finally, at a time when we must be on our guard against all foreign isms, he has coolly announced his belief in altruism—and his fervent hope that some day this entire nation will be altruistic!

I beg you, my friends, to oppose this man whose life and work and ideas are so openly and avowedly compatible with our American way of life. A vote for him would be a vote for the perpetuation of everything we hold dear.

The facts are clear; the record speaks for itself.

Do your duty.

MINI–CASE STUDY

"I THINK WE SHOULD GO LEGIT... GET OUT OF THE COMIC BOOK RACKET AND INTO EDUCATION..."

Comics as Persuaders

Just as television conveys subtle messages of persuasion as well as overt attempts to persuade, so do comics. While comics, in whatever form—comic books, comic strips, cartoons—are obviously intended to entertain, their role as persuaders cannot be overlooked. Sol Gordon, director of the Institute for Family Research and Education at Syracuse University, has gone so far as to develop a series of comic books designed to educate non-readers about such subjects as premarital sex, drugs, and VD.*

Not all comics are that weighty, of course, but more than ever before comics are attempting to deal with real life and, according to some sociologists, are accurately reflecting our culture. Not satisfied with simple humor or escapist entertainment, more and more cartoonists and comic strip writers are dealing with politics and with social issues, such as discrimination, poverty, and ecology. Changing social patterns are reflected in the comics, which in turn contribute to changing our ideas. The following articles present various views on the comics and on their power to persuade.

* Samples are available at 25 cents each from Ed-U Press, Institute for Family Research and Education, 760 Ostrom Avenue, Syracuse, New York 13210.

FROM

Leapin' Lizards!

WHAT'S HAPPENING TO THE COMICS?

by JOHN CULHANE

After mass, the newsboys would have their stacks of Sunday papers piled up at the bottom of the broad stone steps leading down to the sidewalk from old St. Mary's, competing for our patronage in the good old free enterprise way. My father read The Chicago Herald & Examiner and The Rockford Morning Star, so we kids were assured of their comic sections; but unless we could also persuade him to buy The Chicago Tribune, we could not follow the adventures of "Terry and the Pirates," "Smilin' Jack," "Dick Tracy" and "Little Orphan Annie." Even though Dad disliked The Tribune for being anti-Roosevelt, he would usually indulge us; then we could keep the Sunday boredom at bay until the good radio shows started in the evening, lying flat on our stomachs on the living room rug, with the color comics of three newspapers spread out before us. Believe it or not, we had no difficulty keeping in mind from week to week the continuing adventures of several dozen heroes on land ("Joe Palooka"), sea ("Don Winslow of the Navy") and air ("Smilin' Jack"), and in the past ("Prince Valiant"), present ("Gasoline Alley") and future ("Flash Gordon" and "Buck Rogers, 25th Century A.D.")

But then, at Thanksgiving of 1943, my Dad went into the Army. My mother, trying to get along on his allotment check, stopped getting any Sunday paper except the local one—which was needed to know who had been reported killed, missing or wounded in action. From that time on, I had to wait for the periodic paper drives, when I could collect old newspapers, turn to their comic sections and catch up on the funnies before turning them in up at the schoolhouse. This scrambled continuity didn't make any difference in reading "Blondie," but it made it very difficult for me to follow the adventure strips. For example, it was nearly Easter of 1944 before I found the installment of "Little Orphan Annie" for Christmas of 1943. It sticks in my mind because it seemed to express my political views so perfectly. It showed Annie kneeling before her bed and praying: "Bless Uncle Spike and Auntie Sally . . . and bless 'Daddy' . . . and all our men out there . . . whose courage makes it possible for millions o' us kids to grow up here in decency and *peace!*" In the next picture, "Daddy" Warbucks paused while hacking his way through what in those days we called a "Jap-infested jungle" to look up at the evening star and say to his faithful Punjab and Asp: "Christmas Eve! Back home she'll be saying her prayers . . . From Herod to Hitler and Hirohito! But the prayers of all the Little Annies are greater than all the Herods of all time!"

Leapin' Lizards! Since that wartime Christmas at Easter, 30 years have gone by! Us millions o' kids did grow up here in decency and peace, and we begat many millions more, while Little Orphan Annie stayed the same age (11 or 12) that she was when she first appeared on a comic page 50 years ago next August 5. For all these years, she has faced up to one danger after another with blunked-out eyes. But this year, she finally succumbed to the one kind of danger no comic-strip hero can survive. Two weeks ago [in April, 1974], at the 50-year-old age of 11 or 12, Little Orphan Annie died of circulation trouble.

The condition resulted from complications following television. First, there was the competition from television for the time the audience has to spend being entertained. Why follow one story in "Little Orphan Annie" for eight weeks when you can get eight stories in eight weeks on "Kung Fu"? How can a newspaper adventure strip compete with a television program that is essentially an adventure strip that moves, in color, on a panel eight columns wide and four comic strips high? To make the competition more unequal, television has also caused an economic crisis in the newspaper business; this, aggravated by recent newsprint shortages, has resulted in less space for comic strips—a condition that hits story strips hardest because it takes away the space they need for dialogue, settings and props. And, lastly, television has been a major factor in social changes since the Second World War which have rendered most prewar heroes obsolete.

At least five story men and artists tried to keep Annie alive after the death of her creator, Harold Gray, in 1968. But the formula that made the strip popular for so long belonged to another time. Underscoring this truth was the decision of the Chicago Tribune–New York News Syndicate, which owns "Little Orphan Annie," to offer reruns of old Harold Gray strips to newspapers, starting with her 1936 adventures on the road during the Great American Depression. This decision to "go to reruns," as they say in TV-land, served to make "Little Orphan Annie" a thing of the past

LITTLE ORPHAN ANNIE—FOR THIS THEY FIGHT

even more than her simple disappearance might have. For the syndicate's idea, according to its president, Robert S. Reed, is to appeal to "the current mood of nostalgia for the good things of the past."

The decline of "Little Orphan Annie" is no small event, for it was one of the most popular comic strips of all time. A survey conducted by the Opinion Research Corporation in 1962 found it the third most popular strip in the comics—after "Blondie" and "Dick Tracy." In those days, when The Washington Post tried to drop the strip, angry Annie fans picketed the paper. At its peak (in the forties) it was running in over 500 papers.

Furthermore, Annie's demise is part of a wider trend—the general decline of the serious adventure serial comic strip. Last year, for example, on Feb. 25, the Chicago Tribune–New York News Syndicate ended the 38-year run of "Terry and the Pirates" rather than seeking a successor for the artist, George Wunder, who resigned. Wunder conceded that the strip's readership had been declining for some time. "People just don't seem to follow continuity strips any more the way they used to," he says. And less than two months later, on April 1, the syndicate also ended the 40-year run of its other flying-adventure strip, "Smilin' Jack." Its creator, Zack Mosley, in his sixties as was Wunder, was retiring, and the syndicate did not name a successor.

Those who put out surviving adventure strips are far from sanguine these days. Chester Gould, 73-year-old creator of "Dick Tracy," warns that adventure strips will have to be better and better to stay alive. "The strip that stands still will be tossed out in the face of competition," he says. And Milton Caniff, who had created the syndicate-owned "Terry and the Pirates" but abandoned it in 1946 for the chance to own his own story strip, "Steve Canyon," has admitted that he is running scared. He says he's cut the length of his episodes from 12 weeks down to eight in an effort to hold readers.

Robert Gillespie, promotion director of the Chicago Tribune–New York News Syndicate, says flatly that "the comics are in a state of change. The joke strip is in, the story strip's in trouble. The strong ones still survive, but the weaker ones die or run in fewer papers, and there have been few new continuity strips over the last five years."

. . .

In 1957, Leo Bogart, director of research for the American Newspaper Publishers Association, made a study of New York readers and found that "Annie" had " a strong appeal to persons who feel weak or frustrated. For them, the strip . . . permits regression to the happy days of childhood by introducing an all-powerful father-image who can always be counted upon to set things right." Well, that fits me, all right. I loved "Little Orphan Annie" at a time when I wanted my own daddy to come home and take charge and make everything come out all right. But he was off to war, so my mother and us kids had to do the best we could. As a result, I couldn't justify my actions with "Father Knows Best," and could hardly understand the Watergate defendants who justified actions they would ordinarily consider wrong by pleading that the President's office had authorized them, and the President should know best.

Instead of the authoritarianism of the unfunny funnies, there is about the sophisticated funnies a skepticism that I find healthy. You see it in Pogo's famous comment when he found his beloved swamp polluted with garbage. Instead of blaming it on any of the hate objects and objects of righteous superiority feelings that Gray used as enemies (politicians, bureaucrats, spies and other foreigners), he simply said, "We have met the enemy, and they is us."

Kelly, of course, was more than a cartoonist; he was a philosopher. He expounded his philosophy in fun—his goal was always the laugh that liberates—but he had as much common sense in his strips as Harold Gray had humbug. As president of the National Cartoonists Society in 1954 (his peers had chosen him cartoonist of the year for 1952), he campaigned to cut down on the crime and horror in comic strips. It was an idea whose time had come: "Superman was created in the Depression as an icon, a Nietzsche superman," Carmine Infantino, editorial director of National Comics, explained in 1970. "At that time, people needed a perfect being." In other words, we were scared. As Walt Kelly wrote, "Laughter can always be depended upon to well up out of the balanced mind and the courage of truth, right where it started many thousands of years ago. Wit shrivels and laughter dies when we submerge ourselves in images of perfection, in fear and trembling." And as harsh experiences have destroyed our innocence, we have seen that the heroes of the unfunny funnies are the real jokes.

"Doonesbury" is the perfect example of the new generation of sophisticated funnies. The artist, Gary Trudeau, was born in 1948, the year that Walt Kelly launched "Pogo," and he has grown up on comics that get their laughs out of wit rather than slapstick. "Charles Schulz and Walt

Kelly had the most profound influence on me as far as the writing goes, and Jules Feiffer had the most important influence on me as far as drawing goes—particularly in my early cartoons," says Trudeau. His early cartoons were for The Yale Daily News in 1969, when he was a Yale undergraduate majoring in art. "The strip was called 'Bull Tales' and it was about a football player named B.D., who was based on Brian Dowling, the Yale quarterback. Most of the episodes took place in a huddle."

The strip was a campus sensation, which was duly noted in a story in The New York Times, and that story was duly noted by John McMeel, who was about to become president of the Universal Press Syndicate, which was founded in 1970 and which acquired Sheed & Ward, the religious publishing house, and led it into secular pastures. "We had just launched Garry Wills as a columnist and we were looking for good young talent. So we subscribed to college newspapers, trying to find a writer who deserved to be syndicated nationally. My partner, Jim Andrews, who is the editor of the syndicate and is about my age [38], spotted this strip in The Yale Daily News and wanted to syndicate it, and I remembered the story in The Times, so we decided to gamble. We started selling it in 1970 with a release date of Oct. 26. We started with only 27 or 28 papers, but they included The Washington Post, The Boston Globe and The Chicago Tribune, which went all the way in promoting it."

"Doonesbury" now runs in 347 papers, with an estimated daily readership of 18 million persons. "'Doonesbury's' well-earned popularity is based on the pithy way its characters sink their teeth into contemporary subjects," said The Washington Post. "The strip is created with sure-handed sophistication." An example was during the Vietnam war, when B.D. dropped out of school and joined the Army to avoid a term paper. B.D. got sent to Vietnam, where he got lost and was captured by a Viet Cong terrorist named Phred. They became dependent upon each other for survival, and Phred saved them both from starvation by finding a cache of Schlitz that the Viet Cong had stolen from the U.S. supply depot. In the end they become the best of friends. "It seemed the way I could make a statement about the war most effectively," said Trudeau. "I placed two individuals who, under normal circumstances, would be the bitterest of enemies into a situation where their mutual survival depended on their understanding of their common humanity."

"Sweetness and light—who the hell wants it?" groused Harold Gray in 1964, as the trend toward joke strips got stronger and stronger. "What's news in the newspapers? Murder, rape and arson. That's what stories are made of."

That's true enough; but the kind of heroes the comic page offers no longer provide us with images of our aspirations. We no longer believe in the hero as soldier, as fighter pilot, as astronaut: Television has shown them all too close up. The hero as detective is bigger than ever in this guilt-ridden society, so Dick Tracy survives; but life-styles have changed, and it is hard to imagine him sharing a squad car with Frank Serpico. And as for "Daddy" Warbucks, the hero as billionaire is absolutely out. To the newspaper reader of the thirties and forties, Howard Hughes was a dashing aviator-movie producer who won round-the-world airplane races and pioneered depth cleavage in a Jane Russell movie called "The Outlaw." To the readers of the seventies, Hughes is a comic and/or sinister recluse who makes huge, anonymous political contributions and served as a model for the kidnaped billionaire saved by James Bond in "Diamonds Are Forever." What My Lai and Watergate have shown is that Americans have grown up from being blind hero-worshipers. We no longer confuse the man with his role, and we believe in the man only as long as he acts ethically. (Is that the reason that Gray wouldn't let Annie grow up—because she might have caught on to "Daddy"?) What we need now is not heroes but lots of citizens with a respect for truth, a sense of balance and a sense of humor.

So good-by, "Little Orphan Annie," living symbol with blunked-out eyes; and hello, "Little Orphan Annie," shade of Gray. And welcome back to the funnies, funnies. Perhaps, in whatever Valhalla is reserved for defunct comic-strip heroes, there is Depression, World War and Cold War forever, and "Daddy" can spend eternity justifying the ways of robber baron capitalism to God. As for me, I'll take the living present and "Doonesbury." Nostalgia for the way we were doesn't mean we want to go back. We been there before.

Cartoonist

With a Conscience

by LOUIE ROBINSON

The changing face of America may be reflected, as much as any place else, in the changing faces of its comic strips. For the funnies, like any other art form, have always mirrored life in these United States. Just as discrimination, for instance, barred black people from most of the country's institutions, so it did from the cartoon strips of the nation's newspapers. Thus generations of black kids grew up tacking unlikely identities to the white faces of their earliest literary interests. And from the hi-jinks of the *Katzenjammer Kids* to the dashing heroics of *Dick Tracy* to the outer space adventures of *Flash Gordon* and *Buck Rogers,* it was a lily-white universe.

To be sure, there were some rare exceptions: *Mandrake the Magician* had an African strongman sidekick, Lothar; a giant East Indian wizard named Punjab frequently turned up as a friend of Daddy Warbucks to help *Little Orphan Annie* out of a jam; and *Terry and the Pirates* and *Steve Canyon* sported Oriental types on occasion.

Today, black characters sometimes turn up in otherwise white comic strips, but breaking the cartoon strip color barrier has been done most forcefully by Morris (Morrie) Turner, a 49-year-old Oakland, Calif., cartoonist with a conscience, whose *Wee Pals* now appears in more than

70 newspapers across the country. The strip, syndicated by King Features, has been so successful that it now appears as a Saturday morning network show, *Kid Power,* on ABC.

While uncounted millions catch the weekly electronic presentation, an estimated 40 million are on hand for the daily newspaper version. Thus while Turner's cartoon characters are not the only blacks now represented in the medium (the Harlem Globetrotters and the Jackson Five, two real life groups, both have their TV cartoon counterparts, and *Friday Foster* and *Hard Core* are both black-dominated comic strips) his creation is certainly the most widely viewed.

Actually, *Wee Pals* is far from an all-black strip, featuring instead a multiracial cast of small fry whose theme is, appropriately enough, "rainbow power." It is a cast that is ever expanding. It was a while before Turner started calling the kids in the strip by name. "The biggest kick was when Letha started calling them by name," Turner says, nodding towards his wife. "Now, other people do too."

The star of *Wee Pals* is Nipper, a small black youth whose face is perpetually half-masked under a confederate hat. "He's the most forgiving guy in the strip," explains Turner, who took the name from comedian Nipsey Russell. Furthermore, says Turner: "Nipper is me. For a long time, I didn't know he was me." Then, there is Oliver, "the resident intellectual; he doesn't know it all, but he thinks he does." Oliver is white, as are the inquisitive Wellington, who wears his hair down to his eyes Beatle-style, Ralph ("He could very well be Archie Bunker's son.") and Jerry, a freckled-face, Jewish kid ("He looks like a childhood friend of mine," says Turner. "I'd never seen a red-headed, freckled-face Jew before.").

Other black boys in the strip are Diz, who wears a dashiki, dark glasses and a beret ("He's the hippest thing around."), and Randy ("He's my son, very athletic," says Turner, who has a grown, married son. "Everybody likes Randy."). Then there are two black girls: Sybil, the peacemaker and problem-solver, whom Turner refers to as "the black mama" of the strip, and Mikki, a recent addition in honor of the Turners' new granddaughter, Michele.

Wee Pals has another female character, Connie, "a real women's lib type; she's for women's rights—she doesn't *understand* women's rights and she overdoes it most times. . . ."

Turner has been careful to try and balance out the ethnic scales in his strip with George ("He was just Oriental at first, but he became very Chinese, he started quoting Confucius, and everything. I didn't intend for that to happen but it did."), Rocky, an American Indian whom Turner found in a book on Sioux Indians ("I was looking for something that said 'Earth.' "), and Paul, a Chicano.

In addition to parading across television screens and through newspaper pages, these comic characters are also collected in nearly a dozen

hardcover and paperback book originals and reprints. Although Turner's earlier work indicated he was aiming his humor primarily at adults, his later material shows more awareness of youth audiences. Thus *Wee Pals* avoids the subtle psychological thrusts of *Peanuts* and goes for the simple jokes and interracial messages more easily understood by children.

. . .

by D. KEITH MANO

Sometimes, perhaps too often, I dream of my high-school class. We gather in a time pocket: formal as our yearbook snapshots, acne retouched by the kindly photographer. Once and again we meet in a football huddle; I can dream-smell the sweat that none of us now has the time to raise. And 15 years' trouble is unanticipated. No November 1963; 1968 gone altogether. A second opportunity for Vietnam, Watergate: events still avoidable. Things change. My son tackles me now. Hard. But, on Sunday, there is a pocket very like the one I dream. Not the Christian liturgy, that has become a fashionable item: People fashion and refashion it. I mean the funnies. Their people, too, gather in a time lapse without future or the chance of doom. Comedy is static. It conserves.

They appear in strict rectangles. There is an aptness to that. Isolated; I remember a hotel in Venice surrounded by water. I perceive a self-sufficiency, a wholeness in islands. Venice isn't too convenient for street rioting. The funnies have a tough, impermeable cell wall. Very little of the Sixties, the Seventies has filtered through. What does filter through is caught by antibodies, made harmless. There are exceptions, but surprisingly few. The newspaper comics mock Relevance.

Dagwood has that inexplicable navel in his shirt. Someone still waffle-irons the rear of Archie's head and he has been left back at Riverdale High for twenty years. Dick Tracy's Moonmaid manages to ignore

Funnies: From *National Review* (June 22, 1973). Reprinted with permission of *National Review,* 150 East 35th Street, New York, New York 10016.

the giant step for mankind: There are, she tells us, ungeological hot springs on the moon. Dondi is a pathetic casualty of the Korean War, stunted at age seven or eight by shell shock. After all these years Little Orphan Annie still can't arrange a pupil transplant. Styles change, but they wear the clothing of morality play figures: simplified, easy to draw. God knows they're more resilient than the Latin Mass or illegal abortions. They continue.

I have noticed changes. Smilin' Jack is no more. Terry and the Pirates was a late victim of the Vietnam war, Dragon Lady outpirated by the VC. For some months in my morning paper a small, black ghetto child, Quincy, appeared. He was pleasantly unradical, a sort of line drawing high yellow, too young to mainline or join the Black Liberation Army. How much poverty can you draw into a three by four rectangle anyhow? Quincy didn't last. Sesame Street replaced him, stupidly teaching the sovereign mysteries of Up and Down, Inside and Outside. And, except for the Sunday edition, Sesame Street is gone now as well. Replaced by Hagar the Horrible, a middle-class barbarian, drawn by Dick Browne, co-author of the middle-class Hi and Lois. Sesame Street was out of place, also boring. Simply: The newspaper comic strips aren't meant for children.

There is no urban humor. Serious strips tend to be set in the city, but a comic comic requires lawns, storm windows, golf, two-car garages—and neighbors. The comic strip cast of characters is a community; it's separate, a dead-end suburban street. And unintegrated. Cameo parts are available only for mailmen and door-to-door sales people. There are no manageable communities in the city; new influences impinge constantly, uncontrollably. The comic strip is semi-pastoral. Blondie, Hi and Lois, Archie, Peanuts, Gasoline Alley. Even, by extension, Hagar the Horrible and Snuffy Smith. It's the American small town, though a city may be implied some few commuter minutes away. Yet newspaper readership is overwhelmingly urban. An escape, of course, but not an expensive one: No more than a short Sunday's drive away. And therefore credible enough.

The family survives here: game preserved. Divorce is unthinkable, unthought of. The comic strip zeitgeist has a moral force to make popes jealous. Margaret Mead should spend time here, squatted on her haunches: Coming of Age with Mr. and Mrs. Dennis the Menace. Humor is the side effect of petty intramural skirmishes, a sex war fought with biface tools. But for Andy Capp—anyhow a crass foreigner—the woman is monotonously more cunning. Victories, though, that would give Gloria Steinem an inflammation of the bile. Blondie gets a new hat; Lois gets the grass cut; Lucy demoralizes Charlie Brown. Some profound earth upheaval has shut the generation gap to a hairline fault: Allowances, broken windows, messy rooms are the small change of father-son antagonism. After all, these people are islanded and must learn to coexist. A rectangle's penstroke border keeps them down on the farm. America's open society is closed to them. Even the stormy Louds, comic-stripped, would have come to love one another.

There is no death; they don't even pass away. Newspapers land on the roof, but you can't make out a headline. Golf games are unimproved. They go twenty years without a cost-of-living raise from Mr. Dithers. They never reach puberty; or, having reached it, they cannot consummate their loves. And the comic strips get penalized for safety: To be honest, they are often not that funny. Our superstar jokes, jokes that rip the diaphragm with laughter, are about sex and death and the ephemerae of politics. How many ways can you cut the lawn? Yet the comic strips endure; they train for distance.

Most of us break even, going all out: mortgage payments, thinning hair, chest pain, a transmission job. No headline surpasses the yellow journalism of an abscessed tooth. Crabgrass transcends Vietnam; hell, it's in my front yard. These are the opiate of the masses: a whining child in your kitchen; a bounced check; leaks through the basement wall. We read the comics because they are relevant, not Relevant. Though we suffer, there is no tragedy. Our hearts are refused burial at Wounded Knee, at Selma, at the ten dozen great confrontation places of our time. We are human, but never somehow human enough for the activists. And that's why there are no funnies in the *New York Times*.

Comeback of the Comic Books

by DAN CARLINSKY

Not so long ago, comic books were almost the exclusive domain of younger kids—mostly boys, at that. But along with many other pieces of American popular culture, comic books have changed.

Now, for the first time in the forty-year history of comic books, there are thousands of readers in high school and college. What's more, female interest is higher than ever.

It's not so much that young people have changed: it's simply that the comic books themselves have undergone a radical transformation. During the late 1950s the comic book business, once a thriving, rich industry, began to sag, as parents protested against the graphic violence of some comics and young readers turned more and more to that relatively new invention, television. Over the next decade sales figures spiraled downward to a fraction of their glorious heights: kids just weren't interested anymore. Then, several years ago, things picked up.

During the past two years, for instance, dozens of new comic titles have appeared, and comic book sales have jumped to 300 million books a year—still only half the number sold in the heyday of comic books, twenty years ago, but a healthy improvement. What caused it?

It isn't that more eight-to-twelve-year-olds are reading *Donald Duck* these days—that scene is about the same. But there's a whole new audience of comic book readers that didn't exist in years past—the high school and college crowd who used to be considered "too old for funny books." That audience exists because there's a new breed of comics being produced today, in addition to the old standbys.

Over the 1960s, a few of the industry's biggest publishers slowly developed a group of more mature, better written, better drawn, better *conceived* comic books, aimed at an older audience—and the readers appeared and grabbed them.

Kids growing up in the 1960s were bombarded with cosmic problems, mistakes, doubts, differences. In most of the comics they read as children, these real-life matters weren't represented. Comic books were a fairy-tale land. Then some writers and editors latched on to the idea of trying to bring their books into the world as it existed.

Stan Lee, the chief at Marvel Comics, which produces the superest of today's comic book superheroes, explains the thought process: "We tried to be realistic. When we were starting with this idea twelve years ago, we thought of our stories as fairy tales for grown-ups. They would all have some one thing unrealistic about them, of course—like a hero who had the strength of a hundred men or could fly—but we thought everything else should be realistic. Heroes should be like normal people who happen to have a superpower or two. Maybe they're super, but they might still be greedy, they might still have halitosis."

So Marvel created stars like the Fantastic Four, who were once evicted from their headquarters because their leader lost so much money in the stock market he couldn't pay the rent, and Spider-Man, a teen-ager who can trap evildoers in his spider-like webs but can't seem to keep from tearing his own costume. Except for his superpowers, Spidey is a typical fellow, with girl-friend problems and one identity crisis after another ("*Some* superhero *I* am!" he tells himself after a particularly bad blunder). He has troubles cashing checks ("Do you have a Social Security card or a driver's license in the name of Spider-Man?" the bank teller asks). In short, except for one fairy-tale premise, he's as real as the boy next door.

It seems now like a simple design—make comic books realistic, authentic. But it was daring then. And it took a while to catch on, with numerous different heroes and stories being tried. But finally the audiences began to grow faithful and large. And, as Marvel intended, they were older.

"For a while everybody was laughing at Marvel," says Stan Lee, "because we were going after the college crowd. But I've always felt comics were a very valid form of entertainment. There's no reason to look down on telling a good story in the comic book medium. It's just dialogue and illustrations, after all, like film, except that it's a little harder than film because our action is frozen. If Ernest Hemingway had written comic books, they would have been just as good as his novels."

Other publishers got into the act too, creating their own new comics and updating old ones. The venerable old Superman, the invulnerable caped hero from the planet Krypton who had been thrilling kids since 1938, was given a face-lift. His earthly alter ego, newspaper reporter Clark Kent, became a more up-to-date TV broadcaster. Superman's problems and language became more with-it and story plots began to hit at all angles of the world; in one tale, Clark's girl friend, Lois Lane, becomes temporarily black; in another, Superman fights pollution instead of the traditional bank robbers.

Batman and Robin began to pacify street-fighters in the Spanish section of Gotham City. Green Arrow was urged to wage war on slumlords. Black characters began springing up all over comicdom and comic books became so contemporary that even illegal drugs began making their way into stories. (As a result, the Comics Magazine Association of America, the publishers' self-policing group, revised its code of acceptability to include a warning that in comic books "narcotics or drug addiction shall not be presented, *except* as a vicious habit.")

Eventually the snowballing "relevance" cooled down a bit. But its mark had been made, and a good portion of the comic book market today feels the influence of this up-to-date approach to comic entertainment.

More skilled writers and artists entered the field of comic book production, and as high quality comics were made, they attracted still more topflight talent. Now, says Leonard Darvin, who, as administrator of the Comics Code Authority, probably reads more comic books per month (about a hundred) than any other adult in the world, comic book writers are better than they've ever been. He insists that when it comes to the artists "there's just no comparison with those of twenty years ago—the art is far superior." (Still, every publisher is crying for new talent. "If any kids come to us able to draw or write like what they see in our books, we want them!" says Marvel's Lee.)

Few are about to insist that the people who create comic books today—even the best of them—are Ernest Hemingways. But comic books are at least taken more seriously. To anyone who hasn't read anything but old issues of *Yogi Bear* and *Betty and Veronica,* it might come as a shock to learn that several full-length books on comic strips have appeared in the past half-dozen years. Sociologists now write studious essays on comics as an authentic expression of American culture; scholarly journals now discuss the theory of "the flawed hero" and rhapsodize over comic writers' use of irony, satire, hyperbole and other English-class literary topics. One author went so far as to make serious comparisons between the newspaper strip *Little Orphan Annie* and classic writers like Charles Dickens and Victor Hugo.

According to a recent count, some twenty colleges and junior and senior high schools in all parts of the country either give a separate course on comics or study them in a course on the mass media. Says Steve Balzarini, an English teacher who leads a nine-week course called The Comic Book at Holmdel High School in New Jersey: "Some people still chuckle at the idea of a course on comics. But comic books are a very powerful mass medium. They reach a large segment of society. Like any other medium they reflect that part of society's thinking and its ideals. Today's comics have art work that's very refined and some of the best writing being done today. We study the writing, characterization, plot and theme. We study comic book characters as folklore. Did you ever stop to think that Superman is probably as well known to Americans as Hercules was to the Greeks? He's as much a part of our culture."

Can anyone deny that comics have come of age?

Today, National Periodical Publications (publisher of *Superman* and others) and Marvel dominate the field of comics for older readers. Other publishers are more traditional, continuing with younger-oriented animated cartoon books, little-boy Westerns and television spin-offs like *The Partridge Family* and *The Flintstones* comic books. There has been some updating of the immensely popular *Archie* series (Archie's pals all say, "Right on!" and "Groovy!" a lot). But the stories remain more fifties than seventies, and the readers are heavily in the nine-to-twelve bracket.

Then there are the so-called underground comic books. The "undergrounds," once low-circulation books privately distributed, have now grown into a huge industry, separate from regular comics. There are possibly as many "underground" titles as regular ones published today—about three hundred. "Undergrounds" are characterized by an irreverent reaction to middle-class values that results in frequent blunt references to drugs and sex, and heavy-handed satire and moralizing. They generally sell in college stores for fifty cents, with a meaningless but tantalizing "For Adults Only" printed on the cover. The most successful of them, like Robert Crumb's *Zap Comics*, outsell the biggest of the overground comics.

Where do girls fit into all this?

Since the beginning, before World War II, more boys than girls have read comics. Presumably that was because girls were less interested in the superhero, adventure type of story that fit so well into the medium. Girls have always done their fair share of reading *funny* comic books—the animated cartoon stories, the lighter things—but more and more of the publishers' output has grown to be action-oriented. Yet today there are some superheroes the editors direct, at least partly, to female readers.

The best known, perhaps, is Wonder Woman, the 1940s heroine who recently made a reappearance. "As lovely as Aphrodite—as wise as Athena—with the speed of Mercury and the strength of Hercules," Wonder Woman is princess of the Amazons on Paradise Island. In her modern form, she is a strong, independent woman, vitally concerned with her sisters' well-being. Gloria Steinem loves her.

Women's lib, incidentally, has made inroads into comic books for younger readers. Witness this conversation:

> *Archie:* No kidding, now! Level with us! Do you girls believe in Santa Claus?
> *Betty:* Well sure! *I* do! Don't *you,* Ronnie?
> *Veronica:* Of course! Doesn't *everyone* believe in *her?*

Then there have been *Shanna the She-Devil, The Cat!* and others. Lois Lane, who would still love to marry Superman, also has her own comic book. But while all of these have heavy female readership, none is a best seller.

Publishers also report that romance comic books, definitely the domain of female readers, continue to sell well. Although even adult women buy such titles as *Young Romance, Just Married* and *Love Diary,* wishful preteens are still the number-one romance buyers.

The most usual way that young women barge into the comic book picture, publishers agree, is through their boy friends. Girls of high school and college age, says Carmine Infantino, head of National Periodical Publications, make up a large chunk of the attendance at comic conventions. There the faithful fans discuss, buy and see comic books and listen to talks by top artists and writers. Infantino guesses most of the girls are there not because they're really into the new comic books, which are still heavily male-oriented, but for more practical reasons. He says that like the woman who learns a little about football so she can converse with her husband during the Sunday-afternoon game, "they do it to zero in on their boy friend's head."

Liberated? Perhaps not. But practical.

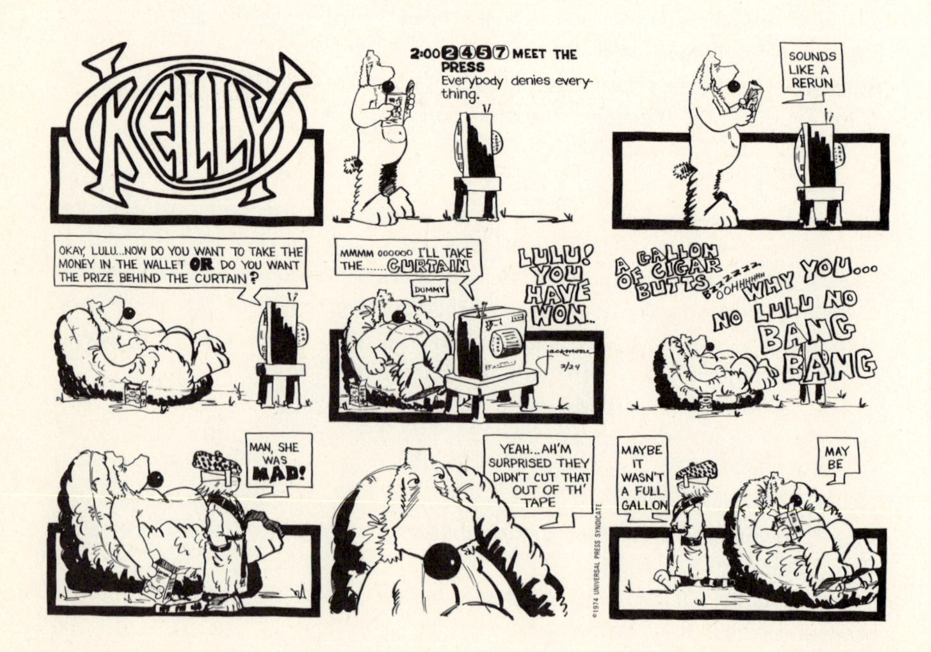

MAGAZINE

WITNESS FOR THE PEOPLE

by RICHARD REEVES

My son is a wiseass. He answers the telephone with cracks like "Do you know where your children are tonight?" He answers most questions with questions—"How was school today?". . . "School?"—half the time you laugh, half the time you want to kick his teeth in.

He thinks Richard Nixon is a crook and a clown—and he does a fair Nixon imitation, for an eleven-year-old. He thinks George McGovern is just a clown and Teddy Kennedy should become a swimming coach. He suspects "Exxon" is the Greek word for rip-off. His favorite work of art is a photograph of the White House with a huge "Nixxon" sign in front and the caption, "But it's still the same old gas!" That was in *Mad* magazine's April issue.

He doesn't just read *Mad*—he memorizes, quotes, collects, and fondles it. So, he tells me, do all but one of the boys in Miss Piper's sixth-grade class at Main Street School in Denville, New Jersey. As far as I can tell, *Mad* is all he reads except for the TV schedule.

And, as far as I can tell from an informal but intensive survey of friends, so does every kid in the country. Certainly more kids than ever are, even though *Mad* has been an adolescent phenomenon since I was fighting acne and surging hormones twenty years ago. Not only has it gotten bigger, much bigger, but its circulation has suddenly begun surging up again in the past year.

Mad may be the most influential magazine in the United States—if you assume teenagers and other children are worth influencing. Assume it or not, Jeffrey Richard Reeves gets his information from television and his viewpoint from *Mad,* and he and his friends will start voting and doing other things in 1980.

The people at *Mad*—they call themselves "*Mad*men"—are not in the influence business. They are out of the comic book business, out of Brooklyn and the Bronx and Music and Art High School, mostly Jewish with New York strains of street-tough Irish and Italian; the same people who gave you Sid Caesar's lines and, hero of heroes, Neil Simon. *Mad* may be New York's most successful export.

"We don't really know who our audience is," said William M. Gaines, the publisher who describes himself, accurately, as "a maniac." "We kind of publish for ourselves. We publish things because we like them."

Knowing something about the magazine business, I cleverly asked about market research. "Oh!" said Gaines, a huge rumpled man who looks like a fat Karl Marx and plans to vote for John Marchi for mayor, reaching into a desk drawer for a maroon leatherette folder. The pages were literally yellowed: it was the statistical breakdown of answers to four questions tacked onto a Hires Root Beer survey done in 1957 by Eugene Gilbert Youth Research. The sum total of the information was that twice as many boys as girls were then regular *Mad* readers, and thirteen- and fourteen-year-olds read it more often than fifteen- and sixteen-year-olds.

This time *I* said, "Oh!" But Gaines had more: a six-inch-wide sheet of dirty graph paper recording the sales figures for each issue since *Mad* was first published in 1952. Following the bouncing ballpoint dots, I figured out that the latest issue of *Mad* sold more than 2.4 million copies, a jump of more than 300,000 over the year before. From 1968 through 1972 circulation averaged under 2 million. (The circulation of *National Lampoon,* a satirical monthly, is also growing—from 486,000 last year to about 750,000 recently. *Mad*men call it the *Mad* of "the iconoclast crowd.")

Who are the new readers? "I think we're reaching a younger group," said Gaines. "I think we're holding onto young readers longer and getting back some old *Mad* readers, adults," said Al Feldstein, the editor, a Flatbush boy who got into comic books at Music and Art when he found out you could get $18 a page for drawing strips.

Gaines and Feldstein are 20 per cent of the *Mad* staff, ten people working in an eight-room suite at 485 Madison Avenue. That's publisher, editor, art director, production manager, two associate editors, three women handling subscriptions, and a stockboy. Gaines doesn't like to talk exact money figures, but suffice it to say that *Mad* makes a couple of hundred thousand dollars in profit per employee per year.

There are also "the usual gang of idiots," as the masthead calls them, the twenty or so free-lance writers and artists who are each paid $300 a page for their words and drawings in the eight regular issues *Mad* publishes each year. The artwork in the magazine is superb and *Mad* artists—

especially Jack Davis and Mort Drucker whose *Time* and *Newsweek* covers often compete—are not doing it for the cash. Part of the attraction is the yearly trips—comic caravans to Europe, Africa, and Japan—that Gaines takes with his staff and regular contributors because he thinks it's good for morale and because he likes traveling and loves the best food and wine with his best friends.

Gaines's friends produce 48 pulpy pages every 45 days under the steady control of Feldstein—the publisher says he's not "the creative type," but he's the dominating type and Feldstein says he edits to make Gaines laugh —and inside a slick cover almost always graced by the grinning face of Alfred E. Neuman. The *Mad* symbol, ("What, me Worry?") Neuman, is a lop-headed, jug-eared, gap-toothed idiot boy—on the current issue he's sitting on the beach, building an elaborate sand castle when a large wave hits; when the wave goes down, the castle is still there and Neuman has been reduced to a pile of wet sand.

Besides the 2.4 million copies sold here for 40 cents each, the staff and usual gang of idiots produce seven foreign language editions, three 75-cent "Super Specials" a year with a mix of old features, and collect royalties on eight "Best of Mad" paperbacks. That's it, conglomerate fans, no advertising and no spin-offs—no posters, sweat shirts, records, key chains or Madboy clubs.

One conglomerate which might wish it were different is Warner Communications, which owns *Mad* after a series of corporate mergers that began in 1960 when Gaines's accountant told him no individual could pay income taxes on the kind of money *Mad* was making even then. "Warner leaves us alone because we're very successful and I'm very cantankerous," said Gaines, a 51-year-old multimillionaire. "We could make millions merchandising, but we don't want to rip off our kids and their parents. Warner's would love it, but I always chase away the smart boys by telling them to fire me. There are obvious advantages to being a maniac when you deal with corporate types."

The insides of the magazine are predictable and unpredictable. There is a potpourri of linear slapstick, sight gags on the pie-in-the-face level, and features like "The Lighter Side of Crime in the Streets," and parody and satire that my son sometimes needs help to memorize. ("Venus Envy," a women's lib satire, was a little beyond him.) If the magazine is changing, Feldstein says, it is a trend away from "Ha! Ha!" and toward a more knowing "Oh, boy!"

The most regular features (and I think the best) are television, movie, and magazine satires: "Gall in the Family Fare" . . . "The Heartburn Kid". . . "Passionate Gun Love—the magazine for the devoted gun worshipper."

In "Gall in the Family Fare," by a moonlighting television writer named Larry Siegel, Starchie Bunker, "America's Beloved Bigot," gets a visit from his "old World War II buddy," who turns out to be Adolf Hitler.

Next come two official types who want to see "Dolf"—they look like F.B.I. but it turns out they're CBS offering Hitler his own series with his own "adorable TV family . . . like a dumb wife, two moronic children and a pet wolf!"

In "The Heartburn Kid," the honeymooning not-so-nice Jewish boy from the Bronx meets his dream WASP girl on the beach and . . .

"Look, Kooly, I realize I have a wife! But I'll leave her for you! I'll get a divorce!"

"Benny, you don't understand! I come from a God-fearing, religious home! We believe in certain rock-bound principles . . . among which is the sanctity of Marriage and the Family Unit! Divorce is wrong . . . and cruel . . . and unthinkable! It's just NOT the American Way!"

"Then how do you feel about fooling around with a married man?"

"Now, THAT'S the American Way!"

In "Gun Love," featuring articles like "Tracking the Wily English Sparrow Through Brush and Blind," there is an editorial, "Opening Shots!", attacking gun registration legislation:

"You take away guns and people will find other things to kill with . . . like sticks and rocks, and ax-handles, and axes! . . . Every citizen has the right to bear arms. It was written into the Constitution by our forefathers in the 1700's. Take away the people's guns, you Washington Finks, and who's going to stop the Redcoats! . . . Why DO those Washington Pinkos want us to register our guns? . . . They want to hand us pens, and forms to fill out. And then they want to *embarrass* us! Because they know that many gun-owners can't write!"

And it goes on and on: in a "Near Future" strip, a fisherman chops a hole in the garbage to drop his line in the Hudson River; there are potshots at Joe Namath, Kung Fu, Bell Telephone, millionaires, waiters, parents, children . . . and everything. In "Boredom-12" one of the cops tries to save a suicide on a window ledge with this dialogue:

"Why would a nice guy like you want to kill yourself?"

"What's there to live for? Work is hard! Pay is low! Taxes are high! Politicians are crooked! Morality is crumbling! God is dead! And the world is about to explode in an Atomic War!"

"Is there room on the ledge for me? Move over and we'll jump together!"

Some of the best shots, of course, are at Richard M. Nixon—each week, two of the magazine's 100,000 subscribers cancel in rage at attacks on the White House—and some of them have been eerily prescient. In December, 1971, pre-Watergate, *Mad*'s back cover was a likeness of Nixon in the classic three monkeys pose with the inscription, "See No Evil . . . Hear No Evil . . . Well, Two Out of Three Ain't Bad!"

What does it all mean to me, to Jeff and his thirteen-year-old sister, Cindie, an occasional *Mad* reader, to you, to your kids? "It means . . . it isn't boring, that's what it means . . . like, you know, like the stuff you write," said my son the wiseass in the only usable quotes in a two-hour interview. It means good—to some extent, the kid can spot the sham piling up all around him. *Mad* is true; at least it tells a lot of truth that he doesn't hear from Nixon, Exxon, CBS, Miss Piper . . . and from me.

"The one thing we do know around here is that we have a tremendous responsibility to those kids, there might be 10 million of them if five see each magazine," said Gaines, with Feldstein nodding in agreement. "We hope we're not telling them anything except to think for themselves and not believe everything they read and hear on television or from politicians."

Have you ever thought that you might be turning them into hopeless little cynics?

"Maybe. I hope not. But we all need some cynicism. It's easier to get it from us than being smacked in the head 30 times before you know what the world is like. . . . We're fair, we knock everybody, regardless of race, color, or creed."

One parent I talked with, a 46-year-old editor with a twelve-year-old daughter, thought that discovering *Mad* might have been one of the best things that could have happened to her. "I think it made her secure in being skeptical," he said. "The questions about basic premises were already there. She was already aware that someone out there was always trying to manipulate her. One reaction to that would be to withdraw and she would have been inclined to do that, but *Mad* makes it easier to counter . . . it really strengthens a young ego. On one level, she couldn't handle people, other kids, who were nasty, but *Mad* provides a range of comebacks. Kids quote them, they use them. In fact, *Mad* is a comeback at the whole world. . . . It's really a shortcut to a kind of sanity-preserving sophistication. . . . It does for them what the Marx Brothers, even the Three Stooges, did for my generation. It points up the difference between reality and appearance; it's that simple."

*Mad*men get a little antsy over that kind of philosophical or psychoanalytical crap. "Gee, the Marx Brothers," said Feldstein, "I mean that's going pretty far out. . . . No one, I mean no one here would compare us to . . . (his voice dropped) . . . the Marx Brothers are special, greatness . . . I don't know."

They're real people—Gaines dressed like a newsstand guy, Feldstein more Seventh Avenue with shiny clothes and a gold ID bracelet with a diamond chip, Jerry De Fuccio from my old neighborhood in Jersey City—they're still in touch, like the old editors I used to know at *The Daily News* who really watched television, really read and were interested in the stuff they put in the paper in those days. The *Mad*men are on Madison Avenue—they moved up from Lafayette Street a few years ago when Gaines became convinced there was a Phantom Thief in the old building—but they're not with it, and they weren't fooled for a minute by Woodstock, Rap Brown or Richard Nixon. When you look back, their viewpoint of the passing parade has often been clearer than *Time*'s or *Newsweek*'s.

When you look closely, *Mad* also turns out to be a magazine of old-fashioned morality. A couple of years ago, Vernard Eller, a professor of religion at LaVerne College in California, did a little treatise arguing that *Mad* was doing more to propagate the Ten Commandments than the churches of California.

"*Mad* magazine shows at least something of the same understanding of freedom that the Ten Commandments do," Dr. Eller wrote. "Their magazine is dedicated to helping kids become free and stay free . . . the negativity of (the Commandments') wording is indeed the invitation for man freely to find whatever style of life suits him—as long as he avoids these few pitfalls that would destroy his freedom altogether. . . . The difference is that the Ten Commandments, upon seeing these, warn against them, while *Mad* makes fun of them."

A little too pompous for *Mad,* and it leaves out the magazine's eleventh commandment—"Thou Shalt Not Commit Hypocrisy"—but the good doctor's going in the right direction, even if Gaines and Feldstein felt compelled to write a brief introduction to his book that said:

"Criticism we can take; praise from his kind could kill us . . . We reject the insinuation that anything we print is moral, theological, nutritious or good for you in any way, shape, or form. We live in the midst of a corrupt society and intend to keep on making the best of it."

THE PERSUADERS

STUDY QUESTIONS

1. What implications do Joseph Klapper's theories about the ability of the media to influence opinions have for educational television? for advertisers? for the possibility of media helping to bring about social changes?

2. Basing your opinions solely on television commercials, list the subjects that seem to be of greatest concern to Americans today. Would you reach the same conclusions from a study of printed advertisements? Do you feel it is valid to draw such conclusions merely from advertising content?

3. By what specific means could advertisers help the public to cope with the kinds of change that Toffler cites? Is the responsibility of advertisers to do so increased by the environmental crisis and the energy shortage, for example? If so, why?

4. Richard Heffner, along with several other critics represented in this book, warns of the subtle persuasion of value patterns reflected on television. Study prime-time network television shows for a set period of time—a week, if possible. Identify the attitudes and values underlying each program. Make the same kind of study of commercials.

5. What do you see as possible social consequences of the government's use of the kind of doublespeak Newman illustrates? of educator's?

6. What is television's potential for formal education using technological developments like cable and videocassette? What attempts have been made so far to provide educational programming?

7. How accurately do you think current comics reflect the society and the times? What do you think is the primary role of today's comics?

8. From reading the reviews of **Network,** what sort of information do you need to know about the publication to be able to interpret the review? Do you sense that the reviewers are attempting to persuade a particular segment of the film-going audience?

BIBLIOGRAPHY FOR FURTHER STUDY

Advertising Age. (Chicago: Crain Communications Inc.) Weekly newspaper reporting trends and developments in advertising and marketing.

Baker, Samm Sinclair. *The Permissible Lie.* Boston: Beacon Press, 1971.

Baker, Stephen. *Visual Persuasion.* New York: McGraw-Hill, 1961.

Braun, Saul. "Shazam! Here Comes Captain Relevant." *The New York Times Magazine* (May 2, 1971), 32ff.

Buxton, Edward. *Creative People at Work.* New York: Executive Communications, 1975.

Carnegie Commission on Educational Television. *Public Television, A Program for Action.* New York: Harper & Row, 1967.

Crist, Judith. "The Day TV Went Mad." *Saturday Review* (November 13, 1976), 44, 46.

Denisoff, Serge. *Sing a Song of Social Significance.* Bowling Green, Ohio: Bowling Green University Popular Press, 1972.

"Doonesbury: Drawing and Quartering for Fun and Profit." *Time* (February 9, 1976), 57ff.

Ewen, Stuart. *Captains of Consciousness: Advertising and the Social Roots of Consumer Culture.* New York: McGraw-Hill, 1976.

"Female Image in Children's TV Commercials." *Journal of Broadcasting* 19 (Summer, 1975), 301–09.

"A Fourth 'Network' the Others Might Not Want to See." *Broadcasting* (November 22, 1976), 30.

Freberg, Stan. "The Freberg Part-time Television Plan." *Mass Media in a*

Free Society, Warren K. Agee, ed. Lawrence: The University Press of Kansas, 1969, 63–79.

"Heavy Comics." *Saturday Review of Education* (May, 1973), 83.

Horowitz, Susan. "Paddy Chayefsky Speaks Out." *Saturday Review* (November 13, 1976), 45.

Hulteng, John L. *The Opinion Function.* New York: Harper & Row, 1973.

Key, Wilson Bryan. *Subliminal Seduction.* New York: New American Library, 1974.

Kimball, Penn. "Who Needs Gavel-to-Gavel Convention Coverage?" *Columbia Journalism Review* 15 (September/October, 1976), 28–30.

Kraus, Sidney, and Dennis Davis. *The Effects of Mass Communication on Political Behavior.* University Park: Pennsylvania State University Press, 1976.

Lacassin, Francis. "The Comic Strip and Film Language." *Film Quarterly* 26 (Fall, 1972), 11–23.

Loevinger, Lee. "The Politics of Advertising." Speech to International Radio and Television Society (January 4, 1973). Available from Television Information Office, 745 Fifth Avenue, New York, N.Y. 10022.

"Mass Media in Election Campaigns." *Public Administration Survey* (January, 1973), 1–6.

Mendelsohn, Harold, and Irving Crespi. *Polls, Television, and the New Politics.* Scranton, Pa.: Chandler Publishing Co., 1970.

"New Look on the Funny Pages." *Newsweek* (March 5, 1973), 76–77.

Nickels, William G. *Marketing Communications and Promotion.* Columbus, Ohio: Grid Publishing, 1976.

Park, Leland M. "Radio, TV and the Evangelist: The Mass Media at Work." *Christian Century* (August 15–20, 1973), 804–07.

Robinson, Jerry. *Comics: An Illustrated History of Comic Strip Art.* New York: Putnam, 1974.

Rubin, Bernard. *Media, Politics, and Democracy.* New York: Oxford University Press, 1977.

Sandage, Charles H., and Vernon Fryburger. *Advertising Theory and Practice.* Homewood, Ill.: Irwin, 1967.

Sinclair, John, and Robert Levin. *Music and Politics.* New York: World Publishing Co., 1971.

Stanton, William J. *Fundamentals of Marketing.* 4th ed. New York: McGraw-Hill, 1975.

Stevens, J. D. "Reflections in a Dark Mirror: Comic Strips in Black Newspapers." *Journal of Popular Culture,* X (Summer, 1976), 239–44.

Toffler, Alvin. *Future Shock.* New York: Bantam, 1971.

Tyler, I. Keith. "Opportunity and Responsibility in Educational Broadcasting." *Educational Broadcasting Review* (April, 1973), 86–92.

White, Theodore H. *Making of the President—1972.* New York: Atheneum, 1973, 375–78, 386–87.

Wright, John S., Daniel S. Warner, and Willis L. Winter. *Advertising.* New York: McGraw-Hill, 1971.

Part Four
Mass Communications: Theories and Practices

One of the basic human characteristics is the need to share attitudes, ideas, and information—to communicate. In today's mass society, interpersonal communication alone cannot disseminate all the information required by the citizens of a democracy. It is the mass media that convey such messages, and as a result they have become important forces in shaping our society.

Numerous attempts have been made to analyze and describe the process, meaning, and significant effects of communication in general and mass communication in particular. Authoritarian and libertarian theories of communication, along with their contemporary counterparts, soviet communist and social responsibility theories, represent attempts to define the role of mass communications in its political context.

To understand how a communication system operates, we must examine its environment. As Wilbur Schramm wrote:

> A social system like communication always reflects the social and political structures within which it operates. In trying to understand why mass communication develops as it does in different societies, then, we begin by looking at the societies. And we start with a look at certain basic assumptions which any society holds—assumptions concerning the nature of man, the nature of society and the state, the relation of man to the state, the nature of knowledge and truth and moral conduct.*

Because it was to an authoritarian society—Europe in the 1450's—that Johann Gutenberg presented his first book, it may have been inevitable that mass communication came to be regarded as primarily a servant of government. This has been the most influential and widespread concept of mass communication and it endures today in the Soviet Union and in other authoritarian societies.

Two centuries after Gutenberg, the English poet John Milton joined in the struggle for intellectual, religious, and political freedoms. In his pamphlet **Areopagitica** (1644), Milton argued eloquently for freedom of the press:

> And though all the winds of doctrine were let loose to play upon the earth, so Truth be in the field, we do injuriously by licensing and prohibiting to misdoubt her strength. Let her and Falsehood grapple; who ever knew Truth put to the worse, in a free and open encounter.†

In the next century Milton's argument was further developed in America by Thomas Paine and Thomas Jefferson. In fact, it is because of such strongly libertarian influences on our nation's founders that the American press enjoys Constitutional protection.

* Wilbur Schramm, **Responsibility in Mass Communication** (New York: Harper & Row, 1957), p. 62.

† John Milton, "Areopagitica," in Merritt Y. Hughes, ed., **John Milton: Complete Poems and Major Prose** (New York: Odyssey Press, 1957), p. 746.

With the print media becoming big business and with the development of electronic media, the theory of a free marketplace of ideas has become less and less workable. The diminished accessibility of the media to minority opinions and the lessened chances of truth and error meeting in an open encounter brought about a modification of the libertarian theory: the social-responsibility theory, which holds that the press has a responsibility to maintain a balance between the government and the public.

J. Edward Gerald has described the media as

> social institutions that serve the society by gathering, writing, and distributing the news of the day. They take their character principally from our political and economic institutions, offering information and entertainment in the market place to uncoerced buyers. Uncoerced means that the diverse mass public is able voluntarily to choose anew each day the media it will purchase and to which it will devote its time.*

While granting that the public is free to choose among media offerings, Gerald deplores the lack of social responsibility shown by the mass media in their attempts to attract the public: "When journalism abandoned politics for business as a way of making a living it switched its personality from that of crusader trying to organize, teach, and change the people and the community to that of entrepreneur trying to make a good living with a minimum of trouble."† In short, the social-responsibility theory holds that it is the responsibility of the media to provide balance in an unbalanced marketplace of ideas.

We need to know more, though, than the nature of the government–press–public relationship in order to understand the impact that the mass media have on individuals in a society. Many theories have been put forth, emphasizing technical, economic, or semantic views of the media. Certain technical considerations like encoding (which concerns the communicator), transmitting (the channel or medium), and decoding (the audience) have received much consideration in studies of the communication process, as have the semantic aspects, which concern the ways in which meaning is conveyed. A better understanding of the interrelationship of all these aspects of communication will lead to a more acute awareness of the media's effects on us—individually and collectively.

The following selections attempt to clarify these interrelationships from different perspectives. No brief treatment can adequately cover the theoretical and practical, but these essays will serve as an introduction to communications theory and as stimuli for further study of this important area.

* J. Edward Gerald, **The Social Responsibility of the Press** (Minneapolis: University of Minnesota Press, 1963), p. 3.
† **Ibid.**, p. 100.

THE NEW LANGUAGES

by EDMUND CARPENTER

In this selection anthropologist Edmund Carpenter treats media as "languages" for expressing ideas and emotions. He compares the lineality, causality, and chronology of the old media with the simultaneity of the new, concluding that each has valuable uses.

Brain of the New World,
What a task is thine,
To formulate the modern
. . . to recast poems, churches, art

WHITMAN

English is a mass medium. All languages are mass media. The new mass media—film, radio, TV—are new languages, their grammars as yet unknown. Each codifies reality differently; each conceals a unique metaphysics. Linguists tell us it's possible to say anything in any language if you use enough words or images, but there's rarely time; the natural course is for a culture to exploit its media biases.

Writing, for example, didn't record oral language; it was a new language, which the spoken word came to imitate. Writing encouraged an analytical mode of thinking with emphasis upon lineality. Oral languages tended to be polysynthetic, composed of great, tight conglomerates, like twisted knots, within which images were juxtaposed, inseparably fused; written communications consisted of little words chronologically ordered. Subject became distinct from verb, adjective from noun, thus separating actor from action, essence from form. Where preliterate man imposed form diffidently, temporarily—for such transitory forms lived but temporarily on the tip of his tongue, in the living situation—the printed word was inflexible, permanent, in touch with eternity: it embalmed truth for posterity.

This embalming process froze language, eliminated the art of ambiguity, made puns "the lowest form of wit," destroyed word linkages. The word became a static symbol, applicable to and separate from that which it symbolized. It now belonged to the objective world; it could be seen. Now came the distinction between being and meaning, the dispute as to whether the Eucharist *was* or only *signified* the body of the Sacrifice. The word became a neutral symbol, no longer an inextricable part of a creative process.

Gutenberg completed the process. The manuscript page with pictures, colors, correlation between symbol and space, gave way to uniform type, the black-and-white page, read silently, alone. The format of the book favored lineal expression, for the argument ran like a thread from cover to cover: subject to verb to object, sentence to sentence, paragraph to paragraph, chapter to chapter, carefully structured from beginning to end, with value embedded in the climax. This was not true of great poetry and drama, which retained multi-perspective, but it was true of most books, particularly texts, histories, autobiographies, novels. Events were arranged chronologically and hence, it was assumed, causally; relationship, not being, was valued. The author became an *authority;* his data were serious, that is, *serially* organized. Such data, if sequentially ordered and printed, conveyed value and truth; arranged any other way, they were suspect.

The newspaper format brought an end to book culture. It offers short, discrete articles that give important facts first and then taper off to incidental details, which may be, and often are, eliminated by the make-up man. The fact that reporters cannot control the length of their articles means that, in writing them, emphasis can't be placed on structure, at least in the traditional linear sense, with climax or conclusion at the end. Everything has to be captured in the headline; from there it goes down the pyramid to incidentals. In fact there is often more in the headline than in the article; occasionally, no article at all accompanies the banner headline.

The position and size of articles on the front page are determined by interest and importance, not content. Unrelated reports from Moscow, Sarawak, London, and Ittipik are juxtaposed; time and space, as separate concepts, are destroyed and the *here* and *now* presented as a single Gestalt. Subway readers consume everything on the front page, then turn to page 2 to read, in incidental order, continuations. A Toronto banner headline ran: TOWNSEND TO MARRY PRINCESS; directly beneath this was a second headline: *Fabian Says This May Not Be Sex Crime*. This went unnoticed by eyes and minds conditioned to consider each newspaper item in isolation.

Such a format lends itself to simultaneity, not chronology or lineality. Items abstracted from a total situation aren't arranged in causal sequence, but presented holistically, as raw experience. The front page is a cosmic *Finnegans Wake*.

The disorder of the newspaper throws the reader into a producer role. The reader has to process the news himself; he has to co-create, to cooperate in the creation of the work. The newspaper format calls for the direct participation of the consumer.

In magazines, where a writer more frequently controls the length of his article, he can, if he wishes, organize it in traditional style, but the majority don't. An increasingly popular presentation is the printed symposium, which is little more than collected opinions, pro and con. The magazine format as a whole opposes lineality; its pictures lack tenses. In *Life,* extremes are juxtaposed: space ships and prehistoric monsters, Flemish monasteries and dope addicts. It creates a sense of urgency and uncertainty: the next page is unpredictable. One encounters rapidly a riot in Teheran, a Hollywood marriage, the wonders of the Eisenhower administration, a two-headed calf, a party on Jones beach, all sandwiched between ads. The eye takes in the page as a whole (readers may pretend this isn't so, but the success of advertising suggests it is), and the page—indeed, the whole magazine—becomes a single Gestalt where association, though not causal, is often lifelike.

The same is true of the other new languages. Both radio and TV offer short, unrelated programs, interrupted between and within by commercials. I say "interrupted," being myself an anachronism of book culture, but my children don't regard them as interruptions, as breaking continuity. Rather, they regard them as part of a whole, and their reaction is neither one of annoyance nor one of indifference. The ideal news broadcast has half a dozen speakers from as many parts of the world on as many subjects. The London correspondent doesn't comment on what the Washington correspondent has just said; he hasn't even heard him.

The child is right in not regarding commercials as interruptions. For the only time anyone smiles on TV is in commercials. The rest of life, in news broadcasts and soap operas, is presented as so horrible that the only way to get through life is to buy this product: then you'll smile. Aesop never wrote a clearer fable. It's heaven and hell brought up to date: Hell in the headline, Heaven in the ad. Without the other, neither has meaning.

There's pattern in these new media—not line, but knot; not lineality or causality or chronology, nothing that leads to a desired climax; but a Gordian knot without antecedents or results, containing within itself carefully selected elements, juxtaposed, inseparably fused; a knot that can't be untied to give the long, thin cord of lineality.

This is especially true of ads that never present an ordered, sequential, rational argument but simply present the product associated with desirable things or attitudes. Thus Coca-Cola is shown held by a beautiful blonde, who sits in a Cadillac, surrounded by bronze, muscular admirers, with the sun shining overhead. By repetition these elements become associated, in our minds, into a pattern of sufficient cohesion so that one element can magically evoke the others. If we think of ads as designed solely to sell products, we miss their main effect: to increase pleasure in the consumption of the product. Coca-Cola is far more than a cooling drink; the consumer participates, vicariously, in a much larger experience. In Africa, in Melanesia, to drink a Coke is to participate in the American way of life.

Of the new languages, TV comes closest to drama and ritual. It combines music and art, language and gesture, rhetoric and color. It favors simultaneity of visual and auditory images. Cameras focus not on speakers but on persons spoken to or about; the audience *hears* the accuser but *watches* the accused. In a single impression it hears the prosecutor, watches the trembling hands of the big-town crook, and sees the look of moral indignation on Senator Tobey's face. This is real drama, in process, with the outcome uncertain. Print can't do this; it has a different bias.

Books and movies only pretend uncertainty, but live TV retains this vital aspect of life. Seen on TV, the fire in the 1952 Democratic Convention threatened briefly to become a conflagration; seen on newsreel, it was history, without potentiality.

The absence of uncertainty is no handicap to other media, if they are properly used, for their biases are different. Thus it's clear from the beginning that Hamlet is a doomed man, but, far from detracting in interest, this heightens the sense of tragedy.

Now, one of the results of the time-space duality that developed in Western culture, principally from the Renaissance on, was a separation within the arts. Music, which created symbols in time, and graphic art, which created symbols in space, became separate pursuits, and men gifted in one rarely pursued the other. Dance and ritual, which inherently combined them, fell in popularity. Only in drama did they remain united.

It is significant that of the four new media, the three most recent are dramatic media, particularly TV, which combines language, music, art, dance. They don't, however, exercise the same freedom with time that the stage dares practice. An intricate plot, employing flash backs, multiple time perspectives and overlays, intelligible on the stage, would mystify on the screen. The audience has no time to think back, to establish relations between early hints and subsequent discoveries. The picture passes before the eyes too quickly; there are no intervals in which to take stock of what has happened and make conjectures of what is going to happen. The observer is in a more passive state, less interested in subtleties. Both TV and film are nearer to narrative and depend much more upon the episodic. An intricate time construction can be done in film, but in fact rarely is. The soliloquies of *Richard III* belong on the stage; the film audience was unprepared for them. On stage Ophelia's death was described by three separate groups: one hears the announcement and watches the reactions simultaneously. On film the camera flatly shows her drowned where "a willow lies aslant a brook."

Media differences such as these mean that it's not simply a question of communicating a single idea in different ways but that a given idea or insight belongs primarily, though not exclusively, to one medium, and can be gained or communicated best through that medium.

Thus the book was ideally suited for discussing evolution and progress. Both belonged, almost exclusively, to book culture. Like a book, the idea of progress was an abstracting, organizing principle for the interpretation and comprehension of the incredibly complicated record of human experience. The sequence of events was believed to have a direction, to follow a given course along an axis of time; it was held that civilization, like the reader's eye (in J. B. Bury's words), "has moved, is moving, and will move in a desirable direction. Knowledge will advance, and with that advance, reason and decency must increasingly prevail among men." Here we see the three main elements of book lineality: the line, the point moving along that line, and its movement toward a desirable goal.

The Western conception of a definite moment in the present, of the present as a definite moment or a definite point, so important in book-dominated languages, is absent, to my knowledge, in oral languages. Absent as well, in oral societies, are such animating and controlling ideas as Western individualism and three-dimensional perspective, both related to this conception of the definite moment, and both nourished, probably bred, by book culture.

Each medium selects its ideas. TV is a tiny box into which people are crowded and must live; film gives us the wide world. With its huge screen, film is perfectly suited for social drama, Civil War panoramas, the sea, land erosion, Cecil B. DeMille spectaculars. In contrast, the TV screen has room for two, at the most three, faces, comfortably. TV is closer to stage, yet different. Paddy Chayefsky writes:

> The theatre audience is far away from the actual action of the drama. They cannot see the silent reactions of the players. They must be told in a loud voice what is going on. The plot movement from one scene to another must be marked, rather than gently shaded as is required in television. In television, however, you can dig into the most humble, ordinary relationships; the relationship of bourgeois children to their mother, of middle-class husband to his wife, of white-collar father to his secretary—in short, the relationships of the people. We relate to each other in an incredibly complicated manner. There is far more exciting drama in the reasons why a man gets married than in why he murders someone. The man who is unhappy in his job, the wife who thinks of a lover, the girl who wants to get into television, your father, your mother, sister, brothers, cousins, friends—all these are better subjects for drama than Iago. What makes a man ambitious? Why does a girl always try to steal her kid sister's boy friends? Why does your uncle attend his annual class reunion faithfully every year? Why do you always find it depressing to visit your father? These are the substances of good television drama; and the deeper you probe into and examine the twisted, semi-formed complexes of emotional entanglements, the more exciting your writing becomes.[1]

[1] *Television Plays,* New York, Simon and Schuster, 1955, pp. 176–78.

This is the primary reason, I believe, why Greek drama is more readily adapted to TV than to film. The boxed-in quality of live TV lends itself to static literary tragedy with greater ease than does the elastic, energetic, expandable movie. Guthrie's recent movie of *Oedipus* favored the panoramic shot rather than the selective eye. It consisted of a succession of tableaux, a series of elaborate, unnatural poses. The effect was of congested groups of people moving in tight formation as though they had trained for it by living for days together in a self-service elevator. With the lines, "I grieve for the City, and for myself and you . . . and walk through endless ways of thought," the inexorable tragedy moved to its horrible "come to realize" climax as though everyone were stepping on everyone else's feet.

The tight, necessary conventions of live TV were more sympathetic to Sophocles in the Aluminium Hour's *Antigone*. Restrictions of space are imposed on TV as on the Greek stage by the size and inflexibility of the studio. Squeezed by physical limitations, the producer was forced to expand the viewer's imagination with ingenious devices.

When T. S. Eliot adapted *Murder in the Cathedral* for film, he noted a difference in realism between cinema and stage:

> Cinema, even where fantasy is introduced, is much more realistic than the stage. Especially in an historical picture, the setting, the costume, and the way of life represented have to be accurate. Even a minor anachronism is intolerable. On the stage much more can be overlooked or forgiven; and indeed, an excessive care for accuracy of historical detail can become burdensome and distracting. In watching a stage performance, the member of the audience is in direct contact with the actor playing a part. In looking at a film, we are much more passive; as audience, we contribute less. We are seized with the illusion that we are observing an actual event, or at least a series of photographs of the actual event; and nothing must be allowed to break this illusion. Hence the precise attention to detail.[2]

If two men are on a stage in a theatre, the dramatist is obliged to motivate their presence; he has to account for their existing on the stage at all. Whereas if a camera is following a figure down a street or is turned to any object whatever, there is no need for a reason to be provided. Its grammar contains that power of statement of motivation, no matter what it looks at.

In the theatre, the spectator sees the enacted scene as a whole in space, always seeing the whole of the space. The stage may present only one corner of a large hall, but that corner is always totally visible all through the scene. And the spectator always sees that scene from a fixed, unchanging distance and from an angle of vision that doesn't change. Perspective

[2] George Hoellering and T. S. Eliot, *Film of Murder in the Cathedral,* New York, Harcourt Brace Jovanovich, 1952, p. vi; London, Faber & Faber, 1952.

may change from scene to scene, but within one scene it remains constant. Distance never varies.

But in film and TV, distance and angle constantly shift. The same scene is shown in multiple perspective and focus. The viewer sees it from here, there, then over here; finally he is drawn inexorably into it, becomes part of it. He ceases to be a spectator. Balázs writes:

> Although we sit in our seats, we do not see Romeo and Juliet from there. We look up into Juliet's balcony with Romeo's eyes and look down on Romeo with Juliet's. Our eye and with it our consciousness is identified with the characters in the film, we look at the world out of their eyes and have no angle of vision of our own. We walk amid crowds, ride, fly, or fall with the hero and if one character looks into the other's eyes, he looks into our eyes from the screen, for, our eyes are in the camera and become identical with the gaze of the characters. They see with our eyes. Herein lies the psychological act of identification. Nothing like this "identification" has ever occurred as the effect of any other system of art and it is here that the film manifests its absolute artistic novelty.
>
> . . .
>
> Not only can we see, in the isolated "shots" of a scene, the very atoms of life and their innermost secrets revealed at close quarters, but we can do so without any of the intimate secrecy being lost, as always happens in the exposure of a stage performance or of a painting. The new theme which the new means of expression of film art revealed was not a hurricane at sea or the eruption of a volcano: it was perhaps a solitary tear slowly welling up in the corner of a human eye.
>
> . . .
>
> Not to speak does not mean that one has nothing to say. Those who do not speak may be brimming over with emotions which can be expressed only in forms and pictures, in gesture and play of feature. The man of visual culture uses these not as substitutes for words, as a deaf-mute uses his fingers.[3]

The gestures of visual man are not intended to convey concepts that can be expressed in words, but inner experiences, nonrational emotions, which would still remain unexpressed when everything that can be told has been told. Such emotions lie in the deepest levels. They cannot be approached by words that are mere reflections of concepts, any more than musical experiences can be expressed in rational concepts. Facial expression is a human experience rendered immediately visible without the intermediary of words. It is Turgenev's "living truth of the human face."

Printing rendered illegible the faces of men. So much could be read from paper that the method of conveying meaning by facial expression fell into

[3] Béla Balázs, *Theory of Film,* New York, Roy Publishers, 1953, pp. 48, 31, 40; London, Denis Dobson, 1952.

desuetude. The press grew to be the main bridge over which the more remote interhuman spiritual exchanges took place; the immediate, the personal, the inner, died. There was no longer need for the subtler means of expression provided by the body. The face became immobile; the inner life, still. Wells that dry up are wells from which no water is dipped.

Just as radio helped bring back inflection in speech, so film and TV are aiding us in the recovery of gesture and facial awareness—a rich, colorful language, conveying moods and emotions, happenings and characters, even thoughts, none of which could be properly packaged in words. If film had remained silent for another decade, how much faster this change might have been!

Feeding the product of one medium through another medium creates a new product. When Hollywood buys a novel, it buys a title and the publicity associated with it: nothing more. Nor should it.

Each of the four versions of the *Caine Mutiny*—book, play, movie, TV—had a different hero: Willie Keith, the lawyer Greenwald, the United States Navy, and Captain Queeg, respectively. Media and audience biases were clear. Thus the book told, in lengthy detail, of the growth and making of Ensign William Keith, American man, while the movie camera with its colorful shots of ships and sea, unconsciously favored the Navy as hero, a bias supported by the fact the Navy cooperated with the movie makers. Because of stage limitations, the play was confined, except for the last scene, to the courtroom, and favored the defense counsel as hero. The TV show, aimed at a mass audience, emphasized patriotism, authority, allegiance. More important, the cast was reduced to the principals and the plot to its principles; the real moral problem—the refusal of subordinates to assist an incompetent, unpopular superior—was clear, whereas in the book it was lost under detail, in the film under scenery. Finally, the New York play, with its audience slanted toward Expense Account patronage—Mr. Sampson, Western Sales Manager for the Cavity Drill Company—became a morality play with Willie Keith, innocent American youth, torn between two influences: Keefer, clever author but moral cripple, and Greenwald, equally brilliant but reliable, a businessman's intellectual. Greenwald saves Willie's soul.

The film *Moby Dick* was in many ways an improvement on the book, primarily because of its explicitness. For *Moby Dick* is one of those admittedly great classics, like *Robinson Crusoe* or Kafka's *Trial,* whose plot and situation, as distilled apart from the book by time and familiarity, are actually much more imposing than the written book itself. It's the drama of Ahab's defiance rather than Melville's uncharted leviathan meanderings that is the greatness of *Moby Dick.* On film, instead of laborious tacks through leagues of discursive interruptions, the most vivid descriptions of whales and whaling become part of the action. On film, the viewer was constantly aboard ship: each scene an instantaneous shot of whaling life, an effect achieved in the book only by illusion, by constant, detailed reference. From start to finish, all the action of the film served to develop what was most central to the theme—a man's magnificent and blasphemous pride in attempting to destroy the brutal, unreasoning force that maims him and turns man-made order into chaos. Unlike the book, the film gave a spare, hard, compelling dramatization, free of self-conscious symbolism.

Current confusion over the respective roles of the new media comes largely from a misconception of their function. They are art-forms, not substitutes for human contact. Insofar as they attempt to usurp speech and personal, living relations, they harm. This, of course, has long been one of the problems of book culture, at least during the time of its monopoly of Western middle-class thought. But this was never a legitimate function of books, nor of any other medium. Whenever a medium goes claim jumping, trying to work areas where it is ill-suited, conflicts occur with other media, or, more accurately, between the vested interests controlling each. But, when media simply exploit their own formats, they become complementary and cross-fertile.

Some people who have no one around talk to cats, and you can hear their voices in the next room, and they sound silly, because the cat won't answer, but that suffices to maintain the illusion that their world is made up of living people, while it is not. Mechanized mass media reverse this: now mechanical cats talk to humans. There's no genuine feedback.

This charge is often leveled by academicians at the new media, but it holds equally for print. The open-mouthed, glaze-eyed TV spectator is merely the successor of the passive, silent, lonely reader whose head moved back and forth like a shuttlecock.

When we read, another person thinks for us: we merely repeat his mental process. The greater part of the work of thought is done for us. This is why it relieves us to take up a book after being occupied by our own thoughts. In reading, the mind is only the playground for another's ideas. People who spend most of their lives in reading often lose the

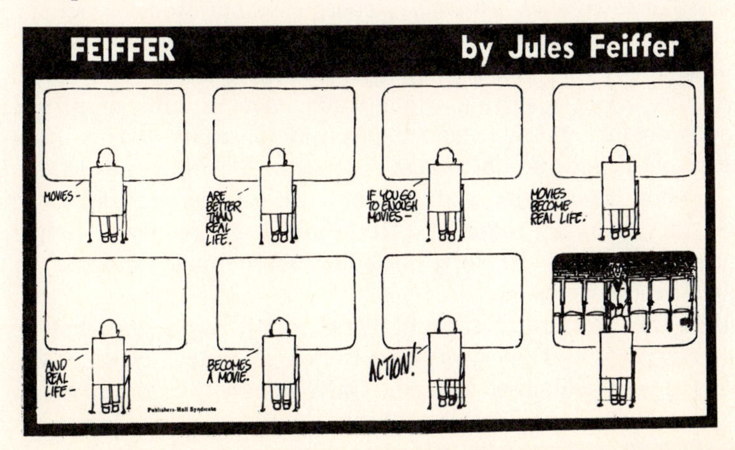

capacity for thinking, just as those who always ride forget how to walk. Some people read themselves stupid. Chaplin did a wonderful take-off of this in *City Lights,* when he stood up on a chair to eat the endless confetti that he mistook for spaghetti.

Eliot remarks: "It is often those writers whom we are lucky enough to know whose books we can ignore; and the better we know them personally, the less need we may feel to read what they write."

Frank O'Connor highlights a basic distinction between oral and written traditions:

> "By the hokies, there was a man in this place one time by name of Ned Sullivan, and he had a queer thing happen to him late one night and he coming up the Valley Road from Durlas." This is how a folk story begins, or should begin. . . . Yet that is how no printed short story should begin, because such a story seems tame when you remove it from its warm nest by the cottage fire, from the sense of an audience with its interjections, and the feeling of terror at what may lurk in the darkness outside.

Face-to-face discourse is not as selective, abstract, nor explicit as any mechanical medium; it probably comes closer to communicating an unabridged situation than any of them, and, insofar as it exploits the give-take of dynamic relationship, it's clearly the most indispensably human one.

Of course, there can be personal involvement in the other media. When Richardson's *Pamela* was serialized in 1741, it aroused such interest that in one English town, upon receipt of the last installment, the church bell announced that virtue had been rewarded. Radio stations have reported receiving quantities of baby clothes and bassinets when, in a soap opera, a heroine had a baby. One of the commonest phrases used by devoted listeners to daytime serials is that they "visited with" Aunt Jenny or Big Sister. BBC and *News Chronicle* report cases of women viewers who kneel before TV sets to kiss male announcers good night.

Each medium, if its bias is properly exploited, reveals and communicates a unique aspect of reality, of truth. Each offers a different perspective, a way of seeing an otherwise hidden dimension of reality. It's not a question of one reality being true, the others distortions. One allows us to see from here, another from there, a third from still another perspective; taken together they give us a more complete whole, a greater truth. New essentials are brought to the fore, including those made invisible by the "blinders" of old languages.

This is why the preservation of book culture is as important as the development of TV. This is why new languages, instead of destroying old ones, serve as a stimulant to them. Only monopoly is destroyed. When actor-collector Edward G. Robinson was battling actor-collector Vincent Price on art on TV's *$64,000 Challenge,* he was asked how the quiz had affected his life; he answered petulantly, "Instead of looking at the pictures in my art books, I now have to read them." Print, along with all old languages, including speech, has profited enormously from the development of the new media. "The more the arts develop," writes E. M. Forster, "the more they depend on each other for definition. We will borrow from painting first and call it pattern. Later we will borrow from music and call it rhythm."

The appearance of a new medium often frees older media for creative effort. They no longer have to serve the interests of power and profit. Elia Kazan, discussing the American theatre, says:

> Take 1900–1920. The theatre flourished all over the country. It had no competition. The box office boomed. The top original fare it had to offer was *The Girl of the Golden West*. Its bow to culture was fusty productions of Shakespeare. . . . Came the moving pictures. The theatre had to be better or go under. It got better. It got so spectacularly better so fast that in 1920–1930 you wouldn't have recognized it. Perhaps it was an accident that Eugene O'Neill appeared at that moment—but it was no accident that in that moment of strange competition, the theatre had room for him. Because it was disrupted and hard pressed, it made room for his experiments, his unheard-of subjects, his passion, his power. There was room for him to grow to his full stature. And there was freedom for the talents that came after his.[4]

Yet a new language is rarely welcomed by the old. The oral tradition distrusted writing, manuscript culture was contemptuous of printing, book culture hated the press, that "slag-heap of hellish passions," as one 19th century scholar called it. A father, protesting to a Boston newspaper about crime and scandal, said he would rather see his children "in their graves while pure in innocence, than dwelling with pleasure upon these reports, which have grown so bold."

What really disturbed book-oriented people wasn't the sensationalism of the newspaper, but its nonlineal format, its nonlineal codifications of experience. The motto of conservative academicians became: *Hold that line!*

A new language lets us see with the fresh, sharp eyes of the child; it offers the pure joy of discovery. I was recently told a story about a Polish couple who, though long resident in Toronto, retained many of the customs of their homeland. Their son despaired of ever getting his father to buy a suit cut in style or getting his mother to take an interest in Canadian life. Then he bought them a TV set, and in a matter of months a major change took place. One evening the mother remarked that "Edith Piaf is the latest thing on Broadway," and the father appeared in "the kind of suit executives wear on TV." For years the father had passed this same suit

[4] "Writers and Motion Pictures," *The Atlantic Monthly*, 199, 1957, p. 69.

in store windows and seen it both in advertisements and on living men, but not until he saw it on TV did it become meaningful. This same statement goes for all media: each offers a unique presentation of reality, which when new has a freshness and clarity that is extraordinarily powerful.

This is especially true of TV. We say, "We have a radio" but "We have television"—as if something had happened to us. It's no longer "The skin you love to touch" but "The Nylon that loves to touch you." We don't watch TV; it watches us: it guides us. Magazines and newspapers no longer convey "information" but offer ways of seeing things. They have abandoned realism as too easy: they substitute themselves for realism. *Life* is totally advertisements: its articles package and sell emotions and ideas just as its paid ads sell commodities.

Several years ago, a group of us at the University of Toronto undertook the following experiment: 136 students were divided, on the basis of their over-all academic standing of the previous year, into four equal groups who either (1) heard and saw a lecture delivered in a TV studio, (2) heard and saw this same lecture on a TV screen, (3) heard it over the radio, or (4) read it in manuscript. Thus there were, in the CBC studios, four controlled groups who simultaneously received a single lecture and then immediately wrote an identical examination to test both understanding and retention of content. Later the experiment was repeated, using three similar groups; this time the same lecture was (1) delivered in a classroom, (2) presented as a film (using the kinescope) in a small theatre, and (3) again read in print. The actual mechanics of the experiment were relatively simple, but the problem of writing the script for the lecture led to a consideration of the resources and limitations of the dramatic forms involved.

It immediately became apparent that no matter how the script was written and the show produced, it would be slanted in various ways for and against each of the media involved; no show could be produced that did not contain these biases, and the only real common denominator was the simultaneity of presentation. For each communication channel codifies reality differently and thus influences, to a surprising degree, the content of the message communicated. A medium is not simply an envelope that carries any letter; it is itself a major part of that message. We therefore decided not to exploit the full resources of any one medium, but to try to chart a middle-of-the-road course between all of them.

The lecture that was finally produced dealt with linguistic codifications of reality and metaphysical concepts underlying grammatical systems. It was chosen because it concerned a field in which few students could be expected to have prior knowledge; moreover, it offered opportunities for the use of gesture. The cameras moved throughout the lecture, and took close-ups where relevant. No other visual aids were used, nor were shots taken of the audience while the lecture was in progress. Instead, the cameras simply focused on the speaker for 27 minutes.

The first difference we found between a classroom and a TV lecture was the brevity of the latter. The classroom lecture, if not ideally, at least in practice, sets a slower pace. It's verbose, repetitive. It allows for greater elaboration and permits the lecturer to take up several *related* points. TV, however, is stripped right down; there's less time for qualifications or alternative interpretations and only time enough for *one* point. (Into 27 minutes we put the meat of a two-hour classroom lecture.) The ideal TV speaker states his point and then brings out different facets of it by a variety of illustrations. But the classroom lecturer is less subtle and, to the agony of the better students, repeats and repeats his identical points in the hope, perhaps, that ultimately no student will miss them, or perhaps simply because he is dull. Teachers have had captive audiences for so long that few are equipped to compete for attention via the new media.

The next major difference noted was the abstracting role of each medium, beginning with print. Edmund M. Morgan, Harvard Law Professor, writes:

> One who forms his opinion from the reading of any record alone is prone to err, because the printed page fails to produce the impression or convey the idea which the spoken word produced or conveyed. The writer has read charges to the jury which he had previously heard delivered, and has been amazed to see an oral deliverance which indicated a strong bias appear on the printed page as an ideally impartial exposition. He has seen an appellate court solemnly declare the testimony of a witness to be especially clear and convincing which the trial judge had orally characterized as the most abject perjury.[5]

Selectivity of print and radio are perhaps obvious enough, but we are less conscious of it in TV, partly because we have already been conditioned to it by the shorthand of film. Balázs writes:

> A man hurries to a railway station to take leave of his beloved. We see him on the platform. We cannot see the train, but the questing eyes of the man show us that his beloved is already seated in the train. We see only a close-up of the man's face, we see it twitch as if startled and then strips of light and shadow, light and shadow flit across it in quickening rhythm. Then tears gather in the eyes and that ends the scene. We are expected to know what happened and today we do know, but when I first saw this film in Berlin, I did not at once understand the end of this scene. Soon, however, everyone knew what had happened: the train had started and it was the lamps in its compartment which had thrown their light on the man's face as they glided past ever faster and faster.[6]

[5] G. Louis Joughin and Edmund M. Morgan, *The Legacy of Sacco and Vanzetti*, New York, Harcourt Brace Jovanovich, 1948, p. 34.

[6] Béla Balázs, *op. cit.*, pp. 35–36.

As in a movie theatre, only the screen is illuminated, and, on it, only points of immediate relevance are portrayed; everything else is eliminated. This explicitness makes TV not only personal but forceful. That's why stage hands in a TV studio watch the show over floor monitors, rather than watch the actual performance before their eyes.

The script of the lecture, timed for radio, proved too long for TV. Visual aids and gestures on TV not only allow the elimination of certain words, but require a unique script. The ideal radio delivery stresses pitch and intonation to make up for the absence of the visual. That flat, broken speech in "sidewalk interviews" is the speech of a person untrained in radio delivery.

The results of the examination showed that TV had won, followed by lecture, film, radio, and finally print. Eight months later the test was readministered to the bulk of the students who had taken it the first time. Again it was found that there were significant differences between the groups exposed to different media, and these differences were the same as those on the first test, save for the studio group, an uncertain group because of the chaos of the lecture conditions, which had moved from last to second place. Finally, two years later, the experiment was repeated, with major modifications, using students at Ryerson Institute. Marshall McLuhan reports:

> In this repeat performance, pains were taken to allow each medium full play of its possibilities with reference to the subject, just as in the earlier experiment each medium was neutralized as much as possible. Only the mimeograph form remained the same in each experiment. Here we added a printed form in which an imaginative typographical layout was followed. The lecturer used the blackboard and permitted discussion. Radio and TV employed dramatization, sound effects and graphics. In the examination, radio easily topped TV. Yet, as in the first experiment, both radio and TV manifested a decisive advantage over the lecture and written forms. As a conveyor both of ideas and information, TV was, in this second experiment, apparently enfeebled by the deployment of its dramatic resources, whereas radio benefited from such lavishness. "Technology is explicitness," writes Lyman Bryson. Are both radio and TV more explicit than writing or lecture? Would a greater explicitness, if inherent in these media, account for the ease with which they top other modes of performance?[7]

Announcement of the results of the first experiment evoked considerable interest. Advertising agencies circulated the results with the comment that here, at last, was scientific proof of the superiority of TV. This was unfortunate and missed the main point, for the results didn't indicate the superiority of one medium over others. They merely directed attention

[7] From a personal communication to the author.

toward differences between them, differences so great as to be of kind rather than degree. Some CBC officials were furious, not because TV won, but because print lost.

The problem has been falsely seen as democracy *vs.* the mass media. But the mass media *are* democracy. The book itself was the first mechanical mass medium. What is really being asked, of course, is: can books' monopoly of knowledge survive the challenge of the new languages? The answer is: no. What should be asked is: what can print do better than any other medium and is that worth doing?

The Ambiguous Mirror

The Ambiguous Mirror

the reflective–projective theory of broadcasting and mass communications

by LEE LOEVINGER

Former FCC Commissioner Lee Loevinger examines some major theories of mass communications and broadcasting. He then sets forth his own theory, which emphasizes the importance of the individual's self-image in determining the impact of the media.*

In contemporary society more people spend more time in communication than in any other waking activity. If there ever was a period when man spent more time manipulating physical objects rather than symbols it is irretrievably past for us. Even in our organization of work we now have more white collar than blue collar workers, and our leisure time activities have long since become predominantly vicarious and communicative rather than manipulative and participant. However, communications is a very broad concept that includes such diverse activities as talking, from gossiping to lecturing, reading and writing, including reading and writing of

* Loevinger's fellow commissioner Kenneth Cox disagreed; he did not regard self-image as crucial and felt it was likely that the broadcast media would become effective tools for achieving social goals. See Kenneth A. Cox, "Can Broadcasting Help Achieve Social Reform?" *Journal of Broadcasting,* XII (Spring, 1968), 117–30.

The Ambiguous Mirror: The Reflective-Projective Theory of Broadcasting and Mass Communications: From *Journal of Broadcasting,* vol. 12, no. 2 (Spring, 1968).

numbers and figures, scanning newspapers and magazines, perusing books, chatting on the telephone, attending the theater, listening to radio, and watching television.

Mass communication, particularly radio and television, is usually the focus of current attention. It has become such a widespread and ubiquitous phenomenon that communication about mass communication has become a mass production enterprise itself. One can scarcely read a newspaper or magazine today without encountering a critique of the mass media in one aspect or another and one cannot listen long to radio without hearing some comment about television. However, when we search the literature for data or scholarship what we find is not impressive. There are innumerable critics of the mass media, especially broadcasting, a few objective observers, and almost no working scientists. Indeed the comments and arguments about broadcasting in general and television in particular are at least as stereotyped as the programs.

The most common comment on broadcasting is derogatory criticism. The characteristic comment is that television represents a wonderful potential and a miserable reality.[1] This is almost always based on either the critic's own subjective views or upon material gathered in response to a general invitation to readers of a particular column or journal to send their views in a letter to the columnist or editor. While all these people are surely entitled to hold any views they like and to express them freely, it must be clear that neither the critics nor their pen pals necessarily represent the public. The correspondence received by a particular critic, or even a particular magazine or newspaper, is not a "survey" in any scientific sense. To take such a sampling and report it as a "survey" is roughly equivalent to reporting the results of a survey taken on the steps of St. Peter's in Rome on Sunday morning regarding attitudes towards Christian Science, or reporting the views of a random sample found in the lobby of the Cairo Hilton as to the character or popularity of Moshe Dayan. Those who want to engage in such an exercise have a perfect right to do so, but the results cannot be taken seriously by anyone familiar with survey research or scientific method in general.

The most scientific investigation conducted to date of public attitudes towards television is still the Steiner study published in 1963. The findings were summarized by Lazarsfeld in these terms:

> Dr. Steiner . . . found that a large number of respondents felt ambivalent about their amount of [television] viewing. They were ready to say that television is both relaxing and a waste of time.

[1] "So wonderful a potential, so miserable a reality" is given as the summary of "a reader survey" by the television critic of the *Christian Science Monitor*. (August 18, 1967, p. 9.) The views of the professional critics can be epitomized by a quotation from Bernie Harrison, television critic of the *Washington Star:* "I've been trying to find one critic who wrote something good, or even polite, about the new season of TV series." (September 21, 1967, p. B 13.)

> Their other leisure activities were not surrounded by such a haze of doubt; reading is elevating, playing golf is wholesome, and sitting in a bar is clearly wrong. Among the better-educated, he found a number of respondents who stated frankly that they felt they watched more than they should.[2]

Interestingly enough, this conclusion is corroborated by a 1965 ITA study of the attitudes of managerial and professional classes in Great Britain toward television. The study concluded that these classes

> by virtue of their educational and occupational background, tend more than the other social grades to have views about the meaningful use of time. They begin with reservations about television and the reservations are all the more likely to swell into irritation when they are themselves weak enough, as they see it, to be drawn into spending a good deal of time watching entertainment on television. They feel that television ought to have a tremendous potential for "good," in the sense of spreading knowledge and enlightenment, though it also seems clear that in having this concept of television they are thinking of the good it ought to be doing to *other* people rather than to themselves.[3]

There are a few other studies, mostly reported in the periodical literature, and some general theoretical analyses of mass communication, but there is no mass of empirical data from which we can derive any systematic view of functional theory of mass communications. There is, of course, a vast body of literature to be found under various library classifications beginning with the term "communications." However, these fall into three major classifications, each of which involves an entirely different frame of reference on an essentially different subject matter.

Communications Theories

When considering communications theory we must first distinguish among the engineering or technical, the economic, and the semantic frames of reference. The engineering or technical frame of reference encompasses what is now known as "information theory" and has to do with the modes and instruments of encoding, transmitting, and decoding messages of all kinds. This may involve an analysis of the physical means utilized (the electronic devices); the psychological processes involved; or consideration of linguistic and other symbols as means of encoding and decoding information. Economic analysis has to do, of course, with the financial as-

[2] Gary A. Steiner, *The People Look at Television*. New York: Alfred A. Knopf, 1963, p. 411.

[3] *ITV 1966*. A Guide to Independent Television, published by ITA, London, 1966, p. 25.

pects of mass communications. The semantic aspect of mass communications is the one that is most discussed and least understood. This is the one that has to do with the meaning and significance of what is communicated, and it is this aspect with which the critics, and most of the theory builders, are concerned.

From an examination of the literature it seems to me that there have been five major theories about the semantic function of broadcasting. The first view of broadcasting was that it was a remarkable and somewhat unbelievable technology that had specialized uses and would affect the public mainly as a hobby. This *hobby theory* of broadcasting was widely held from about the time of World War I until the early 1930's. Although the hobby theory of broadcasting is clearly out-dated, it is still recalled fondly by those of us who used to wind coils on old Quaker Oats boxes, made condensers, or capacitors as they are now called, from wax paper and tin foil, and used galena crystals as rectifiers.

In the early 1930's a great battle was fought between broadcasters and newspaper publishers over the right of broadcasting to transmit news.[4] The details are now only of historical interest and the outcome is well known. For many years after that, and up to the present time, broadcasting has been thought by many to derive its social significance from its effectiveness as a journalistic medium.[5] On occasion I have said that the *journalistic function* of broadcasting was its most important role.[6] A Roper survey indicating that more people look to television as a source of news than to newspapers, and that a substantial number rely on radio, gives support to this view.[7] Nevertheless, the journalistic theory of broadcasting seems to be more a normative view expressing what is thought to be the socially most important activity of the medium rather than an empirical view based on evidence encompassing all the functions broadcasting performs for its audience.

The "Social Reform" Theory

A third view that has gained some currency is the *social reform view* of broadcasting. This is the view held by people who see broadcasting as an immensely popular medium of communication, having a potentially vast influence and therefore offering an irresistible opportunity to achieve

[4] Mitchell V. Charnley, *News by Radio*. New York: Macmillan, 1948, p. 5 et seq.

[5] For a recent and very literate statement of the journalistic theory by a sophisticated and distinguished mind, see Raymond Swing, "Radio: The Languishing Giant," *Saturday Review*, August 12, 1967, p. 51.

[6] Lee Loevinger, "The Role of Law in Broadcasting," *Journal of Broadcasting*, VIII:2:113–126 at 121 (Spring, 1964).

[7] Burns W. Roper, *Emerging Profiles of Television and Other Mass Media: Public Attitudes 1959–1967*. A report by the president of Roper Research Associates on five national studies, April 5, 1967. (Published by the Television Information Office.)

a variety of social goals and ideals. This is the official attitude in many countries, particularly those of the Communist world. In this country there are those who see broadcasting, particularly television, as a means of doing quickly and easily what home, school, and church have been trying to do slowly and painfully for many years. This is the basic philosophy of those who feel that the FCC should exercise greater influence or control over broadcast programming.

The argument for government control of programming—whether extensive or limited—is usually ostensibly based upon the limitations of the spectrum and the consequent limitation of licensed broadcasting facilities. However it is noteworthy that those who are most eager to set official program standards are also among those who support most strongly the limitation of channels of mass communication on the grounds of harmful competition with existing broadcasting facilities. Both the doctrine of the Carroll case[8] and the rationale of the present CATV regulations[9] are based upon limiting the channels of mass communication in order to protect presently licensed enterprises. Regardless of whether such protection is justified, these legal rules make nonsense of the argument that program control is necessary or warranted because spectrum limitations impose an artificial scarcity on station assignments. So long as we are unwilling to permit the public to get as much broadcasting service as technology can provide, we cannot rationally say that technology imposes limitations requiring us to exercise control of programs because of technological limitations. Thus the social reform theory rests on the values and assumptions of its advocates rather than on an empirical foundation. In any event, whether or not broadcasting, and particularly television, is adapted to or capable of doing the work of social reform which some would have it undertake remains a question which is not answered merely by postulating the desirability of ideals to be achieved. The social reform theory needs a good deal more empirical investigation as well as philosophical analysis before it can provide a solid basis for acceptance.

McLuhan's "Sense-Extension" Theory

A fourth theory of mass communication is the *sense-extension theory* of Marshall McLuhan. This has become one of the most widely discussed theories of mass communication. It may be overstating the case to say that McLuhan presents a theory, since he is not a scientist and his ideas

[8] *Carroll Broadcasting Co. v. FCC,* 258 F2d 440, 17 RR 2066 (CA DC 1958). Also see *Southwest Operating Co. v. FCC,* 351 F2d 834 (CA DC 1965); James E. Meeks, "Economic Entry Controls in FCC Licensing: The Carroll Case Reappraised," 52 *Iowa Law Review* 236 (October, 1966).

[9] See *Regulation of CATV Systems*—Memorandum Opinion and Order on petition for reconsideration, 6 FCC2d 309, 330 (1967) (esp. dissenting opinion); *Fetzer Cable Vision,* et al., 6 FCC2d 845, 857 (1967) (dissenting opinion).

are expressed more as a series of disorganized observations than as a philosophical system. The widespread interest and popularity of McLuhan's publications really suggests the paucity of original thinking in this field.[10] Nevertheless the insights that McLuhan contributes are sufficiently supported by observation to warrant attention. His significant views may be summarized by some excerpts from his books:

> Printing from movable type created a quite unexpected new environment—it created the PUBLIC. Manuscript technology did not have the intensity or power of extension necessary to create publics on a national scale. What we have called "nations" in recent centuries did not, and could not, precede the advent of Gutenberg technology any more than they can survive the advent of electric circuitry with its power of totally involving all people in all other people.[11]
>
> . . .
>
> Print, in turning the vernaculars into mass media, or closed systems, created the uniform centralizing forces of modern nationalism.[12]
>
> . . .
>
> [Individualism] is a meaningless principle where the uniform processing of minds by the habit of reading the printed word has not occurred. In a word, individualism . . . and self-expression, alike assumes a prior technology of homogenous citizens. This scabrous paradox has haunted literate men in every age.[13]
>
> . . .
>
> Print created national uniformity and government centralism, but also individualism and opposition to government as such.[14]
>
> . . .
>
> [I]n operational and practical fact, the medium is the message. This is merely to say that the personal and social consequences of any medium—that is of any extension of ourselves—result from the new scale that is introduced into our affairs by each extension of ourselves, or by any new technology.[15]

[10] Charles S. Steinberg, "The McLuhan Myth," *Television Quarterly*, 6:7 (Summer, 1967).

[11] Marshall McLuhan, *The Gutenberg Galaxy*. Toronto: University of Toronto Press, 1962. The quotation is from the summary in the facing page to the prologue in the first U.S.A. edition.

[12] *Ibid.*, p. 199.

[13] *Ibid.*, p. 209.

[14] *Ibid.*, p. 235.

[15] Marshall McLuhan, *Understanding Media: The Extensions of Man*. New York: McGraw-Hill Book Company, 1964. New York: Signet ed., 1966, p. 23. [Copyright © 1964 by Marshall McLuhan. Used with permission of McGraw-Hill Book Company.]

. . .

[T]he medium is the message because it is the medium that shapes and controls the scale and form of human association and action. . . . For any medium has the power of imposing its own assumption on the unwary. . . . [O]ur human senses, of which all media are extensions, are also fixed charges on our personal energies, and . . . they also configure the awareness and experience of each one of us. . . .[16]

. . .

There have been countless . . . men who know nothing about the form of any medium whatever. They imagine that a more earnest tone and a more austere theme would pull up the level of the book, the press, the movie and TV. They are wrong to a farcical degree. They have only to try out their theory for fifty consecutive words in the mass medium of the English language. . . . Suppose we were to try for a few sentences to raise the level of our daily English conversation by a series of sober and serious sentiments? Would this be a way of getting at the problems of improving the medium?[17]

. . .

[T]he critics of program "content" have talked nonsense about "TV violence." The spokesmen of censorious views are typical semiliterate book-oriented individuals who have no competence in the grammars of newspaper, or radio, or of film, but who look askew and askance at all non-book media. The simplest question about any psychic aspect throws these people into a panic of uncertainty. Vehemence of projection of a single isolated attitude they mistake for moral vigilance. Once these censors became aware that in all cases "the medium is the message" or the basic source of effects, they would turn to suppression of media as such, instead of seeking "content" control. Their current assumption that content or programming is the factor that influences outlook and action is derived from the book medium, with its sharp cleavage between form and content.[18]

. . .

Each new technology creates an environment that is itself regarded as corrupt and degrading. Yet the new one turns its predecessor into an art form. When writing was new, Plato transformed the old oral dialogue into an art form. When printing was new the Middle Ages became an art form. "The Elizabethan world view" was a view of the Middle Ages. And the industrial age turned the Renaissance into an art form . . . the electric age taught us how to see the entire process of mechanization as an art process.[19]

[16] *Ibid.*, pp. 24, 30, 35.
[17] *Ibid.*, p. 187.
[18] *Ibid.*, p. 274.
[19] *Ibid.*, p. ix.

Stephenson's "Play Theory"

An entirely different view of mass communications has been offered by William Stephenson, a behavioral scientist, under the name of "the *play theory* of mass communication."[20] Stephenson distinguishes play from work, with play being activity that is self-sufficient and pursued for the pleasure in it, while work is activity involving effort for a purpose regarded as gainful and to produce goods, services, ideas, or other ulterior objectives. He distinguishes between social control, which comprises the devices society employs to establish involuntary categorical imperatives and secure conformity, from what he calls "convergent selectivity," which is the relative freedom of individual choice among alternatives.

Stephenson shows how his theories explain otherwise unnoticed or inexplicable phenomena. For example, he concludes that people read newspapers primarily for pleasure rather than information. As evidence he notes the fact that people read most avidly what they already know about. They go to a football or baseball game, then read about it in the newspaper. People look first in the newspaper to read events they have been involved in and already know about. Furthermore, we all read accounts of the same thing over and over again. This is because newspaper reading is play and involves the reader in projection, or self-identification as a story teller. Thus newspaper reading is an example of convergent selectivity, or voluntary activity, rather than of social control. Similarly the mass media, plays, art, and the theater generally offer opportunity for convergent selectivity, or communication pleasure, rather than work, which is communication effort or pain. Mass communication, he says, is best understood as being manipulated by its audiences, who thoroughly enjoy what they are being offered for the first time in man's history. The media are not manipulating or oppressing their audiences, and they should not make work out of what should be pleasure. Says Stephenson:

> Social scientists have been busy, since the beginnings of mass communication research, trying to prove that the mass media have been sinful where they should have been good. The media have been looked at through the eyes of morality when, instead, what was required was a fresh glance at people existing in their own right for the first time. It is my thesis that the daily withdrawal of people into the mass media in their after hours is a step in the existential direction, that is, a matter of subjectivity which invites freedom where there had been little or none before.[21]
>
> • • •
>
> The fill of mass communication is not a flight from reality, escapism, or the like; nor is it debasing or seducing the masses as the

[20] William Stephenson, *The Play Theory of Mass Communication.* Chicago: University of Chicago Press, 1967.

[21] *Ibid.*, p. 45.

> critics suppose. Rather it is seen as a buffer against conditions which would otherwise be anxiety producing. Without question a constant barrage of political propaganda would find few listeners or viewers, or, if it found many, would arouse deep anxieties in an unsettled world.[22]
>
> . . .
>
> The process of developing national character is no doubt basically rooted in social controls . . . , in which church, home, school, work, and all else mediate. But national character is also what a nation *thinks* of itself, as something to talk about, to sustain ongoing social or national conditions. It is best regarded as communication-pleasure, which has little effect on anything but gives self-satisfaction all around.[23]

It follows from this that separation of the elite from the culture at large creates a separatist culture within a country which bodes no one any good. What is most required for a national culture is something for everyone to talk about. The daily "fill" is far more important than the education of professionals. This is how social culture and character is formed, in songs, gossip, sports, dances, competition, or whatever is required to give people communication pleasure. Stephenson concludes that ". . . mass communication . . . should serve two purposes. It should suggest how best to maximize the communication-pleasure in the world. It should also show how far autonomy for the individual can be achieved in spite of the weight of social controls against him."[24]

Evaluation of These Theories

Each of these theories has some element of validity in it. After all, theories are simply conceptual schemes that enable us to see and relate the various aspects of phenomena under examination. Theories enable us to understand observations and to predict and make reasonable inferences beyond observation. In this sense theories are not true or untrue but more or less useful. Each of the theories, hobby, journalistic, social reform, sense extension, and play, points to an aspect of mass communications by broadcasting that has some significance. The journalistic and social reform theories focus on the medium and its message. The hobby, sense extension, and play theories focus on the audience and its reaction to the medium. However, none of these theories is entirely adequate to account for empirical data that can easily be observed. There are at least half a dozen observable and important facts about broadcasting that I think must be encompassed and explained by any mass communications theory before it may be accepted as adequate:

[22] *Ibid.*, p. 49.
[23] *Ibid.*, p. 91.
[24] *Ibid.*, p. 205.

First, broadcasting is extremely popular with the public and attracts a larger audience than any other mass medium in history, both relatively and in absolute numbers. In some individual cases both radio and television seem to be truly addictive. *Second,* the appeal of American-type broadcasting is universal. Even though much of our programming, such as TV westerns, is indigenous, it is popular throughout the world. Similarly American popular music has captured much of the world radio audience. Where state-controlled broadcasting systems have sought to use broadcasting for propaganda or educational purposes—and the difference is of interest to scholars rather than to audiences—they have been forced either by lack of audience or by competition from pirate, outside, or commercial stations to show more American or American-type programming, that is primarily entertaining. This has been the case in countries as diverse as Britain, Holland, Yugoslavia, Russia, and Japan. *Third,* during a period of increasing population, prosperity, and literacy, newspapers have not increased in number, and have declined in overall economic strength and competitive vitality, in Britain as well as in America, while reasonably reliable reports indicate that the general public relies more on television than on newspapers as a source of news.[25] Broadcasting now performs the journalistic function for most of the public part of the time and for much of the public most of the time. *Fourth,* broadcasting, especially television, arouses strong emotional reactions in most of those who either watch or listen and discuss it. In my experience, no other subject, not even religion, arouses such quick and violent emotional responses from people. *Fifth,* broadcasting, particularly television, is largely rejected or denigrated by intellectuals, and those who consider themselves intellectuals. Indeed, it is scarcely regarded as respectable to write or speak in public about television without deprecating its low intellectual estate. *Sixth,* broadcasting has become a part of ordinary living in contemporary society in a way that no other mass medium or art form has approached. Television or radio are in the home, in the car, in the office, on the beach, on the street, and constantly in company with the majority of the population. Broadcasting is about as ubiquitous as printing and for some people is a far more intimate and constant companion. The theater, pictorial art, and either contemporary or classical literature are none of them a part of everyday living for most people; they are not really an element of our communal experience. Not even the newspapers are a component of our common

[25] Burns W. Roper, *Emerging Profiles of Television and Other Mass Media: Public Attitudes 1959–1967.* A report by the president of Roper Research Associates on five national studies, April 5, 1967, p. 7 et seq. Also see A. H. Raskin, "What's Wrong with American Newspapers?" *New York Times Magazine,* June 11, 1967, p. 28; John Tebbel, "Britain's Chronic Press Crisis," *Saturday Review,* July 8, 1967, p. 49; Henry Raymont, "4 Chicago Newspapers Are Fighting Desperately to Regain Lost Readers," *New York Times,* September 5, 1967, p. 38. Mr. Raskin says, inter alia: "There is disturbing skepticism among large groups of readers, including many of the best educated and most intellectually alive, about whether what they read in their newspapers is either true or relevant."

culture in the sense that broadcasting has become. Any theory of broadcasting as mass communication must be consistent with and adequate to explain at least these data. Testing the five theories mentioned on this basis shows that none of them is wholly adequate.

The hobby theory is, of course, clearly outdated and is really quite inadequate to explain any of the observed data. The journalistic theory is somewhat more relevant and is at least consistent with the popularity of broadcasting, its journalistic function, and, possibly, its place as a cultural component. However, the journalistic theory is not consistent with the universality of broadcasting programs, with the emotional involvement of the audience, or with the attitude of intellectuals toward the medium. The journalistic theory is partially empirical, but is also in part a normative judgment as to the function that broadcasting should be performing rather than an empirical conclusion as to the function that it actually does perform or the need that it does meet. By its own terms, the journalistic theory is an incomplete account of broadcasting as mass communication.

The social reform theory explains the emotional involvement of those who either attack or defend broadcasting, as well as the attitude of the intellectual elite toward television. However, the social reform theory is not at all consistent with the popularity of broadcasting, with its universality, with its journalistic function, or with its observable role as a cultural component. The social reform theory must be judged to have very little empirical basis and to be almost wholly a normative ideal.

The sense-extension theory of McLuhan seeks to be empirical rather than normative and is consistent with the popularity of broadcasting, its universality, and its role as a cultural component. McLuhan explains the emotional involvement of the television audience by saying it is a "cool" medium which conveys little information and so requires audience participation to provide the links necessary to complete the message. I find this unconvincing because the theory strains the observable facts and simply does not apply to radio. Further, the McLuhan theory is neither consistent with nor adequate to explain the journalistic function of broadcasting or the attitude of the intellectual group generally. The play theory of Stephenson, similarly, is empirical and descriptive rather than normative. It is quite consistent with the popularity of broadcasting, with its universality and with its journalistic function. However, the play theory is not adequate to explain the emotional involvement of the audience, the attitude of the intellectual elite, or the place of broadcasting as a cultural component.

The "Reflective-Projective Theory"

A broader theory which seems to encompass all of the aspects of broadcasting mentioned, as well as others, is what I call the *reflective-projective theory* of broadcasting and mass communication. This theory postulates that mass communications are best understood as mirrors of society that reflect an ambiguous image in which each observer projects or sees his own vision of himself and society. This theory not only explains the observable facts about broadcasting better than the other theories but also differentiates the social and the individual aspects of the semantic significance of mass communications, which the other theories do not.

It is apparent that mass media reflect various images of society but not of the individual. However, broadcasting is not a simple, plane mirror but rather a telescopic mirror reflecting an image of what is distant and concentrating and focusing on points in a vast universe. Broadcasting is an electronic mirror that reflects a vague and ambiguous image of what is behind it, as well as of what is in front of it. While the mirror can pick out points and aspects of society, it cannot create a culture or project an image that does not reflect something already existing in some form in society. Further, the mirror can project an accurate or a distorted image and it can reflect an image that is very vague and ambiguous or one that is more clearly defined. These are matters of degree and there is always a significant amount of ambiguity in the image projected.

The ambiguous mirror of broadcasting obviously reflects not a single image but a variety of images of society, as it is turned toward one or another sector or aspects of society. As with a telescope or camera, the broadcasting mirror may be focused broadly or narrowly. So the reflective-projective theory, unlike the earlier theories, takes account of and allows for the variety of broadcasting. Educational television and what is now called "public broadcasting" help to present a broader, and therefore more complete, reflection of society. However, this theory also warns us not to expect too much of educational television or public broadcasting. They can supplement and expand the broadcasting image, but, like conventional broadcasting, so long as they are mass media they can perform only a reflective-projective function and are most unlikely to become instruments of social reform or great public enlightenment.[26]

[26] See Howard K. Smith, "Don't Expect Too Much from Public Television," *Washington Star,* October 1, 1967. Mr. Smith, an experienced broadcaster and social observer, says, "People who understand television but little, . . . are premature and hyperbolic in seeing a new age of wonders about to open. . . . Criticizing the fare on commercial TV is without doubt America's chief popular avocation, ... But for an exercise Americans indulge in so much, it is odd how ill thought out are their assumptions. There is not going to be any hegira away from commercial to public TV. There is nothing magic in public TV that is going to increase the quality of genius or imagination in our nation." I have supported and do support the establishment of a corporation for public broadcasting, not on the grounds that commercial broadcasting is deficient or has failed but on the grounds that the proposal will promote diversity, provide a potential for innovation and excellence, and afford the public a wider choice in broadcasting. See letter to Senator John O. Pastore in *Hearings* before the Subcommittee on Communications of the Committee on Commerce, U.S. Senate, 90th Congress, 1st Session, on S. 1160, The Public Television Act of 1967, Serial 90–4, p. 678.

This view is consistent with observation of national differences in broadcasting patterns. A substantial element of violence in American television reflects a tolerance and taste for violence in American society. This is somewhat offensive to Europeans, who have a different attitude toward violence, and there is less of violence in European broadcast programming. On the other hand, European television has fewer sex and religious taboos than American television and this corresponds to European attitudes, which are looser in these fields than American attitudes. Basically all mass media are censored by the public since they lose their status as *mass* media if they become too offensive or uninteresting to a large segment of the public.[27]

While the mass media reflect various images of society, the audience is composed of individuals, each of whom views the media as an individual. The members of the audience project or see in the media their own visions or images, in the same manner that an individual projects his own ideas into the inkblots of the Rorschach test or the pictures of the Thematic Apperception Test, commonly used by psychologists.[28] Projection is a process that has been well known in psychology for many years. Essentially it consists of an observer attributing his own attitudes, ideas, or feelings to the perceptions he receives from the environment. There is some element of this in all perception. Perception itself is both selective and interpretative, as we never see all the details of any scene and necessarily interpret or impose preconceived patterns on our sensations when we perceive anything as having meaning. All media, including those exalted by the term "art," offer selected sensations which provide the basis for individual interpretations that vary with intellectual, emotional, and sensory responses. What is pure story-telling to one may be allegory or metaphor to another. Well known examples are such classics as *Gulliver's Travels, Alice in Wonderland,* and *Don Quixote*. However, it is not only literary classics that have this mixed narrative-allegorical-metaphorical quality. A recent sociological study of television comments:

> Television series such as *Bonanza,* and *The Virginian,* and most popular films and fiction are in reality morality plays, that show how a hero confronts a moral dilemma and how he finally makes a moral choice. These dilemmas are often quite contemporary and controversial; I have seen *Bonanza,* one of the most popular TV programs, deal with questions of racial intolerance and intermarriage, albeit in a 19th-century Western setting. Programs like

[27] See Wilbur Schramm, *Mass Media and National Development.* Stanford, Calif.: Stanford University Press and UNESCO, 1964. Basically Schramm argues that mass media cannot proceed far in advance of other social developments that relate to and support the media with an internal national culture.

[28] Although there is some dispute among psychologists as to the effectiveness of the Rorschach inkblot test as a clinical diagnostic tool, there is no disagreement as to the phenomenon of projection and the fact that this response is elicited by the inkblot test. See Patricia McBroom, "The Rorschach Tested," *Science News,* 92:182 (August 19, 1967).

> *The Law and Mr. Jones, East Side/West Side,* and *The Defenders* have discussed pertinent social issues in contemporary settings, although they have been less popular from a rating standpoint. And even the innocuous family situation comedies such as *Ozzie and Harriet* deal occasionally with ethical problems encountered on a neighborhood level; for example, how to help the socially isolated child or the unhappy neighbor. Although the schools argue that they are the major transmitter of society's moral values, the mass media offer a great deal more content on this topic.[29]

Thus broadcasting is an electronic mirror reflecting an ambiguous image of its environment in which the audience sees its vision of society. This view explains the several aspects of broadcasting that have been noted above. It also points to another fact which is of substantial significance. In the field of communications media, technology reverses psychology in order of development. The technologically most advanced media are psychologically the most elementary and primitive. Psychologically man has advanced from simple sensation to perception, and then to abstraction which is expressed in gestures, sounds, symbols, verbal signs, and, finally, developed language. Technologically, hieroglyphics were the first form of writing, and we have progressed from them to more sophisticated signs, to alphabet writing, to printing, followed by books and periodicals, and then through the electronic media from the telegraph to the telephone to radio and through the movies to television. The most highly abstract of the technological media is alpha-numeric writing which requires considerable effort and interpretation by the reader. Speech conveyed by telephone or radio is understood more easily and is a psychological regression from the abstraction of printed language to the more elemental level of oral language. Finally, television is a medium which, contrary to the theories of McLuhan, conveys the most information in the most literal form by giving us oral language combined with visual perception and requiring the least effort to interpret the abstractions. Thus television is a multichannel communication which is more elemental and therefore has greater immediacy and impact than other media.

This theory fully explains the aspects of broadcasting mentioned above. Broadcasting is popular and universal because it is elemental, responsive to popular taste, and gives the audience a sense of contact with the world around it which is greater than that provided by any other medium. Broadcasting is increasingly performing the journalistic function for the public not because it is superior by any abstract intellectual standards but because it is immediate, personal, and comprehensive. Television views of a scene may be and often are better than personal observation, in their ability to focus telescopically on details of interest, in their ability to move from place to place, and in their ability to select the scenes of action and

[29] Herbert J. Gans, "The Mass Media as an Educational Institution," *Television Quarterly,* 6:20–37 at 22 (Spring, 1967).

interest. Television and radio duplicate and overlap each other to a great extent, but apparently television has the greater popularity because its multichannel communication with the audience conveys a sense of greater involvement and a closer apprehension of reality.

The reflective-projective theory makes it easy to understand why people are so strongly attached to and upset by broadcasting and react so emotionally to it. It is because each projects his own ego into what he sees or hears and is frequently dissatisfied when he finds the picture unflattering. This reaction can easily be verified by a simple experiment. Take a picture of any individual with an ordinary camera and then ask him, or her, whether the picture is altogether attractive and pleasing. Virtually no one, man or woman, is ever wholly pleased with a picture or reflection of himself. When it is possible to blame the photographer or someone else, that is the easiest course and therefore most frequently followed. On the other hand, people are fascinated by pictures and are invariably more interested in pictures in which they appear than in pictures of others. Another empirical verification is the relationship between people and mirrors. Almost no one can resist at least a glance into a mirror no matter how often and how recently he has inspected his own reflection. Thus the mirror theory of broadcasting explains not only the emotional involvement of the audience but also the popular appeal and universality of the medium.

The reflective-projective theory also explains the democratic paradox that in the field of mass communications the greater the appeal to the mass the more alienated the majority of intellectuals seems to become. Most of those who articulate the demand for democracy and service to the public interest, and who are accustomed to influence policy and social action in this manner, are of an intellectual elite. Such leaders think of democracy as a system in which *they* define the public interest and the public is persuaded to accept or acquiesce in leadership views. But in fact the public wants to see its *own* image in the mass media mirrors, not the image of intellectual leaders. Consequently when the public gets what it wants from the mass media this incurs the wrath of an intellectual elite and the slings and arrows of outraged critics who have been demanding service to the public . . . but who have been expecting their own rather than the public's views and tastes.

Finally, the reflective-projective theory is wholly consistent with the observation that broadcasting has become an important component of contemporary culture. A nation or a community is not formed by lines on a map or even by geographical unity or natural boundaries, as we are learning anew each day. A nation or a community is formed by common interests, ideas, and culture—by a common image or vision of itself. But to have a common image or vision there must be one that is seen, understood, and accepted by most of the people, not merely by a minority or by an elite. This requires that the social image reflected in the media mirrors be one that truly reflects the mass.

The common interest in entertainment, sports, news, and even advertising is likely to be more universally understood and effective in providing common ties of association and conversation than more esoteric and aesthetic material. It seems probable that a television showing of the World Series or of a popular western or other entertainment show will do more to promote a sense of national unity than a lecture on morality by some nationally known clergyman or a performance of *Hamlet* starring some great Shakespearean player. A family is not formed by recollections of a prettily posed, neatly dressed, tinted studio shot of the group on grandmother's birthday. A family is formed by shared experiences of skinned knees, trips to the doctor, hurried meals, mended pants, and all the million and one mundane commonplaces, hardships, and irritations of everyday living together. Perhaps the smudged, commonplace, homely, slightly unattractive picture that we get of ourselves from our mass media is providing us with a common image and a common cultural bond that we could not get from a more elegant and more attractive portrait.

In analyzing the role of mass media, or any other social phenomena, we must distinguish the judgments expressed in empirical and normative theories. Empirical theories are those which are purely descriptive and seek to explain and harmonize observed facts. Normative theories are those which set norms or standards and imply obligations to conform. Of course we need both. However, the first task is to understand before we undertake to judge. It is silly to condemn a camel for having a hump and praise a horse for having a straight back, or condemn a horse for requiring frequent drinks of water and praise a camel for his ability to travel without water. These characteristics are simple facts of existence and are not rationally the basis for either praise or blame. These are things for which normative standards are irrelevant and the only reasonable course is to observe and understand. Once we observe and understand the nature of camels and horses we can then decide the use to which each is best put.

When we understand broadcasting it appears that the mission for which it is best fitted is the creation of a common contemporary culture and a sense of national (and perhaps international) unity. This also appears to be the function which now most needs to be performed. The creation of a common national culture embodying a spirit of national unity must surely rank as a foremost need of the present era. Of course, national unity does not require or imply unanimity of views on all issues or suppression of dissent. It does imply a common bond or mood as well as agreement on some basic ideas and principles. Indeed, national agreement on support of basic American constitutional principles is essential if dissent and its free expression are to survive.

On the other hand, the medium that provides the common denominator to promote national unity and community culture is not necessarily the one that can also provide general adult education, social reform, or even news and information, although these may be provided in some degree in the process of creating and disseminating a national culture. We should remember that Shakespeare in his day was a popular entertainer who wrote fanciful and escapist stories about royalty and nobility, about wars and violence, and not about the common people and ordinary experience.

Even among our mass media there are differences in the ability to perform the function of unification and common culture building. Magazines to an outstanding degree, and even newspapers, are written and published for particular groups and classes of society. Evidence of this is proudly paraded by the publishers in their analyses of the income and educational status of readers. Evidence of this can readily be observed by comparing such newspapers as the *New York Times* and the *Wall Street Journal* with the *New York Daily News,* and by comparing the *New Yorker* with *True Story* magazine. Even more obvious stratification is evident in magazines which appeal to particular ethnic or religious groups as well as those with specific vocational and economic specialization. In contrast, broadcasting is relatively universal and equally available to all members of the public. One can hardly imagine an underprivileged slum dweller buying a copy of *Fortune*. However, the poor, the middle class, and the rich are about equally exposed to news of business and finance given on television news summaries or transmitted by the implicit message of popular entertainment.

It appears that much of the dissatisfaction that is voiced with broadcasting media is really an expression of basic dissatisfaction with society. To a large extent in past history the intellectual elite have lived in a separate world from the great mass of people and have neither confronted the mass or mass views and tastes nor sought to impose their own views and tastes upon the mass, except with respect to a few political issues. Broadcasting, as a universal medium, changes this. To the degree that the intellectual elite pay attention to radio and television they inescapably confront mass tastes and desires. That this does not satisfy their own standards is not only to be expected but, indeed, is inherent in the very nature of things. It is also socially useful to have the elite thus exposed to mass culture.

What we urgently need today is a larger concept of community—to see the community of which we are part not merely as a town, city, metropolitan area, or state, but as a country, a unified, civilized, orderly national society.[30] This is an image that cannot be created by art, but that must grow in the minds and hearts of men. We cannot say with certainty just what will nourish and what will poison its growth. Yet it does appear that the growth of a unified and cohesive national community will be promoted by the presentation of highly popular programs on mass media, especially broadcasting. Our survival as a free nation may depend upon development of a truly common culture. That is a task worthy of any medium.

[30] See Jefferson B. Fordham, *A Larger Concept of Community*. Baton Rouge: Louisiana State University Press, 1956.

FROM counterblast

by MARSHALL McLUHAN

In this brief selection, media theorist Marshall McLuhan discusses some of the profound cultural changes that result from changes in means of communication.

Media are artificial extensions of sensory existence.

each an externalized species of the inner genus sensation. The cultural environment created by externalization of modes of sensation now favours the predominance of one sense or another. These species struggle through mutations in a desperate attempt at adaptation and survival.

Accidents foster an uneven rate of development of communication facilities. Circumstances fostering in one age painting, sculpture, music, may produce a bulwark against the effects of, say, printing. But the same bulwark may be quite useless before the impact of movies or TV.

Improvements in the means of communication are based on a shift from one sense to another. This involves a rapid refocusing of all previous experience. Any change in the means of communication produces a chain of revolutionary consequences at every level of culture and politics. Because of the complexity of this process, prediction and control are impossible.

John Donne and George Herbert transferred to the new printed page of the 17th century many effects which had previously been popular in the pictorial world of the later Middle Ages. For them print had made the visual arts recessive and quaint. In this century the sudden predominance of the graphic arts has made print recessive. We filter one past culture through the screen of others and of our own—a game we play with whole cultures and epochs as easily as we could previously combine phrases from two languages.

With writing comes inner speech, the dialogue with oneself—a result of translating the verbal into the visual (writing) and translating the visual into the verbal (reading)—a complex process for which we pay a heavy psychic and social price—the price, as James Joyce puts it, of ABCED-minded-ness. Literate man experiences an inner psychic withdrawal from his external senses which gives him a heavy psychic and social limp. But the rewards are very rich.

Today we experience in reverse, what pre-literate man faced with the advent of writing. Today we are, in a technical if not literary sense, post-literate. Literacy: a brief phase.

Aristotle described speech as the arrest of the flowing of thought. Today speech begins to look like an obsolete technology. The sounds we utter are structured in acoustic space by noise spaced in silence. What silence is to acoustic space, darkness is to visual space. Speech structures interpersonal distances. These distances aren't just physical, but emotional and cultural. We involuntarily raise our voices when speaking to those who don't understand our language. Entering a silent house, we call a name in a tone intended to extend throughout that space.

Words are an orchestral harmony of touch, taste, sight, sound. Writing is the abstraction of the visual from this complex. With writing comes power: command over space.

Manuscript culture, based on parchment and the scarcity of writing materials, made for a high degree of memorization—the inevitable result of the scarcity of manuscripts, the slowness of reading them and the difficulty of referring to them. Everybody leaned heavily on oral means for the intake of information. Publication of a poem meant its oral delivery by the author. Teachers gave out texts, commented on variants and discussed the figures of speech, wit and decorum of the author phrase by phrase. This involved providing etymologies of the words, the history of their various meanings and their social backgrounds and implications. Each student, therefore, made his own grammar, his own dictionary, rhetoric and commonplace book. Such was the practice in classrooms even in Shakespeare's day, a century after the invention of printing.

But, so far as the classroom was concerned, printing was decisive. Uniform texts became available along with grammars and dictionaries, not only of Latin but of Greek, Hebrew, and the vernacular tongues. Print made not only many more past texts available, but also large quantities of chronicle and historical matter which the medieval classroom could not possibly have found time to copy or discuss. From the point of view of previous education, this made a shambles. The flow of information shifted from wit, memory, and oral dialectics to multilingual erudition. When the main channel of information became the printed page, the critical powers of the young couldn't be trained in the same way. Print isolated the reader. The student who had formerly recited the lecture in a group and had then joined another group to discuss and dispute the points of the lecture was now alone with a text. In the same way, print isolated cultures, each in its own vernacular frame, where before all learning was in a single tongue.

Yet 16th century prose still retained many of the rapidly shifting perspectives of multiple levels of tone and meaning characteristic of group speech. It took two centuries of print to create prose on the page which maintained the tone and perspective of a single speaker. The individual scholar, alone with his text, had to develop habits of self-reliance which we still associate with the virtues of book culture. More and more learning was left to the unassisted industry of the individual. People were consumed by an "immoderate hydroptic thirst for humane learning and languages," in Donne's phrase, which went along with the first discovery of the smooth speedways of the printed page. No more stuttering pilgrimages through the crabbed columns of manuscript abbreviations. But it was a long time before people got to be at home with print. And by that time the newspaper page layout had begun to disturb the precarious equilibrium of 18th century book culture. The format of the 19th century newspaper page was like a dozen book pages set on a single sheet. The telegraph made this format the instantaneous global cross-section of a single day. This was no longer the book. Nor could the book stand up to this new cultural form born out of technology. The book tried to swallow this rival: Joyce in **Ulysses,** Eliot in **The Waste Land**—non-narrative epics which incorporate the newspaper art form.

The newspaper was merely the first of a quick succession of new information channels which challenged the cultural balance. But only the artists of our time have met or understood this challenge. With the arrival of print, Erasmus and his humanist colleagues saw exactly what had to be done in the classroom—and did it at once. But with the arrival of the press, nothing was done to accommodate its new modes of perception to an obsolete curriculum.

Education must always concentrate its resources at the point of major information intake. But from what sources do growing minds nowadays acquire most factual data and how much critical awareness is conferred at these points? It's a commentary on our extreme cultural lag that when we think of criticism of information flow we still use only the concept of book culture, namely, how much trust can be reposed in the words of the message. Yet the bias of each medium of communication is far more distorting than the deliberate lie.

What if He Is Right?

Tom Wolfe

COMMUNICATIONS

COM
MU
NI
CA
TIONS

by NORTHROP FRYE

Northrop Frye, literary critic, Professor of English at Toronto University, and member of the Canadian Radio Television Commission states that print not only made technological efficiency possible, as McLuhan has said, but also, through its durability, created the conditions of freedom in Western society. "Democracy and book culture are interdependent," he concludes, and the electronic media represent "not a new order to adjust to, but a subordinate order to be contained."

I am on an advisory committee concerned with Canadian radio and television, and so I have been trying to do some reading in communication theory. I find it an exciting subject to read about, because so much of the writing is in the future tense, with so many sentences beginning: 'We shall soon be able to . . .' But I have also become aware of a more negative side to it, as to most technology. The future that is technically feasible may not be the future that society can absorb. There is a great gap now between what we are doing and what we have the means to do, and many writers regard this as a disease peculiar to our time that we shall get over when we feel less threatened by novelty. But I doubt that the gap can be so soon or so easily closed. When I read symposia by technical experts telling me what the world could be like 100 years from now, I feel a dissolving of identity, with all the familiar social landmarks disap-

Communications: From *The Listener* (July 9, 1970). Reprinted by permission of the author.

pearing, as though I were in Noah's flood climbing a tree. As I imagine that this is what most people feel, I suspect that the world 100 years from now will be much more like the world today than the experts suggest.

Plato was much concerned with the revolution brought about by writing in his day. He felt that the oral tradition was done for, and that the poets, the great rememberers, were on their way out as teachers, and would have to give place to the writing philosophers. But Plato's Socrates, of all people, was unlikely to overlook the ironic side of this. In the *Phaedrus* we are told that the Egyptian god Thoth invented writing, and explained to all the other gods how greatly his invention would transform the memory. The other gods looked down their noses and said that on the contrary it would only destroy the memory. Thoth and his critics were talking about different kinds of memory, so they couldn't get any further. The deadlock between the enthusiasm of a technological expert and a public digging in its heels to resist him has never been more clearly stated.

All the mass media have a close connection with the centres of social authority, and reflect their anxieties. In socialist countries they reflect the anxiety of the political Establishment to retain power; in the United States they reflect the anxiety of the economic Establishment to keep production running. In either case communication is a one-way street. Wherever we turn, there is that same implacable voice, unctuous, caressing, inhumanly complacent, selling us food, cars, political leaders, culture, contemporary issues, and remedies against the migraine we get from listening to it. It is not just the voice we hear that haunts us, but the voice that goes on echoing in our minds, forming our habits of speech, our processes of thought.

If people did not resent this they would not be human, and all the nightmares about society turning into an insect state would come true. My hair prickles when I hear advertisers talk of a television set simply as a means of reaching their market. It so seldom occurs to them that a television set might be their market's way of looking at them, and that the market might conceivably not like what it sees. If the viewer is black and sees a white society gorging itself on luxuries and privileges, the results can be explosive. But this is only a special case of a general social resentment against being always treated as an object to be stimulated. As with erotic stimulation, or should I say as with other forms of erotic stimulation, there is a large element of mechanical and involuntary response, for all the resentment. The harder it is to escape, the more quickly the resentment turns to panic, and it seems clear that a great deal of the shouting and smashing and looting and burning of our time comes from this panic. Many other things are best understood as forms of resentment, or at least resistance, to mass communication, such as the rock music which wraps up its listeners in an impermeable cloak of noise. I often wonder, too, how far the users of drugs have been affected by a feeling that they have been cheated out of genuinely new sensory impressions by the mass media.

More important is the political resistance. When I read articles on satellite broadcasting and the like I am often told, with a teacher's glassy smile, that the increase in the range of broadcasting will lead to far greater international understanding, because very soon now we can have all the problems of Tanzania or Paraguay brought to us by touching a button, and won't that be nice? One answer from the public which is remarkably loud and clear is that they don't want all those people in their living-room. If the world is becoming a global village, it will also take on the features of real village life, including cliques, lifelong feuds and impassable social barriers. In spirit I agree with the optimists: it is the destiny of man to unite rather than divide, and as a Canadian I have little sympathy with separatism, which seems to me a mean and squalid philosophy. But I can hardly ignore the fact that separatism is the strongest political force yet thrown up by the age of television.

The direction of most of the technological developments of our time has been towards greater introversion. The automobile, the passenger aeroplane, the movie, the television set, the multi-storey block [apartment building], are all much more introverted than their predecessors. The result is increased alienation and a decline in the sense of festivity, the sense of pleasure in belonging to a community. Even our one technically festive season, Christmas, is an introverted German Romantic affair, based on a myth of retreat into the cave of a big Dickensian cuddly family of a type that hardly exists. The one advantage of an introverted situation is privacy; but for us the growing introversion goes along with a steady decrease in privacy. This means that the psychological conditions of life, whatever the physical conditions, become increasingly like those of life in a prison, where there is no privacy and yet no real community. In this situation the easy defences of introversion, such as apathy or cynicism, are no defences at all.

We hear of meetings broken up and speakers howled down by organised gangs; we try to phone from a tube [subway] station and find the telephone torn out; we read of hijacked planes and of bombs in letterboxes; hoodlums go berserk in summer resorts and adolescents scream all the words they know that used to be called obscene. We realise that these acts are in too consistent a pattern to be mere destructiveness, and yet they are too irresponsible to be serious revolutionary tactics, though they may be rationalised as such. However silly or vicious they may be, they are acts of counter-communication, acts noisy enough or outrageous enough to shout down that voice and spit at that image, if only for a few moments. But hysterical violence is self-defeating, not merely because it is violence but because, as counter-communication, it can only provoke more of what it attacks. Every outbreak of violence releases more floods of alarm, understanding, deep reservations, comment in perspective, denunciation, concern, sympathy, analysis and reasoned argument. Violence, however long it lasts, can only go around in the circles of lost direction. There is a vaguely Freudian notion that there is something therapeutic in releasing inhibitions; but it is clear that releasing inhibition is just as compulsive, repetitive and hysterical an operation as the repressing of them.

To go back to Plato and the god Thoth's invention: an oral culture, before writing develops, is heavily dependent on individual memory. This means that the teachers are often poets, because verse is the easiest verbal pattern to remember. With writing, and eventually printing, continuous prose develops. With prose, philosophy changes from aphorism and proverb to a continuous argument organised by logic and dialectic, and history to a continuous narrative. Such metaphors as 'the pursuit of knowledge' are based on the sense of the planned and systematic conquest of reality which writing makes possible. In our day the electronic media of film, radio and television have brought about a revival of the oral culture that we had before writing, and many of the social characteristics of a pre-literate society are reappearing in ours. The poet, for example, finds himself again before a listening audience, when he can use topical or even ephemeral themes: he does not have to retreat from society and write for posterity.

One common interpretation of this fact, strongly influenced by Marshall McLuhan, is that print represents a 'linear' and time-bound approach to reality, and that the electronic media, by reviving the oral tradition, have brought in a new 'simultaneous' or mosaic form of understanding. Contemporary unrest, in this view, is part of an attempt to adjust to a new situation and break away from the domination of print. This view is popular among American educators, because it makes for anti-intellectualism and the proliferating of gadgets, and I understand that for some of them the phrase 'p.o.b.', meaning print-oriented bastard, has replaced s.o.b. as a term of abuse. It seems to me that this view is not so much wrong as perverted, the exact opposite of what is true.

The difference between the linear and the simultaneous is not a difference between two kinds of media, but a difference between two mental operations within all media. There is always a linear response followed by a simultaneous one, whatever the medium. For words there is the participating response of turning the pages of a book, following the trail of words from top left to bottom right, or listening in a theatre or before a radio. This response is pre-critical, and is followed by the real critical response. This latter is the 'simultaneous' response which reacts to the whole of what has been presented. In looking at a picture there is a preliminary dance of the eye before we take in the whole picture; in reading a newspaper there are two preliminary operations: the glance over the headlines and the consecutive reading of a story. Pictures and written literature give us a spatial focus, a kind of projected total recall, to contain the experience. When the communication simply takes place in time and disappears, there has been a purely linear experience which can only be repeated or forgotten.

In verbal communication the document, the written or printed record, is the technical device that makes the critical or simultaneous response possible. The document is the model of all real teaching, because it is infinitely patient: it repeats the same words however often one consults it. The spatial focus it provides makes it possible to return to the experience, a repetition of the kind that underlies all genuine education. The document is also the focus of a community, the community of readers, and while this community may be restricted to one group for centuries, its natural tendency is to expand over the community as a whole. Thus it is only writing that makes democracy technically possible. It is significant that our symbolic term for a tyrant is 'dictator': that is, an uninterrupted speaker.

The most vivid portrayal of an oral society I know is in the opening of *Paradise Lost*. Satan is a rhetorician, an orator, a dictator; for his use of words, everything depends on the immediate mood, where one can express agreement or disagreement only by shouting. The devils are being trained to become oracles, whispering or commanding voices telling man how to act and think. They are also being trained to forget, to cut their links with their past and face the present moment. Eventually they adjourn for a cabinet meeting, for a pre-literate society cannot get politically past the stage of a closed council with its oral deliberations. It is true that when we come to heaven there is another harangue and another listening audience. But there is one important difference: God is thinking of writing a book, and is outlining the plot to the angels.

The domination of print in Western society, then, has not simply made possible the technical and engineering efficiency of that society, as McLuhan emphasises. It has also created all the conditions of freedom within that society: democratic government, universal education, tolerance of dissent, and (because the book individualises its audience) the sense of the importance of privacy, leisure, and freedom of movement. What the oral media have brought in is, by itself, anarchist in its social affinities.

It has often been pointed out that the electronic media revive many of the primitive and tribal conditions of a pre-literate culture, but there is no fate in such matters, no necessity to go around the circle of history again. Democracy and book culture are interdependent, and the rise of oral and visual media represents, not a new order to adjust to, but a subordinate order to be contained.

POSING THE PROBLEM OF EFFECTS

by OTTO N. LARSEN

In a paper prepared for the Media Task Force of the National Commission on the Causes and Prevention of Violence, sociology professor Otto Larsen discusses the frequently posed question of whether violence in the media has harmful effects on viewers' personalities and behavior.

The individual and social effects of mass communications must depend in some way upon: (1) the pattern of content offered by the mass media; (2) the opportunities for access to the media; and (3) the credibility attributed by audiences to media content.

Numerous studies from both commercial and academic research centers clearly support what has long been the contention of many concerned citizens about these elementary points: (1) the menu offered by the mass media is heavily saturated with violent content, including incidents of persons intentionally doing physical harm to one another; (2) more and more people have ready access to the media, with the average American spending between one-quarter and one-half of his waking day attending to the mass media; and (3) for most persons, but particularly for the poor in American society, television is perceived as the most credible and believable source of information on the reality of the world.

These points add up to a statement of one simple effect: *mass media portrayals of violence attract large audiences*. This also implies a much more troublesome question: If models for violent behavior are repeatedly

Posing the Problem of Effects: From *Mass Media and Violence,* A Report to the National Commission on the Causes and Prevention of Violence (November, 1969).

presented with few competing notions, and people, particularly children, repeatedly expose themselves to such materials, what could be a more favorable arrangement for learning *about* violence, if not learning *to do* violence? However, merely to ask this question is not enough. The abundance of violent media content, and the frequency of exposure to the same, do *not* suffice to prove that the mass media can modify attitudes or induce violent behavior.

When expressed in this manner, such questions can hardly be unequivocally answered. Indeed, many of the questions that concern us most intensely involve both fact and value-judgment. More than this, their answers depend on *relations between* different kinds of facts, connections between these relations, and certain value-judgments implicit in the thoughts of the questioner. It is not difficult, for example, to catalog the portrayals of violence on television. It is more difficult to relate such tabulations to personality and behavioral traits of viewers. It is still more difficult to show that such a relation is one of cause and effect, and if this can be established, the effects produced must still be evaluated. When any one of these steps

"As part of the new de-emphasis on violence, play up the line that he's fighting evil because he hates evil, instead of fighting evil because he loves to fight."

Sidney Harris. Copyright 1969 Saturday Review, Inc.

is omitted, basic policy decisions cannot readily be made about the desirability of continuing or changing the existing pattern of media performance.

Mass media, moreover, do not operate alone; they are embedded in a social system which has many other facets. Whatever may be their effects upon the members of their audience, these must be assessed in relation to the way *other* aspects of this larger system affect these same persons.

To speak meaningfully of the role of mass communications media in such critical concerns as the formation of personality, the induction of violent behavior, or in value formation, it is necessary to seek out and chart the main outlines of what is known *in general* about relevant processes of social learning. Because human personality is developed largely through a process of interaction in primary groups (such as the family), and because the various mass media can more or less simulate such primary interaction, they can play a real part in this process. Furthermore, they may do so unintentionally when they only seem to be entertaining or informing, because audience members are engaged in a process of "observational learning" and the mass media contribute to this through "symbolic modeling."

As a child matures physically, he also undergoes a process of social preparation for adult roles. Much of this preparation ordinarily takes place in the family, while some of it occurs in play groups and some of it involves formal education. It occurs all the time the child is awake and active, even when he and the persons with whom he interacts are not consciously concerned with shaping his character. He becomes a residue of what he has done and experienced, which in turn depends on his genetic endowment and the social heritage into which he was born.

As each child grows up, he has a wide range of skills to learn. He has values and customs to embrace, amend, or reject. He has to discover for himself what kind of world he lives in; he gets clues to this from the way others act toward things, toward each other, and toward him. He has to discover who and what he is, and how his identity relates him to the world; again his clues come from the interactions of others with him. He has to find out where he will be going in life, how he will go, who will accompany him, and how they can get together.

It would be surprising indeed if in our society the ubiquitous mass media did *not* play some part in this complex process. And yet until recently, not only has the potential involvement of mass media been relatively neglected, but even the fact that the process is social has sometimes been forgotten.

The mass media enter into this process mainly by providing material for "observational learning," defined as "imitation" in experimental psychology and as "identification" in personality theory. The common denominator for all three terms is a recognition that human beings in certain circumstances tend to reproduce the actions, attitudes, or emotions they perceive in other persons. These other persons may either be live or symbolized models (e.g., a character in a story). As knowledge of the principles of observational learning accumulates, more can be said about *how* groups shape the personalities of their members. The clearer our understanding of these mechanisms, the firmer the ground on which to base statements about the possible effects of symbolized groups, such as those depicted in a television drama.

If the content of mass communications is being widely discussed, perhaps this indicates that it has other effects. One contention is that symbolic violence, whether portraying fantasy or reality, will arouse aggression or increase aggressive behavior, hardening persons to human pain and suffering and leading them to accept violence as a way of life and as a solution to personal and social problems. Another school of thought contends that such exposure has precisely the opposite effect. This view holds that exposure to violence will allow the media user to discharge in fantasy what he might otherwise act out. Thus, watching *Gunsmoke* or reading a *Superman* comic will provide a safe and harmless outlet for human frustrations and aggressive-hostile impulses in much the same manner as hitting a punching bag. A third position holds that violent content has little or no effect. Proponents of this view suggest that in a controlled and relatively secure society, the passive recipient can vicariously live bravely and dangerously through the video hero with no enduring impact on his feeling, attitudes, or behavior in life.

It is, of course the first point of view which has aroused the concern and interest of vast sectors of the general public. However, little is accomplished if one merely notes the presence of undesirable features of some communication medium or art form, and then lets his aversion to both be transmuted into an assumption that the one disliked thing must be caused by the other. Much criticism of the mass media, and especially television, seems to reflect this kind of non-sequitur. This is unnecessary. There are research findings which afford a more objective basis for assessing the situation.

To understand the full implications of the research, it is important to keep in mind just how recent man's experience is with the pervasive presence of mass media. Even now, a decade into the space age, the majority of the world's human beings are illiterate. In our own advanced society, many citizens have first-hand memories of the pre-television and pre-radio era. Some can even remember a childhood in which there was no such thing as a movie theater. Daily newspapers, in fact, have been around for a mere five generations. Since mass communications are so relatively new, it is not surprising that men are not agreed as to the social impact of the various media.

Despite their tender age, mass communications have indeed become a pervasive aspect of our way of life. The media form the core of our leisure time activities, and television is the heart of this core. For the average American, mass media usage occupies almost as much time as does work, and for some, appreciably *more* time is devoted to mass communications. For children, television alone occupies almost as much time as school in their first sixteen years of life. Time-expenditure data by themselves do not prove any of the charges leveled against the media, nor do such data validate the praise the media have received. It is clear that the controversy over the effects of television is unlikely to be the only result of this deluge.

The fact that time devoted to one activity cannot be used in some other way means that the large amount of time allocated by Americans to mass communications must have entailed some redirection of their lives. Although casual radio listening can be done in conjunction with other (presumably inattentive) activities, and newspapers can be read on the commuter train, the mass media must in general have displaced other pursuits.

There are more direct and less incidental ways in which exposure to the mass media could influence persons, and these may have either immediate or long-range impact. Immediate effects include the emotional reactions of a person while he is viewing, listening, or reading, and the ensuing repercussions of these in defensive reactions, fatigue, excitement, dreams, and so on. The long-range effects concern the learning that is produced: both the content (vocabulary, items of information, beliefs) and the strengthening or weakening of personality traits, such as aggressiveness, passivity, and the like. Beyond the psychological level, concern must also be directed to the impact of the media on interpersonal relations, the development of norms, and the acquisition of values. The possibility of a change in behavior without a change in values must also be considered.

These are some of the dimensions of the effects of mass media violence that must be coped with. As with most significant social issues, seemingly straightforward questions become, upon analysis, acutely challenging and do not yield simple solutions. Thus, the following guideline must be set up: when we ask about the effects of the mass media, we must not phrase the question simply in terms of whether the media have an effect; rather, we seek to know under what conditions, how much, and what kind of effect the media are likely to have within specified populations.

We do not underestimate the enormity of the task, nor the necessity of its continuing pursuit. The impact of television in America is difficult to measure because very few people remain unexposed to it, and those few tend to act differently, in ways that pre-date the television era. One solution is to study the way television and other mass media fit into the life cycles of those who use them, without hoping for a comparison group of non-users. We all breathe air, after all, and the unavailability of a control group of non-breathers does not preclude our learning what air does for us.

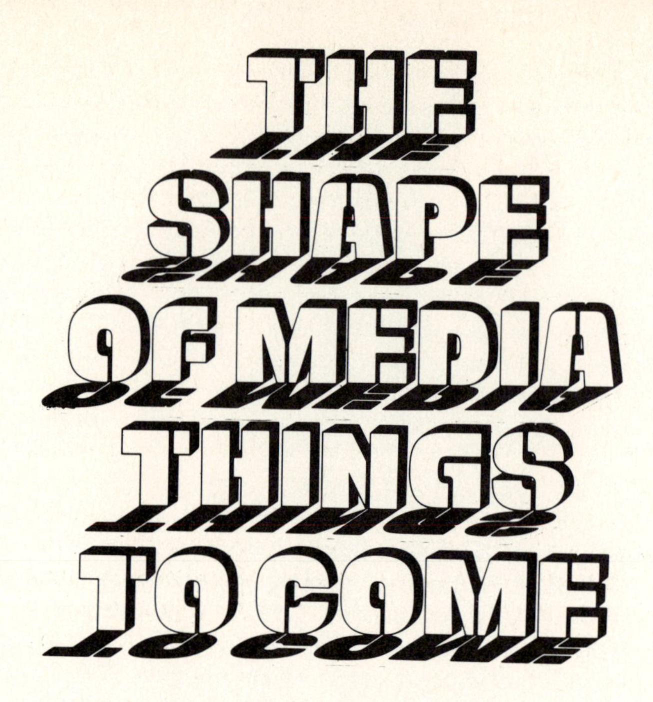

by JON BRADSHAW

In this delightul science-fiction short story from New York magazine, Jon Bradshaw not only traces the technological developments in communications media of the 1970s but also presents his interpretation of the effect these media might have on us.

This is no place to begin. There is no *real* place to begin. Confronted with infinity, with this wonderfully unreal world we have made, it is difficult to conjure up beginnings. Impossible, really. I'll try to recall a few of the less pedestrian memories, but it was all so long ago and the records of the period are sketchy and incomplete.

It is probably best to begin in the middle 1970s. There was an exaggerated concern then that man was becoming plastic, that his best instincts had been somehow pirated, that he had become, in a quaint word of the time, homogenized. Ridiculous, really, in light of what happened later. But an ecology movement had begun. People, usually the young, gorged themselves on natural foods, grew plants and vegetables, jogged, hiked, camped out, and spoke religiously of the environment. Everyone talked about . . . the soil. It was, I imagine, escapist and fun and gave many otherwise uneducable youths something essentially harmless to do.

The Shape of Media Things to Come: From *New York* (April 19, 1976). Reprinted by permission of the author.

But while this movement reeled clumsily backward toward communes and the land, a separate revolution was taking place—accelerating more quickly than anyone could have known then. During the early seventies, world communications were still imperfect, primitive even, little more than common gadgetry. People *communicated*—at least that was what it was called—but with considerable delay and at inconvenient distances. In 1976 people still drove automobiles; they read newspapers, magazines, and books; they traveled to cinemas and listened to stereo systems that were little more than crude machines. They communicated on walkie-talkies and plodded between the earth and the moon on cramped spaceships. They watched an audiovisual contraption called "television," listened to pictureless "radio," and had just begun to toy with the computer in their homes. As the seventies drew to a close, the more affluent members of the society became obsessed with "electronics."

The so-called media room was created in the home and it was stocked with the sophisticated gimmickry of the period. Such rooms had something called the Advent screen, a seven-foot-diagonal television screen, its images projected from an ugly box which dominated the room. There were videotape cassettes with which one recorded television programs, and audiotape decks that played music through huge speakers, in order to give a kind of sense-around sound. There were video disks containing current films, and luminous video art occupied the walls.

Throughout the rest of the home, communications systems were hooked up to a Touch-tone telephone system—the dual-tone multifrequency phone, or D.T.M.F., as it was known. This ancient transmission device enabled its owner to check a bank account, order prescriptions, shop for food, and verify credit cards automatically, without leaving home. The so-called code-a-phone could take messages and be accessed remotely in order to retrieve those messages taken in the owner's absence. A telephonic call-forwarding device rerouted incoming calls. A device called speed-calling connected one instantly, or what was thought of as instantly, to other cities across the world. And add-on conference calls enabled one to plug in three or four callers simultaneously. The telephone could be programmed to wake you up; on cold days, it could pre-ignite the car engine and heater and turn on the heating in your country home. It could, in fact, be made to control all electrical functions in the home—the oven, the doors, lights, radios, television sets, and air conditioning.

Despite the simplicity of these devices, more and more people were becoming, in a phrase of the time, "communications freaks." A huge industry proliferated around them. Automobiles, personal transportation modules, were equipped with telephones and television. Wireless citizen-band radios were an automobile necessity—for highway emergencies and traffic updates. Homes were fitted with video intercoms and video security systems. Wireless telephones and wireless headsets came into general use. Picture phones were available but they were in black and white and were employed, for the most part, in executive conference rooms. There were video tennis matches and hockey games, and video chess games preprogrammed by experts. Many homes contained video synthesizers and colorizers, enabling a child to draw psychedelic pictures on the television screen. Telephonic photostat machines transmitted written words and pictures across the world.

The technology was unsophisticated, but widespread. Already, the functional illiterate of the time was the person who couldn't type, because one *had* to type to work a computer. Due to the digital clock, this was the last generation to know the difference between clockwise and counterclockwise. One early computer device was the DIVA—data input, voice answer—but it was soon replaced by audio computers which translated words into functions. During the late seventies, the stored-program computerized telephone systems, which were replacing the outdated electro-mechanical telephone exchanges, were obsolete on installation, due to improvements in circuitry and miniaturization. A low form of early computer talk, FORTRAN, was being taught in the universities, and elementary schools were teaching computer logic. A new slang sprang up, employing such words as "phase," "out of phase," "interphase," "biofeedback," "biofeedforward," and, when referring to human malfunctions, "gigo" (garbage in, garbage out). The media room was being transformed from an entertainment center to a kind of communications command post. Yet the underlying technology remained at a childish level.

Experts and technocrats were strangely ignorant of the direction technology would eventually take. Since computerized equipment was simply too expensive for the mass of home users, it took many years for a market to be created. And, as elementary as it now sounds, it was the backwardness of communications which produced the major dilemmas of the period—for example, pollution, the preference for living in vertical spaces, the widespread lack of food that led to war and other forms of profiteering, and the obstinate addiction to the old-fashioned wheel.

In retrospect, man's lack of ingenuity is almost unbelievable, and I must continually remind myself that in those dark times he was little more than a barbaric child. The chief characteristics of that culture, particularly the American culture, were immediacy, impact, and sensation. In electronic terms the culture was merely self-indulgent. The future meant instant gratification, which is what instant photographs and videotapes were all about. It was not until copper wires had been replaced with broad-band optical fibers that communications became somewhat more refined. Broad-band optical fibers, activated and enforced by laser propulsion, meant that their users could link up with central information services in order to hear what they wished to hear instead of what someone else wanted them to hear. For example, a universal television retrieval system came into being, attached to the telephone. Wired to a home computer terminal, the system contained a constantly updated encyclopedia of information available to anyone with the ability to press a button. Security systems became computerized and could detect and isolate burglaries instantaneously. All shopping was performed through the computer-telex and all mail and newspapers were now effected through computer-television.

The large TV screen, modern so short a time before, was replaced with a three-dimensional wraparound wall-screen. Even middle-class homes were glutted with voice-activated typewriters, picture phones, hologram-projection machines, and laser burglar alarms set not to kill but to stun. The well-to-do sported decorative computer watches on their wrists and laser scanners in their libraries. Most homes were solar powered. Videophiles had become videomaniacs.

The home had now become a total environment—the ultimate cocoon—and life, its bemused inhabitants believed, was terribly modern. More important, and for the first time, an intimate dialogue had been initiated between man and the machine. The computer had eliminated the merely mechanical. All essentially mechanical movements, in fact, were becoming obsolete, although they had not yet been taken, as you will see, to their purely logical conclusions.

Almost no one "traveled" anymore. More and more business was conducted from the home. Students were educated in the home; and as an alternative to the horrors of enforced holidays, the three-dimensional wraparound screen allowed one to *be* in, say, the South of France, and the sound-around system made soft Mediterranean noises. The wraparound screen also enabled one to link up with live concerts, sporting events, or any other public function. Computer units had become micro-miniaturized, operating on a less-input, more-output ratio. The computer, or Central Processing Unit as it came to be known, controlled everything. The demand for communication between computers was filled by the laser. The portable C.P.U., worn as a watch, was a peripheral device linked by matching light frequencies to the main C.P.U., and it provided a time-divisional highway along which multiplexed information was transmitted. The tiny device functioned as a calculator, watch, telephone, and memory bank. You didn't have to know what you wanted from the C.P.U.; it calculated that for you. It always knew what you wanted because it knew you.

In the home itself, manual lighting had been replaced by glow walls, which stored light by day and emitted it by night. The kitchen had become redundant. In its place, each home was equipped with a photosynthesis module that provided highly enriched liquids for human nourishment. There was no longer any need for old-fashioned "foods." Curiously, to begin with there were grudging complaints that life would never be the same without "cheeseburgers" or "Château Lafite '39," but it soon ceased to be a problem. No one could remember what they had tasted like.

The art world, too, had been revolutionized. Homes of the period were decorated with multiflex neon sculptures, frozen-light murals, and dancing three-dimensional laser paintings. Some homes had image walls on which one could project computerized portraits in color.

No one actually wrote anymore. Books had long since disappeared. As for newspapers and magazines, in the late seventies they were already hopelessly archaic. With the introduction of the new photonic systems, information was now being transmitted by light, almost always when one was asleep, so that on waking one had already "read" the "newspaper."

The computer had become self-evolving, self-sustaining. It performed its own maintenance as well as physical repair. Unlike man, it never required a doctor. Functioning in seconds, it soon sped to microseconds, to milliseconds, and then to nanoseconds, and continued to accelerate.

Computers were used to build computers, of course. Only another computer, in fact, could provide the degree of accuracy necessary to breed a further generation of computers. It was learned that just as human families have generic traits, so do computers. As a result, new breeds of computers came into being, their birth made possible by a much improved generic program.

Although world communications had evolved considerably, one major flaw remained which impeded progress for many years. In pure computer-communicative terms, man had always been beamed into his environment. It was not until man learned to beam the environment into *him* that real progress, as we understand it today, was possible. As early as 1976, scientists experimented with computers that had no external monitor—brain-implanted computers—but they were crude gimcracks.

As everyone now knows, the evolutionary process began to accelerate. All essentially mechanical movements, whether those of machines or of man himself, became slowly obsolete and man, in time, arrived at a new definition of himself. It is interesting to note that man, who had never been as advanced as the computer, relinquished his mechanical grasp of life only after the computer had compelled him to evolve or die.

Given the old dilemmas of environmental pollution, the rising decibel level, and the constant exposure to the new visual age, there had been a steady erosion of purely human senses. The swift advances in computerized communications only hastened the inevitable. The sense of taste was the first sense to disappear, then smell, then touch, and almost immediately thereafter, hearing. Speech had always been a highly mechanical form of communication, tiresome and time-consuming. As long ago as 1984, the spoken vocabulary had dwindled to a few hundred words. I have always been surprised that the spoken word lasted as long as it did, that it had not disappeared with the introduction of the telepathic computer, which permitted one to "talk" in a more direct and efficient manner. Once the telepathic computer—worn as a watch and linked directly to the nervous system—became fashionable, speech was no longer necessary. The new language created instant communication, instant comprehension.

The same electronic potentials that in the old days were used to program the computer were now employed to load the core of the brain, and they could initiate queries to the computer. At first, "speech" was known as "data input" and ultimately was reduced to logic format for purposes of communicating with more sophisticated beings—as computers were now called. They revolutionized the home, of course. Spaces were equipped with ultrasonic mood systems, especially sensitized to their inhabitants, so that intimate communication was possible on every level without people having to move from one room to another.

New thresholds demanded new anatomies. The human body itself, long an awkward weight to cart around, had become little more than a vexatious bore. The crude mechanical functions for which it had been created—hunting, walking, eating, reproducing—were antiquated now. Sex, for example—if history is to be believed—was considered an amiable pursuit, but it never could have been more than a vulgar form of communication. Fortunately it was much improved upon. Once it became a telepathic act, intercourse was purer, more perfect, and, most important, more efficient.

The last of the crude senses to atrophy was sight. Given what seems, even to such a cynic as myself, the really extraordinary developments in cosmic technology, it was soon no longer necessary to open the eyes. Why bother? Entire universes were available when the eyes were shut. It was the last of the old sensory barriers to be overcome.

It is difficult and not a little tedious to catalog the complicated advances that have taken place since then. And I've said much too much already. Suffice it to say that one occupies infinity. And I've not left this particular space for twenty years or more. There is no longer any "time," at least as you would comprehend it, so it is difficult to be precise. There are no "people" as such. There is no "sign of life." Consider it another way. As you must know, the source of all life is light, and we have simply, if I may use so complex a term, become light again. And it amuses me, you understand, to use this primitive form of communication in order to tell you so.

STUDY QUESTIONS

1. In the introductory article to this book (pp. 5–20), Theodore Peterson cites Jay Jensen's criteria for media criticism: the criticism must be objective; it must consider social, political, and cultural forces; and the media must be considered in the context of their environment. Take a recent political or social issue that received attention from the media and apply Jensen's criteria in your criticism of the media's handling of the issue. How well did the media fulfill Jensen's requirements? How effectively did their handling of the issue promote the best interests of society? Were all segments of society served? Was any medium more effective than the others?

2. Edmund Carpenter says that "each medium, if its bias is properly exploited, reveals and communicates a unique aspect of reality, of truth." Marshall McLuhan has also spoken of each medium having a particular bias. Think of a book you have read that has been made into a movie. Do the differences in the two versions seem to stem from intrinsic biases of the two media? Does the book communicate aspects of the story that the movie cannot, and vice versa?

3. Carpenter points out that the three most recent media—film, radio, and television—are dramatic media. What implications does this have in terms of effect on society? Can you give some examples of beneficial effects because a subject was presented by the dramatic media? detrimental effects?

4. Loevinger's reflective-projective theory views the mass media as "mirrors of society that reflect an ambiguous image in which each observer projects or sees his own vision of himself and society." Thus the audience, not the media, is the key factor in social change resulting from mass communication. FCC Commissioner Kenneth A. Cox places more emphasis on the role of the media. He says that "the media can build on existing society and can consciously and significantly influence it."* From your observation of the media today, do you see any conscious attempts to change society? If so, does it seem that the success of such an attempt depends on whether or not the audience has previously accepted the idea of the change? How do the views of Loevinger and Cox, and your own observations, relate to Larsen's opinions about violence in the media?

5. Theorists Loevinger and Frye discuss responses to various media. Loevinger says the response to broadcasting is emotional. Frye claims it is only a written or printed message that make a critical response possible. Does this mean that one cannot make a rational response to the electronic media? Are the electronic media, as Frye says, merely "a subordinate order to be contained"?

6. As have other authors of selections throughout this book, Frye raises significant questions about a human being's changing social condition because of technological developments. How have the new media affected humans sociologically and psychologically? How does Frye's view compare with that of McLuhan (pp. 441–445), Toffler (pp. 343–349), Boorstin (pp. 101–106), and Johnson (pp. 107–121)?

7. Larsen says that whatever the media's effects may be, they must be considered in relation to the total environment—to the ways in which other aspects of our society affect the individual. How important is the media's role in comparison to that of parents, church, or school, for example?

8. Bradshaw sees the possibility of individual use of the media, saying that "users could link up with central information services in order to hear what they wished to hear instead of what someone else wanted them to hear." What implications does this have for our culture? How does this compare to Boorstin's idea that technological developments will have a democratizing effect? How different would this be from the media environment of the 1970s?

* Kenneth A. Cox, "Can Broadcasting Help Achieve Social Reform?" **Journal of Broadcasting,** XII (Spring, 1968), 125.

BIBLIOGRAPHY FOR FURTHER STUDY

Agee, Warren K., ed. *Mass Media in a Free Society.* Lawrence: The University Press of Kansas, 1969.

Anderson, H. Al. "An Empirical Investigation of What Social Responsibility Theory Means." *Journalism Quarterly* 54 (Spring, 1977), 33–39.

Bagdikian, Ben H. "How Communications May Shape Our Future Environment." *AAUW Journal* (March, 1969), 123–26.

———. *The Information Machines.* New York: Harper & Row, 1971.

Boorstin, Daniel J. "Tomorrow: The Republic of Technology." *Time* (January 17, 1977), 36–38.

Carpenter, Edmund, and Ken Heyman. *They Became What They Beheld.* New York: Outerbridge & Dienstfrey, 1970.

Commission on Freedom of the Press. *A Free and Responsible Press.* Chicago: University of Chicago Press, 1947.

DeFleur, Melvin L. *Theories of Mass Communication.* 3rd ed. New York: David McKay, 1975.

Duffy, Dennis. *Marshall McLuhan.* Toronto: The Canadian Publishers, 1969.

Edwards, Verne E., Jr. *Journalism in a Free Society.* Dubuque, Iowa: Wm. C. Brown Co., 1970.

Emery, Edwin, Phillip H. Ault, and Warren K. Agee. *Introduction to Mass Communications.* 5th ed. New York: Dodd, Mead & Co., 1976.

Fore, William F. "Mass Media's Mythic World: At Odds with Christian Values." *The Christian Century* (January 19, 1977), 32–38.

Gerald, James Edward. *The Social Responsibility of the Press.* Minneapolis: University of Minnesota Press, 1963.

Grunig, James, ed. *Decline of the Global Village: How Specialization Is Changing the Mass Media*. Bayside, N.Y.: General Hall, 1976.

Hall, Edward T. *The Silent Language*. New York: Doubleday, 1959.

Hall, Stuart, and Paddy Whannel. *The Popular Arts*. New York: Pantheon Books, 1965.

Innis, Harold A. *The Bias of Communication*. Toronto: University of Toronto Press, 1951.

Katzman, Natan. "The Impact of Communication Technology: Promises and Prospects." *Journal of Communication* (Autumn, 1974), 47–59.

Klapper, Joseph T. *The Effects of Mass Communications*. New York: Free Press, 1960.

Larsen, Otto N., ed. *Violence and the Mass Media*. New York: Harper & Row, 1968.

McLuhan, Marshall. *Counterblast*. New York: Harcourt Brace Jovanovich, 1969.

———. *Understanding Media*. New York: McGraw-Hill, 1964.

———, and Quentin Fiore. *The Medium Is the Massage*. New York: Bantam Books, 1967.

———. *War and Peace in the Global Village*. New York: Bantam Books, 1968.

Merrill, John C., and Ralph L. Lowenstein. *Media, Messages and Men: New Perspectives in Communication*. New York: David McKay, 1971.

Murphy, Robert D. *Mass Communication and Human Interaction*. Boston: Houghton Mifflin, 1976.

Peterson, Theodore, Jay W. Jensen, and William L. Rivers. *The Mass Media and Modern Society*. New York: Rinehart Press, 1971.

"*Playboy* Interview: Marshall McLuhan." *Playboy* 16 (March, 1969), 53ff.

Rivers, William, and Wilbur Schramm. *Responsibility in Mass Communication*. Rev. ed. New York: Harper & Row, 1969.

Rosenberg, Bernard, and David M. White. *Mass Culture Revisited*. New York: Van Nostrand Reinhold, 1971.

Stein, Robert. *Media Power*. Boston: Houghton Mifflin, 1972.

Stephenson, William. *The Play Theory of Mass Communication*. Chicago: University of Chicago Press, 1967.

Wolfe, Tom. "What if He Is Right?" *The Pump House Gang*. New York: Farrar, Straus & Giroux, 1968, 135–70.

(Continued from page iv)

Page 203: (lower right) CBS News

Page 271: Ken Karp

Page 296: Wide World Photos

Page 311: CBS Photo

Page 330: Björn Bölstad, Photo Researchers

Pages 372, 373: Museum of Modern Art Film Stills Archive and United Artists

Page 445: Reprinted with the permission of Farrar, Straus and Giroux, Inc. from **The Pump House Gang** by Tom Wolfe, © 1968

INDEX

A 7
B 8
C 9
D 0
E 1
F 2
G 3
H 4
I 5
J 6